SOLVING POPULATION HEALTH PROBLEMS THROUGH COLLABORATION

Rapid changes in healthcare and public health offer tremendous opportunities to focus on process improvement. Public health departments and agencies increasingly work collaboratively with hospitals and other community partners to promote knowledge and improve collective impact through public and private sector coalitions. *Solving Population Health Problems through Collaboration* brings together population health experts and leaders to examine evidence-based intervention strategies, case studies in health departments and hospitals, health equity issues, core competencies, public health campaigns, step-by-step collaboration advice, and much more. Each chapter is written by a population health leader shaped by his or her experience implementing change in a community's health, to demonstrate innovative methods and tools for building and leading sustainable community coalitions to effect real change. Designed to prepare population health workers in public health and healthcare settings to develop strategies for improved population health, this book is required reading for public health managers and health administrators as well as students enrolled in population health courses.

Ron Bialek, MPP, is President of the Public Health Foundation, Washington, DC.

Leslie M. Beitsch, MD, JD, is faculty at the Florida State University College of Medicine as Professor of Health Policy and Chair of the Department of Behavioral Sciences and Social Medicine, and Center for Medicine and Public Health.

John W. Moran, PhD, is a Senior Quality Advisor to the Public Health Foundation, Washington, DC.

"The collective effort of public health practitioners and the general population is needed to create and sustain the infrastructure to produce and improve large scale health outcomes. As the contributors point out, however, political will is critical for creating and sustaining programs that to some may seem long since resolved. This work provides inspiring and insightful perspectives of what needs to be done and what is being done to improve health outcomes from a practitioner lens."

—**Stephen Williams**, *Director of the Department of Health and Human Services, Houston, Texas, USA*

SOLVING POPULATION HEALTH PROBLEMS THROUGH COLLABORATION

Edited by Ron Bialek, Leslie M. Beitsch, and John W. Moran

Routledge
Taylor & Francis Group

NEW YORK AND LONDON

First published 2017
by Routledge
711 Third Avenue, New York, NY 10017

and by Routledge
2 Park Square, Milton Park, Abingdon, Oxon OX14 4RN

Routledge is an imprint of the Taylor & Francis Group, an informa business

© 2017 Taylor & Francis

Library of Congress Cataloging-in-Publication Data
Names: Bialek, Ronald G., editor. | Bietsch, Leslie M., 1956– editor. |
    Moran, John W., 1944– editor.
Title: Solving population health problems through collaboration / edited by
    Ron Bialek, Leslie M. Bietsch, and John W. Moran.
Description: New York : Routledge, 2017. | Includes bibliographical
    references and index.
Identifiers: LCCN 2016044340 | ISBN 9781498763059 (hbk. : alk. paper) |
    ISBN 9780415793285 (pbk. : alk. paper) | ISBN 9781315212708 (ebk.)
Subjects: MESH: Community Health Planning | Public Health—methods |
    Community Health Services—organization & administration | Cooperative
    Behavior | United States
Classification: LCC RA418 | NLM WA 546 AA1 | DDC 362.1—dc23
LC record available at https://lccn.loc.gov/2016044340

ISBN: 978-1-4987-6305-9 (hbk)
ISBN: 978-0-415-79328-5 (pbk)
ISBN: 978-1-315-21270-8 (ebk)

Typeset in Bembo
by Apex CoVantage, LLC

CONTENTS

ABOUT THE EDITORS

Ron Bialek, MPP, CQIA, has been serving as President and CEO of the Public Health Foundation (PHF) since 1997. He has focused PHF's efforts on developing and implementing innovative strategies for improving performance of public health agencies and systems. Initiatives include developing performance management and quality improvement tools and training for population health professionals; developing the consensus set of Core Competencies for Public Health Professionals through the Council on Linkages Between Academia and Public Health Practice; and creating the nation's most comprehensive population health learning management network—TRAIN. Mr. Bialek serves on the Montgomery County (MD) Commission on Health, and served two years as Chair; is an advisory committee member of the Adventist HealthCare Center for Health Equity and Wellness; and is a member of the Healthy Montgomery Steering Committee. Before joining PHF, Mr. Bialek was on the faculty of the Johns Hopkins University School of Public Health for nine years and spent three years in state government serving as the Executive Assistant to the Assistant Secretary for Health Regulation in the Maryland Department of Health and Mental Hygiene.

Leslie M. Beitsch, MD, JD, joined the faculty at the Florida State University College of Medicine in November 2003 as Professor of Health Policy and Chair Department of Behavioral Sciences and Social Medicine, and Center for Medicine and Public Health. He currently serves as Chair of the Department of Behavioral Sciences and Social Medicine. From June 2001 until November 2003, Dr. Beitsch was the Commissioner of the Oklahoma State Department of Health. In that role he provided oversight for 2,500 employees and a budget of $260,000,000. Dr. Beitsch served as Deputy Secretary and Assistant State

Health Officer for the Florida Department of Health from 1997–2001. He provided guidance and direction for public health programs, the county health departments, and the state laboratory and pharmacy. Prior to this appointment, Dr. Beitsch served as Assistant State Health Officer and Division Director for Family Health Services from October 1991 through August 1997, focusing on maternal and child health. From October 1989 through October 1991, Dr. Beitsch was Medical Director of the Broward County Health Department in Ft. Lauderdale. Dr. Beitsch has been an active member in several organizations. Recent interests have focused on accreditation and quality improvement for state and local health departments through the Multi-State Learning Collaborative and the Centers for Disease Control. He recently completed service on an Institute of Medicine committee studying the future of public health, which issued three reports. Dr. Beitsch served as a Steering Committee member for the Exploring Accreditation Project, and as its Research and Evaluation Workgroup Chair. He is a member of the executive committee of the Public Health Accreditation Board, and just completed a two-year term as Chair. He has participated as a member of committees representing the Association of State and Territorial Health Officials (ASTHO) and committees advising the Centers for Disease Control and Prevention. He is past Chair of the Board of Directors for the Public Health Foundation (PHF) and the Public Health Leadership Society. He has recently been recognized for his contributions by ASTHO (2007 Alumni Award) and PHF (2008 Theodore Erwin Award).

John W. Moran, PhD, is a Senior Quality Advisor to the Public Health Foundation and a Senior Fellow at the University of Minnesota, School of Public Health in the Division of Health Policy and Management 2010–2015; President of the Advisory Board of Choose To Be Healthy Coalition of the Healthy Maine Partnership for York County, Maine, 2011–2016; a faculty member of the CDC/IHI Antibiotic Stewardship project 2011–2012; a member of PHAB's Evaluation and Quality Improvement Committee 2013–2016; and Adjunct Professor at Arizona State University College of Health Solutions' School for the Science of Health 2013–present.

He brings to PHF over 30 years of quality improvement expertise in developing quality improvement tools and training programs, implementing and evaluating quality improvement programs, and writing articles and books on quality improvement methods. Dr. Moran is a retired Senior Vice President of Information Systems, Administrative and Diagnostic Services at New England Baptist Hospital. He was previously Chief Operating Officer of Changing Healthcare, Inc., specializing in management consulting and educational support to healthcare organizations. For 21 years, Dr. Moran was employed at Polaroid Corporation, where he worked in various senior management capacities in Manufacturing, Engineering, and Quality. His last position was as Director of Worldwide Quality and Systems.

ABOUT THE CONTRIBUTORS

Kathleen Amos serves as Assistant Director, Academic/Practice Linkages for the Public Health Foundation (PHF) in Washington, DC. In this role, she coordinates initiatives focused on strengthening the public health workforce, including the Council on Linkages Between Academia and Public Health Practice. Kathleen is engaged in the development of the Priority Competencies for Population Health Professionals and has more than five years of experience in ongoing development of the Core Competencies for Public Health Professionals and resources to help organizations implement these competencies. Prior to joining PHF, she completed the Associate Fellowship Program at the National Library of Medicine, gaining specialized training in health sciences information services and research. Kathleen holds a Master of Library and Information Studies degree and a Bachelor of Arts degree in Sociology and Social Anthropology, both from Dalhousie University (Halifax, NS, Canada).

Yasemin Arikan is a Futurist with the Institute for Alternative Futures. She is a co-author and speaker on the futures of healthcare, society, and technology for a variety of associations and Foundations. Ms. Arikan also co-led the first-ever examination of the U.S. community health centers' role in improving population health by addressing the social determinants of health that underlie and shape the health of patients. Ms. Arikan earned her undergraduate degree in Psychology from the University of Rochester and a master's degree in Sociology from the University of Chicago.

Sonja Armbruster, MA, began her public health career supporting practice-based research and health systems improvement at the University of Kansas School of Medicine's Preventive Medicine and Public Health Department. In

2003 she joined the Sedgwick County Health Department, where she served in a number of administrative roles, including health promotion program management, development of the strategic plan and performance management system, supervision of the quality improvement and accreditation preparation efforts, and leadership of community health assessment and improvement planning. Currently, Armbruster serves as Director of the Center for Public Health Initiatives at Wichita State University's Community Engagement Institute. There she leads a team that provides training and technical assistance to the state health department as well as local health departments and other health services agencies across the state. She occasionally serves as adjunct faculty for both the University of Kansas Master of Public Health program and the Wichita State University College of Health Professions. As a consultant for PHF, Armbruster has provided training and technical assistance for state, local, and tribal health departments in the areas of performance management systems development, workforce development, and quality improvement since 2011. Armbruster served as a past Chair of the National Association of County and City Health Officials MAPP Workgroup. She chaired her community health improvement coalition, the Wichita Health Alliance, for six years and still serves on the leadership team. She began serving as a site visitor for the Public Health Accreditation Board in 2012. Her formal education includes a Bachelor of Arts in Secondary Education and a Master of Arts in Communication, both from Wichita State University.

John Auerbach is Associate Director for Policy at the Centers for Disease Control and Prevention (CDC) and Acting Director of the Office for State, Tribal, Local and Territorial Support (OSTLTS). He oversees the Office of the Associate Director for Policy, which focuses on the promotion of public health and prevention as components of healthcare and payment reform and health system transformation. As the Acting OSTLTS Director, he oversees key activities and technical assistance that support the nation's health departments and the public health system. Prior to his appointment at CDC, he was a Distinguished Professor of Practice in Health Sciences and the Director of the Institute on Urban Health Research and Practice at Northeastern University from 2012 to 2014. He was Commissioner of Public Health for the Commonwealth of Massachusetts from 2007 to 2012. He also served as the Executive Director of the Boston Public Health Commission for nine years. He had previously worked at the State Health Department for a decade, first as Chief of Staff and later as an Assistant Commissioner overseeing the HIV/AIDS Bureau during the early years of the epidemic.

Bill Barberg is President and founder of Insightformation, Inc., a management consulting and technology company based in Minneapolis, MN. He is a globally recognized expert in the Collective Impact, the Balanced Scorecard methodology, collaborative strategy implementation, and community health innovation. Bill has consulted with dozens of communities and organizations and has presented many conference keynotes, workshops, and Web-conferences on Collective Impact and strategy management, often co-presenting with clients. Several of the world's leading experts have publicly recognized the depth and expertise that he brings to the topics of alignment, measurement, and strategy implementation. His clients include regional health improvement efforts like "Live Well San Diego" and Thriving Weld, led by the North Colorado Health Alliance, and Restore Hope, a statewide effort to reduce incarceration, recidivism, and the placement of kids into foster care, all while improving safety and child welfare.

Eric Baumgartner, MD, is a career public health physician engaged in a variety of community and national activities focused on issues of population health and access to care. Currently he serves as Senior Community Health Strategist for the Louisiana Public Health Institute. He also serves as a Commissioner of the Louisiana Health Care Commission. Nationally, Dr. Baumgartner has served as a Technical Assistance Provider for the Georgia Health Policy Center Technical Assistance Program team for HRSA's Rural Health Network Development grantees and has served as Coaching Faculty for the first three cohorts of the National Leadership Academy for the Public's Health directed by the Public Health Institute, Oakland, CA. In addition, Dr. Baumgartner continues to engage in public speaking, facilitation, and community coaching for community health initiatives nationally. Formerly, Dr. Baumgartner served as Director of the Community Access and State Planning Programs of the federal Health Resources and Services Administration in Rockville, MD. Prior to that position, he served in a variety of posts in state public health agencies in the states of Mississippi, Hawaii, Texas, and Louisiana. While in Louisiana, he served as the State Health Officer for three years. In Texas, he served as Chief of the Bureau of Managed Care of the Texas Department of Health, where he shared in the responsibility for converting Medicaid to managed care. Dr. Baumgartner received his medical degree from Louisiana State University School of Medicine and his Master of Public Health from Tulane University School of Public Health and Tropical Medicine. He completed a residency in general pediatrics at the University of Arkansas and completed a second residency in general preventive medicine at Tulane. He received board certification from the American Board of Preventive Medicine and from the American Board of Pediatrics.

Gail R. Bellamy, PhD, is Director of the Florida Blue Center for Rural Health Research and Policy at Florida State University College of Medicine, where she is also a professor in the Department of Behavioral Sciences and Social Medicine. Before joining FSU she was the Director for Community Research at the West Virginia Institute for Health Policy Research in the WVU Health Science Center in Charleston. Dr. Bellamy worked for Scott and White, an integrated delivery system serving a 30-county rural area in Texas, and was a member of the faculty team that created the Texas A&M University School of Rural Public Health, today School of Public Health. Over a 30-year career, she has worked for the state, in the healthcare sector, and in academia. Dr. Bellamy has been a member and leader in three state rural health associations and is a past President of NRHA. She is a current member of the Executive Board of the American Public Health Association. She received her doctorate from the Johns Hopkins University Bloomberg School of Public Health. Her research interests focus on rural and underserved populations. She was part of the early planning team for Rural Healthy People 2010 and is Co-director, along with Dr. Jane Bolin, of the Rural Healthy People 2020 Project.

Kaye Bender, PhD, RN, FAAN, is President and CEO of the Public Health Accreditation Board (PHAB), a position she has held since 2009. Prior to coming to PHAB, she worked in both local and state public health practice in the Mississippi State Department of Health. Her last position there, for 12 years, was Deputy State Health Officer. She served as Dean of the University of Mississippi Medical School of Nursing and Associate Vice Chancellor for Nursing for six years. Dr. Bender chaired the Exploring Accreditation Steering Committee, the precursor study for the establishment of the Public Health Accreditation Board (PHAB), funded by the Robert Wood Johnson Foundation and the Centers for Disease Control and Prevention. She has served on three Institute of Medicine study committees related to public health; is currently on the National Board of Public Health Examiners; is an active member of the American Public Health Association; and is a fellow in the American Academy of Nursing. She is Co-chair of the Population Health Framework Committee for the National Quality Forum. She has numerous publications related to governmental public health systems improvement, and has received a number of awards and recognitions both in nursing and in public health.

Clement (Clem) Bezold, PhD, is Chairman and Senior Futurist at the Institute for Alternative Futures (IAF). Dr. Bezold established IAF with Alvin Toffler to encourage "Anticipatory Democracy." Trained as a political scientist, he has been a major developer of foresight techniques, applying futures research and strategic planning methods in both the public and private sectors. He has done futures work with the World Health Organization, the American Cancer Society, CDC, NIH, and DOD. He has led AFA's (IAF's for-profit subsidiary) work with large corporations. He has authored or edited 11 books focusing on the future of government, work, and health, and he serves on the Editorial Advisory Boards of *Technology Forecasting and Social Change, Journal of Futures Studies, World Future Review* and *Foresight*. In 2011, the World Future Society honored Dr. Bezold with its Lifetime Achievement Award.

Don Bradley, MD, MHS-CL, holds a position as an Associate Consulting Professor in the Department of Community and Family Medicine at Duke, and serves as Executive Director for The Practical Playbook (www.PracticalPlaybook. org). He retired from Blue Cross and Blue Shield of North Carolina (BCBSNC) in April 2014, where he served in a number of roles, including Executive Director for BCBSNC's federally qualified Health Maintenance Organization, and as Senior Vice President, Healthcare, and Chief Medical Officer. Dr. Bradley is a member of the National Academy of Medicine Health and Medicine Division (formerly Institute of Medicine) Roundtable on Obesity Solutions, Chair of the Roundtable's (Interdisciplinary) Provider Training and Education innovation collaborative for development of competencies for the prevention and management of obesity, and a public member of the Academy of Nutrition and Dietetics Board of Directors. His work at Duke includes development of population health competencies, curricula, and tools; leadership development; prevention and management of obesity; and healthcare policy, finance, and transformation.

Brian C. Castrucci is Chief Program and Strategy Officer at the de Beaumont Foundation, whose mission is to strengthen and transform public health in the United States. Brian applies the experiences he gained through a decade of work in governmental public health practice to conceptualize, identify, and implement visionary public health projects. Since joining the Foundation in 2012, he has led the Foundation to the forefront of issues like integrating primary care and public health, assessing the governmental public health workforce, and using partnerships and policy to help solve our most complex health challenges. Brian has shared practice-based, applicable scientific findings through more than 60 articles in peer-reviewed journals and also routinely blogs on the importance of public health in achieving improved health by acting on the undeniable link between individual and community health. Brian graduated summa cum laude from North Carolina State in 1997 with a Bachelor of Arts in Political Science and received his master's degree in Sociomedical Sciences from Columbia University in 2006. He is currently pursuing a doctorate in Public Health Leadership at the University of North Carolina's Gillings School of Global Public Health.

Theresa Chapple-McGruder, PhD, MPH, joined the de Beaumont Foundation in March 2015 as Senior Research and Evaluation Officer. In her current position she is charged with ensuring that the Foundation's grants are measurable and impactful, as well as conducting and facilitating research that will aid in the promotion of the Foundation's mission. The Foundation's mission is to strengthen and transform public health in the United States.

Prior to joining the Foundation, Dr. Chapple-McGruder spent eight years in governmental public health at the local, state, and national levels. Her areas of expertise are decreasing disparities and promoting the health of underserved populations. She has worked in the fields of maternal and child health, chronic disease, and infectious disease.

Her doctoral work was in Maternal and Child Health and Epidemiology from the University of Illinois at Chicago. She received a master's degree in Public Health from the University of North Carolina at Chapel Hill, and a bachelor's degree in Psychology from Clark Atlanta University. She is also on faculty at Emory University School of Public Health and University of Memphis.

Gary Cox, JD, has served as Executive Director of the Oklahoma City-County Health Department (OCCHD) since 2009. Executive Director Cox received a Juris Doctorate from the University of Tulsa. He has previously served as Adjunct Professor of Environmental Law and is presently serving as a visiting associate professor at the University of Oklahoma, College of Public Health. Before joining the Oklahoma City-County Health Department, Cox worked as an environmentalist for the Tulsa Health Department, where he went on to serve as Legal Counsel before eventually serving as Director for 15 years. He brings more than 45 years of public health experience to the Oklahoma City-County Health Department, and his leadership opportunities include past President to both the Oklahoma Public Health Association (OPHA) and the National Association of County and City Health Officials (NACCHO). He has served on various national, state, and local public health efforts including one of RWJF's National Advisory Committees and previously as the RWJF/RESOLVE Transforming Public Health Thought Leaders Project and the Oklahoma Health Improvement Plan. He currently serves as Chairman of the NACCHO Past Presidents Council, the MyHealth Governance Board, and on the OKC Chamber Advisory Board. Executive Director Cox is involved nationally in Public Health, providing testimony and briefings to Congress. Executive Director Cox has dedicated his career to improving health, raising the awareness about health issues at the grassroots level through a community-led coalition representing over 300 partnerships, the Wellness Now Coalition. Executive Director Cox is also committed to developing and leveraging private and public partnerships to improve community health outcomes. This concept is showcased in the NE Regional Health & Wellness Campus, designed to bring together resources in one location for underserved areas of the community. He is committed to a culture of health and continuous quality improvement and has consistently supported transparent governance in local health departmental activities, evidenced by the Oklahoma City-County Health Department designation as one of the first local health departments to pursue and achieve national accreditation.

Lou Anne Crawley-Stout is a Lean Improvement Specialist with NC State University Industry Expansion Solutions. She has 14 years of experience in public health, government, and hospital performance improvement, training and coaching leaders and staff in Lean Six Sigma and Toyota Production System methodologies and tools to foster a continuous quality improvement culture. She also is experienced with developing models and mentoring customers in return on investment analysis for population-based and public health quality improvement initiatives, and she has published a related article. Lou Anne earned a BS in Business Management from Indiana Wesleyan University and an MBA at the Indiana Institute of Technology. She is certified as a Project Management Professional and a Lean Six Sigma Master Black Belt.

Karen B. DeSalvo, MD, is Acting Assistant Secretary for Health at the U.S. Department of Health and Human Services (HHS), where she oversees 12 core public health offices, including the Office of the Surgeon General and the U.S. Public Health Service Commissioned Corps. From January 2014 until August 2016, Dr. DeSalvo also served as National Coordinator for Health Information Technology, where she led the nation's charge to develop an interoperable health IT system to help improve consumers' health. Dr. DeSalvo has dedicated her career toward improving access to affordable, high quality care for all people, with a focus on vulnerable populations. Prior to joining HHS, she was Health Commissioner for the City of New Orleans, a Senior Health Policy Advisor to New Orleans Mayor Mitchell Landrieu, and Vice Dean at Tulane University School of Medicine. Dr. DeSalvo earned her Medical Doctorate and Master of Public Health from Tulane University, and her master's degree in Clinical Epidemiology from Harvard School of Public Health.

Rachel Dixon is a rising senior at the University of Kentucky. She is a Singletary Scholar, Honors Program member, and Fellow in the John R. and Joan B. Gaines Fellowship in the Humanities. She is double-majoring in English and Writing, Rhetoric & Digital Studies (WRD) while also completing the university's Pre-Medicine curriculum. Her research interests include the rhetorical and sociological implications of coal mining in Appalachia, policymaking in the Commonwealth of Kentucky, and partnerships improving healthcare across the United States. She has publications in *Young Scholars in Writing*, *The Oral History Review*, and *Public Health Reports*, and online at the National Issues Forums website.

Deborah Erickson-Irons has led healthcare service organizations including a federally funded community health center, community coalitions, and nonprofits. An experienced group facilitator, she values the art of collaboration and finding common ground to produce action on priority goals. Deborah has conducted three community health needs assessments and published those reports on behalf of York Hospital and The Choose To Be Healthy Coalition in York, Maine. An experienced grant-writer, she has successfully brought hundreds of thousands of dollars of public health funding into Southern Maine. Deborah has been active in supporting community efforts to improve healthcare access, mental health and addiction care services, and expansion of cycling and pedestrian trails. She is the recipient of the Choose To Be Healthy Coalition Apple Award in 2016.

Jamie Clesi Giepert promotes clinical transformation efforts within the primary care setting in her role as a Program Manager with the Louisiana Public Health Institute (LPHI). Jamie holds a BA from of the University of Alabama's Health Care Management program. She is a certified Project Management Professional, who prior to joining LPHI had four years' experience with Our Lady of the Lake Regional Medical Center, working closely with hospital administration in advancing community advocacy and outreach efforts within underserved communities.

Rahul Gupta, MD, serves as West Virginia State Health Officer and Commissioner for the West Virginia Department of Health and Human Resources, Bureau for Public Health. Dr. Gupta is a practicing internist who also serves as Adjunct Professor in the Department of Health Policy, Management & Leadership at the West Virginia School of Public Health and Adjunct Associate Professor at the University of Charleston's School of Pharmacy. Dr. Gupta has authored more than 125 scientific publications in medicine and public health and served as a principal investigator for numerous well-known clinical trials. He presently serves as Secretary and Ex-Officio member at the West Virginia Board of Medicine and as President of the West Virginia State Medical Association. He has also served on several national boards such as the National Association of County and City Health Officials (NACCHO). Currently, he serves as a steering committee member at the National Quality Forum on Population Health as well as at the Institute for Health Metrics Evaluation. He is a recipient of several state and national awards, including the Marie Fallon Award for Public Health Leadership by the National Association of Local Boards of Health; the 2015 Milton and Ruth Roemer Prize for Creative Local Public Health Work by the American Public Health Association; and the 2015 Jay Rockefeller Lifetime Achievement Award presented by U.S. Secretary of Health and Human Services, Sylvia Mathews Burwell, on behalf of West Virginians for Affordable Health Care on the advancements in public policy in healthcare.

Megan Holderness currently serves as Administrator, Data and Grants Evaluation at the Oklahoma City-County Health Department (OCCHD). She oversees the epidemiologists and biostatisticians and supports planning and development efforts through data analysis, strategic planning, and partner engagement. She is board certified in Public Health by the National Board of Public Health Examiners. Before joining Oklahoma City-County Health Department, she served as a Public Health Officer in the U.S. Air Force, where she coordinated medical and environmental threat reduction for warriors, monitored food safety and sanitation, and developed disease containment plans.

Megan received a Bachelor of Science degree in Biology and a minor in Philosophy/Pre-law from Chapman University, where she graduated on the Chancellor's List. She has a Master of Public Health in Epidemiology with a concentration in Leadership from the University of Texas Health Science Center. She has published systematic reviews and clinical trials reports in Public Health peer-reviewed journals.

Edward L. Hunter joined the de Beaumont Foundation as President and Chief Executive Officer in February 2015, having previously served as Director of the Centers for Disease Control and Prevention's (CDC) Washington Office. Mr. Hunter was a principal CDC spokesperson to the Congress, the Administration, and public health organizations, and as a member of CDC's senior leadership, Mr. Hunter directed CDC's legislative strategy and gained valuable insight into public health programs, the intersection of policy and science, and the role of partnerships in our Federalist system. Prior to his work at CDC's Washington office, Mr. Hunter was Associate Director of the CDC's National Center for Health Statistics. He received a Bachelor of Arts in Economics from the University of Maryland, and a Master of Arts in Science, Technology, and Public Policy (emphasis in Health Policy and Economics) from George Washington University.

Denise Koo, MD, is Advisor to the CDC Associate Director for Policy. She is chief architect of the CDC Community Health Improvement Navigator (www.cdc.gov/CHInav), which provides an important unifying framework and tools to support hospitals, health systems, public health, and other community organizations and stakeholders that are interested in improving the health of their communities. Dr. Koo graduated from Harvard University with a BA in Biochemical Sciences. After combining medical school at the University of California, San Francisco, with an MPH in Epidemiology at University of California, Berkeley, she completed a primary care internal medicine residency at Brigham and Women's Hospital in Boston. Dr. Koo is a graduate of CDC's Epidemic Intelligence Service and Preventive Medicine Residency. Prior CDC positions have included running the National Notifiable Disease Surveillance System, serving as Director of the Division of Public Health Surveillance and Informatics, and serving as Director of CDC's Division of Scientific Education and Professional Development. Dr. Koo holds appointments as Adjunct Professor of Global Health and of Epidemiology, Rollins School of Public Health, Emory University, and Consulting Professor, Department of Community and Family Medicine, Duke University Medical Center.

Paul Kuehnert is Assistant Vice President—Program, for the Robert Wood Johnson Foundation where he provides leadership and management direction for the Foundation's work related to leadership and transforming health and healthcare systems. As an executive leader for the past 25 years, Kuehnert has led both governmental and community-based organizations in order to help people lead healthier lives. Most recently Kuehnert was the County Health Officer and Executive Director for Health in Kane County, Illinois, a metro-Chicago county of 515,000, where he initiated and led "Making Kane County Fit for Kids," a public–private partnership to reverse the epidemic of childhood obesity. Kuehnert is a pediatric nurse practitioner and holds the Doctor of Nursing Practice in Executive Leadership as well as the Master of Science in Public Health nursing degrees from the University of Illinois at Chicago. He was named a Robert Wood Johnson Foundation Executive Nurse Fellow in 2004 and inducted into the American Academy of Nursing in 2015.

Allen Leavens, MD, MPH, is a Principal Clinical Quality Analyst at the MITRE Corporation. He supports multiple projects as a subject matter expert in population health and quality measurement. Prior to this, Allen worked as a Senior Director at the National Quality Forum, and as Director of Healthcare Quality Improvement at Resolution Health Inc. Allen received his medical training at SUNY Buffalo, and is board certified in General Preventive Medicine and Public Health.

Amanda McCarty, MS, MBA, MS-HCA, is Assistant Professor in Health Sciences Administration at West Virginia University. Previously, she served as Director of Performance Management & Systems Development at the West Virginia's Bureau for Public Health. At the Bureau, Amanda was a member of the health department's leadership team and was responsible for accreditation, performance management, strategic planning, and quality improvement efforts. Prior to joining the Bureau, Amanda worked for Mountain State Blue Cross Blue Shield/Highmark, Inc., in health promotion, disease prevention, quality improvement, and evaluation for health-related programming and served as a consultant for regional and national accounts. As a consultant for PHF, McCarty has provided training and technical assistance for state and local health departments in the areas of performance management systems development, workforce development, quality improvement, and the development of evaluation plans and logic models since 2013. Amanda holds a BS and MS in Exercise Science as well as an MS in Healthcare Administration from Marshall University, and an MBA from West Virginia University.

Alicia Meadows, MPH, MBA, is the Director of Planning and Development for the Oklahoma City-County Health Department, where she led the agency efforts to become one of the first nationally accredited health departments. She has served in leadership roles at both local metro health departments in Oklahoma. She holds an MPH from the University of Oklahoma, and an MBA from Oklahoma State University. In her current role, she has primary oversight for accreditation, strategic planning, grants, program development, and quality improvement efforts, agency-wide. She is also a consultant for the Public Health Foundation, providing change management, quality improvement, strategic planning, and facilitation support for healthcare organizations in public and private sectors.

Michael Meit serves as a Senior Researcher in NORC's Public Health Research department and as Co-director of the NORC Walsh Center for Rural Health Analysis. He is responsible for NORC projects in the areas of rural health, public health systems research, and public health preparedness. He leads several program evaluations related to rural health, tribal health, and public health systems, and currently leads research projects in the areas of health workforce and the impacts of health reform. Meit has over 20 years of experience in public health systems and rural health. His experience includes work at both the state and national levels, first with the Pennsylvania Department of Health and then with the National Association of County and City Health Officials (NACCHO) in Washington, DC. Following his tenure at NACCHO, he served as the founding Director of the University of Pittsburgh Center for Rural Health Practice and as the Co-director for rural preparedness for the University of Pittsburgh Center for Public Health Preparedness. Meit served on the National Advisory Committee for Rural Health and Human Services from 2004 to 2008, recently completed two terms on the Board of Directors for the National Rural Health Association, and is a current member of the Board of Directors of the Maryland Rural Health Association.

J. Lloyd Michener, MD, is Professor and Chairman of the Department of Community and Family Medicine. He directs a national program for the "Practical Playbook" which facilitates the integration of Primary Care and Public Health, supported by the Centers for Disease Control and Prevention, the Health Resources and Services Administration, and the de Beaumont Foundation. He also leads the technical support services of "The BUILD Health Challenge," a national award program aimed at increasing the number and effectiveness of hospital, community, and public health collaborations that improve health, supported by the de Beaumont Foundation, The Advisory Board Company, the Kresge Foundation, The Colorado Health Care Foundation, and the Robert Wood Johnson Foundation.

Sharon Moffat was appointed as Interim Executive Director for the Association of State and Territorial Health Officials in December of 2015. She has worked at ASTHO for the past eight years as Chief of Health Promotion and Disease Prevention. She has oversight of a broad range of national public health programs, including public health and primary care integration, chronic disease prevention, injury and violence prevention, health information exchange, maternal child health, infectious disease, and health equity. Her work includes leadership roles as Chair of the National Forum Board for Heart Disease and Stroke, Liaison to Community Preventative Services Guide, and Past Chair of Vermont's Cathedral Square Corporation providing housing for the elderly and disabled.

Sharon served for two years as Commissioner of Health for Vermont Department of Health and four years as Senior Deputy Health Commissioner. As Health Commissioner, Sharon led the state public–private executive committee in the strategic development and implementation of Vermont's health reform. In 2009, Sharon was appointed by Governor Douglas to the Vermont Commission on Health Reform.

She began her public health career working in Vermont local health offices in urban and rural settings, providing Women Infant and Children Nutritional services, disease outbreak investigation, refugee health, and community coalition building.

Sharon has led policy and program planning in health system transformation, maternal child health, environmental health, chronic disease, mental health, and substance abuse.

Judith A. Monroe, MD, is President and CEO of the CDC Foundation, which she joined in February 2016. Over her career, Monroe's professional focus has centered on the intersection of primary care and public health. Prior to joining the CDC Foundation, Monroe worked for six years with the U.S. Centers for Disease Control and Prevention (CDC), serving as Director of the Office for State, Tribal, Local and Territorial Support (OSTLTS). In that role, Monroe oversaw key activities and technical assistance that support the nation's health departments and the public health system. Before joining CDC, Monroe served as the State Health Commissioner for Indiana from 2005 to 2010. She was President of the Association of State and Territorial Health Officials (ASTHO) from 2008 to 2009. Monroe has served on many national advisory committees and boards, such as the CDC Surveillance Leadership Board, Global Health Leadership Council, Robert Wood Johnson Foundation's Public Health Leadership Forum, de Beaumont Foundation-sponsored National Advisory Committee for the Practical Playbook, Medicaid-Public Health Expert Committee, and the Institute of Medicine's Roundtable on Population Health.

José Thier Montero, MD, became the VP of Population Health and Health Systems Integration at Cheshire Medical Center/Dartmouth-Hitchcock Keene in May 2015. In this capacity he has the responsibility to forward the mission and vision of the institution by:

- Directing, coordinating, and implementing Population Health interventions.
- Integrating clinical areas with community-based services.

- Developing and implementing approaches to address social determinants of health on the population at large.
- Providing leadership to engage with other senior clinical and administrative leadership colleagues to design and implement a health model that ensures high performing patient and family centered population management.

José served the State of New Hampshire as the State Epidemiologist and as the State Health Official (Public Health Director); in this capacity he was elected to be President of the Association for State and Territorial Health Officers (ASTHO). He also fulfills several national roles by serving in several committees, including the CDC's board of scientific councilors for the Office of Infectious Diseases and the OSTLTS advisory committee. He is a member of the Institute of Medicine (IOM) Roundtable on Population Health and Co-chair of the IOM collaboration for Public Health and Health Care Integration. He is the Chair of the New Hampshire Citizens Health Initiative. José serves as well as a member of Dartmouth Medical School's Leadership Preventive Medicine Residency Advisory Committee. He is Assistant Professor at the Geisel Medical School at Dartmouth, Department of Community and Family Medicine, and an Assistant Clinical Professor at the University of New Hampshire School of Health and Human Services. José received his MD from the Universidad Nacional de Colombia. He specialized in Family Medicine, receiving his degree from the Universidad del Valle in Cali, Colombia, and a degree in Epidemiology from the Pontificia Universidad Javeriana in Bogota, Colombia. He received as well a master's degree in Health Care Delivery Science at Dartmouth College.

Elisa Munthali, MPH, is Vice President of Quality Measurement at the National Quality Forum (NQF). Elisa joined NQF in 2010 and oversees NQF's Consensus Development Process, Measure Applications Partnership, and all other performance measure projects. She has led several Centers for Medicare & Medicaid Services–funded performance measure endorsement projects related to ambulatory care, patient safety, healthcare disparities and cultural competency, behavioral health, and population health. Prior to joining NQF, Elisa worked with the Maryland Hospital Association's Quality Indicator Project for eight years, where she coordinated education and training efforts on national hospital quality reporting requirements for healthcare facilities across the United States. Elisa received a Master of Public Health degree from the George Washington University Milken Institute School of Public Health.

Melanie Nadeau has lived and worked in tribal communities throughout her entire life. Being an enrolled member of the Turtle Mountain Band of Chippewa, she has a personal interest in both research and community engagement because of the many health problems that are not only faced by members of her family, but also by the community in which she is from. Currently, Melanie is Operational Director/Assistant Faculty in Practice at the American Indian Public Health Resource Center (AIPHRC), which is housed at North Dakota State University. This position has given her the opportunity to serve American Indian people utilizing the knowledge, skills, and abilities which she has acquired through years of education and experience working in tribal communities. Melanie is highly educated and trained in epidemiologic methods, mixed methods, public health program evaluation, community health education, and health disparities. Throughout her education she has been given many opportunities to work with tribal communities conducting community-based participatory research and case-control studies. As Operational Director of the AIPHRC, Melanie leads a team that has successfully engaged a multitude of tribal health stakeholders from tribes across the region and other AI health stakeholders using a four-pronged approach to public health that includes addressing issues through a public health policy, research, education, and services lens. As Assistant Professor she is also given the opportunity to guest lecture for the only Master of Public Health program in the nation in which students can specialize in American Indian Public Health. Her first peer-reviewed publication was in 2010, focused on recruiting American Indian women into an epidemiologic study which stemmed from her work as a research technician at a tribal college. While in this position, Melanie recruited over 400 women to participate in the research and was also given the opportunity to translate research findings at the community level for participants, community members, tribal health board members, tribal council members, and tribal college faculty. As part of her service to the profession, Melanie currently serves as the American Indian Section Chair for the North Dakota Public Health Association, a board member for the Turtle Mountain Band of Chippewa Indians Research Review Board, and a board member for the American Public Health Association American Indian, Alaska Native, Native Hawaiian caucus.

Tiffany J. Netters is Program Manager of the Gulf Region Health Outreach Program's Primary Care Capacity Project, working across the Gulf Coast of Louisiana, Mississippi, Alabama, and Florida to enhance the primary care delivery system through funding and technical assistance to community health centers. At the Louisiana Public Health Institute, Tiffany coordinates a team of over 25 technical assistance providers and five project officers to implement this program under this court-supervised settlement project. Tiffany has served as Interim Chronic Disease Director for Louisiana's Chronic Disease Prevention and Control Unit, in which she led the development of several CDC-funded grant programs and the state's Community Transformation Grant. She has extensive experience and training in strategic planning and implementation, project management, team building, and strategic partnership management. Tiffany holds a Master of Public Administration with a concentration in Nonprofit Management from the Louisiana State University's E. J. Ourso College of Business.

Janelle Nichols serves as the Project Associate for Academic/Practice Linkages (APL) at the Public Health Foundation (PHF). In this role, she assists with the management of the day-to-day operations of the Council on Linkages Between Academia and Public Health Practice and other APL activities, including promotion of the Core Competencies for Public Health Professionals (Core Competencies), facilitating the Core Competencies Workgroup, coordinating communications activities, and preparing and disseminating reports and other promotional materials. Ms. Nichols holds a Bachelor of Science degree in Health Services Administration from Ohio University and a Master of Public Health degree from The George Washington University.

Patrick W. O'Carroll, MD, is a Rear Admiral and Assistant Surgeon General in the U.S. Public Health Service (USPHS), serving since January 2003 as Regional Health Administrator for the U.S. Department of Health and Human Services (HHS) Region X (Alaska, Idaho, Oregon, and Washington); and since April 2015 as Senior Adviser to the Assistant Secretary for Health, HHS. As RHA, RADM O'Carroll serves as the principal federal public health leader in the Pacific Northwest, representing the HHS Assistant Secretary of Health. RADM O'Carroll received his medical degree and his Master of Public Health from Johns Hopkins University in 1983. After training in family practice and preventive medicine, he joined CDC as an Epidemic Intelligence Service Officer, and spent 18 years with CDC as an epidemiologist, informatician, and program director. During his 31 years with USPHS, RADM O'Carroll has worked on a great variety of health and policy challenges, including injury prevention; immunization; chronic disease; maternal and child health; environmental health; infectious disease epidemic control; behavioral health; tobacco control; suicide prevention; global health and disease surveillance; and bioterrorism and disaster preparedness. RADM O'Carroll holds Affiliate Professor appointments in the Departments of Epidemiology and Health Services at the University of Washington School of Public Health, and in the Department of Biomedical Informatics and Medical Education, UW School of Medicine.

Alonzo Plough became Vice President for Research and Evaluation and Chief Science Officer at the Robert Wood Johnson Foundation (RWJF) in January 2014. RWJF is the largest private funder solely focused on health and healthcare improvement and research in the United States. He also oversees the two grant-making portfolios focused on innovation and emerging issues: Pioneer and Global Ideas for U.S. Solutions. Dr. Plough came to RWJF from the Los Angeles County Department of Public Health, where he served as Director of Emergency Preparedness and Response from 2009 to 2014. In this role he directed activities in emergency operations, infectious disease control, risk communication, planning, and community engagement. Prior to that position, Dr. Plough served as Vice President of Strategy, Planning and Evaluation for The California Endowment from 2005 to 2009. He also served as Director and Health Officer for the Seattle and King County Department of Public Health for ten years, and Professor of Health Services at the University of Washington, School of Public Health in Seattle. He previously served as Director of Public Health in Boston for eight years. Dr. Plough earned his PhD and master's degree at Cornell University, and his Master of Public Health degree at Yale University School of Medicine's Department of Epidemiology and Public Health. He has held academic appointments at Harvard University School of Public Health, Tufts University Department of Community Medicine, and Boston University School of Management. He has been the recipient of numerous awards for public service and leadership and is the author of an extensive body of scholarly articles, books, and book chapters.

Lawrence W. Prybil retired as Norton Professor in Healthcare Leadership at the University of Kentucky in 2016. He also is Professor Emeritus at the University of Iowa, where he served as Associate Dean and Senior Advisor to the Dean in the UI College of Public Health. Before returning to Iowa to participate in building its new College of Public Health, Dr. Prybil held senior executive positions in two of our country's largest nonprofit health systems for nearly 20 years, including ten years as CEO for a six-state division of the Daughters of Charity National Health System.

Dr. Prybil received his master's and doctoral degrees from the University of Iowa's College of Medicine and is a Life Fellow in the American College of Healthcare Executives. He has served on the governing boards of hospitals, health systems, state hospital associations, the American Hospital Association, and other nonprofit and investor-owned organizations. He presently serves on the national board of the AHA Center for Healthcare Governance. Dr. Prybil has authored or co-authored 108 publications. He is recognized for expertise in governance and executive leadership. He has directed a series of national studies regarding governance practices in nonprofit hospitals and health systems, and recently completed a study of successful multi-sector partnerships focused on improving the health of communities they jointly serve.

Greg Randolph, MD, MPH, is President and CEO of Population Health Improvement Partners and is Professor of Pediatrics and Adjunct Professor of Public Health at the University of North Carolina at Chapel Hill. Dr. Randolph has over 17 years of experience in quality improvement (QI) leadership, implementation, education, and research. He has published extensively on the application of QI in healthcare and public health. He currently provides QI expertise nationally via the Public Health Accreditation Board Evaluation and Quality Improvement Committee, the American Board of Pediatrics Maintenance of Certification Committee, the American Academy of Pediatrics (AAP) Quality Improvement Innovation Network's Steering Committee, and the AAP Chapter Quality Network's Project Advisory

Committee. He has also served on the Institute of Medicine Committee on Quality Measures for the Healthy People Leading Health Indicators, the U.S. Department of Health and Human Services Expert Panel on Public Health Quality, the Executive Committee of the AAP Council on Quality Improvement and Patient Safety, and as Editor of the AAP Quality Connections newsletter. Dr. Randolph received his MD/MPH degree from UNC-Chapel Hill, completed an Academic General Pediatrics Fellowship and Preventive Medicine Residency at UNC-Chapel Hill, and is a CDC National Public Health Leadership Institute Scholar.

Julia J. Resnick, MPH, serves as Senior Program Manager for the Association for Community Health Improvement, a division of the Health Research and Educational Trust of the American Hospital Association, where she has worked since 2013. Julia oversees relationships with external partners, develops ACHI's strategy and educational curriculum, and plans the ACHI National Conference. Julia has published numerous guides and works on a variety of projects with HRET that address population and community health topics. Prior to joining HRET, Julia worked as a Research Coordinator at NorthShore University HealthSystem. While on a fellowship in Israel, Julia worked in a community clinic and coordinated perinatal care for pregnant African refugee women. She received a Master of Public Health degree at Hebrew University's Braun School of Public Health and Community Medicine and a Bachelor of Arts in sociology from Bates College.

Rudy Ruiz is a nationally recognized social entrepreneur, multicultural advocate, and award-winning author. As CEO of the advocacy marketing agency Interlex Communications, Mr. Ruiz has led the development and implementation of numerous public health awareness and behavior change campaigns on issues including nutrition, obesity, immunizations, and smoking cessation and prevention. Through these efforts, he has successfully pioneered multicultural marketing techniques to address health disparities. His writings have been published in books, academic papers, and major media outlets. Mr. Ruiz earned his bachelor's degree in Government from Harvard College and his Master of Public Policy from the Harvard Kennedy School. He serves on the Board of Directors of the Center for Science in the Public Interest.

Renata Schiavo, PhD, MA, is a public health, healthcare, global health, and social innovation specialist with more than 20 years' experience in a variety of settings around the globe. Currently, she is Founding President, Board of Directors, of Health Equity Initiative, a member-driven nonprofit membership organization dedicated to building and sustaining a global community that engages across sectors and disciplines to advance health equity. Dr. Schiavo is also Senior Lecturer at Columbia University Mailman School of Public Health, where her courses focus on topics at the intersection of society, health equity, and communication; and the Editor-in-Chief of the peer-reviewed *Journal of Communication in Healthcare: Strategies, Media, and Engagement in Global Health*, which is published by Taylor & Francis. In addition she is Principal, Strategic Communication Resources, a global expert consultancy she established in 2004, where her work has been focused on building the capacity of different strategic approaches to health, equity, and social issues, strategic counsel, qualitative research and review studies, participatory planning and human-centered design, and intervention design and/or evaluation as related to many health and social topics. An accomplished leader and well-published author, Dr. Schiavo has served on advisory/expert panels for the World Health Organization, U.S. National Institute of Health, and American Public Health Association. Throughout her career, Dr. Schiavo has designed and led numerous consensus-driven processes and multisectoral interventions for behavioral, social, organizational, and system change. She was recognized as one of 300 Women Leaders in Global Health (2015), and is an elected Fellow of the New York Academy of Medicine.

Thomas Schlenker, MD, MPH, is a physician and public health leader who has practiced clinical pediatrics in the United States and Latin America; directed local health departments in Milwaukee and Madison, Wisconsin, Salt Lake City, Utah, and San Antonio, Texas; and researched, lectured, and published on population health topics ranging from measles to infant mortality to health financing to obesity and diabetes. With degrees in Political Science from Antioch College, Medicine from Northwestern, and Public Health from Harvard, he has been CDC national faculty in childhood lead poisoning prevention, Fulbright Senior Fellow in Mexico, and member of a U.S. commission reporting on health conditions in El Salvador. Following four years directing the San Antonio Metropolitan Health District, Dr. Schlenker became in 2015 Medical Director of Interlex communications.

F. Douglas Scutchfield, MD, is the initial incumbent in the Peter P. Bosomworth Professorship in Health Services Research and Policy at the University of Kentucky. He holds faculty appointments in the University of Kentucky College of Public Health and the College of Medicine. He received his MD from the University of Kentucky, where he was elected to AOA medical society honorary. He completed postgraduate medical education at Northwestern University, The Centers for Disease Control and Prevention, and the University of Kentucky. Dr. Scutchfield is a diplomate of the American Board of Preventive Medicine and was, from 1972 to 1985, a diplomate of the American Board of Family Practice. He holds fellowships in both the American College of Preventive Medicine and the American Academy of Family Practice. He holds honorary doctoral degrees from Eastern Kentucky University and the University of Pikeville. He was one of the founders of the College of Community Health Science at the University of Alabama, he founded the Graduate School of Public Health at San Diego State University, and he founded the School, now College, of Public Health at the University of Kentucky. Dr. Scutchfield has held many national positions in professional organizations, including President of the American College of Preventive Medicine, and received several awards from those organizations, including the American Medical Association's Distinguished Service Award. He is a skilled editor and has served as editor, guest editor, and on the editorial board of many journals. He is the author of over 200 refereed papers, book chapters, and technical reports and has edited several books. He is a valued consultant and has consulted broadly both in the United States and abroad.

Julie Sharp is a Performance Improvement Specialist for the Public Health Foundation (PHF) in Washington, DC. In that role, she works on a number of performance improvement initiatives, including the Public Health Improvement Resource Center, and Development of Competencies for Performance Improvement Professionals. Prior to joining PHF, Julie worked for over a decade in local public health in Kane County, Illinois, serving as the Accreditation Coordinator for the department's successful application to the Public Health Accreditation Board in 2013. She also developed and implemented the department's first quality improvement and performance management systems. Julie holds a bachelor's degree in Psychology from Rockford College (Rockford, Illinois), and an MPH from Benedictine University (Lisle, Illinois).

Kenneth D. Smith, PhD, is a health economist and public health practitioner. His research in health economics in academia and private industry has focused on healthcare financing, physician practice behavior, and the evaluation and evaluation design of large national healthcare demonstration projects for persons with chronic disease. Dr. Smith became a public health practitioner after he was appointed Director of Chronic Disease Prevention, Philadelphia Department of Public Health. There, he oversaw the City's Tobacco Control Program; helped implement the City's Clean Indoor Air Act and trans fats ban; and drafted a plan for improved access to fresh, affordable produce. As a result of Dr. Smith's efforts, and with the assistance of community stakeholders, Philadelphia passed the nation's most comprehensive menu-labeling ordinance. Dr. Smith was Lead Analyst for Chronic Disease and Environmental Health for the National Association of County and City Health Officials, where he built a national-level portfolio of projects around Health Impact Assessment, Health in All Policies. Dr. Smith was appointed Interim Director for the Center to Eliminate Health Disparities in 2014, where he is charting a new path for the Center to be a catalyst for systems changes that promote health equity.

Michael A. Stoto, PhD, Professor of Health Systems Administration and Population Health at Georgetown University, is a statistician and health services researcher.

He also holds faculty appointments in the Department of Family Medicine, where he is Associate Director of the Population Health Scholars Program, and the Georgetown University Law Center. Dr. Stoto is an expert on public health systems research (PHSR), applying and developing rigorous mixed-methods approaches to studying and evaluating federal, state, and local public health systems. Dr. Stoto's recent PHSR work has focused on public health emergency preparedness, regionalization in public health, the evaluation of biosurveillance methods, and the development of methods for assessing emergency preparedness capabilities based on exercises and actual events. Dr. Stoto is a recognized expert on population health and public health assessment, and has developed methods for evaluating community health assessments and performance measures, and helped to develop Community Health Needs Assessments (CHNAs) for hospitals as well as state and local health departments in the Washington, DC, metropolitan area. He is currently leading a project to evaluate the impact of new federal requirements that nonprofit hospitals conduct CHNAs.

Trevor Thompson focuses on intersections of human health, emerging technologies, and climate change. His recent work in strategic foresight has spanned the areas of public health, healthcare, sustainability, cyber security, and artificial intelligence. Prior to joining IAF, Trevor interned with the World Health Organization (WHO) in Switzerland, and also worked on a leishmaniasis policy and prevention project in Bahia, Brazil. Trevor received his AB in Environmental Science and Public Policy from Harvard University in 2011, along with a secondary in African and African-American Studies and a Spanish Language citation. Trevor is currently pursuing a joint Master of Environmental Management (MEM)/Master of Business Administration (MBA) at Yale University, with a focus on climate change, health, and sustainability issues.

Julie Trocchio is Senior Director of Community Benefit and Continuing Care for the Catholic Health Association of the United States. She coordinates CHA activities related to community benefits and tax-exemption of not-for-profit healthcare organizations and leads the association's programs for Catholic-sponsored long-term and elder care. Julie has nursing degrees from Georgetown University and the University of Maryland.

Kerri Ann Ward, MHA, is a Program Manager at Population Health Improvement Partners, where she provides quality improvement expertise and coaching to healthcare and public health organizations across the country. She also has experience managing quality planning projects and adapting quality improvement curriculum for large-scale training programs. Kerri received her BS in Business Administration and her Master of Healthcare Administration from the University of North Carolina at Chapel Hill and completed her Lean Six Sigma Black Belt training at Villanova University.

Donald Warne, MD, is Associate Professor and Chair of the Department of Public Health in the College of Health Professions at North Dakota State University, and he is Senior Policy Advisor to the Great Plains Tribal Chairmen's Health Board. Dr. Warne is a member of the Oglala Lakota tribe from Pine Ridge, SD, and comes from a long line of traditional healers and medicine men. He received his MD from Stanford University School of Medicine and his MPH from Harvard School of Public Health.

Professional activities include:

- Member, National Board of Directors, American Cancer Society;
- Member, Minority Affairs Section and Association of American Indian Physicians Representative to the American Medical Association;
- Member, Advisory Committee on Rural Health and Human Services, U.S. Department of Health and Human Services;
- Member, Advisory Committee on Breast Cancer in Young Women, Centers for Disease Control and Prevention;
- Member, National Institutional Review Board, Indian Health Service.

Marcia Wilson, PhD, MBA, is Senior Vice President of Quality Measurement at NQF. She leads the core NQF activities of measure endorsement and measure selection through the multiple-stakeholder consensus process. Prior to joining NQF, Marcia's primary work focused on quality improvement initiatives in healthcare, with an emphasis on ensuring equitable care for minority patients. Marcia was Associate Director for Aligning Forces for Quality, the Robert Wood Johnson Foundation's signature effort to improve the quality of healthcare in 16 communities across the United States. In this role, she led the team responsible for overseeing and supporting all activities of the 16 Aligning Forces' communities working to make changes in performance measurement and public reporting, quality improvement, patient experience, consumer engagement, and reductions in healthcare costs. Prior to Aligning Forces, Marcia was responsible for the development and implementation of two nationwide hospital initiatives—addressing disparities in cardiac care and reducing emergency department crowding by improving hospital-wide throughput. Marcia has an additional 20 years of experience in healthcare working primarily with medical groups. She received her PhD from the George Washington University School of Business in health services administration and her MBA from the University of San Diego.

PREFACE

It's difficult to see the picture when you're inside the frame.

—Eugene Kleiner

This book is designed to help those trying to improve a community population health issue with unique ideas and tools from respected population health experts. These experts will explain how they have approached population health with ideas that are outside the frame. Each chapter is written from that author's perspective of population health shaped by their experience implementing change in a community's health.

The goal of this book is to help those trying to engage their community in a population health issue to demonstrate how new innovative methods and tools can facilitate building and leading community coalitions that are sustainable and able to make real improvements. Leadership skills needed to become a Community Chief Health Strategist, using a driver diagram to engage the community, understanding "What is in my backyard," or becoming an Exemplar Organization are some of the innovative approaches discussed in this book. To really improve population health we need to do some *Innovative* things well to reach the desired future state of health. We simply cannot reach that "new" state unless the organization is prepared culturally, has stable and reliable processes that can transform into a population health model, and has a workforce possessing the competencies to perform population health interventions. This book provides you with the means and ways to reach this state.

So what is Innovation in Public Health as it moves to be a force in Population Health? Is it brought about by many incremental advances in technology or processes, as Quality Improvement was designed to do, or is it revolutionary innovation, which is often disruptive because everything will change? We throw around the word *Innovation* as if it is a panacea for making things better in an easier and simpler way. In reality innovation only occurs with a stable organizational platform to build from; one with competent workers and processes that deliver what the customer wants/needs in an efficient and economical manner. This requires an organization to be constantly and continuously improving everything they do—even in the innovative state. The false prophets that start pushing innovation as the new way and tell you to discard or minimize quality improvement because "innovation will leapfrog your organization to a new and improved state" miss the point that whatever state you are in, you must do the hard enduring work of quality improvement every day in every one of your processes. If you do not continuously improve yet jump to "Innovation" you will find that your innovative state looks identical to the state you left, only masked by the veneer of an innovation panacea.

The culture of Public Health must be transformed to break from the doldrums of "the business as usual" model to one where new and truly innovative ideas may thrive. We can feel good by putting "Innovation" in our strategic plan but only if we are mindful of what Peter Drucker used to say: "Culture eats strategy for breakfast." People are loyal to a culture, not a strategy. Culture is the way things get done, and people become comfortable in the status quo.

For Public Health to become a real linchpin in its community's Population Health will require it to change its culture, develop new strategies, implement those strategies, measure the impact, consistently and continually improve its processes, and develop new workforce competencies. This book is designed to orchestrate that change.

1

PUBLIC HEALTH FUTURES

Clement Bezold, Yasemin Arikan,
and Trevor Thompson

Introduction

The public health community is currently situated at the fulcrum of many of
society's greatest challenges. Population health, chronic disease, emergency preparedness, and even the more familiar ground of infectious disease are all fraught
with uncertainties to which public health will need to respond in the years to
come. Such responses will often require significant changes from the kinds of
responses public health agencies have utilized in the past. The four alternative
public health scenarios presented in this report invite readers to recognize that
the future is uncertain, but can be bounded using the knowledge we have today.
Further, public health leaders have an opportunity to influence which future
unfolds and how. This report seeks to equip these leaders with a broader awareness of the relevant trends and forces so that they can more adroitly shape the
future of public health.

Why Scenarios?

Given the multiple uncertainties facing public health, scenarios are needed to consider plausible alternative paths for the field in order to choose the best way forward.
Scenarios are parallel stories describing how the future may unfold (in ways both
good and bad). They help us view the dynamic systems around us in more complex
terms that accept uncertainty, and then clarify and challenge the assumptions about
what we can do. While the future is inherently uncertain, scenarios help us bound
that uncertainty into a limited number of likely paths. Some paths may lead to

futures we want to avoid while others point to surprisingly favorable outcomes. Once these alternatives have been articulated, we can more easily explore the inherent uncertainty to find opportunities and challenges we might otherwise miss. These insights can then inform strategic planning processes.

To find more creative options for public health and improve strategic planning in and for public health, the Institute for Alternative Futures (IAF) developed a set of four alternative scenarios of public health in the year 2030. These consider the range of forces, challenges, and opportunities shaping public health in the United States.

Origins and Development of the Public Health 2030 Scenarios

This project to develop scenarios of public health emerged from IAF's earlier work with the Kresge Foundation and the Robert Wood Johnson Foundation (RWJF). RWJF had turned to IAF to explore the future of vulnerable populations and to produce a set of Vulnerability 2030 scenarios (www.altfutures.org/vulnerability2030) that were published in 2011. The following year the Kresge Foundation funded IAF's Primary Care 2025 scenario project (www.altfutures.org/primarycare2025), which made clear that the population health agenda would prove vital. The Kresge Foundation then suggested that it would be beneficial to develop scenarios for public health. At around the same time, RWJF sponsored a scenario exploration of health and health care in 2032 (www.altfutures.org/health2032) as part of its 40th anniversary recognition. For RWJF, these projects set the stage for a project on the future of public health to explore this vital component of the evolving health landscape in the United States. Hence the Kresge Foundation and RWJF joined forces to have IAF explore the future of public health in the United States.

For this project we recruited a small advisory committee of public health leaders from APHA, ASTHO, NACCHO, academia, and CDC and state and local health departments. These advisors gave us invaluable input and guidance on design and directions and reviewed draft forecasts and scenarios. They also took part in the national Public Health 2030 workshop. Likewise, our project officers—Phyllis Meadows from the Kresge Foundation and Sallie George and Paul Kuehnert from the Robert Wood Johnson Foundation—gave us important input in the development of the scenarios. We interviewed a wide range of experts in public health and the surrounding fields, both individually and within assembled public health groups. Our advisors, interviewees, and national workshop attendees are listed in the full scenario report at www.altfutures.org/publichealth2030. We also worked with four health departments to develop 2030 scenarios for their jurisdictions: Fargo Cass Public Health (ND), the Boston Public Health Commission, the Virginia Department of Health, and the Cuyahoga County Board of Health. These state and local scenarios are available at the same location.

Our scenario development used IAF's Aspirational Futures[1] approach that considers expectable (or most likely), challenging (exploring some of the many things that could "go wrong"), and visionary (or surprisingly successful) space for public health.

Four Public Health 2030 Scenarios

Overview of the Four Scenarios

Scenario 1: One Step Forward, Half a Step Back

Amidst continued fiscal constraints, public health agencies and health care slowly advance their capabilities. Many use automation and advanced analytics to improve services and community and population health. However, climate change challenges continue to grow, and there is little progress in improving the social determinants of health. Great variations in technological capabilities, funding, and approaches to prevention—along with a continuous rise in health care costs—significantly limit public health gains.

Scenario 2: Overwhelmed, Under-Resourced

Funding cuts and a hostile political context undermine the role of public health agencies, which subsequently fail to attract talented young people. Public health crises grow worse and more frequent, largely due to climate change. Private sector initiatives produce significant innovations for health and wellness, but these primarily benefit the middle-class and affluent groups. Technological, economic, educational, and health disparities grow, and the institutions of public health have little capacity for doing anything about them.

Scenario 3: Sea Change for Health Equity

National and local economies gradually grow, and changes in values and demographics lead to "common sense" policies and support for health equity. Public health agencies develop into health development agencies (HDAs) that use advanced analytics, gamification, and diverse partnerships to identify problems and opportunities, and catalyze and incentivize action to improve community health. While some disparities persist, in 2030 the vast majority of U.S. residents have attained greater opportunity for good health through quality improvements in housing, economic opportunity, education, and other social determinants of health.

Scenario 4: Community-Driven Health and Equity

Public health agencies, partners, and local health improvement initiatives coalesce via technology and social media into a national web of community health-enhancing networks. These networks help communities exchange their innovations and best practices, and leverage the expertise of public health agencies and others. The nation also strives to come to terms with its racial and socioeconomic histories, and supports real changes and legislation to create a more equitable society. This value shift to equity is accelerated by the proliferation of new community economic models that help households sustain themselves and improve health and wellbeing. Public health sheds many functions and facilitates these movements to improved health.

Scenario 1: One Step Forward, Half a Step Back

Life in This Scenario

"Alright, let's start this month's strategy session by going over the latest numbers and maps." Karla, who had been County Health Department director for more than a year now, pulled up the latest health maps for the others to see. Under Karla's direction, the department had become a leader in "big data" analytics for community and population health improvement. This included ensuring that the electronic health records used by health care providers were interoperable and secure, and that the aggregations were accessible to the County Health Department and linkable to data from environmental monitors, reimbursements, and other sources. Using this data, health care providers collaborated with Karla's staff to conduct community health needs assessments and to support community groups to address the findings.

George, a pediatrician at a local Accountable Care Organization, could not contain himself. "That's great progress!" he exclaimed, pointing to a few neighborhoods where the average resident had lost more than four pounds over the past six months. Tobacco sales had also declined, largely due to improved access to cessation programs through health care providers, and the work of the County Health Department with faith-based and community groups in creating positive peer pressure to reduce smoking rates among teens and young adults.

Raymond chimed in. Raymond was the executive director of the local YMCA. "We've been named one of the best counties in emergency preparedness." As extreme weather events grew frequent, Karla's team used online games and simulations and advanced mapping to better prepare their communities for emergencies, which also included outbreaks of vector-borne diseases like Lyme disease and dengue fever. Funding these efforts was possible due to the automation of many traditional monitoring and inspection activities, which now required fewer employees.

In health care, the patient-centered medical home (PCMH) model was widely adopted in the county, and the vast majority of residents now had access to affordable and effective care. This change reduced the need for personal clinical services from the County Health Department. The department shifted to put a stronger focus on prevention in order to improve preconception health, increase birth outcomes, lower obesity rates, and reduce injuries.

Karla frowned as she looked at a low-income section of the county. "What will need to happen to make a dent over here?" she asked. George and Raymond gave no answer. They knew that public health in the county had become smarter, leaner, and faster over the past two decades, but that the county's consistent overall gains in nutrition, physical activity, and other key health indicators, as well as continued decreases in rates of smoking, had not been distributed evenly. Investments in the broader social determinants of health such as housing, education, and economic opportunity had remained few. The three were distraught by the persistent health disparities in the county.

"Clearly, we still have a long way to go," Karla noted. "What should we do next?"

FIGURE 1.1 Scenario 1

Scenario 1 Highlights

Public health agencies (PHAs) slowly advanced their capabilities in technologically enhanced monitoring of health across populations, emergency preparedness, and inspections. As the Patient Protection and Affordable Care Act expanded health care coverage, PHAs stepped back from personal clinical health services and focused on prevention and improving community conditions. PHAs used automation, diverse data streams, and big data analytics to improve community and population health, and demonstrated positive returns on investment for the services they still offered. However, great variations in their capabilities, funding, and approaches to prevention—along with a continuous rise in health care costs—held back public health from advancing as far as it should have by 2030.

Scenario 1 Details

The two decades leading to 2030 were largely characterized by recurring fiscal and health challenges. Public health programs and technologies improved only slowly. In terms of the opportunities for all to be healthy, there were improvements overall in some health measures (especially reductions in obesity and some chronic diseases). Nevertheless, several disparities continued across race and class in almost all measures. Public health agencies (PHAs) tried to address them, but varied widely in their access to the funding, capabilities, and services needed to make a difference. Most consistently, however, public health continued to shift away from personal clinical services, and moved toward prevention, health promotion, advocacy, advanced analytics, and emergency preparedness. Some states confined PHAs to provide only legislatively required or mandated services (e.g. infectious disease control, restaurant inspection, and other regulatory activities) or aspects of emergency preparedness. Where this was the case, PHAs could do little prevention or community-focused activities.

While PHAs were forced to reduce or put a strain on their prevention and community-focused activities, their roles expanded in emergency preparedness and response, particularly as climate change took its toll on the nation. The 2020s saw increasing frequencies of extreme weather events such as droughts, floods, tornadoes, hurricanes, and other storms that challenged communities. Vector-borne infection outbreaks, such as Lyme disease and dengue fever, became more frequent and severe. Many PHAs used ever better games and simulations to prepare their communities for these and other types of emergencies. Federal, state, and local health and other agencies, as well as nonprofits and the business community, got better at successfully coordinating their preparation, response, and recovery. PHAs also increasingly automated their monitoring and inspection activities, focusing on designing and approving monitoring and inspection systems, and providing quality control for these systems, these data streams, and the analyses based on them. Thus, fewer but more technically savvy employees were needed to manage these systems and to deal with potential food-borne contaminations, air pollution, and environmental toxins.

Most PHAs sought to keep pace with "big data" and advanced analytics to improve coordination in disaster preparedness, response, and recovery, as well as ongoing public health improvements. These PHAs ensured that the electronic health records (EHR) systems used by health care providers were interoperable and secure, and that the aggregations were accessible to PHAs. PHAs also strongly advocated for privacy and discrimination protections, which were ultimately put in place. Personal health information in EHRs was thus effectively integrated with environmental monitoring, social media data, Medicare and Medicaid reimbursement data, motor vehicle records, employment records, and other government data. Most PHAs accessed the anonymized data through cloud computing services for health surveillance.

Analyzing the increasingly larger and more diverse data, however, required well-trained staff who were often at risk of being hired away to better paying jobs. Many PHAs (particularly those with small staff sizes, or those which could not share advanced analytics with other PHAs) thus left big data analytics to private sector contractors and local Accountable Care Organizations (ACOs). In any case, the growth of increasingly complex and sophisticated analyses strengthened emergency preparedness, response, and recovery efforts, and improved PHAs' ability to target community needs, to monitor health trends, to provide better forecasts, and to plan. PHAs collaborated with health care providers and private companies to improve public health analyses and the design of public health services, and interventions aimed at individuals and behaviors. For example, one emerging challenge for PHAs was the fact that next-generation social networking platforms facilitated intensive and continuous interaction among people, and this interaction often reinforced negative health behaviors. PHAs spent significant time and effort using advanced analytics to understand the social dynamics that played out in these networks and "nudge" the conversation toward better health.

Technological advances improved the clinical services provided by PHAs and others, but the successful implementation of the Patient Protection and Affordable Care Act (PPACA) was even more influential. By the end of the 2010s, over 90 percent of U.S. residents had health care insurance. This gave them affordable access to a health care system that had become more effective through the widespread adoption of the patient-centered medical home (PCMH) model. The PPACA assured age-appropriate preventive services without co-pays and enhanced financial incentives for primary care, effectively doubling the volumes of federally qualified health centers. Providers in PCMHs anticipated patients' needs by routinely analyzing large pools of data, including genomic and bio-monitoring data (often transmitted to the EHR from the patients' smartphones and wearable devices). Patient protocol systems became more sophisticated through the expanded use of cognitive computing tools, such as IBM's "Doc Watson" and its successors. Most ACOs and community health centers also provided their patients with some form of digital health coach that used personal health information to help them make healthier choices in their daily lives.

Ultimately, the PPACA reduced the need for personal clinical services from PHAs. For example, in the states where Medicaid expansion covered mothers and children, PHAs' maternal and child health programs shifted away from being the payer or the provider of last resort for that care toward primary prevention in order to improve preconception health, increase birth outcomes, lower obesity rates, and reduce injuries. Similarly, federal funding for HIV/AIDS programs provided by PHAs declined as health care providers routinely treated the newly insured HIV/AIDS patients.

In addition to improving the quality and per capita cost of clinical care, health care providers played larger roles in improving population health. However, their relationships with PHAs for this purpose varied widely. Most providers were part of ACOs that were required to conduct community health assessments and address the resulting findings. Based on the assessment and findings, most ACOs funded or otherwise supported community groups to improve population health. On one end of the spectrum, PHAs led the analysis, and collaborated with ACOs in conducting the needs assessment, facilitating community priority setting, and joining community groups and others in addressing the priority needs (including issues such as housing, education, neighborhood safety, physical activity, and access to food). At the other end of the spectrum, however, ACOs did not see the PHA as having much to offer in terms of analysis or as a cost-effective supplier of programs.

Another jigsaw puzzle was state and local public health funding. Virtually all states continued to face severe fiscal constraints. Many cities and counties teetered on the brink of bankruptcy, with some falling over the edge. Cost pressures on PHAs, the automation of several functions, and the ability to serve communities in digital and virtual spaces led to more sharing of services and consolidation among local health departments.

Funding for some federal programs was stable or slightly expanded, whereas funding for health services programs (e.g. Ryan White, Maternal and Child Health, cancer screening) was reduced. PHAs still complained about the restrictions of categorical funding, particularly for building infrastructure across their programs. However, the Centers for Disease Control and Prevention (CDC) allowed PHAs to use up to 5 percent of some CDC grants to pay the costs associated with the public health agency accreditation process. Most PHAs pursued accreditation. Many also implemented a uniform chart of accounts, which enabled agency-to-agency comparability and recurring quality improvements. PHAs increased their evaluation activities and showed positive return on investment for many programs. What's more, big data studies showed that addressing the social determinants of health was far more cost-effective in reducing health care costs, improving community economies, and strengthening the overall wellbeing of populations, than investments in health care. Yet decisive and sustained investments to improve housing, education, and economic opportunity remained few.

Given all of the developments in technology and health care reform, one of the biggest surprises in the field of public health between 2014 and 2020 was the absence of so-called "game-changers." While "big data" had proven useful in many contexts, including disease surveillance and health needs assessment, it had not transformed society in the ways that some in the mid-2010s had expected. While genomic data is now included in most EHRs, it rarely provides a "smoking gun" for health researchers working on a specific disease or condition, or for population health researchers to identify useful genetic markers that would positively affect community prevention efforts. While the PPACA was a significant step toward universal access and health equity, there were no parallel improvements in the social determinants of health (such as housing, education, and economic opportunity) that would have been necessary to fundamentally improve the nation's health. In 2030, late-career public health officials can look back on a series of important successes for the field, while at the same time recognizing that the field never made it as far as it should have. The consensus in the field is that public health made gains, but the continuous rise in health care costs had limited these gains to half steps or "baby steps." PHAs and public health leaders recognize that they still have a long way to go to improve population health, reduce disparities, and optimize their use of emerging technologies.

Scenario 2: Overwhelmed, Under-Resourced

Life in This Scenario

As Allison read over the latest round of budget cuts, David could see anxiety and exhaustion in her face. David had joined the City Public Health Institute (CPHI) only three months earlier, eager to apply his new MPH and specialty in data analysis. Allison had joined the city health department in 2015. She became the Executive Director of CPHI in 2024 when the city fell into bankruptcy. The City Health Commission was abolished and the commissioner resigned. CPHI was created as a nonprofit to take over the city's public health functions. CPHI had lower pay, fewer benefits, and an employee-funded retirement plan rather than a city pension, but David had hoped that he would at least have the resources he needed to put his new knowledge to work.

A phone call notification interrupted the silence, and David answered it. It was Rob McCall from the local online newspaper, wanting to interview Allison. Since the 2020 flu pandemic, health agencies had become an easy political target, often blamed for their allegedly inadequate responses to everything from floods to dengue fever. The reporter told

David he was doing a series on the poor performance of the state's health agencies and the nonprofits like CPHI that had replaced them in many jurisdictions.

Allison took the call, and explained to Rob that she had been hired to work on smoking and obesity, but that both of those programs had been severely cut back after the 2016 recession. In the 2023 recession, health programs faced even heavier cuts, and many programs were eliminated altogether. That's when CPHI was created to provide basic public health services for the city.

Allison became agitated as she continued her story. "Those cuts may have done the trick for the city's public finances," she said, "but those changes had real consequences for the city's health. Obesity and chronic diseases have increased, especially in poor neighborhoods. Tobacco use has increased cigarette taxes and smoking restrictions have been rolled back. Now vaping is what so many teens start with before they move to tobacco."

"But what are you doing about it?" Rob asked. "And I should add that we're also seeing historically high rates of infectious diseases, in addition to extended drought and devastating hurricanes, floods, and heat waves. How is CPHI addressing these issues? You know, State Representative Carey recently said that public health agencies and the nonprofits that replaced some of them are doing nothing to improve health and emergency preparedness—that they are in her words 'a complete waste of tax dollars.' How would you respond to that comment?"

"I have responded, Rob. Over and over again. Listen, our hands are tied," Allison explained. "And State Representative Carey should know, since she consistently votes against increasing health funding. With budget cuts and layoffs, we just don't have the staff and resources to do what needs to be done. I mean, you've seen our budget. On that budget, how could we possibly analyze health data, coordinate community action, perform mandatory inspections, enforce regulations, deal with climate change—you see where I'm going with this. No wonder our Environmental Health Director threw in the towel last week after thirty years of dedicated service to the community."

David put his head in his hands. He was starting to understand why everybody at CPHI was so down all the time. He started to wonder if he'd ever be able to put his degree to use to improve health in his hometown. Did the public even care? It didn't look like they did. David made a note to himself to reply to the job posting from the biomonitoring company for entry-level big data analysts.

FIGURE 1.2 Scenario 2

Scenario 2 Highlights

Funding cuts and a hostile political context undermined the role of public health agencies (PHAs) that subsequently failed to attract talented young people. Public health crises grew worse and more frequent, largely due to climate change, and created short-term infusions of resources targeted to the problem. Yet the political "blame game" justified further cuts in core public health functions. Private sector initiatives produced significant innovations for health and wellness. However, the most vulnerable populations could not afford the new means for getting healthy, and fell further behind middle-class and affluent groups. Technological, economic, educational, and health disparities grew, and the institutions of public health had little capacity to do anything about them.

Scenario 2 Details

Given how many Millennials[2] and Globals[3] had obtained degrees in public health by 2030, it is shocking in retrospect how few young people actually chose to *work* in public health. But then again, this might have been inevitable given the overwhelming problems in public health over the past two decades. Funding was cut repeatedly at the federal, state, and local levels. When public health calamities erupted—such as a disease outbreak, an extreme weather event, or food and water contamination—public health agencies (PHAs) bore the blame in legislative hearings and in the press for lack of preparation or ineffective responses. Then politicians would announce new funds to fight each problem, hire new "problem solvers" (often their friends from the private sector), and then undermine those very efforts the next fiscal year with budget cuts. No wonder so many young MPHs decided to apply their skills in the private sector where they could make better salaries.

The situation outside the field of public health was not particularly rosy either. Severe recessions in 2016 and 2023 dashed the economic hopes for most Americans and shrank public budgets at the state and local levels. Many cities followed Detroit into bankruptcy, and some replaced their public health departments with nonprofit institutions to continue offering public health services. Political polarization and one-upmanship continued to block any substantive legislation. The health care crisis continued to monopolize the public's attention, particularly after the 2020 election when the federal government finally abandoned the reforms of the Patient Protection and Affordable Care Act, hoping to save costs during the prolonged period of economic recession.

The economic recessions were mirrored by declining social conditions, especially for disenfranchised and vulnerable populations. Higher unemployment led to higher rates of depression, homelessness, substance abuse, violence, and crime. Chronic illness became more prevalent, while mental and behavioral health worsened. Health disparities became starker as safety nets were cut and access to health care declined. "Critical resource theft" (the stealing of food, water, etc.) became almost commonplace in most major urban and suburban areas. The economic downward spiral drove American politics, social bonds, and public health into a sustained period of regression.

Social media and online network users in part fueled this regression by spreading misinformation and vitriolic propaganda against government programs, including public health. The refusal of many Americans to get flu shots was one of several trends that reflected growing distrust of the federal government and the health care industry among the public. By 2020, this trend had ballooned out of control and a particularly virulent and powerful strain of the flu that emerged that year led to a flu pandemic breakout. PHAs tried their best to address the sudden demand for an instant and comprehensive response to this pandemic. However, they were underfunded, overworked, and very limited in their ability to communicate and coordinate with other governmental agencies and with residents. PHAs were unable to effectively analyze real-time data emerging in their communities and coordinate optimal flu vaccine distribution within and across cities and states. As a result, tens of thousands of people died. Congressional committees and news pundits scapegoated PHAs for not doing more to control the pandemic. PHAs' claims of inadequate funding, overworked staff, and poor support from other agencies did little to assuage a public looking for someone to blame.

The flu pandemic disaster cemented the public perception of PHAs as ineffective bureaucratic strongholds for people who could not find jobs elsewhere. This reputation made it all the harder for PHAs to recruit and retain top people. PHAs had previously tried to improve their public image during the 2010s through the accreditation process. However, accreditation had failed to reach "critical mass" because many PHAs either could not afford the fees or could not provide all the services required to meet the standards for accreditation.

While many PHAs struggled to adequately perform their responsibilities, and public distrust of public health, health care, and the government grew, "citizen science" services and activities expanded and advanced throughout the 2010s and 2020s, particularly in surveillance and monitoring. More and more residents decided to take community matters into their own hands. These networks and the data they produced raised the visibility of problems in the community, but they focused disproportionate attention on the affluent and middle-class areas where these individuals lived. Problems in poorer areas remained largely invisible because the networks did not connect marginalized populations. For example, poorer areas were more subject to high levels of air and soil toxins and pollutants, but there were few citizen science networks coming from or focusing on these communities. However, wealthier communities were able to reduce levels of toxins and pollutants in their own vicinities because strong data was coming from their own citizen science monitoring and surveillance efforts. Through this and other examples of citizen science disparities, an evidence base was created that justified allocation of resources to the well-to-do, particularly in the areas of health and wellness, whereas evidence on conditions in low-income areas was not as consistently gathered or analyzed.

These technological disparities were just another tourniquet cutting off the most vulnerable populations from the better future that the affluent and middle class would enjoy. As smartphones, wearable devices, and real-time social networking were becoming staples of mainstream American life in the 2010s, they reinforced economic and educational disparities that undergirded many of the nation's most critical public health challenges. For example, by 2020 personal biomonitoring technologies were integrated into the electronic health record (EHR) systems of many high-end health care systems. Patients who could afford the higher insurance and the biomonitoring tools gained access to real-time personalized care. However, health care providers for most Medicaid patients and other vulnerable populations were stuck with more primitive EHRs that did little more than reduce the amount of time required for clinicians to talk to patients during a visit.

Health care's disinterest in the wellbeing of vulnerable populations reflected a broader trend in the reduction of population health and prevention activities. Funding cuts combined with the highly publicized climate-related disasters and increase of infectious diseases, which reduced PHAs' focus on prevention activities as they reeled from crisis to crisis. For many in public health, the historical familiarity of infectious disease provided a more understandable challenge than the more complex issues of community health change that were driving the nation's chronic disease burden. The end of the Tobacco Settlement funds in 2025, for example, was a death knell for many PHA-led anti-tobacco programs. The tobacco industry got some restrictions weakened and aggressively renewed its advertising and promotion efforts. PHAs did not have the budget or political support for chronic disease prevention and community health improvement.

Disasters, however, periodically brought PHAs increased funding for disaster preparedness. Looking back from 2030, it is clear that the more newsworthy outbreaks of infectious disease diverted PHAs' attention from the much greater burden of chronic illness that grew relentlessly during the 2020s. Mold and mildew exposure and carbon monoxide poisoning (from overutilization of and damages to portable generators) had become common as a result of climate change. Combined sewer systems in many cities produced major outbreaks of gastrointestinal illnesses, food and water contaminations, and water-borne illnesses, killing thousands. Rates of asthma, hay fever, and allergies increased every year, and air quality got so bad in some cities that residents wore protective air masks whenever they were outdoors.

New and re-emerging diseases became more common as well. To the surprise of many, malaria and dengue fever became more prevalent in some states. A robust strain of West Nile Virus emerged in seemingly unrelated parts of the nation in the summer of 2024. Increasingly antibiotic-resistant bacteria caused intense co-infections with new and re-emerging diseases, and also resulted in more intense infections and even deaths for more "traditional" diseases. Alarm spread across the nation, and an exposé on "CDC Flunks Epidemiology" pressured Congress to hold more hearings and appropriate new funds for public health. This did little to prevent public health and health care from being overwhelmed by the multifaceted health impacts of climate change.

By 2025, the cycle of droughts, floods, tornadoes, and superstorms increased and worsened. Dramatic Arctic methane releases had produced what is now called "runaway climate change." Emissions of methane, a much more powerful greenhouse gas than carbon dioxide, had rapidly accelerated with the melting of the permafrost and other frozen deposits in the Atlantic Ocean, Siberia, and the Arctic, thanks to anthropogenic global warming. By 2030, sea levels across U.S. coastal areas had risen by a staggering average of 14 inches over levels in the year 2000. Many residents of Florida, Alaska, Hawaii, and other low-lying areas were forced to evacuate so often that many simply relocated altogether, not returning to their original homes. In many areas, flash floods became more common and intense, and were more frequently associated with water contamination and deterioration of buildings, roads, runways, and other infrastructure. Some towns and small cities were rendered completely uninhabitable within a matter of weeks. This flooding was regularly preceded or followed by devastating drought.

Thus, conflicts intensified between states and within communities for water resources. Food security diminished as plants and animals died from illnesses, extreme weather events, wildfires, droughts, and hotter summers. These events, as well as water scarcity, rising food and energy prices, and worsening physical and mental health, contributed to violent conflicts within many local communities for food and water. The millions of "climate refugees" worldwide who had relocated to less environmentally stressed areas were particularly susceptible to new and re-emerging diseases, violence, and sexually transmitted infections. Many communities proved hostile to climate migrants, whether from within the United States or abroad. By the mid-2020s, another wave of undocumented migrants began to move into the United States (or attempted to) as climate refugees. The United States instituted new immigration restrictions for individuals who came from nations with severe outbreaks of climate-related infectious diseases, while not allocating resources to assist international climate refugees residing in the United States.

The worsening health of these immigrants was paralleled by the worsening health and economic conditions of many U.S. residents. Violent conflicts and discrimination escalated. Police, emergency responders, and firefighters across the nation were overworked and overstressed, and endured more disease and depreciating mental health. Amidst two recessions, budget cuts, and shrinking of the public health workforce, PHAs struggled to prepare for and mitigate the physical and mental health impacts of climate change. Many did not have the insurance to recover from damages in their buildings and infrastructure caused by extreme weather events, and their governments could not afford to rebuild.

In this tempest of highly complex challenges, PHAs could do little but provide some pre-disaster preparedness and futile post-event mitigation. As the value of PHAs further declined in their eyes, the public and policymakers looked to the private sector to apply newly available technologies to solve problems in both communicable and non-communicable diseases. Without fail, each year's flu scare resulted in criticism for PHAs, supporting political efforts to reallocate PHAs' funding to private sector health surveillance efforts. PHAs that retained a modicum of enthusiasm for their work struggled to replicate these private sector efforts with the little funding they had available.

For good reason, talented young people with a public health education preferred to work in the private sector rather than join a PHA and spend their career in demoralized offices responding to public criticism. With a steady supply of talented employees and investment capital, the private sector yielded innovative approaches to health challenges, particularly in advanced analytics, online health education, and preventive self-care. These innovations improved health for those with the ability to pay for them. Meanwhile, however, many universities shut down their schools of public health in the 2020s. A few merged their public health departments with their business schools. PHAs, as a result, downsized and deteriorated over the years leading to 2030. Many local health departments were consolidated, eliminated, or subsumed into other government agencies. Those that remain by 2030 are underfunded, isolated, often politicized, and uninterested in taking any chances that might subject them to further public scrutiny. Some PHAs are led by the "cronies" of elected officials, or by physicians who no longer want to practice medicine but lack the financial resources necessary to retire. The health aspirations of the public are pursued not through the traditional public health establishment but through private sector innovations that overlook the needs of the most vulnerable members of society, who by 2030 lack access to quality health care, effective prevention, and other public health services. Ultimately, these members of society have lost hope for the future.

Scenario 3: Sea Change for Health Equity

Life in This Scenario

"Let's hear it, Mr. Nguyen!" It was near the end of her second four-year term when Mayor Hayes began to prepare for her 2028 annual state of the city address. Mr. Nguyen, head of the city's health development agency, was about to brief her on the city's state of health and the agency's contributions. Eliminating health disparities had been a major goal of the mayor since she came into office. Mr. Nguyen outlined the advances that Mayor Hayes would review in her state-of-the-city address:

- Resilience in the face of superstorms—Last year's superstorm hit the city hard. However, this time the city was better prepared. The health development agency helped combine increasingly better understanding of how to serve those in greatest need with public gaming activities and investments in mixed-income neighborhoods and access to healthy and affordable food. Together, they built the city's capacity for and equity in rapid citizen response and recovery teams and made communities healthier and more resilient in the first place.
- Health equity—As values and attitudes shifted, particularly with the growth of the Millennials and younger generations, the health development agency facilitated the growth of health equity as a shared goal for the city. This included adapting the PRIVILEGED game to the city's context. The game was originally developed by the Boston Public Health Commission, and allowed players to role-play the lives of different hypothetical residents, ranging from the homeless to the wealthiest in the area. Players demonstrated significantly increased awareness for social justice and participation in equity efforts after playing the game. Now a few years later, the city saw important reductions in health

disparities, and health indicators in low-income neighborhoods were improving fastest.

- Community co-production and household self-sufficiency—Unemployment had grown in the city as more jobs were automated or digitized. To improve household self-sufficiency, the health development agency facilitated the growth of time banking and resource sharing, including community gardening and bartering of services such as home repairs and child care.
- Demonstrating effectiveness and positive return on investment (ROI)— The health development agency had joined a national network of public health agencies (PHAs) that demonstrated a strong ROI for their programs. Collectively, the results from these PHAs convinced Congress to support a 2 percent tax on medical services to fund prevention and public health.

The mayor felt proud of the agency's accomplishments. Reflecting on her own experience, she had come from a low-income background and had been unemployed at various times in her 20s. With so many city residents struggling to make ends meet, she had helped lead and coordinate a movement for community co-production in the city. That organizing had instilled in her a recognition of the importance of health for a thriving city, and led her into politics to effect broader change. She had appointed Mr. Nguyen as head of the health development agency, which served as chief health strategist for the city.

Over the course of her two terms, the agency came to successfully use big data and advanced analytics to determine risks, needs, and opportunities; find best practice options from around the country; foster consideration of health in all the city's policymaking; and engage the public in priority setting, community involvement, and emergency preparedness, often through games. In the process, the health development agency staff had become more analytical and strategic in their focus, and somewhat smaller in their numbers. However, the public and businesses in the city looked up to the agency to lead the city in adapting to new and different opportunities for health.

Scenario 3 Highlights

National and local economies gradually grew, and large-scale changes in values and demographics over time pushed for "common sense" policies and support for health equity. Public health agencies became health development agencies that identify problems and opportunities to improve community health, and catalyze and incentivize action by community, business, health care, and other sectors. Their success

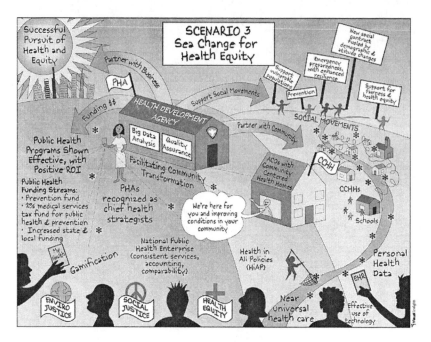

FIGURE 1.3 Scenario 3

as chief health strategists using advanced analytics, gamification, and diverse partner-ships led to quality improvements in housing, economic opportunity, education, and other social determinants of health. Although some disparities persisted, in 2030 the vast majority of Americans had attained greater opportunity for good health.

Scenario 3 Details

The 2010s and 2020s saw dramatic changes in the United States. The nation's working population changed rapidly as Baby Boomers retired from elected office and government jobs, making room for younger cohorts that brought innovation and new technologies for improving outcomes. These younger cohorts generally held more tolerant attitudes towards lesbian, gay, bisexual, transgender, and questioning (LGBTQ) rights, and also brought a clear and surprisingly rapid growth to governmental and private sector support of equity and fairness in the late 2010s.

By the mid-2020s, political scientists described a new social contract that had emerged in the United States over the previous decade. Americans expected their government to be effective, and were overtly willing to pay taxes to support the government functions that they saw as relevant to the nation's wellbeing. They supported government efforts in using the technologies that had become available to become transparent in its operations and to continuously innovate to do more good at less expense. The people expected that government agencies coach, lead, and cheerlead for fairness, including health equity.

The value shift and demographic change helped transform politics. Voters rewarded candidates that brought pragmatism and a "can-do" optimism to improve fairness and opportunity for the nation and its communities. Disagreements remained on many issues, but common sense and a spirit of cooperation became the norm. This included agreement on the value of and support for collaborations across sectors to achieve mutually beneficial goals, and the aggressive implementation of the "Health in All Policies" approach. Congress adjusted its "anti-lobbying legislation" to allow the Centers for Disease Control and Prevention and other agencies to engage in research, advocacy, and program planning related to legal products (e.g. sugar and guns) that could harm health. Congress also adjusted legislation for all public health agencies (PHAs) to use up to 10 percent of their categorical program funding to develop their foundational capabilities and achieve accreditation.

During this time, the national economy resumed its slow growth, with minor recessions. Federal finances gradually improved, as did the finances of most states and many cities and counties. Evaluation of public health interventions became routine and regularly demonstrated a positive return on investment for health interventions and programs. Public support for health programs and evidence of the interventions' effectiveness continued to grow, which led all levels of governments to stabilize or increase public health funding. In 2020, Congress restored the Prevention and Public Health Fund to the $2 billion level called for in the Patient Protection and Affordable Care Act, adjusting funding upward for inflation.

While the economy and public health funding improved, however, structural unemployment continued to grow. Globalization, automation, and knowledge technologies fundamentally changed the economic reality for the United States; robotics, 3D printing, and digitization had taken over many manufacturing and service jobs by the mid-2020s. As structural unemployment grew, millions of Americans and their communities turned to themselves and to each other to produce and co-produce basic necessities for sustaining their households—including food, home repairs, child care, and other shared services.

Public health was subject to the same larger economic forces. In environmental health, for example, automated monitoring (e.g. for toxins and pollutants) and inspections (e.g. for restaurants and health facilities) required fewer and better trained PHA employees to oversee regulated establishments, licensing activities, and worker training and testing in food safety; to provide quality control and improvements of the reporting systems; and to deal with regulatory violations and food-borne illness outbreaks. Moreover, the licensing process integrated assurance that the business is in compliance with labor pay and worker safety regulations—but this too was largely automated.

As the public health workforce became smaller and more technologically savvy, PHAs increasingly drew on advanced informatics to transform the nation's health. In the realm of PHA operations and capabilities, most PHAs implemented a uniform chart of accounts and achieved accreditation during the 2010s. These changes improved their ability to compare and learn from their peers in other jurisdictions, provide comparative cost analysis, and secure state and local funding. To improve the science and art of public health, PHAs partnered with Accountable Care Organizations (ACOs), universities, and citizen scientists to explore the dynamics of health and prosperity. PHAs converted data from a wide range of medical, social, behavioral, environmental, and economic sources into real-time virtual simulations of public health in communities. PHAs could now explore the implications of trends shaping communities, and quantify the costs of events such as a flu pandemic using indicators such as lost work time and business income or reduced educational attainment. Policies, programs, and expenditures could now be routinely assessed for their effectiveness and return-on-investment (ROI). These modeling and analytics capabilities led to sweeping advances in epidemiology, community interventions, and the guidance of behavior change that were key to reducing the country's chronic disease burden.

Highly energized cohorts of public health leaders built on the growing consistency and effectiveness of PHAs throughout the 2020s to develop an increasingly interrelated network of PHAs into "health development agencies." These PHAs performed strong fiscal management, learned and applied innovation principles from each other and other sectors and organizations, and leveraged other stakeholders and resources from other sectors to improve health and well-being. Their staffs had the interdisciplinary training and skills needed to work with other stakeholders and to support the agencies' role in fostering and promoting prevention strategies. These PHAs identified problems and opportunities to improve community health, and catalyzed and incentivized action by multiple sectors. They targeted highly sophisticated and effective messages and interventions. They led in the analysis and dissemination of best practices for community interventions, and in the identification of the most cost-effective and appropriate providers of a program or service. Sometimes the PHA itself was the optimal provider, but for many efforts other community groups were more appropriate. By the early 2020s, most PHAs had demonstrated a positive ROI for their remaining services and programs.

PHAs were using a uniform chart of accounts, pursuing accreditation, sharing best practices, and generally cooperating. Noting similarities to private franchise models, many leaders referred to this collaborative network of PHAs as the "public health enterprise." The public health enterprise helped accelerate program activities and enabled the enhanced, targeted creation of opportunities for all to be healthy.

Their move to become health development agencies and the resulting achievements in improving community health over the years to 2030 earned PHAs public recognition for their role as chief health strategists for their communities.

Based on their analyses and evaluations, PHAs had raised additional resources for public health activities from the business community, foundations, and their local health care providers. Some had developed "pay for performance options" that allowed gain sharing for effective health promotion that reduced health care costs (this was an important factor when Congress created the health services tax for public health in 2022). Based on the leadership and evidence of effectiveness provided by PHAs, all levels of government ultimately realized that if budgets needed to be reduced, public health spending was too important to be cut. If public health spending ultimately had to be reduced, governments sought to minimize its cuts.

Simulations and predictive analytics also contributed to the spread of games that changed communities' awareness of and commitment to achieving health. One such game, named PRIVILEGED, quickly went viral after 2020 and prompted a major public conversation about fairness. The game allowed players to role-play the lives of different hypothetical residents—from the most privileged to the more vulnerable—in virtual communities. Players thus explored their degree of privilege and hardship, and worked with other players to devise equity-enhancing strategies. Although communities varied widely in the needs and goals that they identified, factors that emerged most often included support for mixed-income neighborhoods and community development, employment, community resilience, and the promotion of alternative community economic models such as self-production, co-production, community and home gardening, and Time Dollar exchanges.

While the existence and strength of equity-enhancement initiatives varied among communities, nearly all U.S. residents gained access to capitated and effective care during the 2010s and 2020s. Preventive services no longer required co-pays. Primary care evolved to the "Community-Centered Health Home" model where health care providers—particularly ACOs—worked to improve population health. As care and access thus improved, federal funding for public health programs in screening and treatment were cut. Nevertheless, HDAs continued to receive funding for the provision of supportive services for HIV/AIDS, maternal and child health, and primary care (for the small percent of those still lacking access to health care).

Unfortunately, health care costs remained far too high. In 2022, this prompted Congress to implement a recommendation that the Institute of Medicine had made a decade earlier. Given the continued evidence on the ability of community-focused prevention programs to reduce illness and health care costs, Congress instituted a 2 percent tax on medical services. State health departments were tasked with distributing this tax revenue to communities for community prevention purposes. PHAs led most communities in facilitating the analysis and shared goal-setting that targeted this funding. In some cases, the funds went to PHA programs. In most cases, however, they went to other community organizations or community development efforts. Many people strongly opposed this tax or debated how it should be implemented. By 2030, however, this policy has begun to show health improvements and reduce demand for health care.

Taken together, opportunities for all to be healthy improved dramatically in the decades leading up to 2030, and public health played important roles in leading this transformation. PHAs lead coalitions of stakeholders in a wide range of activities that promote health. They work with developers and urban planners to ensure the availability of safe, attractive places where people can be physically active. They foster mixed-income neighborhoods, entrepreneurship, and job matching and training programs, as well as self-production and community co-production. PHAs also work with app and game developers and health care providers to ensure that new technological developments are made affordable and culturally appropriate for vulnerable populations. While some disparities have persisted, there is greater equity in 2030 than in previous decades. Almost all communities have improved opportunities for good health and health equity by advancing quality improvements in housing, economic opportunity, education, and other social determinants of health.

Scenario 4: Community-Driven Health and Equity

Life in This Scenario

Priya finished her morning run around the local community gardens and aeroponics facility, all within "reduced emissions" and "no emissions" zones. She thought of her next health equity and resilience Time Bank assignments as she checked the data from her run. The environmental monitoring apps on her subsidized smartphone had sent the data in real-time to the local health department, where it was factored into big data analytics on the community's health.

It was hard to believe that a year earlier the area had been hit by a powerful hurricane. Back in the 2010s, this kind of hurricane would have wreaked much more havoc on a "poor" community such as Priya's. However, throughout the early 2020s, Priya and other residents had been participating in emergency preparedness games and simulations facilitated by the local health department. They had built resilience into the neighborhood, among other things, growing mixed-income neighborhoods, fostering co-production of food, and getting the Time Bank ready to exchange rebuilding services. Recovery from the last hurricane was swift because of these pre-storm efforts.

Changes in Priya's neighborhood also include the growth of networked local initiatives, community co-production, and collective self-care efforts to reduce disparities, strengthen community health, and improve neighborhood resilience. As chief health strategist, the local health department played a key role in facilitating community health and resilience. It also served as a network facilitator with Groupnets as part of its health equity and prevention efforts, as well as co-host of the Truth and Reconciliation hangouts. Hangouts were informed by social monitoring apps and designed to improve indicators such as the ratio of pleasant to hostile exchanges between community members of different racial and ethnic backgrounds. The data regularly fed into the health department's community health dashboard on indicators for the community's physical, social, mental, nutritional, and spiritual health.

After a quick shower, Priya tuned into the Groupnet session using both audio and video feeds. Her husband Marcus was already tuned into the session. To make time for it, they had been trading their citizen science hours for child care offered by other Time Bank members.

MarcusLee98:	"David, how's it all look?"
Yourfriendlyneighborhood DataMan:	"Good news, the 'uMonitor' app has just been integrated with our remote sensor network. That bumps our data acuity up by another 10 percent. The aggregated time-specific results from all the apps now show about the same carbon and NOx levels around the gardens as our remote sensors network."
Priya2020:	"Are we still on track for meeting emissions targets?"
Lucky City_Prevent_Promote_Protect:	"We need a few more sessions to confirm, but it looks like the local air pollutant levels are down 35% from 2020! DataMan, can you share with us a verified screenshot of your comparisons?"
Yourfriendlyneighborhood DataMan:	"Done. The results are pretty similar."
Lucky City_Prevent_Promote_Protect:	"Fantastic. We'll be asking you all to do some monitoring assignments to feed into the early-warning forecasts and community health dashboard. We'll need to specifically check if the improved air quality is helping reduce asthma, allergy, and hay fever reductions. Great job, everybody!"

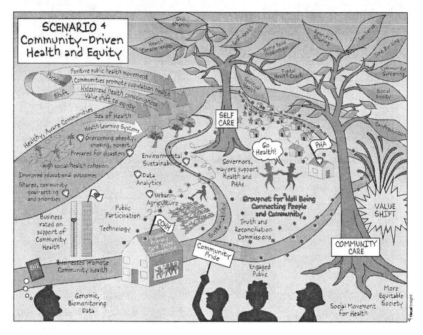

FIGURE 1.4 Scenario 4

Scenario 4 Highlights

Public health agencies, partners, and local health improvement initiatives coalesced via technology and social media into a national web of community health-enhancing networks. These networks helped communities exchange their innovations and best practices, and leverage the expertise of public health agencies and others. The nation also strived to come to terms with its racial and socioeconomic histories, and supported real changes and legislation to create a more equitable society. This value shift to equity was accelerated by another major recession and the ongoing transformation of the economy, including significant digitization of jobs. New community economic models helped households sustain themselves and improve health and wellbeing. As chief health strategists, public health agencies shed many functions, and facilitated these movements to improved health.

Scenario 4 Details

Excitement gathered as President Thompson, the first African American woman to win the White House, began delivering her 2030 State of the Union address to a holoconference of more than 200 million American viewers. There was much for the speech to celebrate given the nation's achievements over the previous 15 years, particularly in public health. These improvements had become a foundation of strength supporting the broad-based reinvention of the country's economy and society.

This societal change had its roots in the late 20th century. New technologies and new ways of organizing around health had been producing encouraging results in many communities since the 1990s through the Healthy Communities movement, federal programs for communities such as REACH and Community Transformation Grants, and extensive support from national and local foundations. As the 2010s progressed, a combination of economic and environmental challenges, evolving technologies, and changing values accelerated community transformations while advancing health and equity.

As chief health strategists, state and local public health agencies (PHAs) played a major role in stimulating more intelligent and collaborative health generation in their communities. For example, PHAs used new trends in social media to influence and generate better behavioral health at the micro-level. In the late 2010s and early 2020s, social media had evolved as more and more people joined "Groupnets," circles of around ten people who interact with one another in real time and with great intensity. Such online engagement proliferated as cities provided their own free wireless networks, and as access to smartphones and data plans were subsidized.

PHAs sought to improve community health and personal health behavior through "peer uplift," and through effective collaborations and interactions with and within Groupnets. Groupnets had created new kinds of good and bad "peer pressure" or "friend pressure," as people in the Groupnets influenced group behavior much more directly through real-time video and audio interaction. PHAs supported the fusing of Groupnets into a vast and organic social network that was much more influential than any social network in the past. Consumers and communities were using Groupnets and other forms of social media to organize, evaluate, rate, and share activities and experiences across a wide range of areas. These networks, local health improvement initiatives, public health agencies, and partners converged into a broad, national network through which communities could exchange their innovations and best practices, and leverage the expertise of PHAs and their leaders.

Although this national network greatly enhanced and accelerated successful public health activities, there were widespread concerns about the quality of the information being propagated via the network. People were as often impressed by the "wisdom of the crowds" as they were startled by the "insanity of the mob." For health, food safety, and health care, the public increasingly looked to experts in PHAs and academia to help them distinguish good information from bad, and knowledge from opinion. For example, the public expected PHAs to aid Yelp!, Urban Spoon, their successors, and other consumer rating websites in maintaining quality-rating processes (which included the use of PHA-required safety monitoring data for restaurants and other organizations).

In addition to the evolution of social media, public health was also greatly affected by major changes in the health care delivery system. The health care reforms of the early 2010s expanded access to health care insurance, while incentivizing health care systems to take responsibility for population health within their communities. Research and evaluation drew on the spread of electronic health record systems that collected genomic, biomonitoring, and socioeconomic data. PHAs drew on them as well to identify groups and neighborhoods whose social, genetic, and environmental risks could be addressed through targeted prevention strategies. Health care providers used these analytics to direct their funding priorities for population health strategies.

As the field of advanced analytics rapidly evolved, it helped create a "community health learning system" that had been envisioned decades earlier. This system helped PHAs, community groups, local businesses, and health care providers to multiply their collaboration and effectiveness, and to build upon earlier tools like the Robert Wood Johnson Foundation County Health Rankings and CommunityCommons.org (which offered informal "progress reports" using population health metrics that could be tailored for a particular community). By 2020, public health officials and researchers were using sophisticated, real-time, virtual simulations of individual neighborhoods and communities. These models drew data from many sources, including reimbursement, real-time environmental and biomonitoring, and various forms of crowd-sourced data. Interventions could now be modeled and analyzed for impact and cost-effectiveness in virtual space before they were implemented in the real world. This learning system vastly enhanced PHAs' role in population-level analytics and research, particularly in communicable disease surveillance and prevention, emergency preparedness, and environmental monitoring. As their role in community strategy development and facilitation grew, PHAs cut their clinical health services as access to effective health care became nearly universal.

In the background, droughts, floods, heat waves, and severe storms increasingly took their toll on all parts of the country. Part of the "mind-change" that took place in the 2010s was recognition of the threat of climate change, and a national commitment to mitigating its effects. PHAs and others advocated for the integration of environmental resilience, sustainability, and mitigation into all parts of local, state, and federal policies. This was reflected in PHAs' emergency preparedness activities, but also in the results of community goal-setting activities and growing support for Health in All Policies (HiAP). PHAs worked with citizens, businesses, policymakers, and various agencies to reduce environmental impact and expand renewable energy. This included establishing "no emissions" and "reduced emissions" zones. PHAs also encouraged reduced reliance on cars and promoted anti-idling policies for vehicles; worked with private and nonprofit organizations to expand the number of hybrid and electric vehicles in communities; encouraged more biking, car-sharing, and ride-sharing; encouraged and provided quality control for automated and networked citizen science monitoring for and reduction of toxins and pollutants; and fostered greater energy efficiency and renewable energy use in buildings and communities. PHAs were active partners in preparing local neighborhoods to create and implement community health preparedness and resilience plans in the face of extreme weather events. These activities were all part of a shift from traditional views of "environmental health" to one of environmental improvement, listed under the uniform chart of accounts as "Environmental Responsibility and Sustainability," which had also become an important part of PHA accreditation standards by 2022.

Accreditation standards by the 2020s also required PHAs to ensure health equity. For this purpose, a growing number of PHAs advised in the development and dissemination of consumer tools—such as web and mobile applications—to ensure the enhancement of public health and health equity. PHAs monitored these tools and other innovations and emerging knowledge technologies for quality and effectiveness in community engagement, and ensured that they benefited low-income populations as quickly as possible.

One major use of these community engagement tools was to address environmental health and disaster preparedness. PHAs facilitated pre-event resilience games and simulations to minimize the potential costs and impacts of environmental disasters. These simulations and games helped community groups imagine and practice "emergent" roles they could play in disaster response. These engagement and involvement tools proved important in 2024, after Superstorm Richard pounded the coasts of Delaware, New Jersey, and New York. Together with community groups and other responders in the region, members of the Tri-State Time Bank led in quickly collecting, distributing, and delivering food and supplies, and in getting homes and apartments ready for reoccupation.

The advent of Time Bank networks reflected the major economic shift that had been emerging throughout the 2010s and 2020s. Many jobs were lost to automation and distributed manufacturing (e.g. the use of 3D/4D printing) and greater productivity through cognitive computing and knowledge technologies. Declining revenues forced federal, state, and local government to spend smarter and to cut programs and services. Income support programs, including the Earned Income Tax Credit, had expanded, yet remained insufficient to address the growing structural unemployment. Many Americans responded to these trends by creating their own local livelihoods—made up of diverse activities with their own revenue models—rather than relying on a steady paycheck. New community economic models included Time Banks where many Americans exchanged their labor hour-for-hour with their neighbors. Time Banks became important community networks that helped build social coherence as neighbors helped neighbors, and their impacts were widely noted particularly after Superstorm Richard. Many people also joined collaborative consumption schemes (e.g. Zipcar) to rent or share cars, bikes, and other goods rather than owning the items themselves. Community gardening and home food production (including 3D-printed food) offered new opportunities for households and communities to feed themselves. This more distributed economy often supported community members in crowd-sourcing and crowd-funding health improvement efforts that they deemed most important at the local level. Communities that actively sought to improve social coherence by merging the interests of the wealthiest and poorest residents ulti-mately performed far better economically than those communities that maintained the status quo.

During the late 2010s, as this economic and social justice movement pro-gressed, more communities began to understand the practical need to address racial and discriminatory injustices. Leaders in social services realized that it was foolish to expect oppressed minority groups to be capable of full participation in 21st century society if their contemporary and centuries-old wounds continued to be left untended. Many communities therefore undertook a courageous process of "truth and reconciliation" of the nation's racial past and present. These initia-tives focused on open discussion of the long-lasting impacts (for both people of color and whites) of, for example, slavery in the history of African Americans; the torture, forced assimilation, and displacement of Native American Indians throughout the 19th and 20th centuries; 20th and 21st century segregation (including hyperghettoization); the War on Drugs; incarceration; contemporary economic and social oppression; immigration histories; contemporary Islamo-phobia; and lynchings. Discrimination against lesbian, gay, bisexual, transgender, and questioning (LGBTQ) persons was also widely acknowledged and discussed. Foundations funded sessions that held the space for these groups to speak their truths without fear of retaliation or rejection. As this Truth and Reconciliation Movement grew, it offered a deep catharsis as all Americans came to see them-selves in the experiences that were being shared. In conjunction with the increas-ing momentum of the Truth and Reconciliation Movement, awareness of economic injustice grew. These were key factors in generating new legislation to promote social and economic fairness, including more tax fairness, a national living wage requirement, and an expanded Earned Income Tax Credit that effectively created the negative income tax first proposed by the Nixon admin-istration in the 1970s.

These shifts in technology, health care, social media, and the roles of residents and public health called for a new kind of public health worker. Fortunately, schools of public health had been realigning their programs in order to develop a public health workforce with the skills that were appropriate to the times, particularly advanced analytics and community engagement expertise. PHAs thus benefited from a stream of public health graduates equipped with advanced technical and social knowledge.

In 2030, Americans celebrate the movement toward a more equitable society, although there are still gaps and economic injustices. Moreover, they recognize that their efforts must continue and focus more on the spiritual dimensions of health. Those who felt this need most strongly paid great attention to the presi-dent as she beamed herself into living rooms across America. Standing at her podium, she declared, "We, the public, have come together around a shared vision of health. We have begun the journey to that vision by working together and by combining new technologies with the strength, passion, and spirit of our communities. We, the public, must now move more powerfully toward that vision—a bold vision that pulls us into a future where all Americans can enjoy living healthy, productive, and meaningful lives. Will you join me in creating this future?"

Two hundred million heads nodded.

Recommendations

At the national Public Health 2030 Workshop participants explored the scenarios and developed recommendations for the field. These detailed recommendations and related action plans are available in the full Public Health 2030 report and can be summarized as:

Recommendation 1:
Transform Public Health Agencies into "Health Development Agencies" with Dedicated, Sustainable, and Sufficient Funding

> Recommendation 1A:
> Develop Dedicated, Sustainable, and Sufficient Funding

> Recommendation 1B:
> Implement Policies for the Systematic Use and Development of Evidence and Best Practices

> Recommendation 1C:
> Build Public Health Agencies' Role in Fostering Prevention and Health Promotion Strategies

Recommendation 2:
Partner in Health Care Transformation to Facilitate the Evolution from a Health Care System to a Health System

Recommendation 3:
Build the Capacity for Dialogue about Inclusion, Opportunity, and Equity

Recommendation 4:
Dialogue with Other Sectors to Support Innovation

Conclusion

These scenarios of public health in the United States in the year 2030 describe a range of plausible futures worthy of consideration as relevant organizations conduct their own planning. The scenarios highlight both challenges that might otherwise surprise and opportunities that might otherwise be missed. The recommendations presented in the full report represent steps toward better public health futures, and deserve support to promote and develop more effective public health. We encourage organizations and individuals to support these recommendations, to be aware of their own preferred future for public health, and to move forward to effectively create that future.

Since their release in 2014 these scenarios have been used by numerous state and local health departments: state public health meetings in Michigan, Iowa, New York, ASTHO, NACCHO, APHA; the National Governors' Association; the Public Health Accreditation Board; the Association of Public Health Schools and Programs; and individual schools of public health.

Visit www.altfutures.org/publichealth2030 for an electronic copy of this report, driver forecasts, and scenarios for three local health departments and one state health department. You will also find a "toolkit" with which any community or organization can conduct their own scenario workshop. The toolkit includes a workshop agenda, instructions, worksheets, videos, and presentation materials. The scenario workshop enables the groups to "step into" each of the futures and consider implications. Using the scenarios in this way can assure that plans address the larger picture and longer-term futures for public health.

Notes

1. Clement Bezold, Aspirational Futures, http://www.jfs.tku.edu.tw/13-4/AE06.pdf.
2. The U.S. generation born 1983–2002.
3. The U.S. generation born beginning in 2003.

2

POPULATION HEALTH AND COLLABORATION AS EMBEDDED WITHIN THE ESSENTIAL PUBLIC HEALTH SERVICES

Leslie M. Beitsch

Population Health

Prior to passage of the Affordable Care Act (ACA), responsibility for the health of populations was viewed as almost exclusively the purview of governmental public health. Underfunded and largely unreimbursed by third parties, the public health perspective was encompassed within the rubric of the three core functions (assessment, assurance, and policy development) and the Ten Essential Public Health Services (EPHS) (see Figure 2.1).[1, 2] For the broader public health

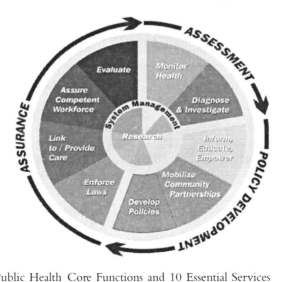

FIGURE 2.1 Public Health Core Functions and 10 Essential Services

Source: Ten Essential Public Health Services: Core Public Health Functions Steering Committee, Centers for Disease Control and Prevention, 1994.

practice, community population health meant serving the entire population of the jurisdiction along with any visitors or temporary residents—in short, everyone. Distinctions between the current view of some health plans and public health remain, yet the central tenet for both is the improvement of health outcomes for groups of people which the entity (public or private, governmental or otherwise) has responsibility.[3, 4]

Largely an historical byproduct of divergent funding sources and conceptual models, public health and health care have endured an uneasy co-existence.[5] One need look no further than our nation's current inflated health expenditures and unimpressive health outcomes to determine that our present bifurcated approach poorly serves our long-term interests. Population health conceptually embraces the potential for shared accountability across both health sectors. Although direct lines of accountability may become blurred in shared accountability models (some may term it an oxymoron by definition), the shared emphasis and combined resources feature better health and prevention far more prominently on the national health agenda. This is the direction underscored by the ACA, and also as put into practice by the Centers for Medicare and Medicaid through the Accountable Care Organizations (ACOs) and various innovation grant models. It is also supported by recent reports recommending professional health sector marital counseling—enabling public health and primary care to collaborate far more closely.[6]

Contemplating a future, one in which public health and health care are collaborators rather than competitors, was envisioned in the late 1990s and framed in the context of the public health system and national public health performance standards (see Figure 2.2).[7] The National Public Health Performance Standards (NPHPS) program is a CDC-led partnership of national public health organizations to improve public health systems through the development and application of local and state-based performance standards. The NPHPS consists of three performance self-assessment instruments, one for state public health systems, one for local public health systems, and one for local governing bodies. The NPHPS are framed as optimal standards using the Ten EPHS framework, and as such constitute a unique resource to examine public health *system* expectations. In a related fashion, Public Health Accreditation Board standards and measures (see Chapter 8) establish a framework for governmental public health. The two models complement one another. Key to understanding the NPHPS is the embedded notion of the *system*, and the critical role that system partners play in building capacity and ultimately improving health outcomes. In many ways, the NPHPS set the stage for the collaboration and partnerships we have today, by establishing and building a science base around the effectiveness of shared system efforts.

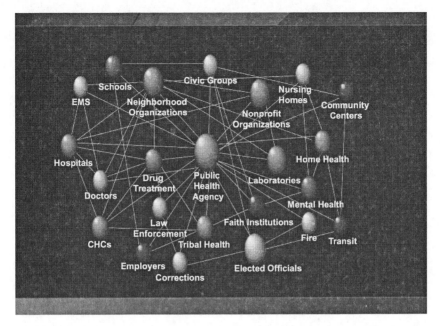

FIGURE 2.2 Public Health System

Source: Public Health Practice Program Office, Centers for Disease Control and Prevention, National Public Health Performance Standards Program, User Guide (first edition), 2002. (Current version available at www.cdc.gov/nphpsp).

A lingering undercurrent of the population health debate fuels concerns that governmental public health may be relegated even further back in the bus, while health care sits ever closer to the front. Still worse, others see a likely ongoing struggle with health care to retain the modest federal and state funding currently allocated to governmental public health, even as health department recovery from the recent Great Recession and associated budget cuts and layoffs remains uneven across the country. The likelihood is that some health care organizations may seek public health funding, but for the most part, these entities have little interest or expertise in environmental health or outbreak investigation, just two of many such examples. Moreover, the simple reality is that neither health care nor public health can achieve the goal of better health outcomes acting alone. Greater coordination between the health sectors will facilitate both contributing in roles that reflect their strengths. In the following sections of this chapter, population health will be described through the lens of the EPHS, with opportunities and leverage points for intersectoral collaboration highlighted.

Essential Public Health Services

EPHS 1. Monitor Health Status to Identify and Solve Community Health Problems

A critical role public health plays in many communities across the nation relates to the ongoing surveillance performed by health departments at the state and local level as part of the assessment core function. This allows public health to gather actionable data about the health needs of the jurisdiction. Various forms of data contribute to this effort to develop a comprehensive portrait of a community's overall health. Vital statistics registrars collect birth and death information that can lead to a rapid understanding of leading contributors to poor health. Disease registries such as cancer registries or practitioner reporting of elevated lead levels also support important dimensions that develop a more complete picture.

Many public health agencies also conduct organizational self-assessments, identifying strengths and weaknesses, and channeling this information into organizational capacity-building plans. The panel of performance expectations for local public health practice in the Assessment Protocol for Excellence in Public Health (APEX-PH) served as an early blueprint for many public health agencies seeking to focus and strengthen their roles in their communities.[8] APEX-PH adoption and implementation experience was substantial, although not universal. Where APEX-PH was implemented widely, public health practice performance was found to be substantially higher than areas where it was less frequently used.

In communities across the country others have also been engaged in various forms of community health monitoring, although typically viewed through a narrower lens. United Way agencies, for example, are using frameworks that overlap considerably with public health. With the enactment of the ACA, nonprofit hospitals are required to conduct community needs assessments every three years or face Department of Internal Revenue penalties. The convergence of missions for these three organizations (local public health, philanthropy, and hospitals) in the current environment offers distinct opportunities to provide more comprehensive community monitoring and to facilitate resource allocation toward priorities and pockets of high health need.

The evolution of the internet and the rapid, often real-time, ability to gather health data is leading to a new era in the capacity to provide active and timely surveillance and monitoring. Whereas in the past health data was published incrementally, typically annually or even less often, many states and local jurisdictions now have developed interactive websites that facilitate immediate access to health profiles of communities and even neighborhoods within them. This offers the potential to have meaningful interventions that are targeted and that engage multiple stakeholders with vital interests—inviting greater opportunities for intersectoral collaboration. It also sets the stage for public health departments to transform themselves into "information agencies," organizations that collect and analyze critical data, which can be utilized internally and also shared with partners to guide evidence-based interventions that positively impact health.

EPHS 2. Diagnose and Investigate Health Problems and Health Hazards in the Community

Disease outbreak investigation is one of the more recognized and unique roles of public health agencies. Popularized by recent Hollywood films, threats of bioterrorism, and real-world news events like Ebola in West Africa, epidemiologic investigations are a specialized function undertaken by local, state, and federal public health agencies. Adequate capacity must be maintained in the form of sufficient highly skilled personnel with knowledge of epidemiology and communicable diseases. As pointed out above, few others are offering to fulfill this public health responsibility. ESPH 2 is closely tied with ESPH 1; the surveillance and gathering of data allows public health to be informed about events as they occur. When such data is not collected, it would be difficult to know a cancer cluster or food-borne outbreak is in fact under way.

For diagnosis and investigation to be vigorously pursued, others in the community must also be vigilant and participate—again underscoring the need for partnership and collaboration. Lacking alert and informed health practitioners who report suspicious cases, the anthrax cases of October 2001 might not have been identified.

EPHS 3. Inform, Educate, and Empower People about Health Issues

Health promotion and health education are often under-appreciated contributions of health departments. Such services that may prevent or limit the extent of disease may be far more cost-effective than provision of clinical services occurring after diseases have already developed. The remarkable decline in adult and youth smoking rates over recent decades is one prominent example. This has been a coordinated effort of not only public health, but community activists, voluntary health organizations, and health care—again underscoring the power of partnership and collaboration to achieve desired health ends. Policy adoption accomplished via changes in social norms have made the most significant contributions to the overall decline in smoking rates and tobacco-related deaths. Smoking cessation, likewise important, and as effective as breast cancer screening in terms of disease prevention, actually has been a more modest contributor to the gains in health when compared to tobacco education and health promotion messaging.

Aside from tobacco there are multiple other areas where educational and promotional services may prove to be more effective than disease treatment. This impact may occur before a risk factor has been introduced (primary prevention) or mitigate further risk once a disease process has begun (tertiary prevention). Healthy lifestyles, diet, interconceptional health, proper use of contraceptives, and methods to avoid sexually transmitted infections and environmental hazards are other examples in which health promotion and health education can be adjuncts and supports as clinical care is received. This allows for more effective treatment and prevention, and highlights the possible synergy between public health and health care.

EPHS 4. Mobilize Community Partnerships and Action to Identify and Solve Health Problems

Public health has embraced its role as neutral community convener. Given its community-wide responsibilities to care for the health of the entire population, public health has inherent credibility with all stakeholders around crucial health issues. EPHS 4 acts on the body of information and evidence collected and analyzed under EPHS 1–3. In other words, it is the activity that naturally flows as the logical next step and occurs following identification of pressing public health problems that demand attention.

Being the convener or mobilizer does not necessarily mandate that public health assumes the key leadership role. The various roles will be assigned at the community level, and should reflect expertise and relationships corresponding with the particular issue being addressed. However, ESPH 4 does requires public health to be at the table as partnerships form to address health problems. Viewed in this manner it is an explicit obligation for public health to form dynamic partnerships, or participate in them when formed by others, in order to contribute in a meaningful way as public health challenges are confronted. Continuing with the examples presented earlier, forming coalitions to develop local clean indoor air ordinances might occur following the identification of unexpectedly high rates of asthma-related illnesses in school age children. Further analysis, if it determines that rates are higher in homes of smokers, might call for other partnerships to form and differing approaches in terms of policy development or prevention, depending upon the evidence base for impactful interventions.

EPHS 5. Develop Policies and Plans That Support Individual and Community Health Efforts

As part of their responsibilities, health departments participate in the development of numerous planning efforts. Some relate exclusively to the health department and operational management, such as the strategic plan for the entire agency, or more specific plans for workforce development and quality improvement. Others may involve sister governmental organizations which share similar responsibilities—such as preparedness planning.

Relevant to other EPHS, a major population health function is development of a periodic community health improvement plan (CHIP). Other chapters of this guidebook address this activity and associated collaborations directly. In this particular context, the health department roles as leader and/or convener of the CHIP are derived organically from EPHS 1–4. In fact, the partnerships and actions pursued as a result of EPHS 4 really should be initially developed and proposed in the context of the CHIP. In short, this EPHS is almost by definition a community-driven activity, built on the bedrock foundation of closely facilitated community collaborations and partnerships.

EPHS 6. Enforce Laws and Regulations That Protect Health and Ensure Safety

Health departments have unique regulatory roles in most jurisdictions, typically encompassing environmental and related food safety laws. These important population health functions are unlikely to be assumed by non-governmental organizations, and require specialized expertise and infrastructure. However, it would be a misconception to view these regulatory and enforcement roles as solitary activities conducted without the involvement of others—typically key stakeholders such as affected industries and consumers. Feedback and input is necessary as new regulations are proposed in the face of changing conditions. Septic system failures as climates change or as rural areas become more urbanized might present public health challenges affecting groundwater and sanitary nuisance.

Regulatory and enforcement functions also do not occur in isolation from other EPHS. There are often strong education roles related to regulated entities that precede enforcement action. The data collection, problem identification, and planning efforts occur within the framework of the other EPHS as briefly summarized above. So although the actual inspection and regulatory actions occur under the auspices of the health department acting alone, the events preceding the regulatory roles have been shaped by the give and take of a vigorous process with stakeholders, partners, law makers, and collaborators actively participating.

EPHS 7. Link People to Needed Personal Health Services and Assure the Provision of Health Care When Otherwise Unavailable

In many parts of the country, particularly the South and the West, local health departments have historically played major roles in the provision of health care for underserved populations. This "assurance role" has diminished in recent years with Medicaid expansion, proliferation of community health centers, and passage of the ACA, among other factors. Nonetheless many health departments still provide clinical services related to sexually transmitted infections, tuberculosis, family planning, maternity, and immunizations, spending a disproportionate share of their modest budgets.[9, 10]

In other parts of the United States, for example the Northeast, clinical services are seldom provided. Frequently, however, health departments still maintain certain roles related to care coordination, and linking patients to providers for other needed services. Even as patients formerly seen at the health department transition to care elsewhere, the health department may still maintain this linkage responsibility. Additionally, they may also have roles connecting patients with necessary wraparound services that include social supports. Maternal and infant services often fall within this dimension of public health activity. For example, WIC (Special Supplemental Nutrition Program for Women, Infants, and Children) remains the single largest public health program in the nation and is a key support service for pregnant women and their infants.

With the major seismic shifts in the health care universe, most health departments have opportunistically forged new relationships with clinical sector partners, with some clinical services provided on health department sites by others, or patients being simply referred. Newer models that reflect the spirit of the recommendations within the IOM report incorporate public health as the principal partner within ACOs or managed care plans.[6] A case in point is occurring in the Minneapolis area where several public entities, including public health, have banded together to form a risk-bearing ACO. There is tremendous upside potential when public health can truly partner with health care, allowing both to provide services that constitute their strengths. Public health is enabled to move toward the information functions driven by surveillance and data, while clinical services are provided by those with vastly greater resources and well-trained practitioners.

EPHS 8. Assure a Competent Public and Personal Health Care Workforce

Public health budgets are largely driven by their human capital. Stated another way, public health is only as strong or prepared as its workforce. In the recent cycles of budget shortfalls and staffing reductions, workforce competency was an often ignored secondary consideration. Unfortunately, just as service demands are greater (public health service demands are counter cyclical—growing when economic conditions worsen), with many workers departing and those remaining being called upon to perform even more tasks, the need for ongoing training is even greater. Partnerships between public health departments and schools/programs of public health is one very productive approach to focusing the proper attention on meeting the demands for ensuring requisite workforce skillsets are developed. Regional training centers also are present across the country, and distance learning infrastructure has made opportunities increasingly available. Nonetheless scarce financial resources make these collaborations between practice and academia tenuous.

EPHS 9. Evaluate Effectiveness, Accessibility, and Quality of Personal and Population-Based Health Services

Quality improvement (QI) and evaluation are assuming ever more important recognition within the public health enterprise. They are the cornerstone of the PHAB accreditation program described in a subsequent chapter. For the most part these activities are conducted internally within the health department itself (see Figure 2.3). Expertise in QI and evaluation capacity within public health remains somewhat limited in scope largely due to their relatively recent emphasis. This provides yet another opportunity to tap into the expertise present in other sectors. Non-traditional partners, like manufacturing, or current collaborators in health care have years of QI experience behind them. Because they are well ahead of public health, they can partner to become valued sources for training and/or new hires when resources permit.

QI and evaluation, once embedded within the health department, have major roles in support of the other EPHS and population health. All activities can, of course, be performed better, while a major focus can be partnership development and implementation of shared initiatives like the CHIP. This enables QI to be front and center in the effort to strengthen population health through collaborative

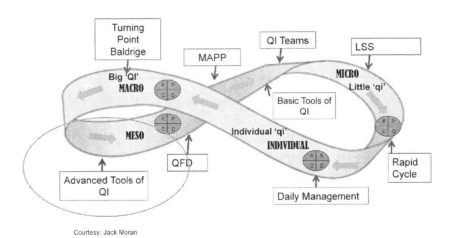

Courtesy: Jack Moran

FIGURE 2.3 Continuous Quality Improvement System in Public Health

Source: Wallace Consulting (with permission).

efforts. By taking this approach and utilizing QI to strengthen population health via strategies like the CHIP, QI is working across sectors—the so-called meso QI depicted in Figure 2.3 within the circle.

EPHS 10. Research for New Insights and Innovative Solutions to Health Problems

Although most health departments are not conducting research, increasingly many across the country are engaged with Practice-Based Research Networks (PBRNs). PBRNs seek to answer questions specific and relevant to public health practice. Many are organized in conjunction with academic partners, providing the research know-how to assist those in the laboratory. Because the research questions are driven by public health practice rather than the traditional grantor process, the learning can be immediately translated into practice. Such topics are more likely to be related to key drivers of population health, thus elevating the importance of these inter- and extra-sectoral partnerships.

Perhaps equally significant, ESPH 10 has been more recently interpreted to also encompass health department use of best evidence and science within its interventions. This can readily be correlated with use of sources, such as the Community Guide, that can assist health departments and partners with appropriate community-level interventions based upon issues identified in the community health assessment and CHIP.

Connecting the Dots

The previous section highlighted the EPHS and the role public health system partnerships and collaborations could assume in order to facilitate population health gains. In some respects, separating out the varying roles and responsibilities that health departments have may not seem altogether meaningful. It is also seemingly artificial. However, in order to fully understand the net impact a health department may have, it is necessary to first grasp the individual roles and contributions. Nonetheless, it is the composite of the mosaic, the net product of the Ten ESPH, coming together in a complementary fashion—in coordination with external partners—that actually drives the potential for improvements in overall health status at the population level. In essence we have deconstructed the model to better understand it in its fully formed state.

In recent years there has been a renewed appreciation of the importance of public health law in catalyzing policy formation. Simply perusing the *Ten Great Public Health Achievements of the Twentieth Century* underscores the clear relevance of policy as a formidable tool for formulating dramatic health impact.[11, 12] This renaissance inspired the development of "health in all policies (HiAP)," which is a "collaborative approach to improving the health of all people by incorporating health considerations into decision-making across sectors and policy areas."[12, 13] Placed into context then, health in all policies is an instrument that in collaboration with partners can be deployed to achieve the objectives derived from the construct of the Ten EPHS—the convergence of community processes facilitated by public health embodied in the Community Health Improvement Plan.

Many jurisdictions around the nation have utilized elements of the HiAP approach to implement evidence-based practices to address identified health needs, often targeting upstream social determinants of health. HiAP at its core calls for policy-makers and stakeholders to consider health implications of every policy action. It can call attention to the unintended health impact, or more proactively, incorporate a policy that improves health through action in a different sector. Facilitating legislation that requires bike trails and sidewalks be included with all new roadway construction encourages a whole host of positive health effects, even as it reduces congestion and fosters alternative transportation modalities—also meeting the needs of other constituents. Minimum wage laws sweeping the country are another profound example of how health may benefit from joining forces with labor. Raising the pay of the lowest compensated workers enhances their purchasing power, offering the potential to relocate them from unsafe housing and the inadequate nutrition offerings of food deserts.

Few would argue that the trend toward real-time data fueled by the internet is now an irreconcilable force to be reckoned with. Public health has the potential to harness these gains through data sources across sectors to realize population health improvements. The momentum around meaningful use and the HITECH Act have brought innumerably more health care settings into the electronic digital age, enabling their clinical data to be harvested by public health. In order to capitalize on these advances, health departments must be well positioned to enter the fray. Relatively straightforward examples of how public health might benefit include preparedness surveillance and clinical prevention. Health departments with ties to data systems from pharmacies or school districts can monitor usage of indicator pharmaceuticals or student absences. Both may help alert health authorities to rapidly evolving events. New York City Department of Health and Mental Hygiene has developed a diabetes registry employing clinical data that tracks hemoglobin A1C levels as a quality of care indicator that also yields real-time population health data about diabetes. Alternatively, other data also could be captured. The movement toward patient-centered medical homes is sweeping across primary care settings, and offers genuine possibilities for improved coordinated care. Collected for an entire jurisdiction, such data could inform a wealth of public health interventions premised upon greater knowledge about the health of local residents. Collaborating across sectors, with managed care, hospitals, ACOs, and others, could facilitate access to such data for public health monitoring purposes.

Some of the largest public health dividends deriving from true intersectoral collaboration fall within the CHIP domain. Arguably these are not single EPHS collaborations, but rather are developed in conjunction with partners as the sequential antecedents of the CHIP are crafted by the larger community through the guidance and facilitation of the health department. Chapter 8 will provide several accreditation case studies that stress how these collaborations led to more robust strategy formulations and health outcomes.

Just as patient-centered medical homes are gaining traction as a viable health care improvement model, a potentially disruptive public health innovation may be arriving at community health centers near you. The Community-Centered Health Home (CCHH) is a concept developed by the Prevention Institute that attempts to build on the foundation of community health centers' centrality as a health home for underserved populations.[13] The underlying intent is to bolster community health centers' capacity to undertake broader public health and population health roles within their catchment areas. For example, the model includes greater analytic capability to collect and examine population data on health metrics as well as local determinants of health. There is a greater emphasis on community engagement and action—which in some fashion resembles the community health assessment and CHIP. Philanthropies (Robert Wood Johnson and Kresge Foundations) are supporting pilots to test the proposed model. More recently as part of the Deepwater Horizon Medical Settlement awarded to the Gulf Region Health Outreach Project, several sites recently received grants to implement CCHHs in Louisiana, Alabama, and Mississippi. Chapter 20 describes these activities as part of the Primary Care Capacity Project of the Louisiana Public Health Institute.

One rational perspective is that the CCHH approach might be threatening to an already challenged and stretched governmental public health system. Community health centers could be perceived as yet another "pretender" seeking to displace governmental public health in much the same way managed care and ACOs might also be considered competitors. Alternatively, CCHH proliferation might be understood as yet another avenue for strengthening collaboration in the population health sphere. CCHHs may offer another powerful voice for those underserved and vulnerable in the community that the health department also serves. In fact, the potential nexus with the CHIP and several other EPHS is relatively direct.

The Robert Wood Johnson Foundation (RWJF) has recently embarked upon an ambitious decade-long commitment to build a national culture of health. The Foundation expects to achieve this end via several key interdependent action areas: fostering intersectoral collaboration; making health a shared value; creating healthier communities; and strengthening integration of systems.[14] Underlying this approach is the recognition that simply reforming the health care system is a necessary but insufficient means to improve overall health for our nation. The emphasis on integration of systems and intersectoral collaboration reflects many of the same underlying foci of several EPHS previously presented. RWJF is a powerful and resourceful influence in the formation of national health policy.

Well-developed and thoughtfully implemented visions like building a culture of health hold the potential to aid public health in efforts at intersectoral collaboration and public health system development. Grants and a funded research agenda supporting these concepts may well incentivize fundamental steps necessary to ensure meaningful collaboration is embraced widely.

Takeaways

The primary message of this chapter is that population health (with its many definitions—very much user-dependent) is embedded and well integrated within the EPHS. So too is the concept of meaningful collaboration as framed through the lens of the public health system. Health reform, among other forces, is dramatically influencing how policy-makers and others now think about health (something greater than mere health care alone). Moreover, research has demonstrated that strong collaboration contributes to greater health investment, and improved health.[15, 16] The opportunity is historic for public health to help shape implementation of a true population health movement, even as some individual health departments struggle to recover from the Great Recession.

References

1. Institute of Medicine, *The Future of Public Health* Committee on the Future of Public Health, ed. I.-o.-Medicine. 1988, Washington, DC: National Academy Press-Institute of Medicine.
2. Public Health Functions Steering Committee. Public Health in America. *Public Health Service*, 1994; Available from: http://www.health.gov/phfunctions.
3. Kindig, D.A. and G. Stoddard, What Is Population Health? *American Journal of Public Health*, 2003. **93**: p. 3669.
4. Berwick, D., T. Nolan, and J. Whittington, The Triple Aim: Care, Health, and Cost. *Health Affairs*, 2008. **27**(3): pp. 759–69.
5. Beitsch, L.M., et al., Public Health at Center Stage: New Roles, Old Props. *Health Aff* (Millwood), 2006. **25**(4): pp. 911–22.
6. Institute of Medicine, *Primary Care and Public Health: Exploring Integration to Improve Population Health*. 2012, Washington, DC: National Academies Press.
7. Centers for Disease Control and Prevention. National Public Health Performance Standards Program, August 31, 2009; Available from: http://www.cdc.gov/od/ocphp/nphpsp/.
8. *An Assessment Protocol for Excellence in Public Health*. 1991, Washington, DC: National Association of County Health Officials.
9. Brooks, R.G., et al., Aligning Public Health Financing with Essential Public Health Service Functions and National Public Health Performance Standards. *Journal of Public Health Management and Practice*, 2009. **15**(4): pp. 299–306.
10. Honore, P.A. and T. Schlechte, State Public Health Agency Expenditures: Categorizing and Comparing to Performance Levels. *Journal of Public Health Management and Practice*, 2007. **13**(2): pp. 156–62.

11. Achievements in Public Health, 1900–1999: Changes in the Public Health System. *Morbidity and Mortality Weekly Report (MMWR)*, 1999. **48**(50): pp. 1141–7.

12. Rudolph, L., et al., *Health in All Policies: A Guide for State and Local Governments*. 2013, Washington, DC and Oakland, CA: American Public Health Association and Public Health Institute.

13. Cantor, J., et al., *Community-Centered Health Homes: Bridging the Gap between Health Services and Community Prevention*. 2011, Oakland, CA: Prevention Institute.

14. *Culture of Health.* January 7, 2016; Available from: http://www.cultureofhealth.org/en/about.html.

15. Mays, G.P., et al., Getting What You Pay for: Public Health Spending and the Performance of Essential Public Health Services. *Journal of Public Health Management and Practice*, 2004. **10**(5): pp. 435–43.

16. Mays, G. and S.C. Smith, Evidence Links Increases in Public Health Spending to Declines in Preventable Deaths. *Health Affairs*, 2011. **30**(8): pp. 1585–93.

3

WHAT IS A POPULATION HEALTH PLAN?

Amanda McCarty and Rahul Gupta

For the past approximately 150 years, governmental public health agencies at local, state, and federal levels have successfully united with others to eradicate some, and control many other, communicable diseases, improve sanitation, and lead the charge for the development of policies such as seatbelt safety and drunk driving reducing. As a result, since the 1900s the average life span in the United States has increased by more than 30 years; 25 years of this gain have been attributed to public health advances. However, the role of public health must evolve in order to be successful for the next 100 years. We as a society must demand a population health approach from public health. The Institute of Medicine's *Future of the Public's Health in the 21st Century* calls for significant movement in building a new generation of intersectoral partnerships that draw on the perspectives and resources of diverse communities and actively engage them in health action—a population health approach. However, much of U.S. governmental public health activity does not have such a broad mandate even in its "assurance" functions, because major population health determinants like health care, education, and income remain outside public health authority and responsibility. Current resources provide inadequate support for traditional—let alone emerging—public health functions.

To further augment the emerging trend, and need, of focusing on population health, the U.S. federal government implemented that National Prevention Strategy as part of the Affordable Care Act. The National Prevention Strategy aims to move the United States from a system fixated on sick care to one focused on wellness and prevention. We know that preventing disease before it starts is critical to helping people live longer, healthier lives and keeping health care costs down.[1] We also know that many of the strongest predictors of health and well-being fall outside of the health care setting.[1] The National Prevention Strategy focuses on integrating prevention into all aspects of our everyday lives. The Strategy prioritizes prevention by integrating recommendations and actions across multiple settings and envisions a prevention-oriented society where all sectors recognize the value of health for individuals, families, and society, and work together to achieve better health.[1] The Association for State and Territorial Health Officials (ASTHO) also recommends utilizing the National Prevention Strategy as one of two strategies to support population health improvement.[2]

The priority areas of focus within the National Prevention Strategy include:

- Tobacco-free living
- Preventing drug abuse and excessive alcohol use
- Healthy eating
- Active living
- Injury- and violence-free living
- Reproductive and sexual health
- Mental and emotional well-being

No single entity in the public or private sectors currently has responsibility for overall health improvement. Addressing population health provides an opportunity for public health agencies, health care delivery systems, education, community-based organizations, economic development, and many other entities to work collectively to improve health outcomes in the communities they serve. Through integrated partnerships, across multiple sectors, we can work together to engage individuals in their health and empower them to make healthier choices, expand clinical and preventive-care services, diminish health disparities, and ultimately create safe and healthy communities.

Population Health and Public Health

Population health requires us to consider ways in which we can maximize health as a denominator and in doing so forces us to not define public health as a sole governmental function. The population health perspective requires the consideration of a broader array of the determinants of health than is typical in either health care or public health. Therefore, successful population health interventions of the future will require active commitments and ongoing contributions from many sectors of the society, including health care, social, economic, environmental, education, transportation, business, faith-based, and many others as co-equals. Government public health agencies, as the backbone of the public health system, are clearly in need of support and resources, but they cannot work alone.[3]

Population health has been defined by Kindig and Stoddart (2003, p. 382) as "the health outcomes of a group of individuals, including the distribution of such outcomes within the group."[4] With an emphasis on outcomes, the measurement of the health of a population utilizing health status indicators and social determinants provides a conceptual framework. The outcomes are ultimately impacted by policy, programs, and resource allocation towards such. However, such an approach allows the social determinants to be measured in order to determine the potential outcomes and perhaps altering policy, practice, and research agendas in a manner that would enhance meaningful measured outcomes for the geographic communities. This "health in all policies" approach would encourage policy makers to weigh the health implications of laws, rules, and policies that would otherwise not be considered health related. This is analogous to fiscal notes considered for legislative agenda all across the nation when new laws, ordinances, and rules are being considered for drafting. Adopting a "health in all policies" approach would consider an analogous "health note" to be considered prior to considering all similar legislation, regardless of its perceived relationship to health. ASTHO also recommends utilizing the National Prevention Strategy's "health in all policies" approach, along with the Triple Aim Framework, which focuses on improving patient care and the health of populations, all the while reducing the cost of health care.[2]

SHIP vs. CHIP vs. Population Health Plan

State Health Improvement Plans (SHIP) and Community Health Improvement Plans (CHIP) are based on the public health system perspective and are typically dependent on the state public health system assessment, with the essential services for public health at the foundation. There has been an increase in the development of state and community health improvement plans with the recently established voluntary system of state and local health department accreditation through the Public Health Accreditation Board (PHAB). Public health agencies can seek to become accredited, measuring the agency's ability to meet the Essential Services of Public Health.

The state's population health plan takes an expanded approach, beyond the core public health issues, addressing population health problems with population health solutions. Population health plans should have a comprehensive approach to health improvement focusing on communities, preventive and clinical care, the health care consumer, and aiming to improve health disparities. Just as with the state and community health improvement plans, the state's public health agency or the local jurisdiction can be the convener of the population health plan. However, the plan should incorporate the SHIP/CHIP and expand to identify unique opportunities to advance and impact population health by seeking to develop intersectoral collaborations with traditional and non-traditional partners. Similar to the SHIP and CHIP planning processes, the population health plan begins with a focus on planning and collaboration, focuses on the population's critical health indicators and determinants of health, and ultimately focuses on prioritized population outcomes. The outcome areas of focus in a population health plan can be related to, but are not limited to, chronic disease, prevention, access to care, social determinants of health, and health care costs (see Figure 3.1).

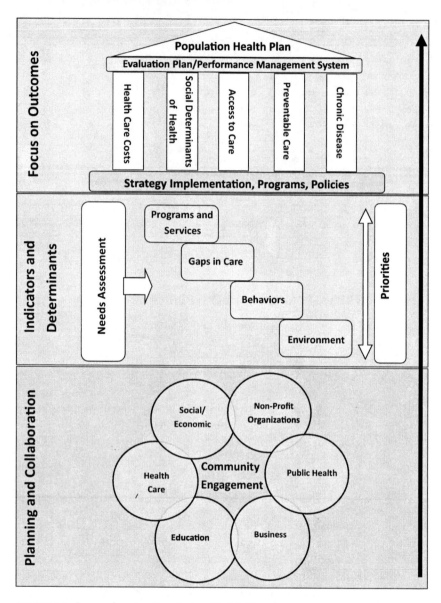

FIGURE 3.1 Comprehensive Population Health Planning

Population Health Plan

The goal of a population health plan is to keep a community's population as healthy as possible, minimizing the need for expensive interventions. When executed appropriately, such a plan not only lowers costs, but also redefines health priorities for the community beyond sick care. The population health plan is a broad plan that covers a vast number of sectors including public health, health care delivery, and non-traditional partners. Population health encompasses a cultural shift from a focus on providing care when individuals are sick to a more comprehensive approach that includes enhancing and improving the health of communities across a spectrum of ages and conditions and a focus on addressing the social determinants of health.[5] Although this may seem broad, it does reinforce that no one sector within the health system can influence the overall health outcomes alone.

The population health plan is an overall representation of and should take into consideration:

- Identified gaps in care, coverage, and resources
- The needs of the population
- A prioritized model of key areas of focus for the plan
- An overview of strategies identified by partners for implementation
- Access to care, including rural populations
- Health promotion and prevention strategies
- Payment systems and moving from fee-for-service models to value-based care
- Data availability and integration
- Information technology and telehealth practices
- Evaluation and outcomes

The plan should include goals, objectives, and interventions that are specific, measurable, achievable in the specific time period, realistic, and time bound. Objectives and associated interventions must address the identified priorities via interventions designed to impact both the health care delivery system and the underlying social determinants of health that contribute to the prioritized health conditions.

In addition to the comprehensive approach for developing a population health plan content covered within this chapter, ASTHO recently published a checklist for population health plans as well as state examples of population health improvement. The checklist provided by ASTHO includes:[2]

- Conduct a coordinated population health needs assessment to identify goals and objectives.
- Develop a priority setting process and identify evidence-based population health improvement interventions for each goal and objective.
- Identify leaders in population health improvement at the state, regional, and local levels
- Develop and implement a population health plan.
- Select a set of metrics to monitor and evaluate the population health plan over time.
- Establish a communications plan for reporting progress on improvements in population health.

Key Elements of a Population Health Plan

Stakeholder Engagement

Establishing a group of stakeholders is one of the first and most important activities in the population health planning process (see Figure 3.2). Recognizing the critical role of improving health in lowering health care costs has led policy makers and payers to shift increased responsibility for the health of populations to health care providers, often blurring the lines between traditional public health and health care delivery roles. Strong partnerships at a community level between local public health agencies, employers, schools, social service providers, and health care providers are essential to the overall success of improving population health through alignment of goals and resources.[5] Thus, the supporting stakeholder group should be a diverse group of dedicated people invested in the population health plan and the overall outcomes of the plan. To assist with the plan being focused on the needs of the population, and not condition or sector specific, all phases of population health plan development from initial planning to priority setting and implementation should include a variety of stakeholders and representation from a variety of sectors. This should include representation from state and local public health agencies, state and local policy makers, state and local health system partners, businesses, community organizations, clinical providers,

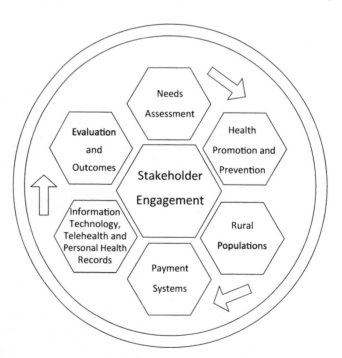

FIGURE 3.2 Key Elements of a Population Health Plan

educational partners, and families. A comprehensive, cross-sector approach will support and champion change at all levels, focusing on improving overall population health within the state. Population health is a shared responsibility, a collaborative commitment, and accountability will drive population health solutions and everyone will benefit from healthier communities.

As noted by the Centers for Disease Control and Prevention (CDC), there are typically three groups of stakeholders in Public Health:[6]

- Those involved in program operations: Management, program staff, partners, funding agencies, and coalition members
- Those served or affected by the program: Patients or clients, advocacy groups, community members, and elected officials
- Those who are intended users of the evaluation findings: Persons in a position to make decisions about the program, such as partners, funding agencies, coalition members, and the general public or taxpayers

Not all stakeholders will fit into just one of the identified categories. These categories are meant to serve as a guide when including partners in planning efforts to help think broadly as well as specifically.

As also noted by the CDC, we should utilize the evaluation standards to help identify those stakeholders who matter most. Priority should be given to those stakeholders who:[6]

- Can increase the *credibility* of your efforts or your evaluation
- Are responsible for day-to-day *implementation* of the activities that are part of the program
- Will *advocate* for or *authorize changes* to the program that the evaluation may recommend
- Will *fund* or *authorize the continuation or expansion* of the program

The National Prevention Strategy encourages partnerships among federal, state, tribal, local, and territorial governments; business, industry, and other private sector partners; philanthropic organizations; community and faith-based organizations; and everyday Americans to improve health through prevention.[1] Just as with population health planning, we must establish cross-sector partnerships in order to achieve an integrated approach to developing strategies for health improvement.

Similar to the stakeholder and partner engagement needed for a successful population health plan, the National Prevention Strategy Council engages a variety of departments and agencies throughout the federal government that are committed to promoting prevention and wellness. As the Council provides the leadership necessary to engage not only the federal government but a diverse array of stakeholders, from state and local policy makers, to business leaders, to individuals, their families, and communities, similar efforts may be undertaken at state and community levels to champion the policies and programs needed to ensure the health and prosperity of Americans.[1]

Needs Assessment

A needs assessment helps to understand the current health care environment. The assessment is often utilized to gather information on programs and services currently available, identify gaps in care and services, and, overall, identify the needs for the target population. The assessment is one of the first steps in planning at local or state level as the information obtained through the assessment provides the foundation for population health planning. It also provides an opportunity to bring together members of the community, partners in public health, and other stakeholders whose participation and commitment will be needed for overall success. Stakeholders are a crucial component in the assessment process, and having the right stakeholders engaged in the assessment process is crucial to informing the overall population health process.

Public health agencies can utilize tools made available by the CDC to assess capacity and the agency's ability to perform the essential services of public health. The National Public Health Performance Standards assessments are available for state public health entities, local public health agencies, and public health governing bodies. A large group of diverse partners and stakeholders will need to be identified to participate in the assessment process, and may sometimes extend beyond the stakeholders already identified in the population health planning process.

Once completed, the results of the assessment will be reviewed by stakeholders to identify gaps in services and resources, and priorities for future public health planning. In addition to the community needs assessment results, the comprehensive assessment report should also consist of a "population profile" providing an overview of the population demographics, education level, average income, disability status, predominant geographic notation, access to health care services, and any other social determinants of health that contribute to overall health status at the population level. Collectively, all of this information will be reviewed by stakeholders and used to determine the targeted priorities of the population health plan for that particular jurisdiction.

Health Promotion & Prevention

Preventing disease and injuries is key to improving America's health.[1] When we invest in prevention, the benefits are vast and broadly shared. Health promotion and chronic disease prevention are at the core of improving population health. Most of our nation's priority health issues and problems can be prevented. In each population health plan there is an aim to identify large-scale population health issues, whether condition or lifestyle behavior based, and determine among the stakeholder group which strategies and evidence-based interventions will work for the target population. Within the United States, health improvement plans and population health plans may focus on some of the same health factors: obesity, tobacco, hypertension, cardiovascular disease, and mental health. We know that eating healthfully and engaging in regular physical activity; avoiding tobacco, excessive alcohol use, and other drug abuse; using seat belts; and receiving preventive services and vaccinations are just a few ways people can stay healthy.[1] Whereas priority areas may be similar across population health plans, the interventions being implemented will likely be different. Interventions that may be successful in highly populated urban areas may not be successful in states that are primarily rural.

Preventing disease requires a multi-faceted approach that includes provider education, the availability of community resources and programs, communities providing the option to make healthy choices, access to fresh healthy food, and an environment supportive of physical activity, individual accountability, and empowerment. Ultimately, we want our communities promoting and encouraging healthy lifestyle choices and behaviors, and providing the appropriate services and programs to improve overall health.

To provide an example, tobacco use is still the leading underlying cause of death in the United States and worldwide. Across the globe, tobacco use kills more than 6 million people per year—more deaths than HIV, tuberculosis, and malaria combined—and nearly 80 percent of these deaths occur in low- and middle-income countries.[7] Without urgent, collaborative action, it is estimated that tobacco use will kill more than 1 billion people in this century alone. Tobacco use in the United States is declining slowly. Smoking-cessation counseling and treatment are effective clinical interventions, but public health interventions, including raising tobacco taxes, expanding smoke-free public places, running hard-hitting anti-tobacco advertising campaigns, reducing images of smoking in movies and television, and increasing the purchase age to 21 years, can reduce smoking rates much more.[8] In its first three years, the "Tips from Former Smokers" advertising campaign from the Centers for Disease Control and Prevention helped at least 300,000 smokers quit and saved at least 50,000 lives, at a cost of less than $500 per smoker who quit, less than $400 per year of life saved, and less than $3,000 per life saved.[9]

Another example is the mandatory childhood immunizations concept. Undoubtedly, immunizations are one of the top accomplishments in the history of public health. There are several life-threatening illnesses that physicians have combated in the past century that are much less common and are much less devastating to patients. Vaccines have been essential in the eradication of deadly diseases, such as smallpox. Although vaccinations have not eradicated all vaccine preventable disease, they have significantly reduced the rates of other diseases. Polio is an example of a now uncommon disease, which used to plague thousands. However, through the utilization of polio vaccines, a case of polio has not been seen in the United States in decades. Although polio is a horrific, distant memory for some, polio is still seen in areas of Pakistan and Afghanistan in 2016.[10] However, there remains a potential threat for this deadly and devastating disease to make its return due to travel. The return of polio to the United States could be as little as an airplane or boat ride away. That is why the continuation of polio vaccine administration in the United States is essential. To accomplish a high level of herd immunity for several such vaccine preventable diseases, states have established compulsory vaccination requirements for school children. Although these laws can vary across states, it is widely accepted that immunization requirements that reach more children through a broad range of facilities, that have detailed requirements for receiving an exemption which is limited to medical reasons, and that are implemented with strong enforcement and monitoring may help promote higher rates of vaccination coverage, and in turn, lower rates of vaccine preventable diseases (Figure 3.3). Currently in the United States, only California, Mississippi, and West Virginia limit vaccine exemptions to medical necessity only.[11]

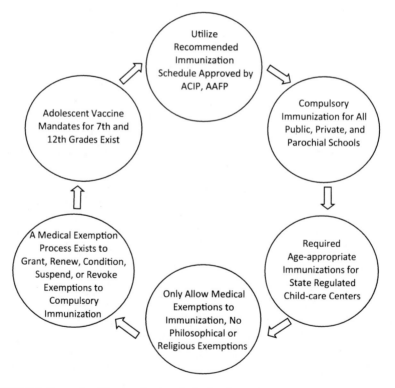

FIGURE 3.3 Strength of Immunization Scale for States

Rural Populations

Many of the strongest predictors of health and well-being fall outside of the health care setting.[1] Social, economic, and environmental factors all influence health.[12] There has been a renewed interest in geographic characteristics within public health, particularly in the areas of rural health. It is noteworthy that the obstacles faced by rural populations in terms of health care access and utilization, cost, and geographic distribution of providers and services in rural areas are vastly different than those in urban areas. Past research has documented that rural America faces a unique combination of factors that create disparities in health care not found in urban areas. As 40 percent of health factors are attributed to social and economic factors, these combined with a lack of robust educational systems and cultural differences often translates into varying levels of health based on zip code.

Additionally, research demonstrates that rural populations are more likely to engage in risky health-related behaviors and to experience higher rates of chronic conditions and activity limitations. The environments in which people live have a tremendous influence on the choices that they make about eating healthy and being physically active. People with a quality education, stable employment, safe homes and neighborhoods, as well as access to high quality preventive services, tend to be healthier throughout their lives and live longer.[1] Rural areas typically have higher rates of chronic disease and poor health behaviors, stressing the need for population health improvement strategies encompassing these individuals. In rural areas 8.2 million Americans (17 percent) live below the federal poverty line.[13] Residents in rural areas or low-income persons—particularly the unin-sured—may have greater problems accessing primary care services than well-insured, suburban residents.[14] Access to quality health care is crucial in supporting a healthy community.

In a population health plan, specific emphasis must be placed towards dif-ferences in population health, public health, environmental health, and the differences between urban and rural health behaviors. In the United States, significant health disparities exist, and these disparities are closely linked with social, economic, and environmental disadvantage (e.g., lack of access to quality affordable health care, healthy food, safe opportunities for physical activity, and educational and employment opportunities).[1] By utilizing a framework that examines determinants of health, planners can identify environment-specific factors that may contribute to different health outcomes for urban and rural residents.

Understanding the differences in rural and urban populations with regards to social and physical environments, as well as access to health and social services, will assist in approaching specific populations with unique, evidence-based approaches to addressing social determinants of health.

Payment Systems

A number of key policy issues are driving the current interest in population health planning. The first is the growing realization that the high level of health care spending in the United States is not producing the value desired in terms of the impact on overall health.[5] The U.S. health care industry is undergoing profound change in financing and service delivery as it shifts from a financial system that pays based on "volume" to one that is based on "value."[5] Today, critical access hospitals (CAHs), rural hospitals, rural health clinics (RHCs), and rural community health centers (CHCs) face the challenge of remaining viable undercurrent payment systems which are largely cost-based and/or fee for service, while preparing for new value-based payment systems that are being adopted in various forms across the nation.[5]

Recognizing that volume-based payment for health care services is fueling unsustainable growth in costs, there has been a renewed focus among payers and policy advocates to address underlying issues such as uncoordinated care, poor chronic disease management, behavioral health, unhealthy behaviors that can drive up utilization and costs, and limited access to evidence-based prevention and wellness services.[5] Provider payment systems can be powerful tools to promote the development of health systems and achieve health policy objectives. Value-based payment systems should help achieve health policy objectives by encouraging access to necessary health services for patients, and provision of high quality care while promoting the effective and efficient use of resources. Alignment of incentives across payers is also critical to addressing the population's health.

To accomplish this, payers and providers will need to change their internal processes and perhaps even organizational structures. Quality measurement and reporting systems may require evolution to meet the expanded needs in each community. Factors such as cost of care, differences in patient populations, and severity of illness must be taken into account when constructing a payment system. Similarly, the risk assumed by patients, providers, and payers must be considered as part of building any reimbursement system.

Population health plans at the state level should include a model design for moving from the traditional fee-for-service payment model to a value-based payment system. Value-based payment systems are being designed to address a three-pronged approach known as the Triple Aim of providing better care, improving health, and lowering costs, a framework developed by the Institute for Healthcare Improvement (IHI).[15]

Information Technology, Telehealth & Personal Health Records

Population health plans should take into consideration how information technology has been and can be utilized to improve health outcomes. The ultimate goal of health information technology (HIT) is to improve the quality and efficiency of patient care in a cost-effective manner. HIT is currently being utilized to improve patient health outcomes by offering electronic access for patients to make appointments, send secure messages to providers, and refill prescriptions. Health providers are able to offer follow-up visits via videoconferencing in remote locations and prescribe remote monitoring devices to assist with managing chronic conditions.

However, population health plans often lack an explicit health information technology strategic plan. The plan should focus on advancing HIT innovation in order to modernize the technology infrastructure. The HIT infrastructure should support dynamic uses of electronic information which should translate into evidence-based informed decisions. Successful development and implementation of an HIT strategic plan will support the cultural shifts necessary to strengthen the collaborative relationships for improving health, health care, research, and innovation. When collaborating with partners during strategy development, it is important to consider populations that are hard-to-reach and may miss appointments due to location, costs, and transportation.

Legislation and policies that impact health information technology (HIT), such as the Health Information Technology for Economic and Clinical Health (HITECH) Act, have had a significant impact on population health by improving access to information to assist providers in better understanding the burden and potential impacts that could improve population health.[5]

With population health data becoming increasingly important it is imperative that the electronic health records (EHR) are optimized to allow for the collection of population health data.[5] A sound health IT infrastructure will allow the advancement of person-centered and self-managed health while transforming the health care delivery system and improving the community's health.

Evaluation & Outcomes

With diminishing budgets and the ensuing restraints being placed on public health, and all public sector programs, public health entities and supporting programs are feeling the pressure to demonstrate accountability and overall effectiveness. Having a strategy for future population health plan operations (strategic plan, project plan, operational plan, etc.), establishing performance measures, having access to integrated and timely data, and a plan for evaluation and demonstrating outcomes is crucial for plan improvement and guided decision making. To demonstrate effectiveness, it is important to establish and maintain an evaluation system that can monitor and document key short-term, intermediate, and long-term outcomes within the population.[16]

An effective evaluation plan:[17]

- Is collaboratively developed with stakeholders
- Is responsive to program changes and priorities

- Covers multiple years if projects are ongoing
- Addresses the entire program rather than focusing on a single funding source, objective, or activity

Throughout the population health planning process it is imperative to engage stakeholders and partners in developing performance measures that will indicate the true performance of implemented interventions and strategies, and to choose measures in which good, quality data is available and will be used to inform policy decision making. The focus should be on developing outcome measures, not activity based measures, and should include measures that can be updated at least bi-annually, although quarterly should be preferred. The more often measures can be updated, the more responsive the population health plan collaborative can be by using this information to guide decision making. As mentioned, a good performance evaluation system or performance dashboard will include:

- Measures that will demonstrate quick action and results which are typically updated quarterly (the noticeable quick-wins will help to gain momentum)
- Intermediate outcome measures representative of strategies that take dedicated effort and resources, but will demonstrate impact after a few reporting cycles; these are measures that may be reported bi-annually to annually
- Long-term outcome measures indicative of long-term commitment, typically measures that are reported on an annual to every two, or even three, years

The information obtained from the overall evaluation plan or performance management system should be used to engage and update stakeholders and partners, inform and guide changes to implemented strategies and interventions, influence policy changes, and most importantly, demonstrate the population health plan's effectiveness.

Transparency in population health planning and implementation is one of the most critical factors to overall success. In addition to a comprehensive, cross-sector approach to population health planning, communication and transparency regarding overall performance is crucial to stakeholder buy-in, accountability, and ongoing support. It is important to share with the community the progress that is being made with the population health plan; this can be done through town-hall meetings, media outlets, the public health agency's website, etc.

Example Population Health Plan Framework

West Virginia

According to data from the Kaiser Family foundation, health care spending in West Virginia (WV) has steadily risen in the past few decades in parallel to the national trend. West Virginia has the tenth highest private health insurance premiums in the nation, and in the eight years between 2003 and 2011, private health insurance premiums rose 62 percent—three times faster than wages—leaving residents of West Virginia paying premiums that exceeded the median incomes of a quarter of the state's workers.[18] West Virginia ranks fourth among states in public health funding per person.[19] Data demonstrates that from 2002 to 2009, WV health care spending increased by nearly 300 percent. If left unchecked, this astounding expenditure may be the single most significant cost driver that cripples the fiscal health of the state. This is especially significant because West Virginia leads the nation in prevalence of tobacco use and obesity with consequential higher rates of many chronic diseases like heart disease, diabetes, arthritis, stroke, hypertension, and disability. Becoming a healthier West Virginia is a real possibility. It begins with no longer tolerating poor health as the status quo.

Tobacco use remains the leading underlying cause of death in West Virginia, the nation, and worldwide. However, as opposed to most states, the adult smoking prevalence has not been declining, although success has been seen with the youth population. Tobacco use rates among pregnant mothers remain the highest in the nation and may be as high 44 percent in some populations. For the first time in the history of our nation, West Virginia and Mississippi have adult prevalence rates for obesity rates exceeding 35 percent. As the aging population of WV combines with an increasingly overweight and obese population, the cost of health care in West Virginia will become unsustainable. In addition, obesity threatens to undermine economic security and communities by creating an increasingly chronically ill and disabled workforce and residents. Public health partners in West Virginia realize that it is time to carefully assess the causes of weight gain and obesity in West Virginia's environment and to take significant steps to ensure those conditions change.

The West Virginia Bureau for Public Health began state health improvement planning efforts in 2012 by forming an advisory group for the initiative and conducting a statewide population health system assessment. The assessment was performed using the National Public Health Performance Standards (NPHPS or the Standards). The Standards provide a framework to assess capacity and performance of public health systems against the essential services of public health and can help identify areas for system improvement.[20] Partners participating in the assessment represented 20 of West Virginia's 55 counties.

As part of the overall baseline assessment process, in addition to the state health assessment being published in 2013, a state health profile was published, and a state public health system partner survey was conducted. The state health profile highlights selected key indicators, in addition to ten other categories: Demographics; Health Behaviors; Infant, Child, & Adolescent Health; Healthcare Access & Quality; Mortality; Mental Health; Communicable Diseases; Cancer;

Chronic Diseases; and Community & Environment.[21] The partner survey served as one of several opportunities to better understand various aspects of existing public health issues facing West Virginia from the perspective of health system partners. The survey collected information related to the barriers to health care, factors influencing barriers to health care, populations having unmet health-related needs, health risks and risky behaviors, community and environmental factors impacting health, and health-related issues being well addressed in the state.

All of the assessment documents are part of an ongoing, collaborative process to improve population health within West Virginia. Assessment information revealed that there were many efforts within the state trying to impact health, some of which are fragmented and duplicative. Rather than creating new programs, the advisory group suggested that the state focus on an innovative collaborative approach that connects programs and partners with a shared vision and switch to planning for population health impacting the system as a whole.

The West Virginia Bureau for Public Health, a division of the West Virginia Department of Health and Human Resources (DHHR), is tasked with creating environments where residents of the state can be safe and healthy, and that is a challenge that must be taken seriously. There has been an increased focus on looking at the programs offered across the state and comparing them to the social determinants of health: the circumstances in which people are born, grow up, live, work, and age, as well as the systems and environments put in place to deal with illness.

In 2014, The West Virginia DHHR launched the West Virginia Health Innovation Collaborative (the Collaborative) to create a statewide partnership strategically focusing on efforts utilizing the Triple Aim Approach to better care, lower costs, and better health. In an effort to summarize population health issues facing West Virginia, summative data from the state health assessment was presented to support initial discussions for consideration and evaluation, and to engage statewide partners to focus on data-driven priority setting for the state's population health plan. Partners were asked to participate in creating the vision for West Virginia's health improvement plan by utilizing data to drive priority setting. As a result of collaborative engagement, a population health framework was developed to use as the focus for the development of the population health plan (refer to Figure 3.4). The framework groups the priority health interventions into three main categories: obesity, tobacco, and mental health. Each of the priority areas includes sub-category areas of focus for strategy implementation and measurement, indicated by the boxes listed beneath. For each of the targeted conditions or behaviors, prevention, patient engagement, and use of data to drive improvement are cross-cutting objectives to improve outcomes.

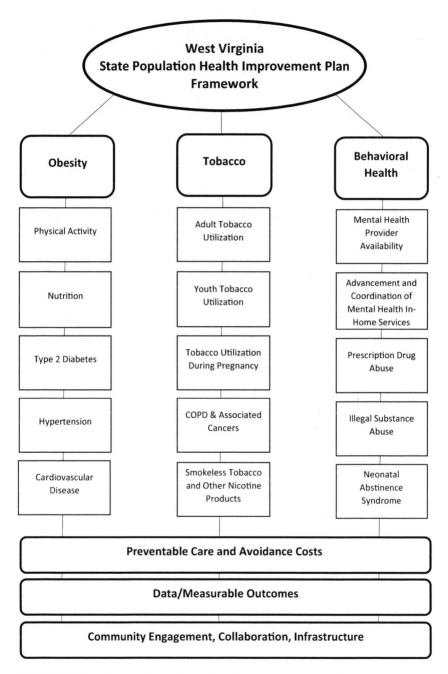

FIGURE 3.4 West Virginia State Population Health Improvement Plan Framework

At the time of this publication, the West Virginia State Population Health Improvement Plan had not been fully developed and implemented.

Conclusion

The health of populations is largely determined by factors and conditions outside the health system. Population health planning aims to improve the health and well-being of whole populations, and to reduce inequities between specific population groups. It takes into account the environmental, economic, political, social, cultural, and behavioral factors that contribute to the health and well-being of communities and populations. Effective and meaningful population health planning requires community, intersectoral, and cross-sectoral engagement, collaboration, and action to address the broad range of determinants that shape health and well-being. It should begin with conducting an assessment of the overall health of the state or local jurisdiction and then identifying measurable goals, objectives, and interventions that will enable the state or jurisdiction to (1) improve the health of the entire population; (2) transform health care delivery systems; and (3) decrease per capita total health care spending. To achieve these goals, it is critical to ensure that the interventions selected for the conditions identified in the needs assessment are grounded in evidence or guidance that supports them as proven, effective, or promising. As we have discussed here, the key elements of a population health plan require a focus on prevention and health promotion with a special emphasis on rural and other vulnerable populations as well as systems transformation with regard to information technology and payment systems. Furthermore, the plan as well as the selected interventions should have strong evaluation and outcomes measures including meeting specified goals and objectives in a timely manner. Finally, an effective population plan will address health concerns with high population burden or societal costs and has the potential to demonstrate improvement in health, quality of care, and decreased costs within a defined timeframe.

References

1. National Prevention Council, *National Prevention Strategy*, Washington, DC: U.S. Department of Health and Human Services, Office of the Surgeon General, 2011. http://www.surgeongeneral.gov/priorities/prevention/strategy/report.pdf
2. Association of State and Territorial Health Officials, *State Health Agencies: Improving Population Health*, 2015. http://www.astho.org/Health-Systems-Transformation/Population-Health-Fact-Sheet/
3. Committee on Assuring the Health of the Public in the 21st Century; Board on Health Promotion and Disease Prevention; Institute of Medicine, *The Future of the Public's Health in the 21st Century*, 2003. http://www.nap.edu/catalog/10548/the-future-of-the-publics-health-in-the-21st-century
4. Kindig, D. and Stoddart, G. 2003. What Is Population Health? *American Journal of Public Health* 93(3): 380–383.
5. National Rural Health Association Policy Brief, *The Future of Rural Health*, 2013. http://www.ruralhealthweb.org
6. Centers for Disease Control and Prevention, *Introduction to Program Evaluation for Public Health Programs: A Self-Study Guide*. http://www.cdc.gov/eval/guide/step1/

7. WHO Report on the Global Tobacco Epidemic, 2015: Raising Taxes on Tobacco. Geneva: World Health Organization, 2015. http://www.who.int/tobacco/global_report/2015/en/

8. Thomas, R. and Frieden, M.D., M.P.H. 2015. The Future of Public Health. *New England Journal of Medicine* 373: 1748–1754.

9. Xu, X., Alexander, R.L., Jr., and Simpson, S.A., et al. 2015. A Cost-Effectiveness Analysis of the First Federally Funded Antismoking Campaign. *American Journal of Preventative Medicine* 48: 318–325.

10. Morales, Michelle, M.D., Tangermann, Rudolf H., M.D., and Wassilak, Steven G.F., M.D. 2016. Progress toward Polio Eradication—Worldwide, 2015–2016. *Morbidity and Mortality Weekly Report* 65(18): 470–473.

11. National Conference of State Legislatures, *States with Religious and Philosophical Exemptions from School Immunization Requirements.* http://www.ncsl.org/research/health/school-immunization-exemption-state-laws.aspx

12. Schroeder, S. 2007. We Can Do Better—Improving the Health of American People. *New England Journal of Medicine* 357: 1221–1228.

13. DeNavas-Walt, C. and Proctor, B.D. 2015. *Income and Poverty in the United States: 2014.* Washington, DC: U.S. Census Bureau.

14. National Institute for Health Care Reform, *Matching Supply to Demand: Addressing the U.S. Primary Care Workforce Shortage.* NIHCR Policy Analysis No. 7, 2011. http://www.nihcr.org/PCP_Workforce

15. Institute for Health Care Improvement, *Triple Aim for Populations.* http://www.ihi.org/Topics/TripleAim/Pages/default.aspx

16. Lavinghouze, R. and Snyder, K. 2013. Developing Your Evaluation Plans: A Critical Component of Public Health Program Infrastructure. *American Journal of Health Education* 44(4): 237–243.

17. Centers for Disease Control and Prevention, *Developing an Effective Evaluation Plan.* Atlanta: U.S. Department of Health and Human Services, Centers for Disease Control and Prevention, National Center for Chronic Disease Prevention and Health Promotion, Office on Smoking and Health, Division of Nutrition, Physical Activity, and Obesity, 2011.

18. Schoen, C., Lippa, J., Collins, S., and Radley, D., *State Trends in Premiums and Deductibles, 2003–2011: Eroding Protection and Rising Costs Underscore Need for Action*, the Commonwealth Fund, December 2012. http://www.commonwealthfund.org/Publications/Issue-Briefs/2012/Dec/State-Trends-in-Premiums-and-Deductibles.aspx

19. United Health Foundation, *America's Health Rankings: A Call to Action for Individuals and Their Communities*, 2012. http://cdnfiles.americashealthrankings.org/SiteFiles/Reports/Americas-Health-Rankings-2012-v1.pdf

20. Centers for Disease Control and Prevention, *National Public Health Performance Standards (NPHPS).* https://www.cdc.gov/nphpsp/

21. West Virginia Department of Health & Human Resources, Bureau for Public Health, *State Public Health Assessment Documents*, 2012. http://www.dhhr.wv.gov/publichealthquality/statepublichealthassessment/Pages/default.aspx

4

ADVANCING HEALTH EQUITY

Population Health and the Role of Multisectoral Collaborations

Renata Schiavo and Kenneth D. Smith

Health Equity: A Multidimensional Issue

We live in extraordinary times. These are times of innovation and ongoing changes in power structures, social organization, economic dynamics, social norms, theoretical and religious perspectives, and human self-knowledge, as well as scientific and medical progress, which has allowed many people to live longer and healthier lives (Schiavo, 2016a). Yet, *health disparities* ("diseases that discriminate and tend to be more common and/or more severe" among disadvantaged groups, and therefore result in preventable "differences in health outcomes") (Health Equity Initiative, 2012, 2014) continue to affect disadvantaged communities across the globe as well as to jeopardize people's ability to thrive and connect with socio-economic opportunities, such as lifting themselves from poverty, changing jobs or cities, or getting married, just to name a few examples (Health Equity Initiative, 2016b; Schiavo, Padgaonkar, Cooney, Cruz Reyes, and Health Equity Initiative, 2016).

Such disparities are avoidable and

> linked to diverse factors—which for the most part are likely to be community- and place-specific—including socio-economic conditions, race, ethnicity and culture, as well as having access to health care services, a built environment that supports physical activity, neighborhoods with accessible and affordable nutritious food, well-designed housing that is sited to minimize community exposure to environmental and other health hazards, efficient transportation that enable vulnerable groups to connect with services and support systems, culturally appropriate health information that accurately reflects literacy levels, and caring and friendly clinical settings.
>
> *(Schiavo, 2013a, p. 102; Health Equity Initiative, 2012, 2014; Schiavo, 2016b)*

Some health disparities are also related to "genetic and biological differences among ethnic groups or between men and women" (Center for Health Equity Research and Promotion, 2005). In other words, over the last decade we have come to the realization that there is more to health than just health *care* (Robert Wood Johnson Foundation, 2016), and that many different professional sectors and disciplines—as well as residents from the geographical communities in which they may operate— need to be involved to create better chances for better health for all.

In urban settings, disparities are further exacerbated by a high concentration of poverty, different urban hazards (e.g., high levels of pollution, poor sanitation), the global health worker shortage, widespread diversity that calls for increased resources to meet the needs of different groups via culturally competent interventions and services, social exclusion and isolation among many underserved and vulnerable groups, and rapid population growth that often outpaces the capacity of cities to build essential infrastructure and services (Alegria, Sribney, and Mulvaney-Day, 2007; Vlahov et al., 2007; Schiavo, 2013b). Examples of urban health disparities include higher infant mortality rate (IMR) among African Americans and Hispanics in New York City, United States (NYC Department of Health and Mental Hygiene, 2015); the widening gap on death rates from heart disease in rich versus poor areas in many cities in England, including London, Liverpool, and Manchester (Asaria et al., 2012); and disproportionate rates of diarrhea, tuberculosis, and child mortality in squatter areas of Manila, Philippines, such as Tondo (Jones, 2015).

Equally pervasive and dream-shattering, *disparities in healthcare* "refer to differences in access and use of healthcare, quality of care, cost, and number of hospitalizations," among others (Schiavo, 2015a, 2015c). Such disparities may often result in poor patient satisfaction and outcomes, high healthcare costs, and suboptimal use of healthcare providers' time in addition to costs associated with loss of productivity and working days (Mayberry, Nicewander, Qin, and Ballard, 2006; LaVeist, Gaskin, and Richard, 2009, 2011). Ultimately, disparities in health and healthcare are interconnected and both affect overall population health outcomes, as shown in Figure 4.1.

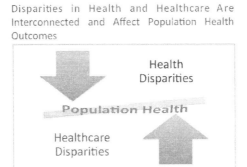

FIGURE 4.1 Health and Healthcare Disparities

Source: Schiavo, 2015b.

Given the many social, environmental, economic, cultural, and/or place-related factors (the "social determinants of health") contributing to health and healthcare disparities, the concept of health equity is intrinsically multidimensional and therefore implies that across our professional and lay communities, we can all contribute to eliminating health disparities by addressing key barriers that prevent people from leading a healthy life. Health equity is defined here as "providing every person with the same *opportunity* to stay healthy and/or effectively cope with disease and crisis—regardless of their socio-economic conditions, race, gender, age, social status, living and working environment, and other socially determined factors" (Schiavo, 2011; Health Equity Initiative, 2012, 2014; Schiavo, Padgaonkar, Cooney, Cruz Reyes, and Health Equity Initiative, 2016).

The concept of "opportunity" is at the core of all kinds of human endeavors within and outside the health field. For example, the idea of equality in America "has traditionally meant equality of opportunity in the sense that the men of the [American] Revolution viewed it" (Van Til, 1978). "Inequality of opportunity for Blacks became a principal political issue" in the civil rights movement that led to the Civil War and Emancipation Proclamation (Van Til, 1978). Similarly, "equal opportunity to participate fully in the political process"—so that different groups are included in the kinds of decision-making processes that affect the well-being of different populations—is at the core of the United Nations' democracy principles (United Nations, 2015).

"Equality of opportunity implies ensuring that progress in the provision of basic opportunities is not biased against anybody because of circumstances" (Paes de Barros, Ferreira, Molinas Vega, and Saavedra Chanduvi, 2009, p. 36), such as gender, race, socioeconomic background, age, birthplace, and other factors that are beyond a person's control. "Equal opportunity levels the playing field," so that "everybody has, in principle, the potential to achieve the outcomes of their choosing" (Paes de Barros, Ferreira, Molinas Vega, and Saavedra Chanduvi, 2009, p. 29). This concept has great implications for both policy and intervention design as it aims to make sure that the correlation "between the pattern of access to, use of, and benefit from public services and the other subcomponents of inequality of opportunity" (Paes de Barros, Ferreira, Molinas Vega, and Saavedra Chanduvi, 2009, p. 37) are considered in the development of global health and development initiatives, programs, and policies.

So, what does equality of opportunity mean for health equity, and why does it suggest that health equity is a multidimensional issue that calls for multi-sectoral approaches? To address this question, we should first ask ourselves how can we ask anyone to eat a healthy diet if they live in a food desert with limited access to supermarkets and/or healthy foods such as fruit and vegetables? Or how can we expect people to exercise if their socio-economic background does not allow them to afford gym fees and/or they live in a neighborhood with high crime rates, which prevents them from going for a run at night after work? Or how could parents protect their children from disease, injury, and death if they live in urban slums that lack clean water and adequate sanitation? Or how could patients who may have strong cultural beliefs and, in some cases, misperceptions about Western medicine comply with instructions by their healthcare providers in the absence of comprehensive efforts to bridge cultural values? By asking ourselves these types of questions, it should become clear that several different professions and sectors need to be involved in removing barriers to health equity. As for the above examples, such individuals may include business owners, architects, urban designers, community residents, community leaders, healthcare providers, hospital administrators, public health professionals, and many more.

In summary, "health equity has many aspects, and is best seen as a multidimensional concept. It includes concerns about achievement of health and the capability to achieve good health, not just the distribution of health care" (Sen, 2002, p. 665). In this context, health equity is a social justice issue as well as a political and economic issue that calls for multisectoral collaborations and solutions. The concept of health equity is intrinsically linked to *population health*, which is defined as "the health outcomes of a group of individuals, including the distribution of such outcomes within the group" (Kindig and Stoddart, 2003, p. 380), and therefore aims for improvements in the entire population and not only within specific segments. This chapter aims to provide a brief overview of the theory and practice of multisectoral collaborations in support of health equity, including case studies and practical steps that we hope will help organizations and leaders to jump-start or advance their efforts to create a "culture of collaboration" within their workplace and communities to improve health and social outcomes.

Why We Need a Multisectoral Approach to Health Equity

Although significant progress has been made on a variety of health and social issues, suboptimal performance in achieving population health goals is well documented both in the United States and globally (Fawcett, Schultz, Watson-Thompson, Fox, and Brembly, 2010; Fehling, Nelson, and Venkatapuram, 2013). For example, only 23% of the objectives established by *Healthy People* 2010—the U.S. public health agenda—were met and another 48% were moving toward the *Healthy People* 2010 targets at the time of the final review (National Center for Health Statistics, 2012). Some indicators (including health disparities in ethnic minorities) actually grew worse (Fawcett, Schultz, Watson-Thompson, Fox, and Brembly, 2010). Although progress toward *Healthy People 2020* indicators is still being evaluated, current data show that 53.9% have either met their target or shown improvement, while 42.3% show little or no detectable change or are getting worse (e.g., suicide rates and percentage of adolescents with depression), and 3.8% are still in the baseline data collection phase (Office of Disease Prevention and Health Promotion, 2016a).

Globally, progress toward the *Millennium Development Goals* (MDGs) has been uneven across indicators and countries. While significant gains have been made in economic conditions, child mortality, and number of children enrolled in primary schools—an important determinant of health—many regions have not been able to meet the estimated MDGs (United Nations, 2012). For example, "an estimated 15.5% of the world population still suffers from hunger, and many countries, particularly on the African continent," could not meet the two-thirds reduction in child mortality within the projected time (Fehling, Nelson, and Venkatapuram, 2013, p. 1109). "The reduction in maternal mortality has been slow and mortality remains alarmingly high (UN, 2012). In sub-Saharan regions and Southern Asia, where 80% of people in extreme poverty live, progress in reaching MDGs has generally been very limited (UN, 2012)" (Fehling, Nelson, and Venkatapuram, 2013, p. 1109).

Many factors usually contribute to poor or slow improvements in health and social outcomes, especially within underserved and vulnerable populations settings. These include "lack of shared responsibility for outcomes" among different stakeholders, and "lack of limited understanding of what works" (Fawcett, Schultz, Watson-Thompson, Fox, and Bremby, 2010, p. 1). In the case of the MDGs, unrealistic objectives and frameworks that in many cases were developed "without adequate involvement by developing countries" have been cited among other important contributing factors (Fehling, Nelson, and Venkatapuram, 2013, p. 1109). Yet, both in the case of *Healthy People* as well as the MDGs, lack of cooperation and collaborations, which often leads to vertical or top-down approaches and may also result in lack of accountability and shared responsibility, is considered a key area for improvement (Fehling, Nelson, and Venkatapuram, 2013; Fawcett, Schultz, Watson-Thompson, Fox, and Bremby, 2010).

Of great importance in looking at the need for multisectoral frameworks for health equity is the renewed emphasis on the importance to address key social, economic, environmental, and place-related barriers (e.g., poor housing, social isolation, limited literacy/health literacy, poverty, racism, lack of access to healthcare, transportation, sanitation, and other essential services, etc.) that may prevent people from leading a healthy life and/or successfully coping with disease and emergencies. Our recognition that there is more to health than healthcare is, or should be, accompanied by the realization that no single sector, organization, community, or individual could make progress toward health equity alone, and that increased awareness of health equity issues and strategies—as well as everyone's role in making progress toward health equity—is needed among key groups, professions, and communities (Health Equity Initiative, 2016b; Schiavo, Padgaonkar, Cooney, Cruz Reyes, and Health Equity Initiative, 2016). By increasing the capacity for multisectoral collaborations and partnerships as well as using a participatory approach to intervention design, implementation, and evaluation that is inclusive of all stakeholders and partners, we are also likely to improve our ability to achieve health and social objectives as part of our professional and community-based endeavors.

Making the Case for Multisectoral Solutions across Multiple Health and Social Areas

Several examples point to the importance of multisectoral collaborations for health equity. First, the global emergence of chronic diseases, and more specifically obesity, in developed and developing countries, including low- and middle-income countries (LMICs), has been associated to the level of "obesoginity" ("the sum of influences that the surroundings, opportunities, or conditions of life have on promoting obesity in individuals or populations") of an environment (Swinburn and Egger, 2002; Lake and Townsend, 2006, p. 126). Shaping the environment in which people live, play, work, and age, and helping support healthful decisions as related to food intake and physical activity requires the involvement of policymakers, residents' committees, investors, foundations, urban designers, architects, supermarket owners, religious leaders, healthcare workers, public health and community development professionals, just to name a few examples. It's only by looking at all kinds of professional and community-based endeavors via a health equity lens that geographical communities not only can have access to much needed services and goods (e.g., recreational facilities and parks, healthy food, buildings that are designed to encourage physical activity, safe streets that encourage walking and biking, mental health services, and others) but also feel supported in adopting and maintaining new health and social behaviors. Recent gains in childhood obesity rates, such as in the case of Kerney, Nebraska, in the United States, have in fact been associated with integrated approaches and multisectoral collaborations among local hospitals, schools, community organizations, campaigns, and fairs, which resulted in a 13.4% decline in obesity among children ages 5–11 (Robert Wood Johnson Foundation, 2015). Key to the intervention results was the integration of strategies that promoted change across different systems (e.g., education, health system, food systems, built environment, etc.) by, for example, improving local parks to create new children-friendly recreational activities, establishing new farmers' markets, promoting and expanding community gardens, increasing school programs dedicated to healthy eating and exercise, and making sure that child health is a priority for kids, parents, teachers, school principals, hospitals, community members, and many others (Robert Wood Johnson Foundation, 2015).

As another example, the recent 2014–2015 Ebola epidemic demonstrated the importance of strengthening health systems by creating health system–community partnerships that resulted in greater ownership of the overall outbreak response by community members. As part of these efforts, community members from at-risk groups worked together with front-line health workers, religious leaders, local ministries of health, and international and local organizations to change social norms and behaviors, operationalize community care centers, and participate in the overall outbreak response (UNICEF, 2015a, 2015b). This type of intervention was largely hauled as the most important factor in Ebola control in most countries (Schiavo, 2014; UNICEF, 2015a, 2015b; Gamhewage, 2016; Schiavo, Hilyard, and Skinner, 2016), and was also integrated in WHO guidance on the control of the Zika virus, which points to the role of communities in the design, implementation, and evaluation of risk communication interventions along with partners from multiple sectors (World Health Organization, 2016).

Finally, as an additional example, recommendations by *Healthy People 2020* for the Maternal, Infant and Child Health area seek to address a variety of conditions, health behaviors, social determinants, and health systems-related factors "that affect the health, wellness, and quality of life of women, children, and families" (Office of Disease Prevention and Health Promotion, 2016b). As many factors (e.g., poverty, preconception health status, chronic stress associated with a history of low socio-economics and/or social discrimination, age at pregnancy, limited emphasis on preconception health within clinical settings, limited community awareness, etc.) can affect maternal, infant, and child health (Schiavo, Gonzalez-Flores, Ramesh, and Estrada-Portales, 2011; Office of Disease Prevention and Health Promotion, 2016b), it is clear that addressing maternal, infant, and child health issues "requires a multidisciplinary and multifaceted effort involving different levels of society" to give mothers, children, and families the chance they deserve (Schiavo, Gonzalez-Flores, Ramesh, and Estrada-Portales, 2011, p. 115). Further corroborating this view, participants in a consensus-driven capacity building experience to build community–campus partnerships and create multisectoral task forces for infant mortality prevention in four U.S. cities also highlighted the importance of going beyond "the usual suspects" (e.g., most affected communities and public health professionals) and to continue to engage a variety of institutions and professionals in intervention design, implementation, and evaluation (Schiavo, Estrada-Portales, Hoeppner, Ormazza, and Ramesh, 2016).

Population Health and the Value Proposition across Different Sectors and Fields

Improving population health outcomes and health equity has also a strong value proposition across different fields and issues. For example, the value proposition of age-friendly communities, which are defined as communities where residents can live and prosper throughout their lifetime, is not only related to improved health outcomes but may also contribute to growing the local tax base as well as to promoting efficient use of infrastructure by allowing people to age-in-place and reduce future treatment and healthcare costs by preventing disease and injury (Grantmakers in Aging and Pfizer Foundation, 2015). Of course, this vision would require adequate investment and multisectoral approaches to create a built environment that is conducive to healthy living as well as opportunities for social inclusion, economic independence, and disease prevention that would allow adults to actually age-in-place.

As another example, within the healthcare system, multisectoral interventions that have connected local communities with hospitals and other healthcare institutions for the provisions of information and services already had an impact on patient outcomes and satisfaction, cost reduction, and better use of physicians' time in areas such as diabetes and other chronic diseases (Walton et al., 2012; Massachusetts General Hospital, 2014; Alliance to Reduce Disparities in Diabetes, 2015).

As vulnerable and underserved populations unfortunately share similar characteristics and histories (e.g., a history of poverty and/or social discrimination, lack of social support or access to essential services, limited literacy) across different settings and countries, multisectoral collaborations and partnerships are essential to addressing the many barriers to health equity.

Theory and Practice of Multisectoral Collaborations in Support of Health Equity

Public health provides a useful starting point for understanding the evolution of theory and practice in multisectoral collaboration for health equity. The roots of public health lie deep in the progressive reform movements of the early part of the 20th century that sought to address the harsh living conditions resulting from industrialization, urbanization, and mass immigration. Public works, sanitation, planning, medicine, and government worked collaboratively to address these social and physical ills. Many of the sources of increased life expectancy over the past century, such as improved sanitation, were the result of these multisectoral interventions. More importantly, these social and population-level interventions often required advocacy for new policies and practices to address transmittable diseases, environmental hazards, and sanitation. For example, mass vaccination and water fluoridation required forming strong alliances to advocate for necessary changes in policies and practices (Colgrove, 2006; Carstairs and Elder, 2008).

There was a movement to formalize these activities into core functions and essential services following the 1988 Institute of Medicine's report, *The Future of Public Health*. Policy development, which is now recognized as a core function of public health, requires mobilizing community partners to identify and solve health problems—one of the ten essential services of public health (Harrell and Baker, 1994). In addition, a number of position statements from national organizations composing the public health, hospital, and nursing communities, just to name a few examples, now recognize health equity as an intrinsic part of their practice. For example, the National Association of County and City Health Officials (NACCHO), the Association for State and Territorial Health Organizations, and the American Public Health Association all have position statements on health equity. Similarly, the American Hospital Association (AHA), in collaboration with the Institute for Diversity in Health Management, support a focus on health equity and coverage. All of the position statements and initiatives stress the importance of addressing health equity and collaboration, particularly with disadvantaged communities. Yet, for this to work we need other non-health sectors to be equally engaged in promoting health equity as well as recognizing the broader social and economic benefits of eliminating health disparities.

Multisectoral collaboration to address health equity, then, is a major concern for many types of practitioners. As a result, public health tools developed to support community mobilization efforts can be used also by other types of organizations outside of the health field and vice versa. For example, Mobilizing for Action through Planning and Partnerships (MAPP) is a model for collaborative community planning developed by the National Association of County and State Health Officials, which represents 2,800 local government public health departments (Fletcher, Knobbs, Lu, and Ritterman, 2003). The process starts with partnership development as a necessary condition for all other stages, such as group visioning, assessment, and planning. MAPP guidance documents recommend "all public, private, and voluntary entities that contribute to the delivery of essential public health services within a jurisdiction" be engaged in the collaborative planning process. This includes both stakeholders from the health (e.g., healthcare providers, and local and state public health agencies) and non-health sectors. Latter stakeholders may include elected officials, or representatives from human services, charity, education, youth development, recreation, arts, economic, philanthropic, and environmental agencies and organizations.

NACCHO has refined this process to better incorporate health equity in the MAPP process. For example, it has released a supplement to its original MAPP guidance document that lists health equity resources and provides recommendations about engaging stakeholders with a health equity and social justice focus (e.g., civil rights organizations, fair housing advocates, etc.), guidance on developing a health equity vision, and instructions for measuring inequity in the assessment process (NACCHO, 2014). This additional guidance is consistent with NACCHO's position statement on health equity, which recommends:

> the incorporation and adoption of principles of social justice into everyday public health practice in order to eliminate the root causes of health inequities; development of long-term relationships with communities based on mutual trust and a recognition of each other's strengths, leadership capacities, and common interests in confronting the social inequalities at the root of health inequities and social injustice; and establishing a movement-building strategy by creating alliances with constituents, community organizers, and relevant institutions as a means toward changing the structures and processes that generate health inequities.
>
> *(NACCHO, 2015, p. 1)*

Finally, several other resources also support a systematic approach to partnership development and management. For example, Schiavo (2013a) has developed a partnership planning model, checklist, and step-by-step approach that intersects with key elements of an intervention's action plan by supporting a consensus-driven and participatory planning approach in which all partners are equally engaged in intervention design as well as the development of assessment parameters. This model has been implemented as part of capacity building and multisectoral intervention design projects to advance health equity issues that were funded by the World Bank (Schiavo, 2008, unpublished data), the Office of Minority Health Resource Center (Schiavo, Estrada-Portales, Hoeppner, Ormazza, and Ramesh, 2016), and others. As another example, the Community Toolbox by the University of Kansas (2015) includes guidance, checklists, and other resources to develop multisectoral partnerships, including the identification of and potential solutions to barriers to successful partnerships via videos and other tools.

These and other tools can be used to support any collaborative effort, notwithstanding a focus on health equity, by organizations from different sectors and disciplines. For example, the Prevention Institute's Collaboration Multiplier, a tool that guides organizations through a collaborative process to develop a common goal with different contributions and to achieve that goal by leveraging expertise and resources, has been utilized successfully to address violence and injury prevention (Pan and Cohan, 2012). Indeed, many of these tools could be used to support collaborative social justice initiatives addressing a wide range of issues from fair housing to civil rights, as the practice of collaboration tends to be universal.

Because much of partnership development and management is practice-based, there has been little theory construction around multisectoral collaboration for health equity. However, observations of collaborative partnerships in action, particularly successful ones, can become the basis for generalization. For example, Alexander and colleagues (2001) collect and analyze qualitative data from 115 site-visit interviews in the Community Care Network demonstration to identify key leadership themes in community collaborative health partnerships. Using content analysis of interview transcripts, they identify five key leadership themes: systems thinking, vision-based leadership, collateral leadership, power sharing, and process-based leadership. These five themes arise from the unique nature of collaborative partnerships, where partnership leaders lack formal control over the members and their actions. Because partnerships are voluntary and egalitarian, traditional hierarchical leadership would be ineffective.

The first two themes, systems thinking and vision-based leadership, form an axis that is remarkably similar to leadership in a learning organization (Senge, 2006). Organizational learning entails approaching complex problems (like inequities arising from upstream social determinants) with a systems approach. Instead of starting out identifying a problem to fix, the emphasis is on developing a compelling vision for the future that is desirable by members of the organization, or in this case, members of a collaborative partnership. The next stage is to understand how complex systems are operating to produce the current reality, and to identify leverage points for action that will lead to systems transformation—changes that will reduce the gap between the current reality and the vision. This approach was promoted to nine grantees of the Kellogg Foundation's Food and Fitness initiative, where the focus was on developing a collaborative vision and identifying policy, systems, and built environment changes to improve access to healthy, affordable food and safe spaces for physical activity and play (Lachance, Carpenter, Emery, and Luluquisen, 2014). The most successful grantees were those whose leaders were able to use the vision to gain the support of critical stakeholder groups and partnering organizations. Moreover, Health Equity Initiative, a member-driven nonprofit membership organization dedicated to building and sustaining a global community that engages across sectors and disciplines to advance health equity, has been advocating for and using a participatory and consensus-building approach to engage professionals and community leaders in consultative processes that aim to identify key strategies, action areas, and priorities toward systems-level change for health equity (Health Equity Initiative, 2016a and 2016b; Schiavo, Estrada-Portales, Hoeppner, Ormazza, and Ramesh, 2016; Schiavo, Padgaonkar, Cooney, Cruz Reyes, and Health Equity Initiative, 2016).

Collateral leadership and power-sharing form another axis. Alexander and colleagues use the term "collateral leadership" instead of "distributed leadership" to focus on the crucial role of both broad-based leadership and designated leadership (Alexander, Comfort, Weiner, and Bogue, 2001). The latter are formally defined leaders with specified roles, such as the grantee organization, the convener, or the evaluator, that may, for example, be required by a funding agency supporting the effort. Staff roles are circumscribed within the context of the designated leadership organizations; however, experts and advocates are critical for translating the vision into a strategy for action. Situational leadership may arise from these experts and advocates who may focus on issues of specific concern to them. Broad-based power-sharing, supported by leadership that focuses on developing a fair process for dialogue and joint decision-making, creates a dynamic whereby all interests and skills combine to create a whole greater than the sum of its parts.

Collateral leadership is not unlike meta-leadership, or leadership of leaders. The Centers for Disease Control and Prevention has fostered the notion of meta-leadership because of its crucial role in emergency preparedness and equitable post-emergency recovery. According to the CDC Foundation, "Being a meta-leader requires a unique mindset and skill set, which often goes beyond the scope of an individual's previous experiences. And it requires building strong alliances with a diverse array of leaders *before* an event occurs" (http://www.cdcfoundation.org/meta-leadership/overview). Meta-leadership has become a model in areas beyond emergency preparedness, however. For example, the Farm-to-School initiatives fostered by a collaborative partnership in Fayette, Kentucky, were a success on account of meta-leadership. Analysis of leadership in the collaborative partnership identified multiple successful meta-leadership strategies and outcomes, including: (1) the ability of individual organizations to transcend their own boundaries to connect to the goals of different stakeholders, (2) emphasis on cooperative decision-making, (3) connectivity through effective communication and coordination, and (4) bridging organizational systems to promote intentional networking and cohesion (Srinivasan, 2012).

The five key leadership themes discussed above were identified inductively based on analysis of multisectoral collaboration in action. However, a structured collaboration model to advance health equity could also be developed deductively based on an understanding of complex systems and social change. For example, "collective impact," developed by the consulting firm FSG, Inc., is based on the premise that sustained solutions to large-scale social problems depend on multisectoral collaboration with a common agenda, shared measurement, mutually reinforcing activities, continuous communication, and a backbone organization (Kania and Kramer, 2013). Collective impact is used to design large multisectoral initiatives in areas as diverse as education and criminal justice reform. More recently, after a convening of collective impact conveners, the originators of collective impact recommended an explicit embedding of a health equity focus throughout any collective impact effort. This means that organizations should apply an equity lens to their internal systems as an initial strategy for broader, multisectoral systems change. This may require navigating through the discomfort of discussions around race, class, privilege, and power. In addition, successful incorporation of a health equity lens will require developing a common language about what health equity means from a social justice perspective (Kania and Kramer, 2013). The idea behind addressing issues notwithstanding discomfort is supported by the concept of systems thinking and organizational learning, as dialogue that avoids information, just because it is uncomfortable, limits the clear understanding of complex systems and, as a result, prohibits the development of successful strategies for systems change.

From Theory to Practice: Lessons Learned from Multisectoral Collaborations

Multisectoral collaborations to advance health equity have focused on engaging sectors that have the most influence over those behavioral and environmental factors with the most negative impact on health, such as tobacco smoking, physical inactivity, and poor nutrition. Indeed, much of the Healthy Communities initiatives funded through government or philanthropy has supported forming relationships with relevant sectors to reduce the availability of tobacco products and spaces for tobacco use, increase the availability of safe spaces for physical activity and play, and improve access to healthy, affordable produce in communities in food deserts. This has included the business community; planning, recreation, transportation, and housing agencies; food producers and retailers; community-based organizations and community advocates, etc. However, as increasing evidence on the social determinants of health becomes available, more sectors are being recognized as essential to achieving health equity.

From Theory to Practice

Multisectoral collaboration involves creating linkages and cultivating relationships among sectors as a critical first step. However, the process for creating those linkages is shaped by the purpose of the multisector engagement effort and the catalyst for those engagement efforts. Once engaged, representatives from the different sectors identify ways to collaborate on a common goal—the second step. We discuss these two steps with examples from the Healthy Communities movement below. We also include examples from other multisectoral experiences outside of public health-led efforts. How various collaborative efforts play out, however, depends on whether health equity is a primary goal as well as the willingness of other sectors to cooperate in achieving these goals. Whatever the case, the evidence suggests the need to address power imbalances that give rise to or maintain health inequities. We discuss some strategies that can be utilized to address some of these power issues in multisectoral collaborations for health equity.

Creating linkages between sectors at the local level can be initiated voluntarily by any given sector as part of its mission, implemented as part of a funded initiative, or mandated by government. Local public health departments form partnerships with other sectors as part of their own strategic plan to improve community health. For example, the Franklin County Health Department partnered with the local YMCA and the school district to address the loss of physical education in elementary schools, which was contributing to youth inactivity and weight gain. Their efforts led to the school district implementing a policy requiring the integration of physical activity throughout the school day using the "Take 10!" curriculum designed by the International Life Sciences Institute.

Prior to engagement, everyone typically focuses on understanding the other sector. This includes learning the other sector's language and terminology, understanding the decision authority and decision-making process, and conducting preliminary research on the role of the other sector in shaping community health outcomes. In the case of Franklin County, the local public health department engaged with the education sector by cultivating relationships with principals at a few schools before scaling up to working at the school district level. The relationship building involved developing an understanding of the school district's policymaking process and the politics that would shape a successful reading and vote on the new policy (http://franklin.oh.networkofcare.org/ph/model-practice-detail.aspx?pid=1672).

Other sectors are increasingly becoming involved with leading multisectoral initiatives in support of health equity. For example, the recently launched Gehl

Institute, the nonprofit spin-off of Gehl Architects, seeks to foster equality by bringing " 'people-first design' to streets, parks, plazas and more. The nonprofit will be a testing ground for how to tailor the Gehl approach to different city settings and encourage broader community participation in planning" to improve health and social outcomes (Mondon, 2015). As another example, Engineers without Borders (EWB) is partnering with underserved communities across the world to provide essential services that are linked to improved health and social outcomes, such as water and sanitation, light, and more (Engineers without Borders, 2016). Also, many hospitals, healthcare insurance companies, and corporate foundations from different fields are prioritizing the interdependence of health equity and community development in their programs and/or grant-making priorities. Finally, by focusing on fighting racism and violence—two important social determinants of health—the people-driven Black Lives Matter organization and movement is a great example of the role multiple sectors and concerned citizens can play in raising awareness of health and social inequities and its many root causes (Black Lives Matter, 2016).

How Collaborations May Start

National funders sometimes utilize their leverage to support cross-sectoral collaboration at the local level. For example, the Centers for Disease Control and Prevention has fostered greater collaboration between local public health departments and local planning agencies at least since 2006. For example, they funded a joint initiative between NACCHO and the American Planning Association (APA) to conduct a survey of their respective members to determine how agency leaders viewed planning/public health collaboration and barriers to collaboration and joint collaborative efforts. The CDC produced and disseminated a guidance document, *Integrating Planning and Public Health*, that included survey results, case studies, and recommendations for integrating planning and public health (Morris, 2006).

In other cases, such as the CDC's ACHIEVE initiative, national organizations representing different sectors become partners in grant-making to local communities to support healthy community planning and implementation. In ACHIEVE, the national leadership included YMCA-USA, NACCHO, the Society of Public Health Educators, the National Association of Chronic Disease Directors, and the National Recreation and Parks Association as well as the CDC. While each national partner funded grantees among its own membership for health assessment, planning, and implementation, they collaborated and coordinated their efforts and helped make linkages across members at the local level.

Multisectoral collaboration is now built into the design of a wide variety of strategies to address the social determinants of health through policy, systems, and environmental change. Often, the funding agency provides tools, resources, and direct technical assistance to support cross-sector coalition development.

However, health equity, if not explicitly incorporated in the design, is often addressed through leadership.

In the case of Health Impact Assessment, multisectoral engagement is incorporated as a practice standard. For example, the *Minimum Elements and Practice Standards for Health Impact Assessment* recommends the following:

> 1.6 Meaningful and inclusive stakeholder (e.g., affected community, public agency, decision-maker) participation in each step of the HIA supports HIA quality and effectiveness. Each HIA should have a specific engagement and participation approach that utilizes participatory or deliberative methods suitable to the needs of stakeholders and context.
>
> *(Bhatia et al., 2014, p. 4)*

Incorporating Health Equity

Whereas some initiatives in health featuring multisectoral collaboration target specific disadvantaged population groups, others do not have a health equity focus as all. In the latter case, however, leadership can steer the coalition toward a greater focus on health equity. In some cases, a health equity lens is included at the very start. Below, we identify initiatives and offer a case study (see Box 4.1) where multisectoral collaboration is a key feature and discuss how they approached health equity. We discuss multisectoral collaborative initiatives funded by the CDC (ACHIEVE and REACH), the Kellogg Foundation (Food and Fitness), and municipal government (Baltimore's Health in All Policies initiative).

Two of CDC's healthy community initiatives provide an interesting contrast in how health equity is advanced in multisectoral collaborations. On the one hand, both the ACHIEVE (Action Communities for Health, Innovation, and EnVironmental change [*sic*]) and REACH (Racial and Ethnic Approaches to Community Health) initiatives entail building large multisectoral partnerships to improve community health. However, whereas ACHIEVE is focused on improving health generally, REACH is focused on reducing health disparities. REACH partners focus on disparity populations and develop interventions to improve health in these populations with a wide variety of culturally appropriate programs. Thus, health equity, at least insofar as inequities manifest as disparities in health outcomes, are addressed as a built-in feature of REACH's design. In addition, REACH coalitions use community participatory methods to ensure that intervention designs have strong community input and buy-in.

Tackling health inequities and addressing health disparities was not a primary feature of ACHIEVE. (Nor was it specifically downplayed.) Instead, the main feature was supporting and providing tools for a local coalition (called a Community Health Action Resource Team or CHART) to work collaboratively in bringing about policy, systems, and environmental change in five sectors: the community at large, community institutions or the organization sector, healthcare, schools, and worksites. A wide range of tools were provided to develop CHARTs reflecting these five sectors, and an assessment tool was used as a way of strengthening relationships among CHART members and between the CHART and the community and local policy leaders.

Despite the lack of an explicit focus on health equity, some CHARTs managed to develop plans that would ultimately reduce health inequities. For example, Putnam, Missouri's CHART identified a low-income neighborhood with low rates of physical activity among school age children. Many of them lived in a low-income housing neighborhood whose park lacked adequate amenities to support physical activity and play. The CHART collaborated with a local university to develop a Park Master Plan and leveraged its ACHIEVE grant funds to implement the master plan. This would not have occurred without the leadership of the CHART and the results of the assessment tool that facilitated priority setting based on needs and was sufficiently flexible to enable CHARTs to identify specific neighborhoods or towns to target.

The Kellogg Foundation's Food and Fitness initiative funded incorporated health equity by focusing the initiative on improving access to food and physical activity opportunities for vulnerable families and children. Children, particularly disadvantaged children, are a primary focus of the foundation. It currently focuses mainly on states with the highest level of childhood health disparities. More importantly, Kellogg offered a two-part funding mechanism. In the first stage, communities were funded to organize a new or engage an existing community coalition to conduct an assessment and develop a plan to improve access to local, affordable produce and safe spaces for physical activity and play. Curiously, youth representation was required on each grantees' coalition to ensure their voice in the assessment and planning phase. In the second stage, communities would be funded for a much larger and lucrative amount depending on their plan and the ability of their coalition to implement the plan successfully. The initiative's Food and Fitness Assessment model was used to determine whether and to what extent a plan's strategic options were feasible, had community impact, and addressed health equity. Thus, health equity was fostered through the initiative at multiple levels.

Another example is included in Box 4.1.

BOX 4.1 CASE STUDY

The Baltimore City's Multisectoral Initiative for Health Equity

In 2010, Mayor Stephanie Rawlings established the Baltimore City Cross Agency Health Taskforce (CAHT) through a directive sent to the heads of all City agencies. The directive requires agency heads to make health a priority in decision-making and identify at least one representative to sit on CAHT. By

2013, CAHT included 25 members from 22 agencies representing planning, transportation, housing, and public works departments. The Baltimore City Health Department (BCHD) was given responsibility for staffing and convening the task force. Given the Mayor's imprimatur, this ensured that all agencies would work collaboratively on developing a health in all policies (HiAP) strategy to improve the health of Baltimore City residents.

The Mayor's directive requires all agencies to consider health in their decision-making and directs CAHT to develop measurable objectives for each agency to help achieve the goals of *Healthy Baltimore 2015*, the City's community health improvement plan. Other BCHD documents, such as Baltimore's *Health Disparities Report Card* and *Neighborhood Health Profile*, also played key roles in developing a strategy. These documents, BCHD leadership, and a new state initiative addressing health disparities played a major role in CAHT implementing a strategy focusing explicitly on health equity. The Mayor's Office recommended CAHT implement a six- to nine-month pilot project to help implement the Neighborhood Health Initiative. This would be the prelude to a neighborhood-based HiAP approach.

CAHT selected the Park Heights neighborhood as the pilot site. Park Heights was selected because of its high rates of chronic disease, violence, and level of community readiness. Park Heights is also located in a Health Enterprise Zone, a state initiative designed—through tax breaks, loan repayment, and other incentives—to reduce racial, ethnic, and geographic disparities; improve access and outcomes for underserved communities; and reduce hospital costs, admissions, and readmissions. However, CAHT had consisted entirely of government agency representatives. This limited its connection with local community and the ability to develop an agenda that had community buy-in. Greater engagement with the Parks Heights community was seen as a necessary condition to implementing the pilot.

Under BCHD's leadership, CAHT initiated a number of engagement activities, which led to a community-supported neighborhood plan that all agencies would collaborate in implementing. First, they identified existing Park Heights community linkages (e.g., Recreation Department community advisory board members), targeted the concept of HiAP to these neighborhood groups, held open CAHT meetings in Park Heights, and invited key community stakeholders to participate in CAHT meetings. The result was a plan that included, for example, building a new free-standing library where gathering space could be used for physical activity and nutrition education, and renovations on a recreation center that included developing trails connecting the park to the recreation center with community involvement.

Building a Culture of Collaboration within Your Organization

We are all influenced by our immediate environment. Therefore, increasing the number of multisectoral collaborations and partnerships in support of health equity research and practice should start with creating a culture of collaboration within our own organizations (Schiavo, 2006–2016; Schiavo, 2013a). Too often, collaboration is "viewed as a one-time or project-oriented activity. An increasing challenge is to help organizations incorporate collaborative values and practices in their everyday ways of working" (Schuman, 2006).

Building a thriving collaborative environment that values both internal and external partnerships doesn't just happen; it takes daily efforts and increased capacity and skills by all involved. In the case of collaborative efforts with external stakeholders, building and maintaining healthy and long-term partnerships must rely on enhanced education and training efforts across different sectors. This is a very important topic in the 21st century; yet, only a limited number of disciplines integrate topics such as partnership development and management, negotiations and conflict resolution, mediation strategies, diplomacy, and other relevant topics as part of their academic curricula or professional development offerings. Namely, this is for the most part limited to schools and programs within the fields of business and/or management. When graduating from programs in public health, healthcare, medicine, community development, urban design, and others, young professionals are too often left only with the option to learn "on the job" about the art and science of strategic collaborations and partnerships (Saltman, O'Dea, and Kidd, 2006; Schiavo, 2006–2016). Similarly, too many organizations struggle with creating a collaborative environment that also values the importance of reaching out to other organizations and truly engaging them in participatory and consensus-driven planning processes. Capacity building, continuing education, and professional development programs are a good starting point also in the case of mid-career or senior professionals who need to refresh or further advance their understanding of what works and what does not work in developing strategic partnerships. At the core of such efforts is the practice of developing and maintaining good relationships both with other internal departments and external stakeholders in health equity issues.

Ultimately, building a culture of collaboration and constituency relations and partnerships is a long-term and constantly renewing process. "A collaborative culture is based on openness, complete transparency and building trust. It also focuses its energy on the search for solutions to challenges and leveraging opportunities rather than on placing blame or searching for [the] 'guilty'" among co-workers and external partners (Caprino, 2014).

Box 4.2 includes some practical steps that may help jump-start the process of encouraging internal and external multisectoral collaborations within your organization.

BOX 4.2   CREATING A CULTURE OF COLLABORATION IN YOUR ORGANIZATION: SAMPLE PRACTICAL STEPS

- Identify and engage internal champions.
- Recognize the legitimacy of and address existing obstacles and concerns to internal and external collaborations.
- Build evidence in support of a multisectoral approach to advance health equity.
- Develop standard processes and models.
- Encourage a culture of participation.
- Hone the skills of internal and external stakeholders.
- Evaluate partnership results.

Source: Schiavo, R. (2006–2016) "Strategies to Build Successful Multi-Sectoral Partnerships." Multiple workshops presented at Support Center for Nonprofit Management, 2006; Strategic Communication Resources, 2007–2010; Health Equity Initiative, 2012–2016; and other organizations. Used by permission.
References: Schiavo (2013a, 2015c).

Future Directions

Although the case for multisectoral and interdisciplinary partnerships in support of health equity has been highlighted by several authors, models, and case studies including those featured in this chapter, a lot of work is still needed. Of great importance to the success of this agenda is to strengthen the capacity of community residents, leaders, and professionals from multiple sectors to (1) become fluent in each other's languages; (2) understand key differences in the mission and objectives of different kinds of organizations, and consider these differences in approaching potential partners; (3) develop adequate "selling points" that would foster multisectoral engagement in advancing health equity; (4) use a systematic approach to partnership planning, which is not only agenda-setting but may help avoid common issues and pitfalls as the partnership progresses; and (5) include mutually-agreed parameters not only for program evaluation but also to assess the level of engagement and satisfaction of all partners with the actual partnership (Schiavo, 2006–2016, 2013a; Health Equity Initiative, 2016b; Schiavo, Estrada-Portales, Hoeppner, Ormazza, and Ramesh, 2016). Of equal importance is to clarify the meaning of health equity in the context of different groups and stakeholders, so that different professionals and communities can comfortably rally around this issue and suitable priorities, as well as recognizing the expert in everyone regardless of their professional background or community association (Health Equity Initiative, 2016b).

In approaching partnerships and collaborations, we also need to redefine the meaning of "community" so it becomes inclusive of everyone who has stake in health and social issues (e.g., local business, religious leaders, hospitals, public health professionals, transportation officers, banks, etc.) and *not only* of community residents (Schiavo, 2013a, 2016b; Schiavo, Padgaonkar, Cooney, Cruz Reyes, and Health Equity Initiative, 2016).

> A *community* is largely defined "to indicate 'a variety of social, ethnic, cultural, or geographical associations, for example, a school, workplace, city, neighborhood, organized patient or professional group, or association of peer leaders,' (Schiavo, 2013a) just to name a few examples. Communities are often made of a diverse group of *stakeholders* ('individuals and groups who have an interest or share responsibilities in a given issue, such as policy-makers, community leaders, special groups, and community members,' Schiavo, 2013a). In a way, we are all *stakeholders* in health and social issues, as we all should care about leaving a better and healthier world to our children, grandchildren and loved ones."
>
> *(Schiavo, 2016a, p. 1)*

By making clear that everyone is or should be involved in creating better chances for better health in our cities, communities, and neighborhoods, we may be able to engage others in advancing population health outcomes and health equity.

Finally, we need to develop suitable mechanisms and forums to address uncomfortable topics, such as race, class, and social discrimination, and how these affect our communities and institutions both in the United States and internationally. Multisectoral collaborations are well suited to provide a safe framework that will allow multiple perspectives to be heard, and ultimately to promote systems-level change as related to these important issues that affect the health and lives of vulnerable and underserved populations.

Summary

This chapter makes the case for a collaborative approach to addressing health equity issues with the participation of multiple sectors and disciplines. It also summarizes key theories, planning frameworks, and lessons learned in support of the integration of a culture of collaboration within our communities and organizations. In doing so, it also points to potential future directions and action areas that may be instrumental in implementing such approach on a larger scale. These include the importance of capacity building at the community, local, national, and international levels as well as across different professions and sectors (Schiavo, 2006–2016; Health Equity Initiative, 2016b; Schiavo, Padgaonkar, Cooney, Cruz Reyes, and Health Equity Initiative, 2016); the need to redefine the meaning of "community" to be inclusive not only of community residents but also of many other key stakeholders who care or should care about the health and well-being of our neighborhoods and cities (Schiavo, 2013a; Health Equity Initiative, 2016b; Schiavo, Padgaonkar, Cooney, Cruz Reyes, and Health Equity Initiative, 2016); and the importance of using a collaborative framework to address uncomfortable topics and address their impact on the health and well-being of vulnerable and underserved populations.

References

Alegria, M., Sribney, W., & Mulvaney-Day, N. E. (2007). Social cohesion, social support and health among Latinos in the United States. *Social Science & Medicine (1982)*, *64*(2), 477–495: http://doi.org/10.1016/j.socscimed.2006.08.030

Alexander, J. A., Comfort, M. E., Weiner, B. J., & Bogue, R. (2001). Leadership in Collaborative Community Partnerships. *Nonprofit Management and Leadership*, *12*(2), 159–176.

Alliance to Reduce Disparities in Diabetes (2015). Participating Sites. Accessed August 2016: http://ardd.sph.umich.edu/participating_sites.html

American Hospital Association. A Focus on Health Equity and Coverage. Webinar. Accessed May 2016: http://www.hpoe.org/resources/hpoe-live-webinars/2826

Asaria, P., Fortunato, L., Fecht, D., Tzoulaki, J., Abellan, J. J., Hambly, P., de Hoogh, K., Ezzati, M., & Elliott, P. (2012). Trends and inequalities in cardiovascular disease mortality across 7932 English electoral wards, 1982–2006: Bayesian spatial analysis. *Int. J. Epidemiol*, *41*(6), 1737–1749.

Bhatia, R., Farhang, L., Lee, M., Orenstein, M., Richardson, M., & Wernham, A. (2014). *Minimum elements and practice standards for health impact assessment*. Version 3. http://advance.captus.com/planning/hia2xx/pdf/Minimum%20Elements%20and%20Practice%20Standards%20for%20HIA%203.0.pdf

Black Lives Matter. (2016). Online Resources. Accessed May 2016: http://blacklivesmatter.com/

Caprino, K. (2014). Six Concrete Steps to Building a Collaborative Culture That Inspires. *Forbes/Leadership*, September, 24, 2014. Accessed April 2016: http://www.forbes.com/sites/kathycaprino/2014/09/24/6-concrete-steps-to-building-a-collaborative-culture-that-inspires/#24ef208d1b04

Carstairs, C., & Elder, R. (2008). Expertise, health, and popular opinion: Debating water fluoridation, 1945–80. *Canadian Historical Review*, *89*(3), 345–371.

Center for Health Equity Research and Promotion. *Intro to Health Disparities*: http://www.cherp.research.med.va.gov/introhd.php Retrieved October 2005.

Colgrove, J. (2006). *State of immunity: The politics of vaccination in twentieth-century America*. Vol. 16. Berkeley, CA: University of California Press.

Engineers without Borders. (2016). Online Resources. Accessed May 2016: http://www.ewb-usa.org/

Fawcett, S., Schultz, J., Watson-Thompson, J., Fox, M., Bremby, R. (2010). Building multisectoral partnerships for population health and health equity. *Prev Chronic Dis*, 7(6), A118. Accessed April 2016: http://www.cdc.gov/pcd/issues/2010/nov/10_0079.htm

Fehling, M., Nelson, B. D., & Venkatapuram, S. (2013). Limitations of the millennium development goals: A literature review. *Global Public Health*, *8*(10), 1109–1122.

Fletcher, K., Knobbs, E., Lu, D., & Ritterman, M. (2003). *Mobilizing for action through planning and partnership: A community-wide strategic planning process for Alameda County*. Alameda County, CA: Alameda County Department of Public Health.

Gamhewage, G. (2016). Socializing outbreak response—Community engagement and other risk communication interventions. *Journal of Communication in Healthcare*, *9*(1), 7–10.

Grantmakers in Aging and Pfizer Foundation. (2015). The Value Proposition of Age-Friendly Communities. Summit Report. Accessed April 2016: http://www.giaging.org/resources/the-value-proposition-of-age-friendly-communities/

Harrell, J. A., & Baker, E. L. (1994). The essential services of public health. *Leadership in Public Health*, *3*(3), 27–31.

Health Equity Initiative. (2012 and 2014). Why Health Equity Matters. Accessed April 2016: http://www.healthequityinitiative.org/hei/wp-content/uploads/2014/04/Why-Health-Equity-Matters-US-and-Global-2014.pdf

Health Equity Initiative. (2016a). Highlights of Accomplishments. Accessed April 2016: http://www.healthequityinitiative.org/hei/wp-content/uploads/2016/04/HEI-Highlights-of-Accomplishments-2016-1-1.pdf

Health Equity Initiative. (2016b). *Implementing systems-level change for health equity: A partnership summit: Summit program*. New York: Health Equity Initiative.

Jones, S. (2015). A lack of clean water and sanitation in the Philippines kills 55 people every day. *Vice News*. Accessed October 2016: https://news.vice.com/article/a-lack-of-clean-water-and-sanitation-in-the-philippines-kills-55-people-every-day

Kania, J., & Kramer, M. (2013). Embracing emergence: How collective impact addresses complexity. Blog Entry, January 21. *Stanford Social Innovation Review*. Accessed May 2016: https://ssir.org/articles/entry/embracing_emergence_how_collective_impact_addresses_complexity

Kindig, D., & Stoddart, G. (2003). What is population health? *American Journal of Public Health*, *3*(3), 380–383.

Lachance, L., Carpenter, L., Emery, M., & Luluquisen, M. (2014). An introduction to the food & fitness community partnerships and this special issue. *Community Development*, *45*(3), 215–219.

Lake, M., & Townsend, T. (2006). Obesogenic environments: Exploring the built and food environments. *Journal of the Royal Society for the Promotion of Health*, *126*(6), 262–267.

LaVeist, T. A., Gaskin, D. J., & Richard, P. (2009). *The economic burden of health inequalities in the United States*. Washington, DC: Joint Center for Political and Economic Studies.

LaVeist, T. A., Gaskin, D., & Richard, P. (2011). Estimating the economic burden of racial health inequalities in the United States. *International Journal of Health Services*, *41*(2), 231–238.

Massachusetts General Hospital. (2014). The Disparities Leadership Program: Case Study for Financial Impact: Kentucky One Health, Louisville, Kentucky. The Disparities Solutions Center, Massachusetts General Hospital. Accessed August 2015: http://massgeneral.org/disparitiessolutions/z_files/Summary_DLP%20cost%20analysis_Final.pdf

Mayberry, R. M., Nicewander, D. A., Qin, H., & Ballard, D. J. (2006). Improving quality and reducing inequities: A challenge in achieving best care. *Proceedings (Baylor University. Medical Center)*, *19*(2), 103–118.

Mondon, M. (2015). New Gehl Institute will bring "people-first design" to more cities. *Next City*. Accessed May 2016: https://nextcity.org/daily/entry/new-gehl-institute-urban-design-placemaking-knight-funding

Morris, M. (2006). *Integrating planning and public health: Tools and strategies to create healthy places*. Washington, DC: American Planning Association.

National Association of County and City Health Officials. (2014). *Mobilizing and organizing partners to achieve health equity*. Washington, DC: NACCHO.

National Association of County and City Health Officials. (2015). *Statement of policy: Health equity and social justice*. Washington, DC: NACCHO.

National Center for Health Statistics. (2012). *Healthy people 2010 final review*. Hyattsville, MD: NCHS.

New York City Department of Health and Mental Hygiene. (2015). Summary of Vital Statistics 2013. The City of New York: Infant Mortality. Accessed January 2017: https://www1.nyc.gov/assets/doh/downloads/pdf/vs/vs-infant-mortality-2013.pdf

Office of Disease Prevention and Health Promotion, U.S. Department of Health and Human Services. (2016a). Healthy People 2020 Leading Health Indicators: Progress Update. April, 28, 2016. Accessed May 2016: https://www.healthypeople.gov/2020/leading-health-indicators/Healthy-People-2020-Leading-Health-Indicators%3A-Progress-Update

Office of Disease Prevention and Health Promotion, U.S. Department of Health and Human Services. (2016b). Maternal, Infant and Child Health. Accessed April 2016: https://www.healthypeople.gov/2020/topics-objectives/topic/maternal-infant-and-child-health

Paes de Barros, R., Ferreira, F. H. G., Molinas Vega, J. R., & Saavedra Chanduvi, J. (2009). *Measuring inequality of opportunities in Latin America and the Caribbean*. Washington, DC: The International Bank for Reconstruction and Development / The World Bank.

Pan, J., & Cohan, L. (2012). Collaboration multiplier: Advancing a multi-sectoral approach to preventing violence and unintentional injury. *Injury Prevention, 18*(Suppl 1), A19.

Robert Wood Johnson Foundation. (2015). Kearney, Nebraska: City Reports 13.4 Percent Decline in Obesity for Grades K through 5. Accessed April 2016: http://www.rwjf.org/en/library/articles-and-news/2013/07/kearney-nebraska—signs-of-progress.html

Robert Wood Johnson Foundation. (2016). Why We Need a Culture of Health. Health Policy Snapshot Series, Robert Wood Johnson Foundation. Accessed April 2016: http://www.rwjf.org/en/library/research/2016/03/why-we-need-a-culture-of-health.html

Saltman, D. C., O'Dea, N. A., & Kidd, M. R. (2006). Conflict management: A primer for doctors in training. *Postgraduate Medical Journal, 82*(963), 9–12.

Schiavo, R. (2006–2016). "Strategies to Build Successful Multi-Sectoral Partnerships." Workshops presented at Support Center for Nonprofit Management, 2006; Strategic Communication Resources, 2007–2010; and Health Equity Initiative, 2012–2016.

Schiavo, R. (2011). Why Health Equity Matters: An International Perspective. Presentation at American University, International Human Rights Week, Washington, DC, October 30, 2011.

Schiavo, R. (2013a). *Health communication: From theory to practice*. Second Edition. San Francisco: Jossey-Bass, an Imprint of Wiley.

Schiavo, R. (2013b). Strategic health communication in urban settings: A template for training modules. In C. Ogkibo (Ed.), *Strategic Health Communication in Urban Contexts*. New York: Springer.

Schiavo, R. (2014). Risk communication: Ebola and beyond. *Journal of Communication in Healthcare: Strategies, Media, and Engagement in Global Health, 7*(4), 239–241.

Schiavo, R. (2015a). Addressing health disparities in clinical settings: Population health, quality of care, and communication. *Journal of Communication in Healthcare: Strategies, Media, and Engagement in Global Health, 8*(3), 163–166.

Schiavo, R. (2015b). Addressing Health Disparities in Clinical Settings: Population Health and the Value Proposition. Health Equity Initiative webinar. New York. October 21, 2015.

Schiavo, R. (2015c). Social innovation as a key imperative in global health. *Journal of Communication in Healthcare: Strategies, Media, and Engagement in Global Health, 8*(2), 86–89.

Schiavo, R. (2016a). The importance of community-based communication for health and social change. *Journal of Communication in Healthcare: Strategies, Media, and Engagement in Global Health, 9*(1), 1–3.

Schiavo, R. (2016b). Welcome: Message from the president, board of directors. In *Summit program: Implementing systems-level change for health equity: A partnership summit.* Accessed April 2016: http://www.healthequityinitiative.org/hei/wp-content/uploads/2015/08/HEI-Summit-2016-Program-Final-website2.pdf

Schiavo, R., Estrada-Portales, I., Hoeppner, E., Ormazza, D., & Ramesh, R. (2016). Building community-campus partnerships to prevent infant mortality: Lessons learned from building capacity in four U.S. cities. *Journal of Health Disparities Research and Practice, 9*(3). Available at: http://digitalscholarship.unlv.edu/jhdrp/vol9/iss3/5

Schiavo, R., Gonzalez-Flores, M., Ramesh, R., & Estrada-Portales, I. (2011). Taking the pulse of progress toward preconception health: Preliminary assessment of a national OMH program for infant mortality prevention. *Journal of Communication in Healthcare, 4*(2), 106–117.

Schiavo, R., Hilyard, K. M, & Skinner, E. C. (2016). Community-based risk communication in epidemics and emerging disease settings. In R. S. Zimmerman, R. J. DiClemente, J. K. Andrus, E. Hosein & Society of Public Health Education (SOPHE) (Eds.), *Introduction to global health promotion.* San Francisco, CA: Jossey-Bass, an imprint of Wiley.

Schiavo, R., Padgaonkar, D., Cooney, L., Reyes, C. C., & Health Equity Initiative. (2016). Implementing systems-level change for health equity: A partnership summit. *Summit Report and Proceedings.* New York: Health Equity Initiative. May 2016. Accessed May 2016: http://www.healthequityinitiative.org/hei/wp-content/uploads/2016/05/HEI-2016-Summit-Report-Final.pdf

Schuman, S. (2006). *Creating a culture of collaboration: The International Association of Facilitators handbook.* Hoboken: Wiley.

Sen, A. (2002). Why health equity? *Health Econ, 11,* 659–666.

Senge, P. M. (2006). *The fifth discipline: The art and practice of the learning organization.* Broadway Business.

Srinivasan, J. (2012). Meta-leadership in a farm to school program: Improving childhood nutrition in Kentucky. *Journal of Public Health, 20*(3), 343–346.

Swinburn, B., & Egger, G. (2002). Preventive strategies against weight gain and obesity. *Obesity Reviews, 3*(4), 289–301.

UNICEF (2015a). Ebola and C4D. Retrieved from http://www.unicef.org/cbsc/index_73157.html

UNICEF (2015b). Community care centers, community dialogue and engagement; Key ingredients in Sierra Leone. Retrieved from http://www.unicef.org/cbsc/files/UNICEF_Community_Care_Centers%281%29.pdf

United Nations. (2012). The Millennium Development Goals Report 2012 (Vol. ISBN 978-92-1-101244-6) 2012. Accessed March 2016: http://www.un.org/millennium goals/reports.shtml

United Nations. (2015). Global Issues: Democracy and the United Nations. Online Resource. Accessed April 2016: http://www.un.org/en/globalissues/democracy/democracy_and_un.shtml

Van Til, L. J. (1978). The Idea of Equality in America. Foundation for Economic Education (FEE). Accessed April 2016: https://fee.org/articles/the-idea-of-equality-in-america/

Walton, J. W., Snead, C. A., Collinsworth, A. W., & Schmidt, K. L. (2012). Reducing diabetes disparities through the implementation of a community health worker–led diabetes self-management education program. *Family & Community Health, 35*(2), 161–171.

World Health Organization (2016). Risk communication in the context of Zika Virus: Interim guidance. Accessed January 2017: http://apps.who.int/iris/bitstream/10665/204513/1/WHO_ZIKV_RCCE_16.1_eng.pdf?ua=1

5

WHY WE DO POPULATION HEALTH TODAY

Julie Trocchio

Obesity and diabetes . . . mental health and substance abuse . . . stroke and heart disease . . . childhood and adult asthma.

These health problems were identified in the majority of Community Health Needs Assessments (CHNAs) surveyed by a group of national hospital associations. These health problems share other commonalities as well: They are especially prevalent in low-income communities and among disadvantaged populations, all would require a multi-faceted approach including upstream/prevention interventions and none could be solved by a single agency or organization.

So the question should not be: "Why do we do population health?" but rather "How can we not?" Today's problems require a population health approach.

Population health has many different definitions and is practiced in different ways by different sectors. But whether you are a state or local health official, hospital CEO or managed care/Accountable Care Organization (ACO) director or community benefit leader, we all share a common understanding that the health of individuals impacts and is impacted by the health of the broader population, that health care is not the only driver of health, and that a collaborative approach is needed to tackle today's most pressing health problems.

Whereas different sectors define and practice population health in different ways, in practice, all seem to share certain core elements. These include paying attention to determinants of health, including social, economic and environmental factors; prevention and health promotion; and community relationships and linkages with community organizations.

Why Hospitals Are Paying Attention to Population Health Today

Four imperatives are driving hospitals to focus on population health approaches: mission, clinical, policy and financial.

The mission imperative: Population health builds on not-for-profit hospitals' historical tradition and mission of bringing health to communities and responding to community health needs. Every not-for-profit hospital was established because religious or civic leaders—and often both—worked to bring health care to America's communities. Our founders and foundresses responded to the needs of their times by working with community members to meet their communities' health needs. This tradition continues today as hospitals and community partners identify community health needs through formal and informal community health needs assessments and develop strategies to address community health problems.

The clinical imperative: Hospital leaders and clinicians are realizing that health care alone cannot solve problems such as obesity, substance abuse, asthma, violence and the other conditions that cause or complicate acute episodes and hospitalizations. They are finding that upstream approaches are needed, such as advocacy for expanded health insurance and efforts to get at the root cause of their patients' health problems. They are realizing that community-based organizations may be the key to keeping people well and out of emergency rooms. Prevention and health promotion, once out of the realm of hospital attention, is now recognized as critical to patient health.

The policy imperative: The Affordable Care Act (ACA) added important new requirements for not-for-profit tax-exempt hospitals. Hospitals must conduct community health needs assessments at least every three years and adopt "an implementation strategy to meet the community health needs identified through the assessment." Internal Revenue Service (IRS) rules, made final in 2014, provided additional details for meeting the ACA requirements. Regulations specify that hospitals must solicit and get input into their assessment and priority setting processes from a state or local health department and members of medically underserved, low-income and minority populations served by the hospital.

In addition to these legal requirements, the IRS rules encourage a population health approach by defining community health needs broadly as "requisites for the improvement or maintenance of health in both the community at large and in particular parts (such as neighborhoods or population experiencing health disparities)." IRS final rule gives, as examples, "the need to address financial and other barriers to accessing care, to prevent illness, to ensure adequate nutrition, or to address social, behavioral, and environmental factors that influence health in the community."

The financial imperative: ACA provisions also provided financial incentives for population health. Through demonstration programs and a series of regulatory carrots and sticks, health care providers are assuming financial risk for health outcomes and cost reductions.

In response to these incentives, many hospitals have developed population health *management* programs to take responsibility for defined or enrolled populations through Accountable Care Organizations (ACOs), medical homes and/or participation in various "bundling" programs. As these population health management programs take on financial risk, they are realizing that in order to manage costs, they must look beyond health interventions, pay attention to what happens between admissions and clinic visits, use preventive care and address the other determinants of health.

How We Do Population Health Today

Health care providers engage in population health by coordinating with community partners, using available evidence and finding new ways to deliver and finance care of populations.

Collaborative Partnerships

Recognizing that many of today's most pressing health problems cannot be solved by a single organization or agency, working with community partners becomes a critical strategy for population health. Health care providers are working with schools, housing programs and a variety of community-based organizations concerned with aspects of community health.

For example, in Cedar Rapids, Iowa, the local health department, mental health authority and hospital are working together to bring services to a low-income apartment building that serves chronically mentally ill persons. This collaborative partnership came about when police and emergency response departments brought attention to many calls originating at the address and hospital staff reported that many repeated emergency room admissions were from the building. The partners' collaborative services now include chronic disease management classes, counseling for residents, and technical and professional support for the housing program's staff.

Use of Evidence

Population health is reinforcing the need for evidence-based solutions to address community health issues. Too much is at stake to "play it by ear." Fortunately, the Centers for Disease Control, Agency for Health Care Quality and others offer resources for these practices which are widely used by hospitals and their partners as they develop implementation strategies and community health improvement plans.

BOX 5.1 SOURCES FOR EVIDENCE-BASED PRACTICES

- *Evidence-Based Practice Centers, AHRQ (http://www.ahrq.gov/clinic/epc/)*
- *Guide to Community Preventive Services, CDC (www.thecommunityguide. org)*
- *Community Health Improvement Navigator, CDC (http://www.cdc.gov/ chinav/database/index.html)*
- *County Health Rankings and Roadmaps (www.countyhealthrankings.org/)*
- *Healthy Communities Institute (www.healthycommunitiesinstitute.com)*
- *National Resource for Evidence-Based Programs and Practices, Substance Abuse and Mental Health Services Administration, U.S. Department of Health and Human Services (www.nrepp.samhsa.gov)*

An example of using evidence can be found in efforts to reduce youth smoking. Many communities are achieving single-digit teen smoking rates by forming coalitions that use the most proven approach: changing public policies. This includes strengthening and enforcing laws about underage purchase of tobacco, forbidding sales near schools and banning flavored tobacco products.

New Ways to Deliver and Finance the Care of Populations

While the use of evidence-based strategies is critically important, now is also the time for innovation and creative thinking. Health care providers, federal, state and local government agencies, and community partners are searching for and trying new ways of delivering and financing the care of populations. As my colleague Ron Hamel said in a recent Catholic Health Association publication, true transformation to achieve population health and other goals of health reform will fail if we merely "pour old wine into new wine skins."

An example of innovative thinking is Baltimore's "Health Enterprise Zone." Bon Secours Hospital in Baltimore, a number of physicians, several clinics and a historically black university within four zip codes of the city are participating in a Centers for Medicare and Medicaid Services (CMS) Health Enterprise Zone demonstration. Participating health care providers have been given a global budget of $1.25 million to prevent and address heart disease of residents in the area. The project includes fitness classes, stocking local grocery stores with healthy food and sponsoring cooking classes. When a person from the community is identified as at risk of heart disease, he or she is assigned a community health worker and recommended for classes in nutrition and behavior change at the university.

What Population Health Looks Like

Across the nation, population health is being practiced by various sectors in various ways. In each instance there is emphasis on prevention and health promotion, community partnerships, attention to determinants of health and a commitment to using both what we know and creative thinking.

Here are some examples.

Maryland Payment Reform

In addition to the Baltimore experiment described earlier, all Maryland hospitals are participating in a CMS capitated payment demonstration. Within the next five years, the demonstration aims to limit hospital per capita spending in the state, and reduce Medicare hospital spending, readmissions and hospital-acquired conditions. Hospitals will receive a global payment and will be expected to reduce their costs and meet quality targets. As a result of the demonstration, hospitals report that they are looking well beyond the hospital stay, reaching out to community partners to find and use community-based services. They are also bringing services into the community, for example, into senior housing programs with historically high hospitalization rates.

Kaiser Permanente Grants

The Kaiser Permanente Community Fund awarded $2.5 million in grant funds to 19 organizations in Oregon and Southwest Washington to address upstream factors that impact health. The awards focus on early childhood development, educational attainment and economic improvements. A wide range of projects include new ways of delivering foster care, strengthening immigrant students' ties to their communities, village gardens and economic development in distressed neighborhoods. Awardees will work with the funder to build internal capacity in their organizations and to evaluate the impact of the programs in order to determine whether social change has occurred.

Mayor's Task Force in Baton Rouge

The Mayor's Healthy City Initiative in Baton Rouge brought together representatives from hospitals, public schools, businesses and social service organizations. The initiative includes "HealthyBR," efforts focused on healthier eating and a more active lifestyle; "MedBR," focused on improving access to care and health outcomes; and an Innovation Center, which is using evidence-based research to assess and improve the healthy city initiative.

Recently representatives from the Baton Rouge hospitals and health department conducted a community health needs assessment and presented the results to the Mayor's Healthy City Initiative. The initiative then prioritized the top four health concerns in the region as obesity, HIV/AIDS, overutilization of emergency departments and a lack of mental and behavioral health resources.

Healthy City Chicago

The Chicago Department of Health has developed a population health vision for transforming the health of the city:

> *A healthy city is a city that*
>
> > *Offers healthier food options.*
> > *Provides places to be physically active.*
> > *Is prepared to respond to public health threats.*
> > *Creates healthy and safe environments.*
> > *Ensures access to care for all its residents.*
> > *Works to eliminate health disparities for all communities.*
>
> > *The Chicago Department of Public Health has created a new public health agenda with an ambitious sense of purpose for Chicago—an agenda that engages our city with bold action and goal-driven results. Together we are going to transform the health of our city. Together we are not just going to walk the talk—we're going to run with it. Together we will make Chicago the healthiest city in the nation.*

Chicago hospitals and other community organizations are working with the city to make this vision a reality.

Hospital Population Health Management Programs and Community Benefit

Population health management programs throughout the country are working with their community benefit programs to build on and enrich their hospital health promotion and prevention programs. They are using community health improvement strategies, such as community health workers and chronic disease education classes, to help their enrolled populations. Population health management programs are helping to conduct or are using findings from community health needs assessments and are taking advantage of community assets identified in community benefit programs that can help their enrollees. Population health management programs are also supporting—financially and programmatically—hospital efforts to address determinants of health, such as safe and healthy housing, access to healthy food and school health programs.

Conclusion

Population health is the approach being taken by health care providers and public health agencies to address their communities' most serious problems. It means looking beyond traditional health care delivery. It means creating new partnerships and new strategies with the goal of truly improving the health of our communities.

Bibliography

Braveman, Paula, and Laura Gottlieb. "The Social Determinants of Health: It's Time to Consider the Causes of the Causes." *Public Health Reports* 129.Suppl 2 (2014): 19–31. Print.

Centers for Medicare & Medicaid Services. *Maryland All-Payer Model to Deliver Better Care and Lower Costs. CMS.gov.* CMS, 10 January 2014. Web.

Frieden, Thomas R. "A Framework for Public Health Action: The Health Impact Pyramid." *American Journal of Public Health* 100.4 (2010): 590–595. *PMC.* 9 September 2015. Web.

Hamel, Ron. "Ethics—More Than Old Wine in New Wine Skins: Reform Means Transformation." *Health Progress* (May–June 2014): n. pag. https://www.chausa.org/publications/health-progress/article/may-june-2014/ethics-more-than-old-wine-in-new-wineskins-reform-means-transformation

Kaiser Permanente Community Fund. *The Kaiser Permanente Community Fund at Northwest Health Foundation Awards More Than $2.5 Million to Improve Health.* Northwest Health Foundation. 9 December 2014. Web.

Kassler, William J., Naomi Tomoyasu, and Patrick H. Conway. "Beyond a Traditional Payer—CMS's Role in Improving Population Health." *New England Journal of Medicine* 372 (2015): 109–111. *New England Journal of Medicine.* 8 January 2015. Web.

Orszag, Peter R., and Ezekiel Emanuel. "Health Care Reform and Cost Control." *New England Journal of Medicine* 363 (2010): 601–603. *New England Journal of Medicine.* 12 August 2010. Web.

6

THE COLLABORATION IMPERATIVE FOR POPULATION HEALTH IMPACT

Julia J. Resnick

The U.S. health care system is rapidly transforming toward a population health paradigm. No longer is it sufficient for hospitals and health care systems to only provide high-quality acute care; they are additionally being tasked with what is arguably a more challenging goal—making people healthy and preventing illness. This approach is in many ways antithetical to the traditional structure of the health care system, which is designed to treat illness and disease in the biomedical model of medicine. But that is starting to change. As hospitals and health care systems take on the new responsibility of improving population health, there is growing recognition that the health care sector alone cannot produce healthy people. Only 20% of health is attributable to medical care; the remaining 80% is attributable to health behaviors, socioeconomic factors and environmental factors (University of Wisconsin Public Health Institute, 2014). It follows that effectively addressing the non-health-care-related factors will require an unprecedented collaborative, coordinated effort between sectors and with communities in order to achieve a shared goal—communities where all individuals can reach their highest potential for health regardless of their race, gender, education level or socioeconomic status. The following chapter will discuss how the U.S. health care and public health systems got to where they are today and present a path forward for hospital–community collaborations to improve population health.

A Legacy of Separate Systems

In order to map a path forward to a more collaborative future, it helps to know how we got to where we are today, with our health care system operating largely separately from our public health system. There is a legacy of separation between these two related yet distinct systems—health care and public health—dating back to the dawn of the 20th century. The Rockefeller Foundation's 1914 meeting set the stage for the future of public health and medical education in America. Two disparate proposals for public health education evolved out of that meeting: (1) emphasis on epidemiology, public health nursing and administration; and (2) emphasis on research and science with the main purpose to be to advance the science of hygiene. Ultimately, the latter proposal was accepted and the first public health school was established, separate from medical education (Ruis and Golden, 2008). This so-called "schism" is the basis for the disparate systems that have evolved separately but in parallel over the past 200 years.

The U.S. health care system's design, and the payment mechanisms that support it, have made it possible for health care and public health entities to operate separately and independently from each other. Because hospitals have traditionally been paid under the fee-for-service model, they are incentivized to fill their inpatient beds, thereby profiting when people are sick. Although health care is a business, health care isn't a normal consumer good—it is also a necessary social service that every individual will need at some point in their life. While the health care system excelled in cutting-edge medical innovation, the overall health of American society waivered, with preventable chronic diseases becoming increasingly prevalent with a health care system ill-equipped to prevent disease.

But, as Nobel Laureate Bob Dylan famously sang, the times they are a changin'. With the implementation of the Affordable Care Act in 2014, financial incentives started to align to encourage hospitals and health care systems to prioritize keeping people healthy by providing high quality care at the right time and place and at the right cost. As the health care system reorients to achieve the "Triple Aim," there is growing recognition that it no longer serves hospitals to act alone and that health care is not the sole determinant of health, a fact that public health has long known. Our 2015 survey of hospitals found that 85% view population health as a key component of their mission (HRET, 2015), a clear indication that the health care field is primed to further engage in population health improvement.

There are natural synergies between health care and public health, and it doesn't serve either sector's goals to continue to operate separately. Independent action doesn't work for population health. In order to succeed in creating healthier communities, it is necessary to address all the drivers of health. And collaboration among stakeholders in the health care, public health, community development and other related sectors is crucial.

Forces Driving Collaboration

Although collaboration to improve the health of a community is not a new idea, it has been gaining traction in recent years due to a confluence of factors stemming from the Affordable Care Act that are driving hospitals and health care systems toward a population health mindset.

1. **Expanded access to health insurance**—Perhaps the most well-known element of the Affordable Care Act, the implementation of health exchanges,

Medicaid expansion and changes to private insurance have expanded health care coverage to 20 million people who did not previously have insurance (Department of Health and Human Services, 2016). The increase in insured individuals has injected more insured people into the health care system, allowing them to seek preventive, primary care before their health needs become emergent. Although insurance alone does not make people healthier, it is a necessary step toward healthier communities.

2. **Changing payment models**—Value-based payment and capitation models are expanding through Medicaid, Medicare and private insurers. By providing financial incentives to provide the best care at the lowest cost and prevent readmissions, these payment models are pushing health care systems to integrate disease prevention and health promotion into their practice.

3. **Redesign of health care**—The expanded patient base and changing payment models are causing health care systems to redesign how they provide care—from primary care to acute care to rehabilitation—to be more seamless and coordinated. Many health care systems are engaging in population health management, the clinical management of a specified population to better manage their chronic diseases and maintain good health. Because health behaviors and environmental and socioeconomic factors have a great impact on health, population health management strategies have to be linked to the elements that impact health outside hospital walls.

4. **Community health needs assessment (CHNA) process**—All nonprofit hospitals are required to conduct every three years a community health needs assessment process—a systemic process involving the community to identify and analyze community health needs and assets, prioritize the needs, and implement a plan to address significant unmet community health needs (Catholic Health Association, 2015). This requirement forces hospitals to think more expansively about the health needs impacting the communities and conduct the assessment in collaboration with other community stakeholders, including public health organizations. The CHNA process acts as a platform to launch community health initiatives that are often well aligned with public health priority areas.

These elements of the Affordable Care Act are making it fiscally viable for hospitals to think and act more expansively to improve health. In order to thrive in the population health environment, hospitals need to be proficient at working outside their walls with community stakeholders to improve the health of their shared community.

The Imperative for Collaboration

Whereas hospitals and health care systems are well-positioned to improve health through their expertise in health care provision, improving the health of communities at scale is complex and multifactorial, requiring a multifaceted approach. Reaching population health goals requires looking upstream to recognize the root causes of health and disease and develop strategies to address them. Often these factors are some of the most complex ones in our society, such as poverty, environmental exposures or unhealthy behaviors. Problems of this complexity and scope cannot be undertaken by a single organization or sector alone. Each organization working independently can have an impact, but by partnering with other organizations around a shared goal, the impact can be much greater.

The Collective Impact Framework shows that large-scale social change—like improving the health of populations—requires broad, cross-sector collaboration and a shared agenda (Kania and Kramer, 2011). Whereas each organization or sector involved in population health improvement work has necessary contributions to make, none can solve this puzzle on their own. Every community has assets that can be leveraged to strengthen population health improvement efforts. Assets can be people, physical structures or places, community services and community organizations, which can be used to improve the quality of life within a community (Community Toolbox, 2015). Collaborative efforts allow organizations to pool their resources and leverage the unique skill sets and competencies of each to work toward a shared goal.

Potential partners for population health improvement are varied, and include both usual and unusual suspects; public health and health care are not the only sectors invested in population health. A nationwide survey of hospitals from the Association for Community Health Improvement/the American Hospital Association (HRET, 2015) found that other hospitals, public health departments, community health centers, universities and school districts were the most commonly reported partnerships. Less common but certainly important partnerships were noted with community development organizations, faith-based organizations, public safety and healthy community coalitions. As population health improvement work grows more sophisticated, the depth and scope of the partnerships will likely be augmented.

Models of Hospital–Community Collaboration

Whereas collaboration around community health improvement seems intuitive, it is often easier said than done. Organizations often struggle to align their interest and approaches, have limited funding, lack structure for partnership, have differing organizational cultures, have limited operational resources or lack leadership buy-in. Oftentimes, a catalyst event is necessary to spur a new partnership or re-energize an existing one. Catalyst events include: the CHNA process, new legislation or policies, new payment models or emerging community health issues (HRET, 2016).

The CHNA process is an ideal platform for initiating or strengthening collaborative work around community health improvement. Maybe even more consequential than the assessment itself are the relationships built in the process. Hospitals routinely partner with public health departments and other stakeholders as part of the assessment process, and those collaborations are growing more robust as hospitals become more sophisticated in their CHNA process. Public health departments conduct community health assessments as well and often identify the same health needs as their local hospitals. These parallels illustrate an ideal opportunity for health care and public health organizations to intersect. Collaborating for the assessment can be the beginning of a long-term partnership if it is sustained through the implementation of community health improvement strategies.

Defining roles can be a tricky element of any partnership, as each organization navigates how it relates to the others. As hospitals and health care systems develop more advanced relationships with community organizations, they need to determine what role to play in population health improvement. The Health Research and Educational Trust (HRET) developed a model (Figure 6.1) that describes roles an organization could play for community health improvement. Each quadrant of the box describes a different role, although the edges are fluid as roles may morph based on the project or strategy.

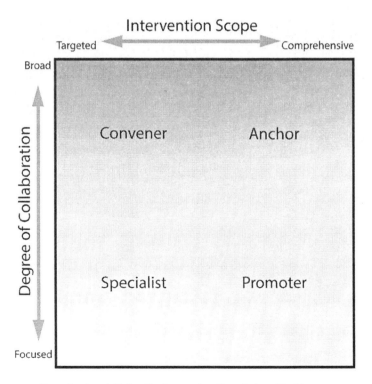

FIGURE 6.1 Organizational Roles for Improving Population Health

Source: Health Research and Educational Trust, 2014.

- **Specialist**—The specialist engages in population health improvement by concentrating on a few specific issues for which the organization is a subject matter or programmatic expert with a focused group of community partners.
- **Promoter**—The promoter plays an active role in population health improvement by supporting other organizations' initiatives through funding or contributing resources (e.g., employees, facility space). The promoter has broad intervention scope but limited community partnerships. Promoters may use their influence in the community and with the government to help shape policy or provide community education.
- **Convener**—The convener fosters collaborations for health improvement by bringing together stakeholders to build collaborative relationships and work toward shared goals. Conveners are influential in their communities and are able to bring together a broad range of multisectoral partners to address community health needs. These organizations target specific issues to address significant community health needs. Conveners may provide funding, facilities, staff expertise or in-kind services to support broader community health programs, but they also empower community stakeholders to take the lead.
- **Anchor**—The anchor serves as a leader in population health within the community. Anchors are influential in their communities, and they have strong, active partnerships with a wide range of diverse organizations to address a comprehensive scope of interventions that encompass both socioeconomic and medical concerns in the community. Population health improvement is a fully integrated part of their mission, with leadership engagement and significant resources allocated to support a broad range of issues that affect health. (HRET, 2015)

Whereas all hospitals should contribute to population health improvement, not all hospitals or health care systems can or should be anchors. Each organization and community needs to determine which model works best with its culture and the other stakeholders.

From Collaboration to Population Health Impact

In our interconnected world, collaboration for population health improvement is more important than ever. Hospitals and health care systems can make a greater impact on population health by aligning their resources, knowledge, skills and expertise with those of stakeholder organizations in their communities. Partnering to address community health needs does not always come naturally. But like any relationship, partnerships between organizations have to be carefully thought out, structured and fostered to promote joint action.

The United States is at a critical juncture as the health care system transforms to prioritize population health. With this shift, hospitals and their community partners have an opportunity to catalyze change in health by jointly addressing the social, economic and environmental factors that contribute to a shared goal—improved population health.

References

Catholic Health Association of the United States: Assessing and Addressing Community Health Needs (2015). Accessed at https://www.chausa.org/communitybenefit/assessing-and-addressingcommunity-health-needs.

Health Research & Educational Trust. (2016, August). *Creating Effective Hospital-Community Partnerships to Build a Culture of Health.* Chicago, IL: Health Research & Educational Trust. Accessed at www.hpoe.org.

Health Research & Educational Trust. (2015, August). *Approaches to Population Health in 2015: A National Survey of Hospitals.* Chicago, IL: Health Research & Educational Trust. Accessed at www.hpoe.org/pophealthsurvey.

Health Research & Educational Trust. (2014, October). *Hospital-Based Strategies for Creating a Culture of Health.* Chicago, IL: Health Research & Educational Trust. Accessed at www.hpoe.org/cultureofhealth.

Kania, J and Kramer, M. (2011) Collective Impact. *Stanford Social Innovation Review.* Accessed at https://ssir.org/articles/entry/collective_impact.

KU Work Group for Community Health and Development. (2015). Community Tool Box. Chapter 3, Section 8: Identifying community assets and resources. Accessed at www.ctb.ku.edu/en/table-of-contents/assessment/assessing-community-needs-and-resources/identify-community-assets/main.

Ruis, AR and Golden, RN. (2008, December) The Schism between Medical and Public Health Education: A Historical Perspective. *Academic Medicine.* Vol. 83, No. 12.

University of Wisconsin Public Health Institute. (2014). County Health Rankings model. Accessed at http://www.countyhealthrankings.org/our-approach.

US Department of Health and Human Services. (2016, March). 20 Million People Have Gained Health Insurance Coverage Because of the Affordable Care Act, New Estimates Show. Accessed at http://www.hhs.gov/about/news/2016/03/03/20-million-people-have-gained-health-insurance-coverage-because-affordable-care-act-new-estimates.

7

PRACTICAL CONSIDERATIONS

Megan Holderness and Alicia Meadows

Evidence-Based Practice: A Starting Point for Implementation

Creating New, Locally Applied Evidence from Adaptation of Evidence-Based Practices

Public health programing and policy is dependent upon sound evidence-based practices in order to drive change. Advanced public health agencies are intentional about leveraging resources from federal, state, local and private organizations in order to collectively drive community health transformation. It's obvious that demographics, culture and behaviors amongst populations can vary depending on the location in which these populations live. Thus, not only are public health professionals tasked with the necessity of identifying needs for improvement, but they must depend on collaborative public health evidence-based practices to help drive programmatic success at their level and in their location. The evidence-based practices must prove the outcome of interest through collection of data at pre-identified intervals during the study process, and maintain protocol fidelity through continuous quality evaluation, data accuracy and thorough evaluation processes. Thus, the public health professional must utilize evidence-based practice to impact their chosen demographic and population of choice.

A local health department that understands and routinely engages in the implementation and adaptation of evidence-based practices is the Oklahoma City-County Health Department. The Oklahoma City-County Health Department serves a population of more than 750,000 residents. The Oklahoma City-County metro area is a diverse community, with more than one-fourth of the population representing a minority group (28%). The largest ethnic minority is

Hispanic (16%), equal to the current African American population. Nearly one-third of the community population is 18 years old or younger (32.4%). In 2013, the United Health Foundation ranked Oklahoma 44th in overall health, an improvement from 46th in 2012. Oklahoma ranked 45th in the nation for obesity, 44th for physical inactivity, 42nd for poor physical health days, 46th in fruit consumption, 42nd for youth obesity (2012 measure), 41st in vegetable consumption and 48th in the nation for cardiovascular health.[1]

The statistics are as staggering at the county level, where the age-adjusted diabetes mortality rate in Oklahoma County was 27.7 deaths per 100,000 people compared to the national rate of 20.8 deaths per 100,000.[2] Also, 34% of adults in Oklahoma County have been informed they have high blood pressure.[3] In order to address, and ultimately reverse, these adverse health needs, the Oklahoma City-County Health Department adapted previously practiced interventions targeting chronic disease reduction and tailored it to most effec-tively utilize its resources and partnerships to bring change in the local com-munity. The Stanford Heart Disease Prevention Program identified that while genetics plays a role in heart disease risk, the environment in which the individual is exposed to also has a high impact on his/her risk of chronic disease.[4] The researchers with Stanford's Heart Disease Prevention Program developed evidence-based practices targeting a community model in order to reduce incidences of chronic disease. An additional evidence-based practice, created through The Centers for Disease Control and Prevention, is the National Diabetes Prevention Program (DPP), a 12-month program utilizing a trained coach to lead those at risk of diabetes towards healthier lifestyles, including improving nutrition, and physical and mental health.[5] Both of these programs provided reliable evidence indicating the success of community-based programmatic approaches in reducing heart disease.

Using the Oklahoma City-County Health Department's Community Health Needs Assessment and the evidence-based approaches of the Diabetes Prevention Program and the Stanford Heart Disease Prevention Program, community partners joined with the local health department to develop My Heart, a cardiovascular disease prevention program in the Oklahoma City-County area.

My Heart

My Heart's pilot program was first implemented in a single zip code. Due to the success and community feedback, the pilot program eventually expanded to seven zip codes strategically selected based on cardiovascular disease mortality rates. The overarching goal of the My Heart program is to prevent the prolifera-tion and exacerbation of cardiovascular disease in the most vulnerable communities in the Oklahoma City-County service area. The program is to be completed in 12 months, and includes both clinical visits as well as visits with a Community Health Worker (CHW).

Similar to the approach of evidence-based practices such as the Diabetes Prevention Program, which requires eligible participants meet certain high-risk categories (to include abnormal biometric screenings and/or high BMI), clients of My Heart must meet the following criteria in order to enroll: have high blood pressure; have high cholesterol; have high blood sugar; are overweight; live in targeted zip code; and be within specified age range. The comprehensive package that the Diabetes Prevention Program offered included a support system and tools to make lifestyle changes. These tools were proven to be a success, and the Oklahoma City-County Health Department adapted them as part of the My Heart package. Additionally, due to the high prevalence of heart disease and uncontrolled chronic disease, the Oklahoma City-County Health Department identified the need of the population to receive additional items unique from the Diabetes Prevention Program. So, utilizing partnerships and data to drive their decision making, the Oklahoma City-County Health Department expanded the toolset of the My Heart program to allow each My Heart participant to receive: health care practitioner visits related to heart disease; lab tests related to heart disease; medications related to heart disease; and some medications related to diabetes. The My Heart program applies the community-based approach to public health, utilizing various public health professionals to influence behavior change at a local level.

Also unique to My Heart, Community Health Workers (CHWs) provide services to clients that help them to take a lead role in their health care. These services include navigation of the health care system from a culturally relevant perspective. CHWs assist the clients in overcoming difficulties (such as lack of transportation) in setting and keeping appointments. CHWs also assist clients in communicating with their health care provider. The CHWs follow established guidelines and meet with the clients according to their needs. Additionally, CHWs are available for clients who may need additional follow-up after completing the My Heart program, similar to the support system identified through CDC's research-based program. CHWs have the unique ability to meet clients in the community when clients are difficult to reach through contemporary means of communication (i.e. telephone, post mail, electronic mail, etc.). Additionally, CHWs attend events in the community in order to network with non-profits, health care entities and other community members.

My Heart participants are enrolled on a continuous basis designated by quarters. The first and second cohorts completed their one-year participation in My Heart in the Summer and Fall seasons of 2015. The results from these cohorts further demonstrate the impact that community models have on reducing disparities in health outcomes and improving the countywide health status. Data collected during the initial year illustrates a successful model that leverages community resources, enhances community health and promotes health and wellness through a unique technical package.

The pilot project of My Heart was so well received by community members and partners that the program expanded to all countywide zip codes in Winter 2015. The overarching goal was to reduce disparities in health outcomes (10% reduction in overall mortality in our jurisdiction between 2010 and 2020). Recent data analysis demonstrates that between 2010 and 2012 Oklahoma City-County realized a 1.2% reduction in overall mortality rates, demonstrating that these strategies are effective at moving the community towards this goal.

Of course, without the efforts of strategic planning, data collection and evaluation protocols, this expansion success would not be possible. Thus, public health professionals need to remain vigilant in the implementation of tailored evidence-based practices at their level, as well as flexible in the approach to constantly evaluate and re-evaluate outcomes of interest in order to arrive at the best practice for the targeted area.

Lesson Learned

In the My Heart experience the Oklahoma City-County Health Department gained some valuable insight into the practice of applying evidence-based programs in diverse communities. Oklahoma City-County is an interesting rural/urban dichotomy, requiring that interventions can be flexible to the contrasting needs of each population. This requires developing a level of cultural competency that meets each resident at his or her place of comfort. Although attention must be given to the importance of evaluation and outcomes, when it comes to community practice, the goals of an outcome evaluation, at least initially, must come secondary to a process evaluation, which guides the quality improvement activities and directs the necessary modifications to successfully implement evidence-based practices within the community. Furthermore, understanding that this flexibility is often an opportunity to expand upon the evidence-based practice is a critical component of public health practice, and one that historically we do not effectively accomplish.

Evaluation Tools: Balancing Evidence-Based Practice with Efficiency at the Local Level

Historically, the Oklahoma City-County Health Department has subscribed to the identification and implementation of existing evidence-based best practices to improve health outcomes for its jurisdiction. These practices were consistently implemented according to guidelines, but largely without coordination across target populations. Efforts have been operating in silos, even within the local health department, with resources scattered throughout the county and without recognition of the need to allocate resources geographically or within specific populations. The initiation of the *Wellness Score* was the first opportunity for the Oklahoma City-County Health Department to begin planning for implementation based on geographic needs, health disparity and with an emphasis on upstream indicators of health outcomes. In addition to implementation based on needs, program evaluations need to be conducted in order to maintain efficiency and process improvement.

Program evaluation is a critical component to measuring an agency's impact on the population it serves. In public health settings, standard and systematic evaluation has been overlooked, largely because of the difficulty in defining "success." The Oklahoma City-County Health Department built its program evaluation protocol from a variety of best practices in the public health community.[6] A comprehensive program evaluation system should incorporate metrics from each of the following categories:

- Input—what you put in (staff time, money, etc.)
- Output—what you do (clients served, meetings attended, etc.)
- Outcome—what impact you have (decrease in smoking rates, increase in physical activity, etc.)
- Process—efficiency of program to deliver (return on investment, customer satisfaction, etc.)

The nature of public health funding often puts significant emphasis on input and output—because they are easy to capture—and marginalizes outcome and process metrics—because they are difficult to define.

Programmatic, specific protocol implementation must be conducted as the program planning and development is under way. The evaluation design ensures that staff is properly trained on the protocol and can implement it in a consistent and uniform manner, data collection is accurate and provided in a timely and consistent manner, participants are aware of their responsibilities, and quality assurance and regular audits are routinely conducted to ensure fidelity to outlined protocol.

Local Health Department Use of Evaluation

A key example of how a local health department used evaluation to efficiently allocate resources and tailored program operations to fit its population of interest is the Total Wellness program at the Oklahoma City-County Health Department. The Total Wellness program was built upon previously designated evidence-based practices, such as the Stanford Heart Disease Prevention Program and the CDC's Diabetes Prevention Program, and began as a 12-week course aimed at reducing risk factors associated with cardiovascular disease and diabetes. Total Wellness classes are provided to all at-risk citizens of Oklahoma County. Health screenings are conducted as part of the My Heart outreach program. In October 2014, Community Health Workers (CHWs) began teaching in target zip codes in order to further integrate community services into the client experience. A participant must complete at least six classes in the session in order to be a graduate from the class.

The initial evaluation of Total Wellness conducted identified no significant health benefits in individuals who completed the 12-week course compared to those who completed at least 6 of the 12 classes during 2011 and 2012. Thus, beginning Summer 2014, sessions were conducted using an 8-week curriculum instead of the original 12-week curriculum, a length of time identified by adapting results from previously discussed evidence-based practices as well as confirmation from local data collection. This change in course length allowed for four sessions per year to be offered with streamlined course content; the more condensed classes were recognized to lead to increased retention rates and more efficient utilization of staffing and available resources. A second evaluation was conducted after a pilot phase of the 8-week course curriculum and examined the effectiveness of the 12-week and the 8-week courses in order to establish a common practice for this program.

There was a total of 64 Total Wellness classes from Spring 2013 to Spring 2015, with 32 held as 12-week sessions and 32 as 8-week sessions. A total of 1,628 community members participated in these Total Wellness classes, with 999 graduates and 629 non-graduates, leading to an overall graduation rate of 61%. As Figure 7.1 illustrates, the majority of graduates realized significant decreases in triglyceride levels, fasting blood sugar levels, total cholesterol levels and systolic blood pressure. Also, 14.9% of graduates achieved the primary goal of at least 5% body weight loss. Logistic regression was conducted to determine the

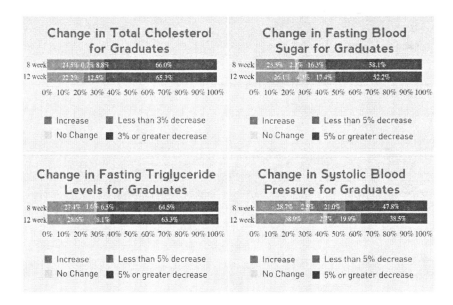

FIGURE 7.1 Total Wellness Course Length Biometric Comparison

effectives of course length on the 5% body weight loss goal. There was not a significant association (p-value = 0.66) with course length on body weight loss. The data collected and analyzed through the evaluation demonstrates that the 8-week curriculum was as effective as the 12-week course when addressing change in graduate biometrics and development of healthy habits. Thus, continuing with the 8-week course curriculum for Total Wellness was ideal for the Oklahoma City-County Health Department to implement.

Creating a culture of evidence-based practice adaptation, continuous program evaluation and quality data collection provide the most efficient use of public health resources and pave the road for strategic community change. Of equal importance is the necessity of public health departments, organizations and professionals to partner together in order to leverage strengths and collectively reduce negative health outcomes and promote community health innovation. Through partnerships and a data-driven culture, public health change on a large-scale is attainable and should be the standard in modern public health practices.

Lessons Learned

Perhaps the most important lesson learned from the comparative effectiveness evaluation conducted for Total Wellness was the impact the change in program operations had on the program staff. A sincere desire to maintain fidelity to the evidence-based practice, as originally designed, led to confusion among staff and concern for their ability to reproduce results. This hesitation was in spite of the very clear data presented through the evaluation team that results were as good or better in the 8-week course when compared to the 12-week course. Public health professionals are trained to utilize and adhere to evidence-based practices and guidelines, and when asked or encouraged to go "off script" are often uncomfortable with forging that path. Providing the program staff the time to acclimate to the change and understand how it would ultimately improve health outcomes by expanding access to the classes was critical to successfully modifying this program.

Place-Based Strategies: Optimizing Practice in Your Jurisdiction

We hear with some regularity now the connection being made between health outcomes and geographic disparities. Particular attention is being given to the role of place-based strategies in addressing health equity concerns and access to resources. Using data to drive where evidence-based and promising practices should be concentrated has emerged as a critical opportunity for impacting these very concerns.

Aggregating community resources to address social determinants of health within or near health care services has been one such strategy to optimize evidence-based practice implementation. The Northeast Regional Health and Wellness Campus, located in Oklahoma City, OK, is one such example of the operationalizing of this approach. In what was the most health disparate zip code in Oklahoma City, the local health department, armed with a $16 million public–private partnership and 54-acres of land, embarked on the development of a campus atmosphere that combined outdoor recreational opportunities with access to primary, mental and public health services. Partnerships to address education, job development, food security and interpersonal violence are also found on this campus, working in a coordinated manner that enables clients coming in for an ear infection to receive information about food boxes, family activities and enrollment in adult education classes all at the same time, and in some circumstances without ever leaving the exam room. Community gardens, meeting spaces, an auditorium and a state-of-the-art demonstration kitchen are available as well to enable community-led events, free of charge if they focus on an aspect of health or wellness. Beginning the spring of 2015, soccer fields and basketball courts also became available for community leagues and pick-up games.

The campus first opened its doors in 2014 and since that time has seen thousands of residents utilize both the indoor and outdoor amenities. At the time of development and construction of this campus, there was no single evidence-based practice that indicated this approach to improving health outcomes would work. However, each component of the planned campus was rooted in independent evidence-based or promising practices. In Oklahoma City, the decision was made to see what would happen if these practices were cobbled together in a systematic manner. The results are undeniable. Since deploying these aggregate resources to the most disparate zip code in Oklahoma City, that zip code has shed that title, moving incrementally out of the poorest health outcome zip code in two years. The local health department makes no claims that these results are attributable just to the Northeast Health and Wellness Campus; however, there is a sense that the campus was a catalyst for interest and investment in an area of the city that had for many years been abandoned and forgotten.

Sources

1. United Health Foundation. (2013). State Public Health Statistics | America's Health Rankings. *America's Health Rankings*. Oklahoma: State Public Health Statistics.
2. Oklahoma State Department of Health (OSDH). (2013). Vital Records 2010–2012. Retrieved from: https://www.ok.gov/health/pub/wrapper/ok2share.html
3. Centers for Disease Control and Prevention (CDC). (2012). Behavioral Risk Factor Surveillance System (BRFSS) City and County Data. Retrieved from: https://www.cdc.gov/brfss/smart/smart_data.htm
4. Maccoby, N., Farquhar, J. W., Wood, P. D., Alexander, J. (1977). The Stanford Heart Disease Prevention Program. *Journal of Community Health, 3*(100). DOI:10.1007/BF01674232.

5. Ma, J., Yank, V., Xiao, L., Lavori, P. W., Wilson, S. R., Rosas, L. G., & Stafford, R. S. (2013). Translating the Diabetes Prevention Program Lifestyle Intervention for Weight Loss into Primary Care: A Randomized Trial. *The Journal of the American Medical Association Internal Medicine, 173*(2), 113–121.
6. Riley, W., Parsons, H., McCoy, K., Burns, D., Anderson, D., Lee, S., & Sainfort, F. (2009). Introducing Quality Improvement Methods into Local Public Health Departments: Structured Evaluation of a Statewide Pilot Project. *Health Services Research, 44*(5 Part 2), 1863–1879. DOI: 10.1111/j.1475-6773.2009.01012.x.

8

AFTER INITIAL ACCREDITATION

The Road Ahead

Kaye Bender

Achievement of initial accreditation for a health department, as important as that is, is not the end; it's the beginning of a journey of performance management and quality improvement that will last a lifetime.

> Terry Cline, PhD, Oklahoma Secretary of Health and Human Services
> and Commissioner of the Oklahoma Department of Public Health

Intentional Linkage between Accreditation and Health Status Improvement

The national public health department accreditation program was launched in September 2011 intentionally based on concepts associated with improving and protecting the health of the public by advancing and ultimately transforming the quality and performance of state, local, tribal, and territorial public health departments. Elements of the accreditation program were created by practitioners for practitioners in an attempt to address the fragmentation in governmental public health department services that was described in a 2003 Institute of Medicine (IOM) report, *The Future of the Public's Health in the 21st Century.*[1] Accreditation standards and measures, designed to capture the capacity of a health department to provide their public health services in alignment with the ten Essential Public Health Services, were developed. A balance between the description of the organizational capacity of the health department to operate and their need to be flexible as they address the specific health status indicators for their jurisdictions was paramount as the program was developed. In short, the national public health department accreditation program assumes that a health department that understands the health status of its jurisdiction and implements, either alone or in partnership, those best and promising practices specifically designed to improve health status, will in fact contribute positively to health status improvement. However, measurement of the health department's contribution to health status improvement continues to be a challenge given the complexities associated with the multiple determinants of health.

Health departments who achieve accreditation under the Public Health Accreditation Board (PHAB) have demonstrated that they have the capacity to:

- Systematically assess the health status of the community it serves, using a variety of both quantitative and qualitative data (community health assessment)
- Work with its partners in the community, and with representatives of the community itself, to use the community health assessment to set health status objectives that can be tracked and measured over time (community health improvement plan)
- Specifically develop strategies for the health department to operationalize so that its specific role in implementing health status improvement is well defined, articulated, and measured (agency strategic plan)
- Document its actions aimed at tracking and controlling communicable diseases as well as communicating risks to its community (all hazards communication plan)
- Develop and maintain a commitment to development of its public health workforce, in spite of budget cuts and other challenges (workforce development plan)
- Develop and maintain a performance management/quality improvement culture (performance management system and quality improvement plan).[2]

Fundamental Cornerstones Related to Achieving Accreditation

Accredited health departments, in responding to external evaluation questions administered by NORC at the University of Chicago under contract with PHAB, have identified the following benefits of achieving national accreditation:

- Documentation of capacity to deliver three core functions of public health and the ten Essential Public Health Services
- Improved management processes used by leadership team
- Stimulated quality improvement and performance management opportunities
- Allowed the health department to identify its strengths and weaknesses
- Stimulated greater transparency and accountability
- Improved relationships with local community stakeholders
- Improved relationships with their board of health or governing entity
- Improved relationships/communication with local policy makers
- Improved competitiveness for funding.[3]

A strong cornerstone of the successful work in achieving accreditation is the work that health departments plan or strengthen with their partners. In today's complex public health environment, collaboration with partners at the state level and/or in the local community is more essential to success than ever. It is important that health departments continue the partnership momentum well after accreditation is achieved. A review of the partnerships that 53 accredited health departments documented as being important to their work in community health improvement planning indicated the following impact:

- Introduction of a variety of examples of tools that can be used for community health improvement planning. Because PHAB does not require a specific tool, health departments working in partnership with their health systems might choose to use the Catholic Hospital Association's Framework for Assessing and Addressing Community Health Needs or the Association for Community Health Improvement Assessment Tool.
- Identification of hospitals and health systems working on their community health needs assessment requirement under the Internal Revenue Service (IRS). Once health departments and health systems understood that PHAB's requirement for a community health improvement plan (CHIP) to be done within the past five years can readily fall within the IRS three-year requirement, then more collaboration between the two organizations can result in ONE CHIP for an entire community.
- Focus on the multiple determinants of health engages health departments with non-traditional partners such as law enforcement, education, faith-based organizations, economic development groups, and the media.[4]

Also, once a health department has become accredited, a partnership in economic development can lead to the community being potentially eligible for increased points under the STAR Communities Rating System.[5]

FOUR CASE STUDIES

Some examples of the specific impact of initial accreditation on health departments include case studies from the Oklahoma and California state health departments, City of Chicago Local Health Department, and the Three Rivers District Health Department in Kentucky. While there are multiple other examples, these are typical illustrations of the types of impact that are described in many jurisdictions.

- The Oklahoma State Department of Health serves 3.8 million people, and was one of the first state health departments to be accredited (2013). According to Dr. Terry Cline, "Being among the first to achieve national standards that promote continuous quality improvement demonstrates that we are delivering services as effectively as possible." The Oklahoma State Department of Health has identified increased awareness of the value of quality improvement and a commitment to an ongoing culture of quality improvement as key benefits of their accreditation journey. In 2014, the Oklahoma State Department of Health received the Quality Crown Award, the top quality improvement award given by the state. This award was given for their use of data to inform activities and decision making. Their data management system includes goals, timelines, and the name of the person responsible for each task. It is updated and monitored regularly to determine progress, or lack thereof, toward each goal. Another aspect of the award was to recognize their work in reducing overuse of antipsychotic medicines in nursing home residents with dementia: Working with nursing homes, advocates, families, and providers, the department was able to reduce overuse of antipsychotics in residents with dementia by 24%, exceeding the goal of 15%. These are just two of the several examples of quality improvement strategies initiated by the health department as they achieved their initial accreditation, but that exemplify their ongoing commitment to a culture of quality improvement post accreditation.[6]

- The California State Department of Health serves approximately 38 million and was accredited in 2014. Dr. Ron Chapman, Director of the California State Health Department when it was accredited, stated, "As a leader you are always looking for a tool, a strategy to take the organization to the next level, and accreditation does that." The California Department of Health embraced the fact that the PHAB standards and measures for accreditation are the first national accreditation standards developed specifically for governmental public health departments. They used their accreditation journey as an opportunity to assess the "health of the health department." Dr. Karen Smith, current State Health Officer for California, describes the impact of accreditation as a total change in the culture toward a commitment of the health department to measuring and tracking their performance in everyday practice in all programs. That shift in organizational culture is aimed at strengthening the health department's commitment to fostering those practices which improve the health of Californians. The California State Health Department operates a strong Office of Quality Performance and Accreditation, which serves as a clearinghouse and strategic leader in ensuring support for the local health departments to achieve accreditation. Their website not only houses their state-level community health assessment and improvement plan, strategic plan, and other similar documents, but it also houses examples of that same work for the local health departments. An annual Accreditation Readiness Conference aims to keep all health departments in the state up to date on best and promising practices, as well as to ensure that their comprehensive public health system works together for all citizens of California.

- The City of Chicago Department of Public Health serves 2.7 million and was the first large city health department to be accredited by PHAB (2013). Dr. Julie Morita, Commissioner of Health for the Chicago Department of Public Health, states:

> We knew that some of our programs were doing well and others not so well. The accreditation process allowed us to level the playing field by providing us with the information to help all programs do a better job in serving the citizens of Chicago. That will ultimately improve their health status.

Chicago identified a key benefit of going through the accreditation process as the peer review. The report from those reviewers gave them useful feedback about improving their work with their partners on their community health improvement plan. Taking those recommendations seriously has allowed them to focus on those areas that will have the most positive impact on the public health issues in their city. They have already identified improvements in immunization coverage; in environmental public health services; and in health services provided in their school system. In addition, the keen focus on partnerships has strengthened their ability to affect policies aimed at improving the health of the citizens of Chicago. The momentum that began with work on accreditation continues today as they build on their successes to identify additional foci for their work using the same successful strategies.

- The Three Rivers Public Health District in Kentucky serves a population of 48,000. Dr. Georgia Heise, Director of Three Rivers Health Department, identifies accreditation as "allowing the health department's good work to be noticed by a lot of people." This small health department district in rural Kentucky admits that it doesn't have a lot of resources, but that doesn't mean that it isn't doing good public health work. Working in lock step with their board of health, Three Rivers credits their accreditation journey with empowering them to document the work they were doing for funders and for policy makers. They have also used this opportunity to be more strategic in their grant planning for the future. Whereas many health departments in the country have admittedly implemented programs because funding was available, Three Rivers has made the commitment to use their accreditation work to prioritize what their citizens need and to apply for funding for those strategic services. They identify their work after accreditation as a paradigm shift. Their board of health also gives the accreditation journey credit for assisting them to better understand the full array of public health services provided by the health department, which in turn enables them to set better policies and make more strategic decisions.[7]

These health departments demonstrate the link between accreditation and a culture of performance management and quality improvement, as well as the use of that culture change to affect health status post their accreditation award. They are truly doing things differently as a result of their accreditation journey.

Accredited Health Department Requirements and Choices

As with any national accreditation process, there must be standardized requirements that health departments should address in order to be successful. PHAB has intentionally developed standards and measures that incorporate "what" health departments should be doing in order to be effective administrators of public health without being prescriptive about "how" health departments should accomplish their mission. There are several key elements of organizational capacity that PHAB considers essential for health departments to address in order to be considered strong health departments, both for initial accreditation and for the way forward post accreditation. Each health department, and its stakeholders, has a myriad of choices, however, in how they address these requirements. Figure 8.1 summarizes those elements. Each will then be discussed in more detail.

Foundational plans include the Community Health Assessment (CHA); the Community Health Improvement Plan (CHIP); and the Agency Strategic Plan (ASP). Components of each plan include the process for the development of the plan; adoption of the plan; implementation of the plan; and evaluation and revision of the plan. The CHA forms the foundation for efforts to improve the health of the population, providing a basis for setting priorities, planning, program development, funding, policy, coordination of community resources, and new ways to use assets to improve the health of the population. The CHA should include data from various sources: population demographics; identification of groups with health issues and disparities; contributing factors; existing assets or resources; community to review and/or active contribution; and ongoing monitoring and analysis of data. Building on the CHA, then, the CHIP provides guidance for improving the health of the population by prioritizing existing activities and setting new priorities, reflecting the results of a collaborative planning process that includes significant involvement by key sectors. The CHIP includes measurable outcomes/indicators and priorities; policy changes; responsibility for implementing strategies; and ongoing consideration of tribal, local,

FIGURE 8.1 Key Elements of Organizational Capacity

state, and national priorities. The ASP then defines and determines the health department's roles, priorities, and direction over three to five years, setting forth what the department plans to achieve, how it will be achieved, and how it will know when it is achieved. The ASP includes the mission, vision, and guiding principles/values; strategic priorities; measurable goals and objectives; key support functions; external trends, events, or factors; agency strengths and weaknesses; and links to the other plans.[2]

Accredited health departments report the following activities/accomplishments from their CHA/CHIP activities:

- Using collective impact model to coordinate with partners.
- Aligning assessment with nonprofit hospital community health needs assessment.
- Engaging new partners (including Tribes).
- Collecting/making available additional data.
- Majority reporting progress towards CHIP health indicators.
- Community coalition working to provide low-income people with vouchers to farmers' market, created city's first bike lane, and partnered with school for a play/exercise facility during cold months. As a result, obesity rates declined.
- Evidence-based, culturally appropriate program resulting in a decrease in Hispanic teen pregnancy rates.[8]

Said another way, accredited health departments have used these foundational plans as they were meant to be used post accreditation. That is, they form the basis for an ongoing assessment, tracking, and priority setting process aimed at improving the health status of their jurisdiction.

Additional significant plans that are closely aligned with the foundational plans as indicators of health department organizational capacity include the Risk Communication Plan (Standard 3.2); Emergency Operations Plan (Standard 5.4); Workforce Development Plan (Standard 8.2); and Quality Improvement Plan (Standard 9.2).

The Risk Communication Plan details the communications and media protocols the health department will follow during a public health crisis or emergency, outlining the decisions and activities that will be taken for a timely, effective response. Included in this plan are elements such as defining protocols; defining roles and responsibilities; providing information 24/7; disseminating information in case of technology disruption; expediting message clearance; working with the media; and dealing with misconceptions or misinformation. The Emergency Operations Plans (EOPs) include collaborative and public health activities for coordinated responses to emergencies; ongoing participation in preparedness meetings; testing plan implementation through exercises and drills; other roles and responsibilities; communication networks; and continuity of operations. Post accreditation, these communications and emergency operational plans continue to be important tools for health departments to use as they stay current in their roles related to the multiple public health threats facing communities today.

The Workforce Development Plan guides the intentional development of a competent workforce with the skills and experience needed to perform their duties and carry out the health department's mission. It includes assessment and updating of the capacity and capability of the workforce; assessment of staff competencies; consideration of advances in technology and public health; and consideration of a variety of education schedules and curricula in an effort to address barriers to closing gaps and planning for future workforce needs. Far too often, workforce needs have been sacrificed under budget cuts and other similar fiscal constraints. Accredited health departments have made a long-term commitment to their staff, regardless of the financial circumstances. This momentum continues into the future, long after initial accreditation is obtained.

The Quality Improvement Plan describes efforts in developing a program that integrates quality improvement into all programmatic and operational aspects, building a culture of quality in the organization.[2] Accredited health departments' annual reports utilize the *Roadmap to a Culture of Quality Improvement*, developed by the National Association of County and City Health Officials (NACCHO),[9] to monitor the health department's ongoing commitment to ensuring a culture of quality. The QI Roadmap provides guidance on progressing through six phases or levels of quality improvement maturity until a culture of quality has been reached and can be sustained. Accredited health departments utilize a variety of quality improvement models and strategies including Plan, Do, Check, Act;

fishbone / cause and effect diagrams; flowcharts and process mapping; and Kaizen. Initially, quality improvement projects may emerge from the accreditation site visit report and/or recommendations from the PHAB Accreditation Committee. Thereafter, accredited health departments provide to PHAB how they select and prioritize their quality improvement projects as well as their ongoing work in doing so. Some examples of accredited health department quality improvement/ performance management projects include:

- Improve office safety for employees.
- Improve staff recycling rates and other energy conservation efforts.
- Decrease human-resources processing time for new applications (decreased by 40%).
- Improve the intake and orientation process for student interns.
- Reorganize shared drive (60% reduction in electronic storage space, reducing need to buy additional servers).
- Better align estimated budgets for federal grants with spending.
- Develop process to share surveillance data with surveillance sites, partners, and staff.
- Respond more quickly to requests for environmental health information.
- Decrease time to share death data.
- Improve outreach and coordination of services for breastfeeding women.
- Increase the proportion of known animal bites reported within 48 hours.
- Increase the percentage of tobacco clerks with valid tobacco permits (increased by more than 30%).
- Decrease frequency of a particular food establishment violation.
- Improve process for gathering/analyzing customer satisfaction surveys.[6]

An accredited health department considering their way forward doesn't complete these documents for initial accreditation just to meet the PHAB requirements. These requirements form the basis for an ongoing commitment to effectively and strategically managing their public health resources to meet the needs of the population they serve. Moving into the future, accredited health departments will not only need to keep these documents updated and used in daily practice; they will also need to be able to address what difference this commitment to planning has made. They will also need to continue to stay abreast of emerging public health issues that have implications for change, innovation, and future accreditation requirements.

Sustaining the Work in Order to Measure the Impact

Whereas initial accreditation captures the health department's capacity to administer the ten Essential Public Health Services, reaccreditation can be viewed as the opportunity to provide evidence that the health department continues to evolve and improve as new and different public health challenges emerge. The design of reaccreditation encourages the health department to continue their effectiveness at improving the health status of the population it serves. Reaccreditation will balance both a demonstration that the health department has processes and capacities in place with its ongoing capabilities and continuous quality improvement. It will be essential for accredited health departments to continue to have the capacity to administer sound public health services while continuing to transform to a higher performing health department. In essence, this is paramount to the survival of the public health department in the 21st century.

In order to successfully navigate the road ahead after achievement of initial national accreditation, health departments will need to focus on:

a.   Continued Conformity with the Initial Accreditation Standards and Measures

Accredited health departments cannot lose ground in ensuring their ongoing capacity to continue to be in conformity with the standards and measures under which they received accreditation. PHAB assumes that health departments can only become transformative if they build on their initial accreditation and progress along a continuum from capacity to capability. Accredited health departments will need to consider the overarching themes embedded in initial accreditation and continue to monitor updates and improvements in those expectations in order to remain in conformity with them.

The overarching themes of the PHAB accreditation standards and measures include the following:

- Planning (such as data collection, analysis, and utilization for decision making; community health improvement planning; agency strategic planning; quality improvement planning; emergency operational planning; and workforce development planning)
- Community Engagement and Partnerships (such as the partnership process for the implementation and revisions of the CHA and the CHIP; other partnerships/coalitions; provision of data to partners; engagement of the population concerning the design of programs and the development of processes and policies; development and implementation of health promotion strategies; and partnerships to address access to care)
- Performance Management and Quality Improvement (such as a department-wide system for managing program performance; "big" quality improvement strategies and associated projects; and staff participation program performance management and in quality improvement)
- Leadership and Governance (such as the health department serving as the primary expert on resources for public health policies, processes, and capacity;

information provision to governing entities, elected officials, and the public about public policies; and ongoing communication with the governing entity)
- Workforce Development (such as promoting public health careers; planning for training needs of staff; and continuous training and development of staff)[2]

Reporting on progress in working on these themes would be similar to and build on the Annual Reports that accredited health departments already submit to PHAB.

Some new areas introduced under Version 1.5 of the PHAB standards and measures which should also be ensured are:

- Populations that are at higher risk for poorer health outcomes and health equity (appears in several places in Version 1.5 of the standards and measures)
- Ongoing revisions of the CHA
- Use of data from multiple databases/sources for decision making
- A planned approach for developing and implementing health promotion programs
- Relationship with the media
- Organizational branding strategy
- Strategic planning that addresses key department support functions (i.e., information management, workforce, communication, and branding)
- Consideration of emerging public health, health care, and reimbursement issues in addressing access to care
- Strengthening the workforce development function
- A supportive work environment for health department employees
- Public health ethics
- Strengthening the information management function[2]

b.   *Foundational Public Health Services*

In April of 2012, the IOM released a report entitled *For the Public's Health: Investing in a Healthier Future*,[10] which was the third in a series of three reports focusing on key issues in public health, including measurement (December 2010), law and policy (June 2011), and funding (April 2012). One significant recommendation in that report was that a detailed description of a basic set of public health services be defined in a manner that allows cost estimation to be used as a basis for an accounting and management framework and compared among revenues, activities, and outcomes. Following that recommendation, a Public Health Leadership Forum, composed of public health leaders from across the country, was convened by the Robert Wood Johnson Foundation and facilitated by Resolve. The forum developed an initial description of foundational public health capabilities and services which could be used for the intended purposes. The March 2014 version of this work is depicted in Figure 8.2.

Other Services Particular to a Community

Programs/Activities Specific to an HD and/or Community Needs
Most of an HD's Work Is "Above the Line"

Foundational Areas

| Communicable Disease Control | Chronic Disease & Injury Prevention | Environmental Public Health | Maternal, Child, & Family Health | Access to and Linkage w/Clinical Care |

Foundational Public Health Services

- Assessment (Surveillance, Epidemiology, and Laboratory Capacity)
- All Hazards Preparedness/Response
- Policy Development/Support
- Communications
- Community Partnership Development
- Organizational Competencies (Leadership/Governance; Health Equity, Accountability/Performance Management, QI; IT; HR; Financial Management; Legal)

Foundational Capabilities

FIGURE 8.2 Foundational Public Health Services

For accredited health departments moving forward post accreditation, some demonstration of the foundational capabilities and services will need to be demonstrated. In conducting an alignment analysis between the foundational public health capabilities and the PHAB accreditation standards and measures, it was determined that a close alignment exists. All of the foundational public health capabilities are included in the accreditation standards and measures, but some of the accreditation requirements go beyond the foundational capabilities. Therefore, accredited health departments should be able to demonstrate this requirement with little to no difficulty. Of course, future iterations of the framework may create some new challenges in this regard.

c. Quality Improvement and Accountability Measures

The Joint Commission has implemented a concept called accountability measures for hospitals. Those measures are quality measures that meet four criteria that produce the greatest positive impact on patient outcomes when hospitals demonstrate improvement on them. The four criteria in that setting relate to the evidence base for the measure; the proximity of the intervention to the outcome; the accuracy of the measure; and the minimization of adverse effects.[9] Given the difference between public health and inpatient care, PHAB has identified ample implications for considering a similar approach for reaccreditation requirements. PHAB would adopt a menu of health status indicators that accredited health departments would be asked to report on—both in terms of their statistics and also in terms of their priority in the health department's CHA and quality improvement work. Some of the potential evidence for adopting this approach include recent publications such as:

- The IOM released a report in April 2015 entitled *Vital Signs: Core Metrics for Health and Health Care Progress*. Following a similar approach to that of the Joint Commission, the IOM proposed 15 measures that together have systemic reach, are outcomes oriented, are meaningful at the personal level, are representative of concerns facing the U.S. health system, and have use at many levels. The core measures proposed by the committee are as follows:

  1. Life expectancy
  2. Well-being
  3. Overweight and obesity
  4. Addictive behavior
  5. Unintended pregnancy
  6. Healthy communities
  7. Preventive services
  8. Care access
  9. Patient safety
  10. Evidence-based care
  11. Care match with patient goals
  12. Personal spending burden
  13. Population spending burden
  14. Individual engagement
  15. Community engagement.[12]

- Whereas not all of these measures are directly applicable to health department reaccreditation, many are and could be considered as measures of population health improvement supported by health departments.
- The University of Washington has worked for several years and with several various local health department sites to develop the PHAST measures. These are a workable set of measures of local public health service delivery in three domains of activity—communicable disease control, chronic disease prevention, and environmental health protection. The MPROVE Study Measures were developed by Practice-Based Research Network (PBRN) investigators from six states: Colorado, Florida, Minnesota, New Jersey, Tennessee, and Washington. These PBRN states represent nearly 300 local public health jurisdictions. PHAST has completed the initial refinement of the MPROVE Study Measures in consultation with public health practitioners, content experts, and public health systems researchers. The revised Measures will serve as the template for a nationwide system for standardized reporting of public health activities and services. The Measures are specific to the following areas:

1. Tobacco prevention and control
2. Obesity prevention
3. Oral health
4. Communicable disease
5. Enteric disease
6. Sexually transmitted infections
7. Tuberculosis
8. Environmental health protection.[13]

- The Robert Wood Johnson Foundation has recently released the Culture of Health metrics. Organized into four Action Areas, the Culture of Health Framework identifies 41 measures (number may increase or decrease over time) that serve to assess the work done by communities to ensure that their citizens lead healthier lives. Whereas not all of these measures are directly affected by public health departments, there are some that are consistently noted in the CHIPs that health departments have submitted for accreditation. Some of them also relate closely to the IOM *Vital Signs* report. The Action Areas and their drivers include:

1. Making health a shared value—sense of community and civic engagement
2. Fostering cross-sector collaboration and well-being—partnerships; investment of cross-sector collaboration; policies that support collaboration
3. Creating healthier, more equitable communities—built environment and physical conditions; social and economic environment; policy and governance
4. Strengthening integration of health services and systems—access to public health and health care (including mental health, dental health, and insurance); consumer experience and quality; and balance and integration.[14]

- The Centers for Disease Control and Prevention (CDC) have identified "Winnable Battles" (Tobacco; Nutrition, Physical Activity and Obesity; Food Safety; Healthcare-Associated Infections; Motor Vehicle Injuries; Teen Pregnancy; HIV in the United States). These have been chosen based on the magnitude of the health problem and the ability to make significant progress in outcomes. By identifying priority strategies, defining clear targets, and working closely with public health partners, significant progress can be made in reducing health disparities and the overall health burden from these diseases and conditions.[15]

No matter which set of population health measures PHAB selects for accredited health departments to report on for reaccreditation, high performing health departments, post initial accreditation, will want to identify their own set of measures from their CHA and community health improvement planning work so that they can measure their progress on them as they monitor their performance over time.

The Institute for Alternative Futures was funded by the Robert Wood Johnson and Kresge foundations to develop scenarios for addressing questions related to describing the greatest accomplishments for public health in the next two decades: identifying the obstacles that may prove insurmountable to public health, and imagining what public health might look like in 2030. Use of the scenarios for planning enables public health leaders to consider what they should be working on today that will help shape public health in 2030. This work included some considerations such as exploration of key forces shaping public health; consideration of the future of public health functions, financing, and sustainability; building expectable, challenging, and visionary scenarios that facilitate preparation, imagination, and aspiration; and providing and widely distributing the scenarios as a tool for public health agencies, organizations, and schools. Throughout the scenarios, public health department accreditation surfaced as both a vehicle for continuing to monitor public health practice and a large contributor to the transformation of public health practice. Growth of accreditation was an underlying assumption in most scenarios, with assumptions of both future challenges and expectations. The scenarios generally reinforce the current focus of accreditation standards but also call for the evolution of accreditation focus/standards as the role, scope, and responsibility of health departments change. In order for PHAB to be successful in continuing to administer an accreditation program that is designed "by practitioners for practitioners" for the purpose of protecting and promoting the health of the public, accredited health departments will also need to continue their active engagement with PHAB to ensure a strong and effective way forward.[16]

Summary Tips for Accredited Health Departments

In summary, accredited health departments have chosen to be viewed as progressive health departments that demonstrate the organizational capacity to do the work they have been charged with doing. Post accreditation, those health departments can continue their pursuit of excellence by attending closely to the following:

- Keep the community assessment, improvement plan, and agency strategic plan alive and active as foundational plans to guide the health department's ongoing work.
- Align the communications, all-hazards, workforce development, performance management, and quality improvement plans with the three foundational plans.
- Stay current and vigilant in monitoring emerging public health issues. If they are important enough to be considered emerging, then they will probably have a long-term effect on the health department in general.
- View the health department's role as the public health conscience and expert in the community it serves and build partnerships that sustain that image.
- Institute regular, credible systems for monitoring selected community health status indicators.

- Continue to learn all that can be learned about managing the performance of the health department. Focus on widely used and tested performance management and quality improvement tools.
- Participate with PHAB on committees, think tanks, expert panels, as peer reviewers, and in various learning communities. This will ensure that accreditation remains focused on "by practitioners for practitioners."

Achieving accreditation requires a lot of work. But sustaining that work becomes a reality if those activities are truly a part of the organizational culture.

References

1. Institute of Medicine. *The Future of the Public's Health in the 21st Century*. Washington, DC. National Academies Press. 2003.
2. Public Health Accreditation Board. *Public Health Accreditation Board Standards and Measures, Version 1.5*. Alexandria, VA. Accessed at http://www.phaboard.org/wp-content/uploads/PHABSM_WEB_LR1.pdf.
3. NORC at the University of Chicago. *Initial Evaluation of the Public Health Accreditation Program*. Accessed at http://www.phaboard.org/wp-content/uploads/PHAB-Evaluation-Brief-2015.pdf.
4. Public Health Accreditation Board. Internal Documents. Review of Accredited Health Departments CHA/CHIP. August 2015.
5. Sustainability Tools for Assessing and Rating Communities. Accessed at http://www.starcommunities.org/.
6. *Planning Your Next Steps: Keeping the Momentum Going after Achieving Accreditation*. Dr. Terry Cline Speech at the COPPHI Open Forum March 5, 2015. Accessed at https://www.youtube.com/watch?v=zP9vTJ4l7eA.
7. Public Health Accreditation Board. *Reaping the Benefits of Accreditation across the Nation*. Video Accessed at https://vimeo.com/138148927.
8. Public Health Accreditation Board. Internal Annual Reports Documents. Accessed November 15, 2015.
9. National Association of County and City Health Officials. *Roadmap to a Culture of Quality*. 2013. Accessed at http://qiroadmap.org/.
10. Institute of Medicine. *For the Public's Health: Investing in a Healthier Future*. Washington, DC: National Academies Press. April 2012.
11. The Joint Commission. *Accountability Measures*. Accessed at http://www.jointcommission.org/accountability_measures.aspx.
12. Institute of Medicine. *Vital Signs: Core Metrics for Health and Health Care Progress*. Washington, DC: National Academies Press. April 2015.
13. Public Health Activities and Services Tracking. University of Washington. Accessed at http://depts.washington.edu/phast/phastweb/?q=node/16.
14. *What Is a Culture of Health?* The Robert Wood Johnson Foundation. Princeton, NJ. Accessed at http://www.evidenceforaction.org/what-culture-health.
15. Centers for Disease Control and Prevention. *Winnable Battles*. Accessed at http://www.evidenceforaction.org/what-culture-health.
16. Institute for Alternative Futures. *Public Health 2030: A Scenario Exploration*. May 2014. Accessed at http://www.altfutures.org/publichealth2030.

9

KEY INGREDIENTS FOR TRANSFORMING COMMUNITY HEALTH

Ron Bialek and John W. Moran

Introduction

The increased demand placed on public health departments and healthcare organizations to perform better and improve health outcomes with less funding cannot be achieved under the design and operation of the current system. In this chapter, community health is defined as having a focus on geographical/ community areas rather than people with shared health characteristics.

Three key ingredients for transforming the health of a community are:

1. Community multi-sector collaborative approach to community health improvement
2. Community Chief Health Strategist
3. Exemplar backbone public health organization

Whereas a health department achieving Public Health Accreditation Board accreditation is a step towards transforming health in a community, this step alone is insufficient. Following accreditation, the accredited health department, working with community partners such as healthcare organizations, businesses, transportation, and others, must continue to grow and improve and not simply rest on its laurels. Too often in many sectors accreditation is considered a hurdle to clear, and once cleared the organization then waits for the reaccreditation cycle to commence before beginning to make or consider improvements. Unfortunately, when these improvements are considered, the improvements often are organization-specific and not aligned to an overall comprehensive community health improvement strategy. What we are suggesting is an approach to transforming community health that overcomes siloed individual organization improvement strategies that are not aligned with the greater community health efforts, and therefore sub-optimize the overall community's health. Under the old fragmented siloed public health and healthcare approach we are constantly winning small improvement battles but losing the overall community health war because resources are sub-optimized.

Community Multi-Sector Collaborative Approach to Community Health Improvement

A *community multi-sector collaborative approach to community health improvement* is the first key ingredient to transforming the health of a community. This may create a seismic chain reaction that is needed in most communities today to achieve the transformational change that is badly needed to improve the overall community's health. This approach engages public health departments, healthcare organizations, and other sectors influencing the health of our communities. This approach will have health promotion, protection, prevention, and treatment working in sync, rather than in silos with little commonality. This approach often leads to or requires a major alteration of the leadership mindset of all organizations involved in impacting a community's health and the introduction of quality improvement (QI) methods to change the teamwork and culture of the community's overall public health and healthcare systems.

The use of QI methods helps the multi-sector collaborative focus on ways that the community's resources can be used strategically and effectively to address the health needs and challenges facing the community. Figure 9.1 shows a graphic of four rings of how to integrate QI and performance management into multi-sector collaborative community health improvement projects that promote and facilitate alignment across community organizations. This alignment helps to achieve improvements in community health and the desired overall vision for a community culture of health.

The innermost ring of Figure 9.1 starts with a clear and crisp vision of the community health need or challenge to be addressed, and the vision for the improvement to be achieved. The second ring focuses on having a performance management system that supports the improvement by understanding and developing a baseline built on solid evidence against which to measure future improvements. The third ring shows a generic process to launch improvement initiatives and to make sure that the solutions implemented are sustained. The fourth ring shows the necessary culture of quality elements that hold together the entire multi-sector collaborative effort that is working to achieve and sustain a community culture of health.

As an initial step towards transforming the public health and healthcare delivery system in a community, it is important to remember that there are individual organizations comprising the system that have their own unique needs, attributes, and accomplishments. For the collaborative to be successful in transforming the

FIGURE 9.1 Integrating Quality Improvement and Performance Management into Community Health Improvement. Developed Collaboratively by the Public Health Foundation and Health Research in Action, 2015.

community public health and healthcare delivery system and improving the community's health, each organization that is part of the multi-sector community health collaborative must contribute to a culture of quality in their individual organizations as well as in their aligned community efforts.

Community Chief Health Strategist

The second key ingredient for transforming the health of a community is to have a *Community Chief Health Strategist*[1] lead this multi-sector collaborative approach. This Community Chief Health Strategist can help with identifying and aligning community resources to gain the optimum health outcome impact. The Community Chief Health Strategist can be a shared position by leaders of various community health organizations, or be a single respected and trusted organization in the community.

The Community Chief Health Strategist's role can be accomplished by using/ employing the following guiding principles:

- Strategic alignment of all community health resources.
  - Align leadership, health improvement plans, and approaches.
- Community customer focus.
- Visible/collaborative leadership.
- Communication/transparency.
  - Internal/external communication.
  - Reporting on progress.
  - Public reporting—Is this making a difference?
  - Accountability.
- Culture of quality.
  - Shared measurement.
  - Shared data.
  - Do data direct action?
- Culture of health.[2]
  - Make health a shared value.
  - Foster cross-sector collaboration.
  - Create healthier, more equitable communities.
  - Strengthen integration of health services.

The difference between a Community Chief Health Strategist and a community manager is that the community manager sets the initial agenda on a community health issue, does most of the talking, makes most of the decisions, and often ignores community input. Whereas this may seem easy and efficient for managers, it is often a waste of people's time and does not tap into their creative talents and abilities. In addition, it does not get their buy-in for implementation of improvements, which is why many managers struggle with success.

Community Chief Health Strategists guide and facilitate community health improvement meetings instead of running them. They are willing to let go of their power and are open to team collaborative outcomes. This is a dynamic change from the community manager model and is needed in the current community health environment. There are 10 basic characteristics of Community Chief Health Strategists that can lead to their success. These are:

1. **Issue Planning and Climate Setting:** They are able to clearly describe the current reality of the health issue and its impact on the community in terms of cost, quality, and equity. They have the ability to lead a collaborative approach to solving a community health issue, starting with planning how to make the case for a full-scale collaborative effort and inviting broad community participation.

2. **Ask Critical Questions:** Great questions stimulate great discussions. What are we each doing now in the community to address the health issue before us? How effective are we? Are we collaborating? Are we winning battles and losing the war? How can we collaborate? What could we do differently that would be more effective? Being able to ask the critical questions, let others answer, encourage debates, and not be defensive define a Community Chief Health Strategist.

3. **Active Listening:** Community Chief Health Strategists know they do not have all the answers so they need to paraphrase, check for understanding, and ask follow-up questions to make sure the group is digging into the community health issue. This will encourage more participation and keep the discussion flowing. They never impose their will unless it is fact-based and will help make the discussion more productive.

4. **Consensus Building:** The Community Chief Health Strategist facilitates the community group to consensus on the health initiative. This does not mean that everybody has to agree with a decision. It means making sure that everyone has had a say, heard each other, and arrived at a decision that they are willing to support. Reaching consensus takes more time, but will usually produce better ideas, more buy-in, and improved outcomes.

5. **Conflict Resolution:** Whenever there is a roomful of people involved in discussing how to solve a problem, conflict is inevitable. A Community Chief Health Strategist understands that constructive conflict can be a productive way for the group to see all sides of the health issue, creating a better environment for constructive problem-solving without avoiding disagreements. By letting disagreements be vented, all members are exposed to opposing views which can be managed in an open forum discussion. A Community Chief Health Strategist needs to understand how to harness the power of conflict in a positive way so that group members can disagree, but remain on task.

6. **Non-Verbal Communication Skills:** While researchers argue over the exact percentages, most would agree that greater than 50% of communication is non-verbal. A Community Chief Health Strategist needs to project the appropriate body language to the group and be able to read the group's tone and body language in order to assess the group's level of engagement, candor, and commitment.

7. **Recording:** A skillful Community Chief Health Strategist understands that group facilitation involves knowing when to turn to a flipchart or whiteboard to capture what people are saying. Doing so enables participants see that their ideas are being heard, valued, and validated. It also serves as a valuable record to be used for action planning and follow-up.

8. **Insatiable Curiosity:** Community Chief Health Strategists recognize that in order to continuously grow and improve themselves they must be curious about possibilities and alternatives and embrace the key concept of learning, not knowing. They do not think or portray that they know everything about

the community health issue being discussed and are open to new information. This insatiable curiosity is continuously conveyed and shared and helps build the collaborative culture.

9. **Customer Focus:** A Community Chief Health Strategist recognizes that there are many customers for any community health improvement initiative. The Community Chief Health Strategist understands that unless the improvement initiative partners have an intense focus on all of their customers and an understanding of what they need, want, and value, the initiative will not succeed.

10. **Authentic, Upstanding, and Respectful:** Community Chief Health Strategists must be authentic in their words, upstanding in their deeds, and respectful to all those around them. These are the traits of any great leader, but they are particularly relevant to the Community Chief Health Strategist. Individuals in these roles must inherently lead by example. Leading by example is not possible without being genuine and acting with high integrity.

Becoming and being a Community Chief Health Strategist requires mastery of many skills. Rate yourself using Figure 9.2 on each of the 10 characteristics of a Community Chief Health Strategist, indicating where you have strengths, weaknesses, and development needs for each characteristic. This analysis will help you

CCHS Characteristic	Strength	Weakness	Needs Development
1. Issue Planning and Climate Setting			
2. Active Listening			
3. Ask Critical Questions			
4. Consensus Building			
5. Conflict Resolution			
6. Non-Verbal Communication Skills			
7. Recording			
8. Insatiable Curiosity			
9. Customer Focus			
10. Authentic and Upstanding			

FIGURE 9.2 CCHS Characteristics

understand where you need additional development or coaching that will help you become a Community Chief Health Strategist in the future or a better Community Chief Health Strategist now.

Exemplar Backbone Public Health Organization

The third key ingredient for transforming the health of a community is to have an *exemplar backbone public health organization* ready to support the Community Chief Health Strategist in the health improvement initiatives to be undertaken. According to *Webster*, an "exemplar" is extraordinary, revolutionary, excellent, perfect, something that one hopes to attain, serves as a model, or one that is worthy of imitation.

An exemplar public health organization is one that through inspired leadership employs QI methods and a performance management system to seamlessly weave and integrate quality into its culture, people, processes, technology, and resources in order to deliver to its customers the best quality public health services they need and desire. This organization is constantly focused on improving the way it conducts its business and delivers its products or services by incorporating both breakthrough and incremental performance and QI at all organizational levels.

In a public health organization with exemplar QI and performance management practices:

- Organizational components and practices are driven by the public health mission and organizational strategy.
- Internal and external activities are integrated into routine public health practices.
- An organizational culture exists in which continuous performance and QI are commonplace and result in better service to the customer.

An exemplar public health organization accomplishes its stated vision and mission, and develops a quality culture throughout the organization, by:

- *Describing* clearly and concisely for the organization's employees the current state the organization is starting from, the direction it is headed, and the timeframe it envisions for becoming an exemplar organization.
- *Employing* a repeatable and deployable planning methodology that is able to deal with the current challenges the organization is facing, the potential changing future economic and political landscape, and future opportunities that may present themselves.
- *Focusing* on the change drivers in the organization and its external environment that will move the organization to higher levels of achievements.

- *Aligning* the activities at every level in the organization with the mission, vision, strategic goals, and future direction of the organization.
- *Instituting* a review process that keeps employees focused on accountability, but also encourages honest discussions of the current realities facing the organization and its impact on the achievement of objectives.
- *Sharing* best practices organization-wide to accelerate learning, knowledge, and continuous improvement in its processes.
- *Measuring* progress at all levels of the organization with aligned indicators of how the organization is progressing.
- *Developing* the organization's workforce competencies to enhance the achievement of its vision, mission, strategic goals, and future direction.
- *Recruiting and retaining* workers who identify with and have the skills to support the organization's stated mission, vision, culture, and future direction.
- *Building* a learning community that is constantly expanding its knowledge and understanding—leading to more focused and targeted improvement efforts throughout the organization.
- *Teaming* for success rather than commanding it.
- *Enabling and empowering* workers at all levels to take responsible improvement actions.
- *Checking* the organization's readiness on a regular basis using self-assessment instruments and establishing improvement targets to keep on track.
- *Involving* community partners to help deliver necessary and aligned services.
- *Re-tooling* the organization on a regular basis to be better prepared for future challenges.
- *Innovating* new ways to please the organization's customers, exceeding expectations.
- *Striving* constantly for excellence in everything the organization does.

The exemplar backbone community public health organization is the neutral convener of stakeholders and partners in the community and supports the efforts of the Community Chief Health Strategist. The Community Chief Health Strategist and the exemplar backbone community public health organization may indeed be, or become, the same organization (see Figure 9.3).

An initial step towards becoming an exemplar backbone community health organization may be to conduct an organization Exemplar Readiness Assessment. Once the Exemplar Readiness Assessment is completed it will help the organization's leadership understand the gaps that have been uncovered and build an action plan to close those gaps. The improvement plan may span a few years because transforming a public health organization into an exemplar organization may require many changes, training, coaching, and a

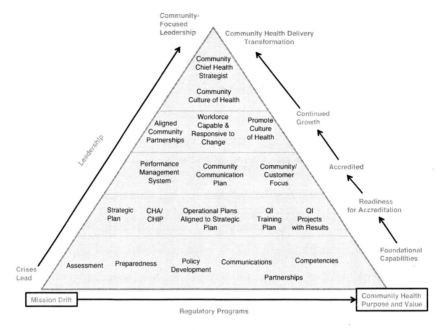

FIGURE 9.3 How an Accredited Health Department Transforms into an Exemplar Community Health Organization over Time

reengineering of their culture and how products and services are identified, developed, and delivered.

The criteria shown in Figure 9.4 can serve as a qualitative assessment or guide for leadership and staff to consider whether or not their public health organization is prepared to successfully become an exemplar. Where criteria appear broad, examples of interpretation are offered.

The Exemplar Readiness Assessment rating scale is (0) Nothing in Place, (1) Beginning Stages, (2) Systematic Approach, and (3) Systematic Approach That Is Fully Deployed. For every score that is recorded the evidence that supports that score should be documented for future reference in the source document column. The maximum score is 57.

The Exemplar Readiness Assessment tool will help identify the areas that are pockets of excellence that can be built upon and areas needing improvement. Lower scores indicate improvements need to be made. Following the assessment, leadership and staff can develop the improvement plan and action steps to be taken for becoming an exemplar public health organization, and an organization that can serve as the backbone public health organization for helping to transform the health of the community.

Criteria	Source Document	Score
1. Commitment exists among leadership for performance, quality improvement (QI), and accountability (leadership could mean health official, Board of Health, QI leadership team, etc.)		
2. Reputation (leadership) for focusing on results		
3. Reputation (leadership) for engaging and/or connecting to community and stakeholders. Educates residents (vis-à-vis Web site/ other); connects to community health, business, and governmental partners; forms strategic alliances, etc.		
4. Key person(s) designated as QI champion, QI leader, and/or network of strategic and innovative intermediaries		
5. Reputation for understanding systems viewpoint (leadership and key personnel)		
6. Poised to move strategically, deliberately, and steadily		
7. Key person(s) designated as QI champion, QI leader and/or network of strategic and innovative intermediaries		
8. Reputation for understanding systems viewpoint (leadership and key personnel)		
9. Poised to move strategically, deliberately and steadily		
10. Deploys strategic plan throughout the organization and requires alignment to strategic goals at all levels		
11. Embraces a performance management system (setting performance standards, measuring performance, evaluating and reporting progress, creating a QI culture)		
12. Embraces self-performance assessment processes (Baldrige, Community Health Assessment, MAPP, National Public Health Performance Standards Program, Performance Management Self-Assessment, state improvement/accreditation assessment, etc.)		
13. History of performance improvement planning and implementation (strategic or performance improvement or community health improvement planning activities, etc.)		
14. History of evaluating and improving programs and services (Examples of embracing QI could be: participating in NACCHO Accreditation Demonstration Sites Initiative, seeking to be a Public Health Accreditation Board (PHAB) Beta Test Site, seeking PHAB Accreditation, conducting PHAB Self-Assessment, implementing QI projects, programs, and/or other improvement oriented strategies, etc.)		
15. Expresses interest in building organizational capacity (innovation, strategy, technology and tools, knowledge and learning, employee satisfaction, physical facility and equipment, etc.)		
16. Personnel reach out locally and nationally and seek to expand expertise (personnel participate in public health national meetings— APHA, ASTHO, ASQ, MLC, NACCHO, NNPHI, NPHPSP, etc.)		
17. Personnel express willingness to build evidence and share knowledge nationally (personnel participate in collecting data to build evidence of improvement, write papers, speak at meetings, leverage/use practice-based research networks, etc.)		
18. Potential exists to work with local and/or regional philanthropic sponsor		
19. Potential exists to identify and invest in innovation and improvement		
Total Score		

FIGURE 9.4 Exemplar Readiness Assessment

Notes

1. Public Health Leadership Forum, *The High Achieving Governmental Health Department in 2020 as the Community Chief Health Strategist*, RESOLVE, Washington, DC, May, 2014.
2. Robert Wood Johnson Foundation, *A New Vision of Health in America*, https://www.cultureofhealth.org/en/about.html, Accessed July 10, 2016.

10

THE OKC STORY—CREATING A CULTURE OF HEALTH, FROM THE INSIDE OUT

Gary Cox

History of Oklahoma City-County Health Department

The public health system within the state of Oklahoma functions as a hybrid of centralized and de-centralized local health departments. Oklahoma City, the largest metropolitan area in the state, along with Tulsa, the second largest metropolitan area in the state, operate independently of the state department of health; the remaining health departments, numbering more than 70 statewide, are operated by the state department of health and focus on the rural communities throughout the state. This is an important distinction as we move forward and consider the challenges and advantages to creating a culture of health in a local health department, and the communities we all support.

In 1954, the Oklahoma City-County Health Department (OCCHD) was created by state statute as an independent public health agency to provide Oklahoma City and Oklahoma County with services needed to protect the health of the community. This distinction as a city-county health department was made in order to recognize the unique health needs present in urban and rural populations. The board of nine professionals from the community governs the Health Department with varied backgrounds as doctors, dentists, educators, lawyers, directors of community-based service organizations, accountants, former state senators and those employed within the healthcare industry. OCCHD employs approximately 260 full-time employees and provides clinic-based services such as Communicable Disease and Maternal and Child Health, as well as population-based services such as Health Promotion, Partnership Development, Epidemiology and Consumer Protection (Sanitation and Restaurant Inspection). The mission of the Oklahoma City-County Health Department is: Working with people, families and communities to protect health, promote health and prevent disease in Oklahoma City and Oklahoma County.

As one of the first nationally accredited local health departments, the OCCHD committed to operational excellence, which meant shifting a workplace culture that would accelerate community health improvement. Change is nearly always preceded by a catalyst, and for OCCHD, this catalyst was a change in leadership at the top level, and among the team surrounding it, in 2009 and the years following. When first assuming leadership of the OCCHD, time was dedicated to observing business operations, understanding who the critical internal players were, and assessing the existing Leadership and program operations staff to determine gaps needing to be filled. Change is not without controversy, and as staff turnover increased, and reorganizations became the norm, the health department that ultimately emerged was leaner, flatter and nimbler; a direct response to board direction and the changing healthcare climate and landscape nationally and locally.

OKC-Specific Challenges

As a state, Oklahoma is not only plagued by poor health in general, but burdened by health inequity and disparity which exists in every imaginable form: rural-urban, education, poverty, access to healthcare, food security, recreational opportunities and crime, to name a few. Oklahoma may in fact be the poster child for "place matters" in regards to health outcomes. In Oklahoma City and County particularly, there are a variety of well-documented health disparities tied directly to zip code of residence, as illustrated in Table 10.1.

The OK County Wellness Score is a measure of how education, poverty, crime and other socioeconomic factors influence health outcomes, and vice versa. The lower scores indicate worse health outcomes and, conversely, the higher the score the better the health outcomes. You will see later in this chapter the actual physical geography of these zip codes, but it is important to note that the low performing zip codes tend to be concentrated in highly urban areas of Oklahoma City, whereas those with higher performing health outcomes tend to be located in more affluent suburbs on the outskirts of the city.

To effectively address these disparities in health outcomes required OCCHD to consider the existing staffing structure and its fit to achieving health improvement. Staff alignment is a particular challenge faced by all health departments, often hampered by funding streams and bureaucratic hierarchies that prevent movement across divisions and departments. This can be further complicated by resistance to innovation, miscommunication and fear that accompanies change to the status quo.

When new Leadership took hold at the OCCHD in 2009, a vision was laid out to the Board of Health (BOH), setting the stage for the planning efforts to come. This vision included a number of commitments and goals for improving health in Oklahoma City and County. Chief among this vision was a commitment to identifying diverse federal, state and local dollars to support policy and

TABLE 10.1 Wellness Score for Select OK County Zip Codes (10 Worst and 10 Best)

Zip Code	Economic Score	Education Score	MCH Score	CVD Disease Score	Cancer Score	Crime Score	Mental Health Score	Overall Score
73108	10.29	9.6	15.17	8.5	2.5	7	10.33	9.62
73111	2.86	20.8	5.83	11.67	5.5	2	2.33	9.79
73129	6.14	12.6	9.67	12	10.5	6.67	9.67	10.82
73117	2.71	23.4	8.4	5.2	5	4.67	1	11.35
73102	11.71	22.4	35.8	1.67	1.5	2	10.5	12.32
73149	9.57	16.6	7	9.25	7.5	14	14	12.82
73109	8.29	11.6	21.17	7.17	18	12.67	10.33	13.52
73105	12.86	30.4	11.17	21.4	20.5	7.33	3.5	14.26
73054	24	25.6	19	6	1.67	28	22.67	14.77
73115	18.57	27.2	8.67	18.5	15.25	18	16.33	14.85
73020	31.43	34.2	28.6	36.67	20.25	40	39	25.73
73120	30.29	36.8	33.17	32.17	33	21.33	28	26.14
73003	34.71	35.6	26	34.17	29.33	35	33.67	26.56
73012	45	22.6	40.67	41.5	48.5	50		26.81
73162	38.57	37	34	30.33	34	24.33	39.33	27
73165	39.29	30	38	31.25	38.5	44	20	27.09
73013	39	33.8	34.17	42	30.5	31	40.67	28.07
73142	38.86	37.2	38.8	32.67	39.5	25	44.5	28.35
73131	34.43	33.4	29.75	43	54	49	35	28.68
73099	35.29	30.6	38	35.5	29.75	29.33	34.67	30.79

environmental changes that focused on creating a culture of health for every citizen. A desire to develop health priorities based on a combination of input from staff, Board, community partners and community residents was clearly delineated, and finally a recognition of the realities facing funding and expectations of public health was articulated. With the recognition of the reality to "do more with less," the vision also included a commitment to leveraging partnerships, investing in quality improvement and becoming an efficient and lean organization from top to bottom.

The first reorganization of the agency occurred in December of 2009, and was followed closely by an agency-wide strategic planning process with external consultants in 2010 facilitating a BOH strategic planning retreat. Of the many actions coming from that initial retreat was the OCCHD commitment to completing a comprehensive community health needs assessment using the MAPP process (Mobilizing for Action through Planning and Partnership). The MAPP process spanned nearly

12 months during which staff at each level were engaged. The MAPP findings informed the development of priorities and goals to recommend to Leadership and the BOH. At its culmination, the strategic plan spanned five years and incorporated four priorities and numerous goals and objectives. Among the priorities was achieving accreditation through operational excellence. The Leadership set in motion a plan to identify redundancies and efficiencies and engage in an intensive internal branding campaign to ensure a clear and consistent message was being received at all levels. The intent of this effort was to remind employees at the agency of the greater mission of public health, and of our responsibility to the communities we serve.

These efforts were met with a number of challenges from agency staff, despite the involvement of all levels in the development of the plan. Employees were used to creating plans, but they were also used to placing them on a shelf and walking away. This time was different. This plan became a living, breathing, dynamic document that Leadership aggressively pursued and expected full support from the agency staff who had been intimately involved in its development. When it became clear that the widespread support was not palpable, the Leadership redoubled efforts on communication and messaging. The internal branding moved into high gear to drive home the message. Not all employees got on board with the direction of the agency, but as you will see in the next few sections, it was hard to argue with the logic, and options for individuals to choose a different path would be made available.

Following the Data

Historically, the OCCHD was limited by a lack of consistent and reliable data to help drive decision-making. In 2009 the Leadership declared this unacceptable and begin to systematically identify opportunities to develop a robust dataset. Beginning with the identification of available data sources, and a commitment to recognize the impact of social determinants of health, the first Oklahoma County Wellness Score emerged in 2010. The Wellness Score represented a zip code level ranking that utilized methodology similar to the large national foundation efforts to rank states and counties according to health outcomes. The first effort of the Wellness Score utilized crude rates and varying data sources, limiting its comparability to future Wellness Scores. The overall Wellness Score was an attempt to determine the extent to which specific social determinants of health impacted health in a zip code. Unequivocally, this demonstrated the impact educational attainment and crime had on health outcomes. It also demonstrated the enormous disparities that existed in Oklahoma County, with variation in Wellness Scores characterized by socioeconomic status and educational attainment. The OCCHD took this data to the community and, in collaboration with locally elected officials, formed the Wellness Now Coalition, then a 25-organization venture led by the Mayor and County Commissioners. The

Wellness Now Coalition undertook the task of developing the first Oklahoma County Health Improvement Plan, which ultimately served as a blueprint for OCCHD in developing strategies and identifying locations for targeted health improvements. These efforts included flooding resources to the most challenged zip code in the County, and building the first regional health and wellness campus in the state. The Northeast Health and Wellness Campus (NE Campus) represents the culmination of several years of planning and building partnerships to meet the community needs and includes an integrated health clinic providing mental health, primary care and public health clinical services in one location (see Figure 10.1). Partnerships with the YWCA provide the community with access to interpersonal violence support, and the Regional Food Bank of Oklahoma provides an on-site food box pantry and a once per month fresh produce mobile pantry that is met with lines all the way around the building. Outside you will find walking trails with fitness stations, a KaBOOM! Playground and community gardens, and the final touches are two professional-grade soccer fields developed with the local minor league soccer team, the OKC Energy. Inside the facility is a commercial-grade demonstration kitchen, training rooms and a large auditorium available to the community at no cost during normal business hours. The NE Campus sits on 54 acres and represents a nearly $16-million investment of public and private partnership in a largely forgotten corner of OKC.

In addition to the capital infrastructure, the OCCHD also embarked on the development of new programs, practices and policies intended to improve the health outcomes of the community. As a successful Community Transformation Grant (CTG) applicant, the Wellness Now Coalition led the way in the development of a city-wide comprehensive health impact assessment that supported implementation of Complete Streets, the effects of which are still seen today in the ongoing construction of sidewalks, trails and pedestrian-friendly communities. Walkability assessments and tobacco-free policies on city land and buildings all expanded and took effect on the heels of the 2010 Wellness Score and the CTG activities. Programming focused in two core areas: our schools and our high-risks communities. In schools, implementation of the Coordinated School Health Model—today the Whole School, Whole Child, Whole Community Model (WSCC)—became a top priority, dispatching teams of nurse case managers, social workers and health-promotion specialists to integrate health and wellness into the school day. Through targeted case finding and case management, Community Health Workers (CHWs) spread out through high-risk communities, helping residents navigate healthcare services and gain access to needed care with a special emphasis on risk factors associated with cardiovascular disease (CVD), the number one killer of OKC-County residents. These efforts did not go unrewarded.

In 2014, the second Wellness Score for Oklahoma County was released, representing a refined methodology, consistent data sources, time periods and age-adjusted rates that will allow comparison to future scores (Figure 10.2).

FIGURE 10.1

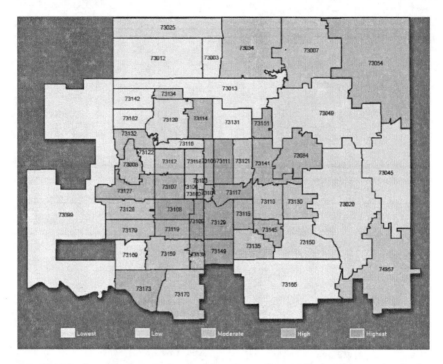

FIGURE 10.2 above illustrates what we hinted at earlier on in the chapter; that is, the highest health burden (darkly shaded zip codes) represents neighborhoods in the urban center of OKC, whereas those with the lowest health burden (lightly shaded) can be found in the suburbs on the far outskirts of the city center.

The 2014 Wellness Score also revealed that the forgotten corner of NE OKC had improved in health outcomes rankings, and no longer occupied the poorest health outcomes zip code in our community. The OCCHD's reliance on data to drive decision-making had served us well, seeing tangible improvements in a number of hard to move health indicators described in Table 10.2.

Whereas there is no doubt the efforts of the OCCHD are not the only factor in the improved health outcomes for NE OKC, and consequently the entire County, it is difficult to deny that the influx of resources to that community had not played a role. However, relying on historic data to drive future decisions left the Leadership at OCCHD unsettled, concerned that we were reacting to events instead of proactively preventing them. The data was consistent; however, it was historic, lagging behind the current calendar year by 1–2 years on average, depending on the data source. This lack of real-time data access presented another challenge to OCCHD in regards to effectively deploying assets and resources to the community in order to *prevent* disease onset, rather than *manage* it once it occurred. Following the release of the 2014 Wellness Score, the OCCHD BOH made an unprecedented decision to invest significant resources into the Public Health Information Technology Infrastructure (PHIT Infrastructure) for the department.

TABLE 10.2 Change in OCCHD Health Indicators

OUTCOME	2010**	2013*	+/-
All Cause (per 100,000 population)	883.8	873.5	-1.2%
Stroke Mortality (per 100,000 population)	43.7	42.0	-3.9%
CVD Mortality (per 100,000 population)	277.0	269.1	-2.9%
All Cancer Mortality (per 100,000 population)	184.9	183.2	-1.0%
Lung Cancer Mortality (per 100,000 population)	54.1	52.2	-3.5%
Breast Cancer Mortality (per 100,000 population)	15.0	14.3	-4.7%
Prostate Cancer Mortality (per 100,000 population)	8.8	8.2	-6.8%
Diabetes Mortality (per 100,000 population)	26.1	27.7	+6.1%
Flu & Pneumonia (per 100,000 population)	19.5	15.2	-22.0%
Homicide (per 100,000 population)	9.2	8.6	-6.5%
Suicide (per 100,000 population)	12.0	16.6	+38.3%

*2010–2012
**2008–2009

The MyHealth Access Network is the foremost Health Information Exchange (HIE) in the state of Oklahoma, with national recognition for its work on population health analytics and infrastructure. In partnership with MyHealth, the OCCHD has invested in the development of a public health electronic record, combining elements of clinical electronic medical records with the needs of case management, referral and tracking capability of social determinants of health, and real-time communication of healthcare utilization and diagnosis. This platform, launched in early 2016, represents a new era for OCCHD in using data to drive decisions, and will, beginning in 2017, provide access to real-time data on incidence and prevalence rates of important risk factors related to chronic disease in our community at the zip code level. This type of data will allow OCCHD to allocate resources to effectively prevent disease onset, enhance appropriate healthcare utilization and, we hope, ultimately provide a tangible opportunity for integrating public health data into traditional clinical decision-making environments.

Business Brains Trapped in a Government Body

Following the data is an expensive proposition, and in order to identify those resources the OCCHD took on the difficult tasks of reducing, regrouping, recruiting, creating a culture of quality and committing to quality.

Reducing and Recruiting

Like many governmental units, over the years the OCCHD had become bloated with programs and staffing that represented mission creep away from the core functions of public health and into arenas better suited for partner agencies, healthcare providers and other community-based organizations. The OCCHD began first with the process of developing a targeted strategic plan, set around priorities identified and developed by the governing (BOH). With direction from the BOH to become as lean and efficient as feasible, the OCCHD included goals in the strategic plan such as implementation of systematic program evaluation, which enabled Leadership to determine programs effectiveness and value. Evaluation revealed a number of inefficiencies agency-wide, resulting in a decision to implement an agency-wide Voluntary Separation Package (VSP). The VSP was specifically geared toward staff who were nearing retirement and/or occupied jobs that could be either regrouped or replaced with improving technology. The OCCHD offered two separate VSPs, one in 2012, and a second one in 2014. In 2012, 39 employees elected to take the VSP, allowing for the elimination of 21.6 FTEs and a two-year net savings of $1,280,418. In 2014, 31 employees elected to take the VSP, eliminating a total of five FTEs and resulting in a two-year net savings of $228,010. Collectively, the two VSP packages resulted in an influx of more than $1.5 million in operational funds put back into the fund for service delivery based on identified gaps and needs of the community. Some of these funds were allocated to expand Community Health Workers into hospitals, clinics and other community settings, others towards increased efforts in our school health programming. Funds were also reallocated to increases in pay for existing employees taking on additional duties and the recruitment of top talent in key areas such as evaluation and workforce development. In 2012, following the first VSP, the OCCHD maintained 75.4 grant-funded FTEs. A commitment was made to diversify funding streams to support additional staff, and as a result in 2016 this number has steadily increased by 14 to 89 FTEs. This increase includes staff to support one large federal grant and one large state grant, each five years in length. In total the OCCHD had 301 FTEs in 2010. Following the second VSP that number was reduced to 246 FTEs. In 2015 an additional 27 FTEs were added, of which 50% (14) were through newly obtained grant funds and associated contracts.

Creating a Culture of Quality

The OCCHD also recognized that maintaining high quality services and outcomes meant investing in quality improvement (QI) not just through traditional training, but by truly integrating it into the daily functions of all employees. Policies and procedures were developed to assure that engagement in QI projects and training is a required element of every employee's job description. This decision demonstrated to agency staff the support from Leadership to engage in the QI Council, participate on project teams and commit to a customer-centric approach. A full-time staff member was provided with intensive training to become the agency QI Consultant and is responsible for leading a team of QI Champions representing program staff from each agency division. The QI Council functions independently of agency Leadership, but has a sponsor from Leadership who serves as a conduit for needs and requests that come from the QI Council. Since 2012, the QI Council has operated with a separate agency budget to support QI projects and training.

Committing to Quality

After making the initial investments to build the infrastructure needed to champion QI throughout the agency, the OCCHD made a commitment to the process by developing a three-year QI Plan that was submitted to both the Leadership Team and the BOH for approval and implementation. The three-year QI Plan outlines expectations of the QI Champions, the Leadership Team and of all agency staff. It commits agency resources to ongoing training for all staff, and annual intensive training for members of the QI Council. Funds are also dedicated to allow members of the QI Council to travel to various quality conferences across the country. The QI Council is the leadership behind the new performance management system that purposefully links QI projects to performance and the strategic plan priorities.

OCCHD's greatest success in regards to achieving a culture of quality is the consistency in which the message was delivered and the commitment to agency staff driving the process. The engagement and buy-in from program-level staff has helped to propel QI from words on a page to an ongoing occurrence in programs. It is not uncommon when a problem arises that we hear statements like, "We should flowchart the process" or "See if the QI Council can come take a look at this." QI tools and processes are seen as resources available to the agency.

Lessons Learned

Changes of this magnitude are not accomplished without lessons to be learned or opportunities to improve. Creating a workplace culture in the public sector that expects business-sector results requires patience and commitment from the top down.

Transparency

No matter how many times you communicate the message, the agency mission or the strategic priorities, there will always be someone who does not hear it. Communicating these using redundant strategies and media were critical to moving the agency from latency to action. Messaging was accomplished through the Executive Director, the Leadership Team and middle management. Forums were formal and informal, written and oral. Organized town halls for all staff became an avenue to voice not only concern and frustration, but excitement and anticipation for what would come with this new vision. The critical theme throughout the process was the requirement for transparent communications.

Everyone Is Not a Good Fit

As difficult as it may be, there are going to be individuals—at all levels—who simply do not share your vision. That is okay, and to be expected. Effective change management is a critical aspect of successfully engaging in the open discourse needed to get the right people on the bus, in the right seat and headed in the right direction. Managing change requires a commitment to transparency and a willingness to provide people the time and environment to change behaviors if the willingness exists. Understanding that people adopt change at varying rates, and need to learn and process change in different ways, is important to ensuring change occurs in a positive and supportive environment. Invest in the book the *Energy Bus* by Jon Gordon and make sure everyone responsible for managing change has read it and discussed it. Developing strategies to recognize the contributions made, and allowing those individuals an opportunity to step away from the agency, are critical in reducing the barriers to successfully cultivating a culture of quality within your organization. Negativity breeds negativity, and there is a sincere need for leaders to recognize those individuals who are detrimental to the organization's success. As you consider creating a culture of quality in your organization, it is important to identify key champions at multiple levels, vertically and horizontally, across your agency. These individuals not only serve as cheerleaders for the culture shift, but they also have the ability to hold their peers accountable in a way that the chain of command cannot. Your champions will help keep everyone "honest" about the process, and encourage those who are not willing or able to share the vision to seek better employment fits.

Quality Improvement Is Not Quality Assurance

Do not confuse the message. Quality improvement is an agency's commitment to examining processes and systems to assure they are producing the intended results. It is not reactionary as problems arise, but anticipatory, constantly reviewing activities to determine if they are the most efficient and effective way to meet the needs of the communities we serve. If quality improvement is not appropriately introduced to your agency, you run the risk of employees feeling as though they are not trusted, or worse, not competent to do the job at hand. Reassuring employees that QI is not about catching the individual doing something wrong, but rather about assessing systematic inefficiencies, is critical. Using projects that strategically demonstrate process issues instead of personnel issues is critical to early buy-in of the benefits of becoming a continuous quality improvement organization.

It Will Take Time

Like most things in public health, if you are hoping to accomplish these activities in one fiscal year, you will be disappointed. Change of this nature must be measured and made incrementally, with careful attention being given to the needs of the employees in your agency, as well as the ability to continue to meet the needs of the community. We made the mistake of undergoing a series of massive organizational overhauls that shifted employees, programs and divisions too quickly. These shifts were made in a span of 18 months, and over that timeframe employee morale took a major nosedive, following which the Leadership Team spent an equal amount of time recovering from. While in hindsight we may not have approached the shifts differently, we might have been more prepared for the shock it would have on employees, and strategies to mitigate that may have been put into place.

Keep Your Governing Board Engaged

Transparency with staff is important, but so is transparent communication with your governing board. One of the things we did really well was anticipating the concerns and complaints of staff during these major reorganizations, and keeping our BOH well apprised of those concerns. Sometimes that meant having hard conversations, sometimes that meant being prepared to shift key members of the team around to accommodate concerns of staff and the BOH, but in the end, we never lost sight of the final goal—improving health for our community, and doing so in an efficient manner.

Final Remarks

Working towards a culture of health in a community begins with taking a hard look at the culture of the local health department (LHD). This is difficult work and not for the faint of heart. It's necessary to take informed risks, to be bold and visionary and to build relationships with staff, partners, the BOH, media, elected officials and the community. The reward is a nimble, efficient, effective LHD which is focused on protecting and improving community health. The prize is a LHD that instills pride and excellence in ourselves and the community.

11

GUIDEBOOK TO HELP SOLVE POPULATION HEALTH ISSUES THROUGH COLLABORATION

York Hospital's Journey to Population Health

Deborah Erickson-Irons

Introduction

In this chapter, we'll share how population health efforts have developed at York Hospital. Whereas our advancement of population health efforts has been in step with public health and value-based health care initiatives in the state of Maine, the question remains regarding how active our role should be in linking these two areas of focus for our organization. Over the past 20 years in the public health arena we have moved from being a Kind Neighbor, to Invested Community Partner, to where we are now—a somewhat reluctant Collaborative Health Strategist. As a Kind Neighbor the hospital has supported local health-related activities such as a grassroots effort to increase access to primary care services. As an Invested Community Partner, York Hospital has helped to lead a comprehensive community health coalition that engages in community disease prevention and health promotion activities. At present, York Hospital finds itself in the role of a Collaborative Health Strategist. It is not a role that we chose for ourselves, but thanks to the Affordable Care Act, we have a Community Health Improvement Action Plan. These roles are not mutually exclusive, nor are they linear in development. Yet, throughout our population health work, the question remains for us, "How active a part should we play in leading community health improvement efforts when our true focus is on patient care initiatives that bring value-based, high quality health care to our patients?"

Background

Starting out as a summer cottage built high upon "Breezy Knoll" in York Village, York Hospital opened its doors on July 22, 1906. It was a 10-room hospital, and among the first patients treated there were diagnoses of typhoid fever, epilepsy, rheumatism, and delirium; with surgical cases including appendectomies, fracture care, carcinoma, endometriosis, and hysterectomies. Today, York Hospital is a thriving 79-bed nonprofit community hospital that offers a full range of health care services including emergency care, birthing and pediatrics, imaging and interventional radiology, surgery and special procedures, oncology, cardiovascular, home care and hospice, physical rehab, laboratory, and pharmacy. Five community sites located throughout the service area offer a menu of services that might include walk-in care, laboratory, pharmacy, and co-location of physician practices, depending on the site. The hospital owns 15 physician practices and employs 120 providers system-wide. We have a clinical affiliation with Massachusetts General Hospital, an hour to our south, which provides us with resources and specialized expertise from a Boston academic medical center. These resources include telemedicine support as well as on-site consulting regarding best practice guidelines, education, and transfer assistance for physicians and staff in Oncology, Critical Care, Emergent Care, Quality Care, Pediatrics, and other York Hospital services.

The community that York Hospital serves includes the nine most southern towns of Maine, a suburban-rural geographic area that is defined by the Atlantic Ocean to our east, New Hampshire to our south and west, and the remaining two-thirds of York County to our north. According to 2014 American Community Survey data, there are a total of 60,377 people living here. The median income by town in our service area ranges from $59,500 to $79,400; the percentage of families living in poverty by town ranges from 8.9% to 1.3%. Although certainly homogenous when compared with many similarly sized geographic areas in the country, socioeconomic differences do exist within our service area—as illustrated by a comparison of the small coastal town of Ogunquit and the inland town of Lebanon. Ogunquit is a town of 1,400 people, only 4.5% of whom live in poverty. The median income is $61,750. A full 40% of the population is 65 years and older, with 19% of these older residents living alone and only 3.5% living in poverty. Lebanon has a population of 6,077, with 10.5% living in poverty. The median income is $62,870. Eleven percent of the Lebanon population is 65 years and older, with nearly 11% of those living in poverty.

Journey to Population Health

For all of its history, York Hospital has invested in community. When many Maine hospitals closed older facilities within the municipality in favor of facilities more visibly located on a highway, York Hospital made the business case for staying within the village of York. The organization has been consistent in its focus on exceptional patient experiences. The facilities are warmly landscaped to create a healing environment that begins before entering. The hospital is known for—of all things—food good enough to warrant a night out, and community members frequently eat out here. Patients, their families, and community members may order from a customized menu that includes lobster rolls. All staff receive consistent messaging from interview to orientation and evaluation regarding the hospital mission, which starts with, *"We are committed to being the best community hospital by providing loving care to our patients and their families. . . ."* Continuous patient-experience surveying has been part of this approach for decades, as has direct access to the hospital President for patient, staff, and community member feedback.

Kind Neighbor

For many years, York Hospital's community health activities could have been characterized as random acts of kindness that reinforced the reputation of the hospital as a good neighbor. School and community events were sponsored. Food and materials were donated to many good local causes. The marketing staff at the hospital budgeted each year for these sponsorships and contributions. Criteria were developed and honed to guide these decisions and eventually the hospital focused on supporting health-related events and causes. Hospital Leaders were encouraged to participate in community organizations. In general the hospital followed the lead of the community and willingly supported others. For a time, employees were paid up to three days per year to volunteer in their communities. We were not the conductor of these health-supporting activities, but preferred to be in the orchestra.

While being a Kind Neighbor, the hospital joined a local committee of organizations led by the Community Action Program, who were interested in assuring access to health care for those with low incomes and no health insurance. The hospital President represented the hospital on this committee. At the time, the agencies had anecdotal evidence of community members who were uninsured or who were covered by the Maine Medicaid program, not having access to care. The group wrote for United Way funding with the hospital as fiscal agent, and a coordinator was hired as an employee of the hospital. A health care access program, Community Health Connection, was established with several social service agencies as entry points to free health care provided by York Hospital and its providers. All participants were defined as "subscribers" and assigned a primary care physician. This program established a model that would be utilized by the hospital in the future regarding community health initiatives, that of the hospital as fiscal agent and employer.

At the state level in the late 1980s to mid-1990s, the Division of Community and Family Health began to support Planned Approaches to Community Health (PATCH) coalitions and Healthy Communities efforts. Locally at York Hospital, staff in the Family Care/Birthing unit noticed that socioeconomically challenged families had trouble accessing helping services. Very few social service agencies had a local presence, with most providing care out of their corporate offices north of the hospital service area, a minimum 45-minute-drive's distance. In addition, there is no state Health and Human Services office in the hospital service area. Nor could helping services for these Southern Maine families be accessed in New Hampshire, which is geographically close but administratively unavailable. The hospital's answer to these problems was to hire a Community Organizer in 1997. This part-time coordinator worked to create the Community Wellness Coalition (CWC), with York Hospital as the fiscal agent and lead partner. The initial coalition was comprised of eight community leaders who oversaw the community coalition funding that was forthcoming from the reorganized state entity, the Community Health Promotion Program in the Maine Division of Community Health.

The CWC established the strong expectation of local community collaboration rather than turf protection. Transparent and inclusive communication was modeled. By design, the CWC brought together purposeful involvement of multiple community sectors to identify community needs, but also to build upon community assets. The York Hospital administrator at the table represented the health care sector. Others represented education, business, law enforcement, youth serving organizations, and social service sectors. CWC members educated themselves in the art and science of developing and maintaining a community coalition. We embraced the concepts of the Healthy Communities movement, based upon the Healthy Cities model. This concept of engaging many community members' perspectives and talents to address complex community problems was adopted.

Invested Community Partner

With the advent of a strong local community coalition, the hospital began to move into the role of Invested Community Partner. In this role, direct and in-kind organizational resources were shared to support this collaborative community work. Until such time when grant funding paid for the Coalition Coordinator, we paid for her salary. Our 501(c)(3) status allowed access to successful requests for state, local, and federal funding. Hospital accounting systems, personnel management, general liability insurance, facilities, and phone and computer system support was given without taking an administrative percentage of the funding from the grants. The hospital representative on the coalition supervised coalition staff.

To develop a shared vision for the future of our community, the coalition held a successful Future Search event that we called "Our Future by Design."

> Future search is a planning meeting that helps people to transform their capability for action very quickly. The meeting is task-focused. It brings together 60 to 80 people in one room or hundreds in parallel rooms.
>
> Future search brings people from all walks of life into the same conversation—those with resources, expertise, formal authority and need. They meet for 16 hours spread across three days. People tell stories about their past, present and desired future. Through dialogue they discover their common ground. Only then do they make concrete action plans.[1]

Priorities were identified and community work groups were established in that Future Search that exist today in some form: a Mental Health Task Force, Physical Activity and Nutrition Committee, Youth Involvement initiatives, and Substance Abuse Prevention, to name a few.

With a defined common vision, the hospital and the CWC wrote a successful request for a small grant to conduct a community health assessment, receiving training from the Maine Community Health Promotion Program. Previously, we had collected data in response to and in support of specific grant requests. These data supported our hunches and what we knew about the story of our communities. Data supplemented the knowledge of the coalition members, but it was not the driver of our efforts at the local level. During this first assessment activity, we chose to assess both the assets and needs of our service area, drawing from John L. McKnight's work on asset mapping for community development.[2] The utilization of socioeconomic, health behavior, disease prevalence, and civic engagement data for planning community health improvement efforts was a true departure from the hospital's Kind Neighbor role and cemented our role as an Invested Community Partner.

Thus, with a shared vision and data gathered, York Hospital's role in community health improvement deepened. However, the successful involvement of many community members following the visioning and needs assessment processes tested York Hospital's role of the Invested Community Partner. With many active participants owning the process of making our community healthier, York Hospital and other coalition members frequently examined the complexities of our role with the CWC. Whereas there were clearly advantages to utilizing the resources of the hospital to support the coalition, how did the hospital remain a coalition partner with equal decision-making authority and not unwittingly exert its influence as an employer and fiscal agent? The answer to this question was one of diligent awareness on the part of coalition members and hospital staff. Oversight of these community health improvement activities remained with the CWC Steering Committee, whereas administrative supervision remained with the hospital.

Our continued and growing investment of coalition infrastructure helped to create opportunities for resources to come to our service area to support priority community health needs. Our community health office grew due to the collaboration with community partners that brought significant funding for youth support and substance abuse prevention. We were prepared to follow the funding stream because we were collaborating with multiple and diverse community partners, we were beginning to understand the use of data, and we had articulated a common vision for a healthy community.

Our position of preparedness led to multi-year federal funding, via the Maine Bureau of Health, to support the activities of a substance abuse prevention coalition, KEYS of Promise (an acronym for the towns of Kittery, Eliot, York, and South Berwick). York Hospital was a primary partner in this coalition and again functioned as fiscal agent and employer.

The most significant resource opportunity that we were prepared to receive came from a new state funding stream—the Fund for a Healthy Maine, Maine's share of the national tobacco settlement. In 2001 Maine created a network of funded Healthy Maine Partnerships (HMPs). These were comprehensive community health coalitions established by a new Maine statute and the Maine Bureau of Health as the backbone of the local public health infrastructure in Maine. Previous to state law Title 22, Maine's public health "system" included two municipal health departments, neither located within the hospital service area, and state epidemiological and health inspection staff dispersed within Department of Health and Human Service offices around the state. The public health law created a system of 27 HMPs as well as nine Public Health Districts in the state, each staffed by one District Public Health Liaison. Healthy Maine Partnerships were tasked with providing many of the Essential Public Health Services at the local level. District Coordinating Councils and a State Coordinating Council were established.

York Hospital staff joined a statewide workgroup of multiple partners to develop the definition of a comprehensive community health coalition. It is statutorily defined as

> a multi-sector coalition that serves a defined local geographic area and is composed of designated organizational representatives and interested community members who share a commitment to improving their communities' health and quality of life and that includes public health in its core mission.

The statewide workgroup established Coalition Core Competencies and Coalition Standards,[3] relying on the growing body of science regarding successful coalition and collaborative community work. These documents helped to bring a higher standard of quality to our local work.

Maine contracted with local HMPs to address chronic disease prevention work including physical activity and nutrition promotion, and tobacco and other substance use prevention. Policy and environmental work was funded, not direct service. As part of this environmental work, state funding to HMPs also supported strengthening and sustaining the coalitions, as well as placing School Health Coordinators within public school districts. York Hospital and coalition partners successfully wrote for these funds, with York Hospital taking the lead for what became the local HMP, the Choose To Be Healthy Coalition (CTBH). The prior coalition, the CWC, continued to work on civic engagement initiatives.

Contracting with the State of Maine brought a new level of sophistication to the hospital's community health work. New staff brought specific expertise in substance abuse prevention and in nutrition. Staffing consisted of a Coalition Director (who also served as the hospital representative to the State and District Public Health Councils), a Chronic Disease Prevention Coordinator, a Substance Abuse Prevention Coordinator, Community Health Specialists, and three School Health Coordinators. Community health work was organized into work plans, with defined completion dates and identified responsible personnel. Evaluation became a part of all community health work.

During this 15-year timeframe, Choose To Be Healthy at York Hospital became the local conduit through which Maine public health funding flowed from many state sources, including the continuation of tobacco settlement funding, but also from cancer, cardiovascular health, and diabetes programs. Funded work included projects to link behavioral health with public health, educate primary care providers about the Patient Centered Medical Home (PCMH) model, identify disparate populations and prioritize them in community health work plans, prevent youth alcohol and drug use, and conduct Rural Active Living Assessments. The newly named Maine Center for Disease Control and Prevention (MeCDC), formerly the Maine Bureau of Health, also provided statewide support in the form of media messaging for our local health promotion efforts, and provided training for our youth leaders responsible for youth-driven initiatives in our service area.

In 2010, Choose To Be Healthy at York Hospital utilized the Community Health Needs Assessment (CHNA) process developed by the National Association of County and City Health Officials to assess health needs in our service area. We worked together with the other HMPs in the York Public Health District and together published a report and Community Health Improvement Plan. The importance of these developments can't be overemphasized in that they set the stage for how York Hospital was to engage in community health work going forward. This process was also the precursor to what is now the Maine District Health Improvement Plan process.

The hospital and CTBH also wrote for and received federal Drug Free Communities funding to support youth substance abuse prevention. Awarded only to coalitions, this additional support encouraged our use of the Strategic Prevention Framework featuring outcomes-based prevention, data-driven decision making and population-level change. What's more, the Drug Free Communities initiative encourages the continuous training of coalition members in the use of the Strategic Prevention Framework as a means of achieving community health goals.

York Hospital's role as an Invested Community Partner was defined by a willingness to remain available to opportunities within an infrastructure maintained via public health funded resources. The hospital could pursue and receive resources from policy mandates, grassroots efforts, or a combination of both. In this role we maintained a model for enhancing the health promotion and disease prevention resources for those living in our service area.

As an Invested Community Partner, York Hospital was extraordinarily supportive of a shared community response to health issues. However, at this point in our journey to population health, our own organization had not defined any community health improvement goals within our internal goals and objectives planning process. Likewise, whereas infrastructure and administrative support was continuously provided, hospital funding for direct expenses was not budgeted.

Successful alignment with state and federal funding priorities wholly funded our community health efforts. It was understood that community health initiatives "lived and died by the grants," and were expected to meet expenses by granted funds. Organizationally, the Community Health Promotion department continued to report to hospital leadership through the Family Care Nursing Leader.

A Collaborative Health Strategist

York Hospital's community health work has entered a new role—that of the Collaborative Health Strategist. Three key changes in hospital involvement in population health can be noted in the Collaborative Health Strategist role. In this role, the hospital is the leader of community health improvement initiatives, the hospital invests direct funding to accomplish them, and the hospital collaborates with partners to establish a continuum of community health prevention activities.

As a Collaborative Health Strategist, the hospital has now taken responsibility for gathering and synthesizing data for the purpose of identifying community health improvement priorities. No longer are these priorities solely generated externally by funding sources. We continue to partner with the Coalition on Health Improvement activities. However, now we also address these priorities with secondary and tertiary prevention efforts within our health care system.

It is unlikely that York Hospital would have intentionally developed into this role. The fact is that multiple external forces brought us here. The passage of the Affordable Care Act required that nonprofit hospitals conduct a Community Health Needs Assessment (CHNA) every three years. In addition, the move toward value-based purchasing and the integration of the PCMH model of care influenced our move to this role. However, our history working in coalition with many partners, our use of data for planning, our experience developing a shared community health future vision, and our developed infrastructure have prepared us for our Collaborative Health Strategist role.

To assess community health needs in the York Hospital service area in both 2013 and 2015, we partnered with Choose To Be Healthy. We based our community health needs assessment process on the NACCHO Mobilizing for Action through Planning and Partnerships model. We invited coalition members, York Hospital Board and staff members, and other key stakeholders to the assessment and planning process. Each CHNA process took us six months.

Priority health issues identified in both the 2013 and 2015 CHNAs are tobacco use, substance abuse, and obesity. These priorities align with grant-funded health improvement activities. York Hospital community health staff members have taken responsibility for leading the work on the Community Health Improvement Plan. Coordination of community health improvement plans with the District Public Health Council and the State Public Health Council health improvement plans has been easily accomplished due to the existing partnerships at the local, district, and state level.

Concurrently, in late 2013 community health staff encouraged the hospital leadership to participate in the Maine State Innovation Model[4] federal grant program. The MaineCare Health Home initiative brought additional value-based reimbursements to the hospital, and the consultation of a statewide quality organization, Maine Quality Counts. York Hospital physician practices began to actively pursue National Commission on Quality Assurance (NCQA) recognition as Patient Centered Medical Homes (PCMH).

The PCMH model brings population health management to health care services. Utilizing searchable electronic medical records, system quality reports, and insurer data, our primary care practices manage the health of their entire patient population. Whereas care is customized for each individual patient, evidence-based clinical decision support is applied to manage chronic disease.

A link is established between PCMH patient care services and community health improvement efforts via the hospital's Community Health Improvement Plan. The following section (Table 11.1) from the York Hospital 2015 Community Health Improvement Plan illustrates this link.

TABLE 11.1 Objective: Reduce Opiate Poisoning (ED Visits) per 100,000 by 10% in Three Years

Strategy	Due Date	Reporting
Continue to partner with Choose To Be Healthy, Sweetser, area school systems and juvenile justice staff to implement the Student Intervention and Reintegration Program (SIRP)	First program offered February 2016; three programs per year through December 2018	CTBH and York Hospital websites
Implement a responsible opiate prescribing policy system-wide	January 2016–March 2016	Policy approved and available in hospital electronic policy manual
Fully implement Screening, Brief Intervention and Referral to Treatment (SBIRT) in all primary care practices	January 2016–December 2018	NCQA PCMH documentation submitted by each primary care practice
Design and implement medication-assisted treatment options, including Suboxone and Vivitrol in the Cottage Program Addiction Treatment Program	January 2016–December 2018	Cottage Program website

Conclusion

In conclusion, York Hospital has been successful in capitalizing on state, federal, and foundation public health funding to the benefit of the health of residents in our service area. Millions of dollars of funding have supported youth prevention work; chronic disease prevention; tobacco-free hospitals, workplaces, and beaches; school health initiatives; trails promotion; and coalition development by working collaboratively with community partners.

When these external public health resources are not available, how do we care for the population's health? As a Collaborative Health Strategist, we specifically target the top three priority health needs identified in our CHNA—in this case tobacco use, obesity prevention, and substance abuse. We are responsible for addressing them on a health care services level. As our community partners take the lead on population health issues with primary prevention work, we will continue to collaborate when resources allow.

In general our experience supports the conclusions of the 2013 Association for Community Health Improvement report, *Trends in Hospital-Based Population Health Infrastructure: Results from an Association for Community Health Improvement and American Hospital Association Survey*: "Thriving in the Affordable Care Act era will require hospitals to transform into organizations that excel at acute patient care alongside population health management."[5]

Citations

1. www.futuresearch.net
2. http://www.abcdinstitute.org/
3. https://www1.maine.gov/dhhs/mecdc/public-health-systems/scc/phwg/documents/icchc-definition-competencies-standards.pdf
4. http://kff.org/medicaid/fact-sheet/the-state-innovation-models-sim-program-an-overview/
5. Association for Community Health Improvement (2013, December). *Trends in hospital-based population health infrastructure: Results from an Association for Community Health Improvement and American Hospital Association survey*. Chicago: Health Research & Educational Trust. Accessed at www.healthycommunities.org

12

POPULATION HEALTH MEASUREMENT

Applying Performance Measurement Concepts in Population Health Settings

Michael A. Stoto

Introduction

Given the broad range of determinants—environmental, social, cultural, behavioral, biological, as well as clinical health services—population health must be seen as the shared responsibility of governmental public health agencies, the health care delivery system, and many other community institutions. To improve population health, communities must establish and nurture partnerships that involve public health agencies, health care providers, and other individuals and organizations. An unprecedented wealth of health data is providing new opportunities to understand and address community level concerns, and the sharing and collaborative use of data and analysis is essential for the alignment of health care, public health, and other efforts. These data, if properly deployed, could form a "shared measurement system" that is one of the five conditions that Kania and Kramer (2011), in their synthesis of effective means of achieving "collective impact," conclude are necessary for large-scale social change. However, despite many calls for better measurement from both the health care delivery sector and public health, there is no consensus on how to measure population health. For example, in their analysis of 12 partnerships between hospitals and public health, Prybil and colleagues (2014) found that even successful partnerships continue to be challenged in developing objectives and metrics and in demonstrating their linkages with the overall measures of population health on which they have chosen to focus.

Thus, the goal of this chapter is to summarize the current status of population health measurement and suggest ways that leaders in public health and the health care system can use data to improve population health. The chapter begins by discussing three major approaches to population health improvement and identifying their population health measurement needs. The next section addresses the development of population health measures, stressing the importance of having the denominator and an appropriate measurement framework, distinguishing between process and outcome measures, and designing measures with a focus on accountability. All of these issues, along with issues of validity and reliability that are beyond the scope of this chapter, are covered in more depth in a longer paper (Stoto 2015) from which this chapter is drawn.

Goals and Objectives of Population Health Measurement

Beyond the Affordable Care Act's (ACA) most prominent provisions to improve access to health care, there are many that aim to improve population health (Stoto 2013), each of which has implications for kinds of population health measures that are needed and how they will be used. This section first looks at two approaches focused on the health care delivery system: "population health management" and Accountable Care Organizations (ACOs). The section then discusses the implications of the requirement that not-for-profit hospitals prepare Community Health Needs Assessments (CHNA) to address the needs of the total population of the geographic areas they serve. Stoto (2015) describes other developments such as value-based purchasing that require new population health measures.

Population Health Management

Many health care delivery systems are shifting from a focus on the treatment of disease to an approach that emphasizes wellness and views acute care as only one component in a delivery system designed to provide value over a patient's lifespan and across targeted populations. The principles and best practices of population health management include data collection, storage, and management; population monitoring and stratification; patient engagement; team-based interventions; and outcomes measurement (Hodach 2014). Populations can be defined in terms of age, income, geography, community, employer, insurance coverage, health status, and by combinations of these factors, but population health management approaches often focus on patients with one or more chronic diseases.

In population health management, data are needed for two purposes. First, patient-level data are needed to identify high-risk patients and to facilitate clinician decision-making at the point of care. This is often accomplished with an integrated electronic medical or health record. Second, population-level performance measures and data analytics are needed to manage the care that the system provides to these groups of patients. To improve the quality of care for the population served, practices are measured at regular intervals and benchmarked against other practices in the network, regional and national practices, and evidence-based standards.

Accountable Care Organizations

One of the most prominent ways that the ACA seeks to improve population health is through changes in the health care delivery system that incentivize providers to take responsibility for population health outcomes. Accountable Care Organizations (ACOs) are groups of health care providers that assume responsibility for the care of a clearly defined population of Medicare beneficiaries. ACOs that succeed in both delivering high-quality care and reducing the cost of that care share in the savings they achieve. Managing this "shared savings" program requires a set of measures of the quality of care provided and the health outcomes achieved in the ACO population (Berwick 2011).

The first set of ACO performance measures was issued by the Centers for Medicare and Medicaid Services in 2011, and includes 33 measures in four domains: patient and caregiver experience, care coordination and patient safety, preventive health, and at-risk populations and frail elderly health (Berwick 2011). This list represents a compromise between the optimal and the feasible. Limitations of current approaches to performance measurement include a focus on individual clinicians and silos of care, inclusion of processes of questionable importance, and burdensome chart reviews and auditing or reliance on out-of-date administrative claims data. The result is a performance measurement system that often provides little useful information to patients or clinicians, reinforces the fragmentation that pervades the U.S. health care system, and reinforces physicians' perception that measurement is a threat. To address these issues, Fisher and Shortell (2010) propose an alternative measurement system based on advances in the science of improvement and progress in health information technology that would build on different levels of ACOs based on different payment models, which would require differing levels of organizational structure.

Community Health Needs Assessments (CHNAs) and Implementation Strategies

Intended to leverage the "community benefits" that hospitals are required to spend (estimated at $12.6 billion in 2008) to improve population health, the ACA requires that non-profit hospitals work with health departments and other community organizations to conduct a Community Health Needs Assessment (CHNA) (Rosenbaum 2013). Parallel developments in public health, including an increasing interest in performance management and evidence-based interventions, as well as the Public Health Accreditation Board (PHAB) and other accreditation requirements calling on health departments to perform community health assessments (CHA), resonate with the new CHNA requirements and increasing focus of the delivery sector on population health. These developments have the potential to leverage and align the strengths and resources of the health care and public health systems as well as many public and private sector agencies and organizations to create healthier communities.

The challenge of managing a shared responsibility for the community's health is that, given the broad range of factors that determine health, no single entity can be held accountable for health outcomes. This calls for two sets of population health measures: (1) measures of population health outcomes for which health care providers, public health agencies, and many other community stakeholders share responsibility; and (2) performance measures capable of holding these same entities accountable for their contributions to population health goals. This same distinction was articulated in *Improving Health in the Community*, where the community health profile is highlighted in Figure 12.1 in the upper "Problem Identification and Prioritization Cycle" in a Community Health Improvement Process (Institute of Medicine 1997). Examples of both types of population health measures are presented in the following section.

Developing Population Health Measures

The world of health care is awash with data, and most people now accept the idea that electronic clinical data and other health records can be used to manage and improve the processes, outcomes, and quality of health care. But although the potential of these data to improve population health is frequently cited by "big data" advocates, the creation of population health measures is neither automatic nor straightforward. To advance the use of these data, this section addresses a number of technical issues that must be considered in the development of population health measures. This discussion begins with the denominator, the most important question to address in specifying population health measures. It then describes the need for a measurement framework, including the careful specification of measures and the target population that clarifies accountability for expected actions. As the old adage goes, "what gets measured, gets done," so measuring the right constructs with valid and reliable indicators is critical.

Population and Denominator

Population health approaches fall along a spectrum based on how that population is defined. At one extreme, the concern is for health outcomes in populations defined by geography. The County Health Rankings (University of Wisconsin Population Health Institute 2014) and most community health assessments conducted by state and local health departments typically take this approach. At the other end of the spectrum are population health management approaches that focus on patients in a health care system with specific chronic diseases. Approaches focusing on accountability for health outcomes in populations defined by health care delivery systems such as ACOs or the Institute for Healthcare Improvement's (IHI) Triple Aim model (Berwick, Nolan, and Whittington 2008) represent intermediate positions along this spectrum. Community-wide approaches to value-based purchasing (Hester, Auerbach, Chang, Magnan, and Monroe 2015) can be seen as a way to broaden the denominator for population health from patients

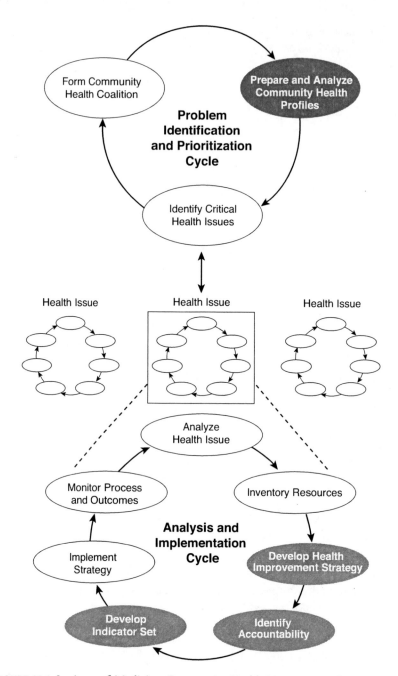

FIGURE 12.1 Institute of Medicine Community Health Improvement Process

Source: Adapted from Institute of Medicine (1997).

defined by their disease status and where they receive care to entire communities. Focusing on implementing the Triple Aim in ACOs, for instance, Hacker and Walker (2013) call for a broader "community health" definition that could improve relationships between clinical-delivery and public health systems and health outcomes for communities.

Measurement systems must begin by determining the denominator that best describes the population whose health is being monitored. Although the ACA and other factors are leading the health care delivery system toward a focus on the communities they serve, different and overlapping definitions of a population currently pose a major challenge. Hospital and ACO service areas generally do not correspond to county or other geopolitical boundaries. Finding ways to bridge these mismatched jurisdictions is one of the primary practical challenges of population health measurement.

The choice of the denominator also has important implications for accountability. For instance, the denominator for the influenza immunization coverage rate could be either (a) patients who have had an encounter with the delivery system between October 1 and March 31, or (b) individuals enrolled with a health plan during that same period. The difference is that the latter denominator holds plans accountable for immunizing all of their members, whereas the former focuses only on those who sought care during the period when immunization is appropriate.

Measurement Framework

Because of the breadth of factors covered by the population health perspective, population health measures require a scientifically valid measurement framework to be maximally useful. This requires that the set of measures be *limited in number*—otherwise users lose sight of the big picture—but yet *comprehensive* enough to cover all of the important issues, including the determinants as well as health outcomes. The individual measures in the set must be *coherent* so that they work together to tell the community's health story, yet *significant* enough to gain policymakers' attention. If the measures cannot be *monitored over time*, they are not very useful for tracking progress so adjustments can be made in population health improvement plans.

Population health measures should also be *disaggregated* to the level of the relevant social unit. For health outcomes, policymakers are interested in addressing disparities among groups defined by race and ethnicity, but also social and economic status, gender, and geography.

In principle, disparities can be identified by comparing the same outcome measures across subpopulations defined by race, ethnicity, socioeconomic status, place of residence, and so on. In practice, however, the ability to calculate disaggregated rates is limited by the availability of racial, ethnic, socioeconomic, and other identifiers in the data, and by small sample sizes. And to the extent that population health measures are needed to drive improvement plans, the data must be disaggregated to reflect the health determinants, from individual health care providers to neighborhood factors.

The primary purpose of a CHNA's community health profile is to identify specific health problems or issues where concerted action by different entities in the community is needed. In other words, the "Problem Identification and Prioritization Cycle" section of Figure 12.1 requires a broad-based measurement framework. Because benchmarking and other comparisons can help to identify priorities, a standard set of measures such as those developed for every county in the United States by the County Health Rankings project is a useful starting point. Based on the latest data for every county in the United States, the County Health Rankings measures collectively describe a community's health in terms of health outcomes (measures of premature death and of quality of life) and four categories of health determinants or factors: Health Behaviors, Clinical Care, Social and Economic Factors, and Physical Environment (University of Wisconsin Population Health Institute 2014).

Communities that have been engaged in health improvement efforts for some time might want to go beyond these basic indicators to develop a community health profile more tailored to ongoing efforts. For example, Healthy Montgomery is a community health improvement process in Montgomery County, Maryland, that includes the county's Department of Health and Human Services, all the hospitals, the Primary Care Coalition of Montgomery County, other health care

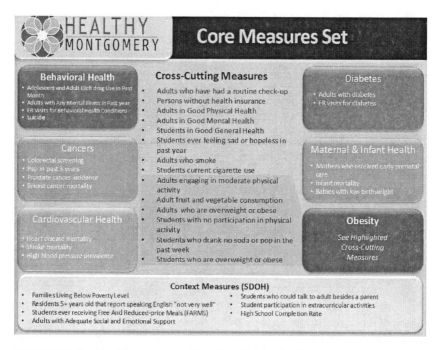

FIGURE 12.2 Healthy Montgomery Core Population Health Measures

Source: Montgomery County Department of Health and Human Services.

providers, government agencies, and community organizations. Six priorities (behavioral health, obesity, diabetes, cardiovascular disease, cancers, and maternal and infant health) have already been identified. To guide ongoing activities, the Healthy Montgomery steering committee recently adopted a set of 37 core measures that include behaviors, health determinants, and health outcomes, and which address the concerns of the hospitals. These measures (Figure 12.2) were also chosen to reflect existing disparities and inequities as well as focus on areas where there is a potential for improvement, e.g. because Montgomery County ranks below the state or national averages, there are factors susceptible to health sector or population-based interventions, and/or the areas identified are matters of community concern (Stoto and Ryan Smith 2015).

Structure, Process, and Outcome Measures

Health care performance measures are often described in terms of Avedis Donabedian's structure-process-outcome triad (Donabedian 1981). *Structure* measures address the factors that affect the context in which care is delivered: organizational characteristics, the physical facility, equipment, and human resources. Structure can be measured in terms of, say, the number of beds in a hospital or the number of physicians per capita in a community or qualitatively.

Process measures describe the activities that make up health care, including diagnosis, treatment, preventive care, and patient education. As long as there is evidence that the process in question improves health outcomes, such measures are regarded as proxies for health outcomes. For instance, because immunization has been shown to be effective, vaccine coverage rates are common process measures.

Outcome measures assess the effects of health care on patients or populations, including changes to health status, behavior, or knowledge as well as patient satisfaction and health-related quality of life. One example is the 30-day mortality rate for adults treated for AMI. This measure is risk-adjusted to account for differences among hospitals in the severity of their patient populations.

The distinction between process and outcome measures is critical to the IHI's Guide to Measuring the Triple Aim (Stiefel and Nolan 2012), which was developed to help health care systems address population health. One of the four basic principles on which the measurement framework is based is the need to distinguish between outcome and process measures, and between population and project measures. Measurement for the Triple Aim can be constructed hierarchically, with top-level population-outcome measures for each dimension of the Triple Aim, and with related outcome and process measures for projects that support each dimension.

The measures based on these principles are summarized in Table 12.1. In particular, the population health component includes measures of health outcomes such as mortality, health and functional status, and healthy life expectancy; disease burden, including the incidence and prevalence of major chronic conditions; and behavioral and physiological factors (Stiefel and Nolan 2012).

TABLE 12.1 Institute for Healthcare Improvement Triple Aim Population Health Measures

Dimension of the IHI Triple Aim	Outcome Measures
Population Health	Health Outcomes: • Mortality: Years of potential life lost; life expectancy; standardized mortality ratio • Health and Functional Status: Single-question assessment or multi-domain assessment • Healthy Life Expectancy: Combines life expectancy and health status into a single measure, reflecting remaining years of life in good health
	Disease Burden: • Incidence (yearly rate of onset, average age of onset) and prevalence of major chronic conditions
	Behavioral and Physiological Factors: • Behavioral factors include smoking, alcohol consumption, physical activity, and diet • Physiological factors include blood pressure, body mass index (BMI), cholesterol, and blood glucose • A composite health risk assessment score
Experience of Care	Standard questions from patient surveys such as the Consumer Assessment of Healthcare Providers and Systems questions on likelihood to recommend to others
	Set of measures based on key dimensions such as the Institute of Medicine's six aims for improvement: safe, effective, timely, efficient, equitable, and patient-centered
Per Capita Cost	Total cost per member of the population per month
	Hospital and emergency department utilization rate and cost

Source: Adapted from Stiefel and Nolan (2012).

Accountability

Given the broad range of factors that determine population health outcomes, the challenge of managing a shared responsibility for the community's health is that no single entity can be held accountable for health outcomes. The roles and responsibilities of different parts of the health system—from governmental public health agencies to schools and hospitals, from transportation networks to local zoning departments, from community-based organizations to local and national businesses—are often not clear. To address this problem, a measurement framework that provides the clear accountability needed to enable decision-makers to understand, monitor, and improve the contributions of various partners in the health system is needed (Institute of Medicine 1997, 2010).

Figure 12.3 and Table 12.2 illustrate this approach in terms of a simplified driver diagram (see Chapter 17, this volume) for a community that has chosen

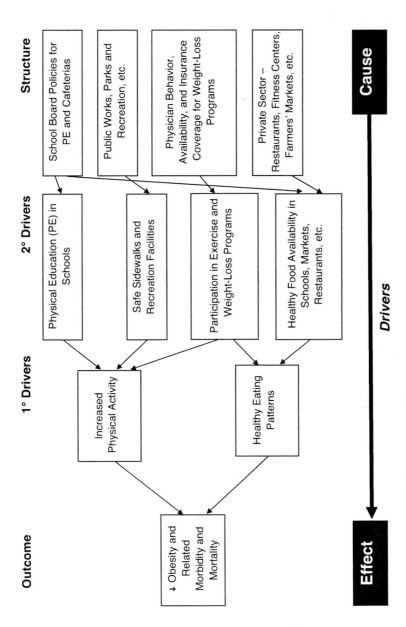

FIGURE 12.3 Simplified Obesity Driver Diagram

TABLE 12.2 Performance Measures Associated with the Obesity Driver Diagram in Figure 12.3. The first three measures reflect the community's shared responsibility, and accountability for the other measures are indicated in italics.

- Obesity and related deaths
- Lack of exercise
- Unhealthy eating patterns
- Counseling by *health care providers*
- Availability of weight loss and fitness / physical activity programs (*hospitals and local organizations*)
- Health plan coverage for weight loss programs; employer-sponsored fitness programs (*health plans and employers*)
- Obesity prevention curricula, physical education, and healthy eating choices in schools (*school board*)
- Local promotion of healthy eating and increased physical activity through fairs, marathons, farmers' markets, etc. (*shopkeepers, storeowners, restaurants, fitness gyms, etc.*)
- Safe sidewalks, recreation facilities, etc. (*public works, recreation*)

to address obesity. The population health goal is to reduce both obesity and related morbidity and mortality, and the primary drivers to achieve this are to increase physical activity and improve eating patterns. The first three performance measures summarize the community's shared responsibility towards meeting these goals: obesity and related deaths, physical activity, and dietary patterns. However, a community's successful efforts to address the secondary drivers and structural impediments might not be reflected in these outcome measures for years. And if progress is not being made in these measures, it is difficult to diagnose the problem.

The other performance measures in Table 12.2 address this by focusing on specific activities addressing the secondary drivers and structural impediments, identifying (*in italics*) which entity has agreed to address each driver and impediment. This approach can help a community align strategies, interventions, policies, and processes; reveal the levels of effort and achievement needed to reach shared objectives; monitor their execution; hold implementing agencies or stakeholders accountable for execution; and help identify necessary revisions to the action plan.

Conclusions

Given the broad range of determinants, population health is the shared responsibility of health care providers, governmental public health agencies, and many other community institutions. Communities must establish and nurture broad-based partnerships that involve many individuals and organizations, some of which do not see health as their primary mission. A shared measurement system incorporating the appropriate population health measures can help to manage this shared responsibility.

To achieve the potential of the population health perspective, public health officials, health system leaders, and others must work together to develop sets of population health measures that are suitable for different purposes yet are aligned so that together they can help to improve a community's health. This begins with clearly defining the purpose of a set of measures, distinguishing between outcomes for which all share responsibility and actions to improve health for which the health care sector, public health agencies, and others should be held accountable.

Depending on the purpose of the analysis, then, measurement systems should clearly specify what to measure—in particular the population served (the denominator), what the critical health dimensions are in a measurement framework, and how the measures can be used to ensure accountability. Building on a clear understanding of the purpose and dimensions of population health that must be measured, developers can then choose specific measures using existing data or developing new data sources if necessary, with established validity, reliability, and other scientific characteristics. Rather than indiscriminately choosing among the proliferating data streams, this systematic approach to measure development can yield measurement systems that are more appropriate and useful for improving population health.

References

Berwick, D.M. 2011. Making Good on ACOs' Promise—The Final Rule for the Medicare Shared Savings Program. *New England Journal of Medicine* 365:1753–1756.

Berwick, D.M., Nolan, T.W., and Whittington, J. 2008. The Triple Aim: Care, Health, and Cost. *Health Affairs* 27:759–769.

Donabedian, A.1981. *The Definition of Quality and Approaches of Its Assessment. Volume 1: Explorations in Quality Assessment and Monitoring.* Ann Arbor, MI: Health Administration Press.

Fisher, E.S. and Shortell, S.M. 2010. Accountable Care Organizations: Accountable for What, to Whom, and How. *The Journal of the American Medical Association* 304:1715–1716.

Hacker, K. and Walker, D.K. 2013. Achieving Population Health in Accountable Care Organizations. *American Journal of Public Health* 103:1163–1167.

Hester, J.A., Auerbach, J., Chang, D.I., Magnan, S., and Monroe, J. 2015. Opportunity Knocks again for Population Health: Round Two in State Innovation Models. Discussion Paper, Institute of Medicine Roundtable on Population Health Improvement. http://nam.edu/perspectives-2015-opportunity-knocks-again-for-population-health-round-two-in-state-innovation-models/ (accessed January 1, 2016).

Hodach, R., ed. 2014. Population Health Management: A Roadmap for Provider-Based Automation in a New Era of Healthcare. Institute for Health Technology Transformation. http://ihealthtran.com/pdf/PHMReport.pdf (accessed January 1, 2016).

Institute of Medicine. 1997. *Improving Health in the Community: A Role for Performance Monitoring.* Washington, DC: National Academy Press.

Institute of Medicine. 2010. *For the Public's Health: The Role of Measurement in Action and Accountability.* Washington, DC: National Academy Press.

Kania, J. and Kramer, M. 2011. Collective Impact. *Stanford Social Innovation Review* 9(1):36–41.

Prybil, L., Scutchfield, F.D., Killian, R., et al. 2014. Improving Community Health through Hospital-Public Health Collaboration. Commonwealth Center for Governance Studies. bit.ly/HospitalPublicHealthPartnerships (accessed January 1, 2016).

Rosenbaum, S. 2013. Principles to Consider for the Implementation of a Community Health Needs Assessment. The George Washington University. http://nnphi.org/CMSuploads/PrinciplesToConsiderForTheImplementationOfACHNAProcess_GWU_20130604.pdf (accessed January 1, 2016).

Stiefel, M. and Nolan, K. 2012. A Guide to Measuring the Triple Aim: Population Health, Experience of Care and Per Capita Cost. White Paper, Institute for Healthcare Improvement. http://www.ihi.org/resources/Pages/IHIWhitePapers/AGuideto MeasuringTripleAim.aspx (accessed January 1, 2016).

Stoto, M.A. 2013. Population Health in the Affordable Care Act Era. AcademyHealth. http://www.academyhealth.org/files/AH2013pophealth.pdf (accessed January 1, 2016).

Stoto, M.A. 2015. Population Health Measurement: Applying Performance Measurement Concepts in Population Health Settings. *eGEMs* 2(4):1132. http://repository.academyhealth.org/egems/vol2/iss4/6

Stoto, M.A. and Ryan Smith, C. 2015. Community Health Needs Assessments? Aligning the Interests of Public Health and the Health Care Delivery System to Improve Population Health. Discussion Paper, Institute of Medicine Roundtable on Population Health Improvement. http://nam.edu/perspectives-2015-community-health-needs-assessments-aligning-the-interests-of-public-health-and-the-health-care-delivery-system-to-improve-population-health/ (accessed January 1, 2016).

University of Wisconsin Population Health Institute. 2014. County Health Rankings & Roadmaps. http://www.countyhealthrankings.org/ (accessed January 1, 2016).

13

PUBLIC HEALTH'S EVOLVING ROLE IN EFFECTING LARGE-SCALE SOCIAL CHANGE

Thomas Schlenker and Rudy Ruiz

Public health has a long and, some might say, glorious history of bringing about large-scale social change. Human life expectancy has doubled over the last 150 years in large part due to public health.(1) Longer span of life certainly is the result of multiple factors, including advances in technology and increased prosperity, but a key driver has been the brilliant thinking and action of public health pioneers like Ignaz Semmelweis, who identified iatrogenic infection as a cause of childbirth-associated maternal death and fought to reform hospital practices; and John Snow, who demonstrated that cholera in London was transmitted by sewage-contaminated drinking water and fought to establish modern sewer and water systems. The construction of public health systems to vaccinate those in need, in an effective time, place and manner, brought to full fruition the revolutionary science invented by Jenner, Pasteur, Salk and Sabin. Identification of vitamin and mineral deficiencies led to fortification of salt with iodine, milk with vitamin D and drinking water with fluoride, benefiting millions. And in the late twentieth century, public health led the struggle to reduce deaths by motor vehicle injury and smoking-related cancers and lung disease.(2)

Historically, there are many examples of public health making large-scale social changes by increasing life span and life quality. But are we still capable of doing so? And is our role taking on new nuances?

Clearly, for the less prosperous, underdeveloped portions of the world, where the average life span is still that of mid-nineteenth-century cholera-ravaged England, we can and we must. But in developed countries like the United States, where considerable infrastructure has long been in place, many of the most important battles have already been won. Today, public health systems exist primarily to preserve the enviable, although not always fully appreciated, status quo that most of us enjoy. One might logically ask: "Is large-scale social change still needed and/or possible in the United States. If so, can public health help achieve it? And what does it mean for our changing role within society and government?"

In fact, the need for continued large-scale social change is urgent and dramatically demonstrated by the marked variation of life expectancy within the United States. According to the Robert Wood Johnson Foundation's web display "Life Expectancy Maps by City," (3) average survival by zip code varies by 13 years in Minneapolis/St. Paul and by 14 years in Kansas City, Missouri. In progressive and highly educated Madison, Wisconsin, black infants die during the first year of life at rates three times those of whites.(4) And in San Antonio, Texas, where 18% of adults have type II diabetes, Hispanics are 23% more likely than whites to be hospitalized with diabetes and 46% more likely to suffer amputations. Some San Antonio zip codes register over 100 diabetic amputations per year.

Health disparities based on race and ethnicity exist not only in specific locations, but across the nation. These may be due to higher levels of poverty, lower educational attainment, cultural barriers, and disproportionate marketing targeted by corporations to Hispanics and African Americans. Regardless of causality, the harsh reality is that these health disparities are life-threatening obstacles to delivering on the American promise of equal opportunity for all. For when a child is sick, he cannot attend school. When a parent becomes hobbled by chronic disease, she cannot earn a living and provide for her family. These public health dynamics play a critical role in the perpetuation of the cycle of poverty and are tied systemically to the broader economic and social issues of income inequality, educational attainment, crime and incarceration rates.

Future large-scale social changes may translate into increased overall life expectancy, currently 80 years in the United States, but that is not our most urgent priority. Health equity that measurably decreases disparities in life expectancy is the prime challenge of our day. But, the question remains, what is public health truly capable of in a society beset by polarization, political gridlock and intensely defended extremes of income and wealth. To suggest a realistic answer to the question, we will review, from the practitioner's point of view, selected large-scale public health successes, as well as failures, in recent U.S. history, while attempting to identify effective strategies. In the process, we inevitably explore the evolving role of public health as an instrument not only for large-scale public wellbeing but also for the pursuit of social justice.

Immunization has saved and improved millions of lives, resulting in worldwide, large-scale social change. In the United States, immunization is considered by the Centers for Disease Control and Prevention (CDC) to be the greatest public health achievement of the twentieth century. Serious diseases of childhood like polio, diphtheria, rubella, measles, H. flu meningitis and hepatitis B have been reduced close to zero. Yet continued progress is not assured. Complacency, due to the generally low level of visible threat, and misguided but vigorous opposition to vaccines, require that vaccination systems be continuously improved and occasionally reconstructed.

Smallpox was conquered in 1978 with complete, worldwide eradication achieved through a decade-long collaborative and coordinated international campaign of vaccination and outbreak response that transcended all cultural, economic and political barriers of the time. In contrast, the more recent campaign for worldwide eradication of polio has been repeatedly thwarted by wars, social unrest and cynical anti-science ideologues who manipulate populations for geo-political ends. Even in relatively stable and well-educated United States, barriers to continued progress in immunizations have arisen.

Twenty-five years ago, the resurgence of measles, following its near elimina-tion, came as a shock to U.S. medical and public health authorities. During 1989–1991, over 50,000 cases, mostly among pre-school age children, rocked urban America.(5) Thousands were hospitalized and over 1,400, mostly children, died. The fact that a majority of those infected had not been vaccinated dem-onstrated failure not of the vaccine but of a system that failed to vaccinate at-risk, urban minority children and the terrible policy decision of the Reagan admin-istration to discontinue vaccination surveillance. Fortunately, physicians and public health practitioners, led by the CDC, responded to this national tragedy and embarrassment by diligently, over the next decade, rebuilding and rejuvenating the U.S. vaccination system.

The struggle, however, continues. As epidemics fade from memory, strident voices of anti-vaccinationist celebrities, politicians and flamboyant practitioners of alternative medicine seek to roll back the clock. Pseudo-scientists like Dr. Andrew Wakefield of London, who was disgraced and lost his medical license for pub-lishing fraudulent research linking MMR vaccine with autism, and other media-savvy anti-vaccinationists, have frightened and confused many parents. Holding the misinformation at bay are thousands of dedicated community physicians, innovative scientist-advocates like Dr. Paul Offit (6), journalists like Seth Mnookin (7) and a few principled politicians like California governor Jerry Brown who, during the summer of 2015, in the face of shrill opposition, signed into law SB277 eliminating the much-abused personal and religious exemptions to school-required vaccination.

In Texas, in-depth research on the varied obstacles to achieving full immuniza-tion of children within diverse segments of the population led to the creation of a highly nuanced, multiculturally targeted behavior change campaign. Spearheaded by the Texas Department of State Health Services, with the collaboration of numerous municipal public health systems and physician associations, the campaign—titled "Vaccines: Build Your Child's Health"—set out to increase the childhood immunization rate. With three different prongs of culturally relevant messaging and imagery as well as a health provider initiative, the campaign connected in distinctively nuanced ways with African American, Hispanic and affluent White parents and their pediatricians and family physicians. By maximizing the relevance of the messaging to address each particular audience's concerns, obstacles and emotional triggers, and by taking into account potential cultural influences which could be brought to bear on increasing motivation to vaccinate, the campaign gained traction. Due to its unique focus on all three demographics, the Texas Health Commissioner commended the creators of the campaign, multicultural advocacy marketing agency Interlex Communications, for "[the] development of a new statewide immunization campaign that in particular looks at the distinct cultures of each target audience." In 2009 Texas was named the nation's "Most Improved State in Childhood Immunizations" by the CDC. Through the campaign, the childhood immunization rates increased by 13.5 percentage points, from 69% to 82.5% from 2004 to 2008, based on National Immunization Survey data of children 19 through 35 months of age.(8)

Examples such as these serve as evidence that collaborative and inclusive multisectoral and multicultural public health initiatives, such as ongoing efforts to immunize against childhood diseases in the United States, have clearly produced large-scale social change directly benefiting all strata of society. But victory is not complete (note the poor acceptance of the HPV cervical cancer vaccine and continued prevalence of whooping cough) and future progress might be harder to come by. For an example of a more complete and permanent transformation, the case of childhood lead poisoning is instructive.

The struggle to eliminate childhood lead poisoning in the United States demonstrates effective collaboration among entities dedicated to public health, environmental protection and safe housing; the U.S. presidency; state and local governments; academic and community medicine; industry, real estate and advocacy organizations; and the U.S. legal system. Over a period of just 30 years the prevalence of childhood lead poisoning has been dramatically reduced. From 1977 to 2007 the proportion of U.S. children with blood lead levels above 10 micrograms/dL was reduced from 88% to 0.8%, whereas the national average of lead in blood dropped from 15 micrograms/dL to 1.3.(9)

In the 1970s and 1980s, researchers identified the widespread nature of childhood lead poisoning and the serious, permanent deficits inflicted by even "low level" poisoning. The CDC responded by leading national, state and local public health in a multi-year, multifaceted effort, working community by community, educating and mobilizing practitioners, the public, local governments, landlords and rehabbers.(10) President George H. W. Bush, on leaving office, ensured that substantial funding was available to reduce the stock of lead-contaminated housing through the Residential Lead-Based Paint Hazard Reduction Act of 1992 (Title X).

Forward thinkers worked hard to educate and gain the cooperation of traditionalists overly focused on the dramatic but rare cases of severely poisoned children presenting with seizures, coma and paint chips in their stomachs. Traditionalists were often reluctant to accept that many children living in lead-contaminated housing who were not overtly symptomatic were nonetheless poisoned, suffering loss of IQ and a range of serious learning and social disabilities. But most came to accept the uncomfortable facts and worked together to overcome the dysfunctional divide between medicine and public health to resolve the problem. An organized and persistent approach produced close and mutually supportive working relationships in which community physicians identified most of the affected children through office-based screening, while local public health responded with mass education, household clean-up and abatement of lead hazards. (11, 12)

Much of the 1990s was spent addressing local housing markets by working with city zoning officials, landlords, rehabbers, lawyers and citizens groups. Local public health took the lead in bringing the often conflicting constituencies to the table. How to abate household lead paint hazards in ways that were both safe for the inhabitants and affordable was the primary challenge. The CDC's in-house expertise and external advisory committees, practicing physicians, advocacy groups like the Center for Lead-Safe Housing and local grassroots activists, especially those with roots in the African American and Hispanic communities, managed to apply the right measures of education and political pressure to sustain the struggle and ultimately achieve large-scale social change.

However, in some areas of great need, public health has failed. Violence in the U.S. continues at high levels while gun violence research at the CDC has been effectively defunded since 1996. Mental illness prevention has rarely gone beyond the concept phase. A good example of large-scale social change in the wrong direction, driven by profit-seeking objectives and lifestyle trends which do not take into account public health consequences, is the increasing prevalence of obesity and diabetes. Obesity rates in the United States have doubled, while the number of Americans living with type II diabetes has quadrupled. Currently, 37% of U.S. adults and 17% of youth are obese. Adults with type II diabetes have skyrocketed from 5.5 million in 1980 to 22 million in 2014.(13, 14) It is predicted, if these trends continue, that U.S. life expectancy may be reduced by 2–5 years by midcentury.(15) Many have tried to reverse these trends. Clinical physicians have always advised their patients on nutrition and exercise. Exercise and active living have been promoted by Jane Fonda and her workout videos and Michelle Obama and her "Let's Move" campaign. Healthy eating is marketed through food pyramids, MyPlate promotions and billion-dollar federal food programs like WIC and SNAP. Nevertheless, fast food and soft drink marketing, consciously directed toward racial/ethnic minorities, youth and the poorly educated, dominates. As a result, stark health disparities can be seen in the higher prevalence of chronic diseases: National obesity rates among adult African Americans, Hispanics and Whites are 47.8%, 42.5% and 32.6% respectively (16), while 9.5% of African Americans, and 8.7% of Hispanics (9.7% Hispanics of Mexican heritage) are diagnosed with diabetes compared to 5.8% of whites.(17) Reversing the obesity/diabetes trends and disparities will likely require a full social-ecological model of social change using individual, relationship, community and societal strategies.(18) And given the disproportionate impact of this epidemic on communities of color, the multicultural approach should also be considered as an effective strategy to align with the goal of eliminating health disparities severely affecting minority groups.

Some signs of hope derive from the 2010–2012 investment of approximately $400 million (part of the American Reinvestment and Recovery Act called "Communities Putting Prevention to Work" (CPPW)) to prevent obesity in 50 communities. Using CPPW-funded school-based interventions in policies, systems and the physical environment, King County, Washington, achieved significant decreases in youth obesity.(19) In San Antonio, Texas, more broadly directed CPPW investments coincided with a significant decrease in adult obesity associated with a parallel decline in daily soda consumption. Within San Antonio, which is comprised of a majority Hispanic population, bilingual and multiculturally relevant branding and communications efforts were also key to engaging diverse audiences and introducing them to new activities and healthy behaviors in culturally relevant manners. It has been estimated that, if improvements in the 50 CPPW communities are sustained, 14,000 deaths and $2.4 billion in health care costs will be avoided by 2020.(20) However, because the CPPW funding was not continued beyond 2012, sustained improvement may not obtain.

Nationally, a new opportunity presents in the realization that obesity rates have increased in tight association with increased sugar in the U.S. diet, now almost 80 pounds per person per year, with half in the form of soda and other sugar-added beverages. Public health entities have begun to militate against excess soda consumption as the logical first step to combat obesity, as have private non-profits like the Center for Science in the Public Interest (21) and Action for Healthy Food.(22) Philanthropists, academics, journalists and cause-based, socially conscientious corporations like Interlex (23) have also taken up the cause. The hope is that this single-issue focus will prove more effective than the shotgun approach. Although the response by the soft drink industry has been—and will continue to be—ferocious, last century's hard-fought war against Big Tobacco and Mexico's recent success with a national soda tax show the power of a single-issue focus to crystallize an idea in order to coalesce and drive an effective movement with broader ramifications. Furthermore, advocates of taxes on sugary drinks in the United States are proposing measures which would specifically direct tax revenues towards prevention efforts targeting the communities most in need due to their higher rates of obesity, diabetes and related chronic disease. This type of approach illuminates the evolving role of public health as an emerging force for social justice in its pursuit of health equity.

Successfully addressing these complex social issues at the local level often requires broad cross-sector coordination. "Collective Impact" is a model that effectively coordinates among individual organizations that have agreed to specific, quantifiable goals by aligning their efforts around common agendas and common measures.(24) In the case of public health's work in achieving the large-scale social change of health equity, this approach embraces the concept that what is good for the few is also best for the whole. There is a growing realization through these kinds of consensus-building initiatives that popular political priorities like economic development cannot be sustained without a healthier workforce. And in highly diverse communities, this interdependence between economic progress and health equity is a crucial motivator to maximizing long-term collaboration driven by a classic American vision which utilizes self-interest to motivate disparate forces to work together towards the common good. In San Antonio, a wide range of organizational stakeholders are using Collective Impact methods to turn back the tide of diabetes, a local epidemic threatening to undermine an otherwise bright future for this burgeoning metropolis. Collective Impact is complemented by a more grassroots, bottom-up approach, developed by John McKnight and Jody Kretzmann, called Asset Based Community Development (ABCD), which is a method to organize communities around issues that matter to them.(25)

Exacerbating the struggle against obesity and diabetes are depression, hopelessness and other mental health conditions. Mental illness is also a mighty contributor to alcohol and drug abuse, homicide and suicide. These taken together are driving down life expectancy even of middle-aged whites.(26) Because individual treatment of the many millions of mentally ill is probably beyond the scope of any health care system, it is up to public health to devise effective approaches to population-based, mental illness prevention. "Cure Violence" is a good example of a population-based program that effectively prevents homicides and assaults by engaging and redirecting the violence prone while simultaneously building neighborhood social capital.(27) Bringing to scale population-based mental illness prevention programs similar in grassroots approach to Cure Violence is an opportunity for public health to have substantial impact.

Finally, pushing public health to the forefront in our nation's efforts for social progress is the persistent failure of the U.S. health care system to rein in costs, improve patient experience and outcomes, and measurably improve population health: the famous "Triple Aim."(28) Health care in the United States continues to be both wasteful and unsustainable in that we spend twice as much per capita as other nations (health care spending consumes 17% of U.S. GNP, predicted soon to be 20%), and still lag seriously behind in life expectancy, infant mortality, the burden of chronic disease and health equity. Recent reforms, such as the Affordable Care Act (Obamacare) and the shift of substantial Medicaid funding away from patient care and into prevention, may be game changers by creating the necessary financial incentives for the large-scale social changes needed.(29) As we continue to tackle these enormous challenges, we must work together across sectors—utilizing the types of proven approaches discussed herein—and acknowledge the evolving role of public health as a champion for social justice. To build on its widespread success in extending average life span and quality of life, public health now has an important role to play in major social change to achieve health equity. Just as governmental intervention has been continuously required through the legal system to address civil rights injustices, it is also required from a public health perspective to enable low-income and minority populations to achieve the healthier outcomes crucial to making our society a place of equal opportunity for all, and empower our economy to sustain growth and prosperity driven by an increasingly diverse workforce.

References

1. OECD (Organization for Economic Co-Operation and Development). 2010. Health Care Systems: Getting More Value for Money. http://www.oecd.org/eco/growth/46508904.pdf
2. CDC. Ten Great Public Health Achievements—United States, 1900–1999. *Morbidity and Mortality Weekly Report* 1999;48:241–243.
3. Robert Wood Johnson Foundation. City Maps.rwjf.org
4. Schlenker, T.L. and Ndiaye, M. Apparent Disappearance of Black-White Infant Mortality Gap—Dane County, Wisconsin, 1990–2007. *Morbidity and Mortality Weekly Report* 2009;58:581–585.
5. Schlenker, T.L., Bain, C., Baughman, A.L., and Hadler, S.C. Measles Herd Immunity. *The Journal of the American Medical Association* 1992;267:823–826.
6. Offit, P.A. *Deadly Choices—How the Anti-Vaccine Movement Threatens Us All.* New York: Basic Books, 2011.
7. Mnookin, S. *The Panic Virus—The True Story Behind the Vaccine-Autism Controversy.* New York: Simon and Schuster, 2011.
8. http://www.dshs.state.tx.us/immunize/CDC_award.shtm
9. CDC. Blood Lead Levels in Children Aged 1–5 Years. *Morbidity and Mortality Weekly Report* 2013;62(13):245–248.
10. CDC. *Preventing Lead Poisoning in Young Children.* Washington, DC: US Department of Health and Human Services, 1991.
11. Schlenker, T.L. Prevention of Childhood Lead Poisoning, Chapter in Pueschel, S.M., Linakis, J.G., and Anderson, A.C. *Lead Poisoning in Childhood.* Baltimore, MD: Paul H. Brookes Publishing, 1996.
12. Schlenker, T.L. Collaborating with Private Sector Physicians: The Example of Childhood Lead Poisoning Prevention. *Journal of Public Health Management and Practice* 1999;5(6):35–40.
13. Ogden, C.L., Carroll, M.D., Kit, B.K., and Flegal, K.M. Prevalence of Childhood and Adult Obesity in the United States, 2011–2013. *The Journal of the American Medical Association* 2014;311(8):806–814.
14. http://www.cdc.gov/diabetes/statistics/prev/national/figpersons.htm
15. Ludwig, D.S. Childhood Obesity—The Shape of Things to Come. *New England Journal of Medicine* 2007;357:2325–2327.
16. Trust for America's Health and Robert Wood Johnson Foundation. Racial and Ethnic Disparities in Obesity—An In-Depth Look at the Inequities That Con to Higher Obesity Rates in Black and Latino Communities 2004–2014. Stateofobesity.org/disparities
17. http://www.cdc.gov/diabetes/statistics/prev/national/figbyrace.htm
18. http://www.healthypeople.gov/2020/about/foundation-health-measures/Determinants-of-Health

19. Kern, E., Chan, N.L., Fleming, D.W., and Krieger, J.W. Declines in Obesity Prevalence Associated with Prevention Initiative—King County, Washington, 2012. *Morbidity and Mortality Weekly Report* 2014;63(7):155–157.
20. http://www.cdc.gov/nccdphp/dch/programs/communitiesputtingpreventiontowork/pdf/community-based-interventions-executive-brief-update
21. http://www.cspinet.org
22. http://www.actionforhealthyfood.org
23. http://www.nterlexusa.com
24. Collective Impact. http://www.ssir.org/articles/entry/collective-impact
25. The Basic Manual—Building Communities from the Inside Out. http://www.abcdinstitute.org
26. Case, A. and Deaton, A. Rising morbidity and mortality in midlife among white non-Hispanic Americans in the 21st century. PNAS 2015:1518393112v1–201518393.
27. Cureviolence.org
28. IHI Triple Aim Initiative. http://www.ihi.org
29. Schlenker, T.L. *Paying for Population Health—A Texas Innovation*. Institute of Medicine, Washington, DC. http://iom.edu/Global/Perspectives?2014/Texasinnovation

14

PUBLIC HEALTH 3.0

Time for an Upgrade

*Patrick W. O'Carroll, Karen B. DeSalvo,
Denise Koo, John Auerbach, and
Judith A. Monroe*

The United States has made enormous progress during the past century in improving the health of its citizens, through aggressive public health action and significant investments in biomedical research and healthcare. However, despite nearly $3.0 trillion in annual healthcare spending—more than twice as much as any other country in the world—the United States ranks 27th in the world in life expectancy, and relatively low in many other measures of health and well-being.[1] Worse yet, trends in increased life expectancy and quality of life in the United States have plateaued.[2] For the poor in this country, life expectancy is actually decreasing.[3]

The Affordable Care Act (ACA) provided an opportunity to dramatically expand healthcare coverage; provide better, more affordable care; and support investments in prevention. This is a necessary step forward to improving health, but it is not sufficient because the major drivers of morbidity and mortality today are non-medical: health-related behaviors, and environmental and social factors such as housing, education, economic opportunity, and the built environment.[4]

Public health has a history of succeeding in improving quality of life and life expectancy by addressing such foundational determinants of health (clean water, safe food, etc.), and expanding into new prevention domains (e.g. vaccination) in keeping with new science and evolving health threats.[5] Given persistent and, in some areas, growing gaps in health status, we believe it is time to boldly expand the scope and reach of public health so that we can effectively address all aspects of life that promote health and well-being, including those related to economic development, education, transportation, food, environment, and housing. In short, it's time for a major upgrade. We call this new era Public Health 3.0.

Public Health 1.0

Public health has its roots in antiquity, but the public health system in its modern sense (as an essential governmental function with specialized federal, state, local, and tribal public health agencies) has a much more recent provenance, developing into its current form after the industrial revolution in the late 19th century.[6] During the 20th century, public health expanded in scope and capacity, empowered by extraordinary scientific advances in our understanding of disease; powerful new prevention and treatment tools such as vaccines and antibiotics; and expanded capability in areas such as epidemiology and laboratory science.[7] We refer to this period as Public Health 1.0.

Yet, by late in the century, the public health system was at a crossroads, encumbered in many communities by the demands of providing clinical care for the indigent, and unprepared and under-resourced to address the rising burden of chronic disease, new threats such as the HIV/AIDS epidemic, and emergency preparedness. Moreover, the capacity and effectiveness of public health agencies varied enormously across the country, with little consensus about what should be expected of public health. In 1988, the Institute of Medicine (IOM) summarized this clearly in its landmark report *The Future of Public Health*, in which they declared "this nation has lost sight of its public health goals and has allowed the system of public health activities to fall into disarray."[8]

Public Health 2.0

We conceive of Public Health 2.0 as beginning with this IOM report and continuing to the present day. In their report, the IOM Committee clearly articulated the mission of public health as fulfilling society's interest in assuring conditions in which people can be healthy, and defined the core functions of governmental public health agencies as assessment, policy development, and assurance. This seminal report was a clarion call to public health and other leaders to develop a strong, focused public health system at every governmental level. It contained a variety of detailed, practicable recommendations for reforming the entire public system, and was enormously influential in shaping and reenergizing public health, e.g., by spurring national deliberations leading to the clear articulation of the essential services of public health.[9] However, the clear focus of the report was on the responsibilities of the public health agency at each level of government, with little emphasis on how public health leaders might work across sectors to address social, environmental, or economic determinants of health.

A Changing Landscape for Public Health

Several developments are driving the need to improve and re-envision public health practice once again.

- Health trends in the last 30 years are such that the leading causes of death and illness are now attributable to behaviors (such as smoking, sedentary lifestyle, and eating patterns) that are powerfully driven by the social and physical environments in which people live, learn, work, and play. Consequently, although we must preserve our traditional public health capacities (e.g., to detect and respond to infectious disease outbreaks), we need to find new ways to build health-reinforcing cultures and environments.

- Today, the largest part of many state and local agency budgets are federal grants tied to specific activities and deliverables. Categorical funding that can be spent only on specific diseases, health events, or preventive interventions (e.g., related to HIV/AIDS and other STDs, tuberculosis, cancer, heart disease, injury control, immunizations, and tobacco control) gives state and local public health departments little flexibility in how best to meet local needs.[10]
- The Great Recession in the United States (2007–2009) resulted in sharp and sustained budget cuts to public health at every level. Most health departments have not seen their budgets or functional capacity fully restored.
- The Affordable Care Act (ACA) addressed in large measure one of our country's most intractable health challenges: assuring access to healthcare for all. Although there is still room for progress, 20.0 million people now have access to affordable healthcare that did not have access before;[11] and the uninsured rate is at its lowest level in 50 years.[12] This development is accelerating public health's transition away from clinical care provider of last resort to primary prevention and health promotion.
- The ACA also catalyzed movement away from fee-for-service to value-based payments, potentiating innovative prevention and health-promoting care models.[13] The ACA's requirement that non-profit hospitals must do community health needs assessments[14] has spurred an increasing collaboration between medicine and public health.
- In the past decade, there has been a widening embrace of health department accreditation as one strategy to improve public health agency performance.[15] As of November 2015, 33 states plus the District of Columbia have a health department accredited by the Public Health Accreditation Board (PHAB). This includes 96 governmental public health departments that reach 45 percent of the U.S. population.[16]
- Finally, there has been increasing recognition in recent years that we—in public health and beyond—must find ways to directly address the broad social and environmental determinants of health, through collaborative, cross-sector efforts. Public health leaders have led or joined a variety of health-relevant collaborative processes with leaders in non-health sectors such as housing, transportation, and community development.[17] Elected and civic leaders have also become more aware of the importance of community health, realizing that a healthy community is one with a strong educational system, safe streets, effective public transportation, and affordable, high-quality food and housing.[18]

Public Health 3.0

In this context, we submit that it is time for a major upgrade in public health practice to Public Health 3.0: a modern version that emphasizes cross-sectoral environmental-, policy-, and systems-level actions that directly affect the social determinants of health. Several pioneering American communities are already experimenting with this expansive approach to community health, but they are doing so in the absence of any broadly accepted framework, inventing processes as they go. The sustainability of their efforts is more dependent upon grant funding or the force of leadership than a systematic, modernized approach to public health. It is time to position *all* local and state public health authorities as leaders in building communities that, by their nature, promote the public's health and wellness and prevent disease.

What Are the Key Components of Public Health 3.0?

Enhanced Leadership and Workforce

An exciting evolving model is one in which local and state public health leaders see themselves not only as the director of their governmental agency and programs but also more broadly as the *chief health strategist* for their communities.[19] Public health leaders must be capable of mobilizing community action to affect health determinants beyond the direct reach of their agencies—and do this in an environment of ongoing resource constraints and constant change. As the chief health strategist, they must be capable of engaging, inspiring, and partnering with diverse sectors in a community to help manage, align, and adapt the resources of the community toward creation of maximum health and well-being.

The role of chief health strategist requires a different mindset and leadership skills necessary to facilitating coalitions and promoting community-wide change. This role also requires a light diplomatic touch that fully acknowledges the contributions of colleagues in other sectors to community well-being. Today's public health leaders must also be able to identify, develop, access, and interpret multiple sources of health-relevant data that are highly localized, timely, and actionable. Curricula in schools of public health should be enhanced to ensure that these skills are developed in their students. At the same time, we also need to ensure that training, technical support, and opportunities for peer learning are available to the incumbent public health workforce.

New Partners

Broad engagement with partners across multiple sectors is inherent to the Public Health 3.0 vision. Whereas such collaborations are necessary at all governmental levels, they may have a particular resonance for local communities where the potential for shaping the immediate environment is most visible. It is especially important to enlist the support of elected leaders, by sharing our vision that health is a fundamental driver of community development.

The business community also has much to gain and give to this effort. For communities to thrive economically, they need a healthy, educated workforce and a safe and healthy community environment. Conversely, safe, healthy communities require robust economic environments to provide employment and support education and other necessary community services.

Members of the general public—including those from the sub-populations at greatest risk of poor health—must also be brought into the process of identifying and deciding how best to respond to community needs. Sustained effort and mobilization over many years will be required to address the social and environmental determinants of health, which in turn will require the ongoing support of an informed and engaged public.

Accreditation

Recent budget and personnel cuts will be a challenge to regain, but this process may be made easier if local communities and funders have confidence in the operational effectiveness of local public health. Through a thorough assessment of an agency's core functions, operations, relationships, and strategic actions, the PHAB accreditation process provides external validation, while institutionalizing a culture of improvement, innovation, and transparency, thereby fostering public trust and support. We encourage continued evolution and improvement of the PHAB process to incorporate Public Health 3.0 elements.

Technology, Tools, and Data That Matter

The success in digitizing U.S. healthcare records means that there is now a vast resource of near-real-time health information that could inform community-level policy and programs. In addition, leading-edge health departments are beginning to use repositories of data from non-traditional sources, sometimes developing predictive models to identify high-risk neighborhoods and target limited resources. We need to develop timely, locally relevant health information systems, instead of relying on data that are outdated, merged across years to improve sample size, and/or not actionable at the neighborhood level. The effective development and use of timely, locally actionable data will require investment in information technology as well as informatics training for the public health workforce.

New Metrics of Success

We need to define what comprises a healthy, sustainable, thriving community and, thus, how to measure success. A limited number of domains should be identified that collectively encompass the conditions and outcomes relevant to measuring the health of a community. Within these domains, communities could then select metrics that are measurable, timely, granular, and appropriate for their own goals, resources, and planned interventions. The diversity of the domains should inherently underscore the criticality of cross-sectoral collaborations.

Funding

Adequate, flexible funding is necessary for a broadly engaged Public Health 3.0 organization. At the federal level, we need to explore ways of funding state and local public agencies to promote an expansive approach to assuring community health. It is likely we will need to continue categorical funding in many areas. However, more flexible funding must also be found to enable health leaders to work toward broad environmental-, systems-, and policy-level changes that promote health and prevent multiple health problems.[20] We must also find ways to work across federal departments to deliver comprehensive support that encourages multi-sector work in local communities.

Ideally, new financial and other support for public health should be developed from state and local sources as well. In the end, communities need to find ways to invest in and manage their own healthful development. Finding ways to reverse the pattern of state and local disinvestment in public health may be one of the most effective strategies for enabling robust, locally driven initiatives to develop safe, healthy, economically thriving communities.

Realizing the Public Health 3.0 Vision

To accomplish this upgrade to Public Health 3.0, we need to engage a broad spectrum of public health thought leaders to better define this vision, and to identify likely challenges to its implementation. We at the federal level must also consider how we can help catalyze progress. It is time once again for the public health community to step up our game: to recognize the changing landscape of health in our country, and to develop and embrace dramatically enhanced, community-wide approaches to assuring the conditions in which all people can be healthy.

Notes

1. National Research Council (U.S.). *U.S. Health in International Perspective: Shorter Lives, Poorer Health.* Washington, DC: National Academies Press (U.S.); 2013. Squires, D. and Anderson, C. *U.S. Health Care from a Global Perspective: Spending, Use of Services, Prices, and Health in 13 Countries.* Commonwealth Fund pub. 1819 (15). The Commonwealth Fund Web site. http://www.commonwealthfund.org/publications/issue-briefs/2015/oct/us-health-care-from-a-global-perspective. Published October 2015. Accessed November 9, 2015.
2. U.S. Burden of Disease Collaborators. The State of US Health, 1990–2010.: Burden of Diseases, Injuries, and Risk Factors. *JAMA* 2013;310(6):591–608. National Research Council. *Explaining Divergent Levels of Longevity in High-Income Countries.* E.M.

Crimmins, S.H. Preston, and B. Cohen, Eds. Panel on Understanding Divergent Trends in Longevity in High-Income Countries. Committee on Population, Division of Behavioral and Social Sciences and Education. Washington, DC: The National Academies Press; 2011.

3. National Academies of Sciences, Engineering, and Medicine. *The Growing Gap in Life Expectancy by Income: Implications for Federal Programs and Policy Responses.* Committee on the Long-Run Macroeconomic Effects of the Aging U.S. Population-Phase II. Committee on Population, Division of Behavioral and Social Sciences and Education. Board on Mathematical Sciences and Their Applications, Division on Engineering and Physical Sciences. Washington, DC: The National Academies Press; 2015.

4. Adler, N.E. and Newman, K. Socioeconomic Disparities in Health: Pathways and Policies. *Health Aff* 2002;21(2):60–76. Walker, R.E., Keane, C.R., and Burke, J.G. Disparities and Access to Healthy Food in the United States: A Review of Food Deserts Literature. *Health & Place* 2010;16(5):876–884. Saegert, S. and Evans, G.W. Poverty, Housing Niches, and Health in the United States. *Journal of Social Issues* 2003; 59(3):569–589.

5. CDC. Control of Infectious Diseases. *MMWR* 1999;48(29):621–629.

6. Rosen, G. *A History of Public Health.* Baltimore, MD: Johns Hopkins University Press; 1993.

7. CDC. Ten Great Public Health Achievements—United States, 1900–1999. *MMWR* 1999; 48(12):241–243.

8. Institute of Medicine (U.S.). Committee for the Study of the Future of Public Health. *The Future of Public Health.* Washington, DC: National Academy Press; 1988.

9. Lee, P. and Paxman, D. Reinventing Public Health. *Annu Rev Public Health* 1997; 18:1–35.

10. Institute of Medicine (U.S.). *For the Public's Health: Investing in a Healthier Future.* Washington, DC: The National Academies Press; 2012.

11. Office of the Assistant Secretary for Planning and Evaluation (ASPE). *Health Insurance Coverage and the Affordable Care Act 2010–2016.* ASPE Web site. https://aspe.hhs.gov/sites/default/files/pdf/187551/ACA2010–2016.pdf. Published March 3, 2016. Accessed March 25, 2016.

12. Martinez, M.E. and Cohen, R.A. *Health Insurance Coverage: Early Release of Estimates from the National Health Interview Survey, January–June 2015.* National Center for Health Statistics Web site. http://www.cdc.gov/nchs/nhis/releases.htm. Published November 2015. Accessed November 10, 2015.

13. Burwell, S.M. Setting Value-Based Payment Goals—HHS Efforts to Improve U.S. Health Care. *New Engl J Med* 2015;372(10):897–899.

14. Internal Revenue Service, U.S. Department of the Treasury. Additional Requirements for Charitable Hospitals; Community Health Needs Assessments for Charitable Hospitals; Requirement of a Section 4959 Excise Tax Return and Time for Filing the Return. *Federal Register* 2014;79(250):78953–79016 (to be codified at 26 C.F.R. pts. 1, 53, and 602).

15. Bender, K., Kronstadt, J., Wilcox, R., and Lee, T.P. Overview of the Public Health Accreditation Board. *J Public Health Management Practice* 2014;20(1):4–6.

16. Nicolaus, T. *Public Health Accreditation Board Awards Five-Year Accreditation to 17 Public Health Departments.* Public Health Accreditation Board Web site. http://www.phaboard.org/wp-content/uploads/PHABNewsReleaseNov1620151.pdf. Published November 16, 2015. Accessed March 25, 2016.

17. Bostic, R.W., Thornton, R.L.J., Rudd, E.C., and Sternthal, M.J. Health in All Policies: The Role of the U.S. Department of Housing and Urban Development and Present and Future Challenges. *Health Aff* 2012;31(9):2130–2137. Trowbridge, M.J., Pickell, S.G., Pyke, C.R., and Jutte, D.P. Building Healthy Communities: Establishing Health and Wellness Metrics for Use within the Real Estate Industry. *Health Aff* 2014;33(11):1923–1929.

18. Trowbridge, M.J., Pickell, S.G., Pyke, C.R., and Jutte, D.P. Building Healthy Communities: Establishing Health and Wellness Metrics for Use within the Real Estate Industry. *Health Aff* 2014;33(11):1923–1929. McKinnon, R.A., Wiedt, T., Hoffnagle, E., and Shrimplin, S. Extended Let's Move! Cities, Towns and Counties Team. Let's Move! Cities, Towns and Counties: Working with Local Elected Officials to Improve Community Food and Physical Activity Environments. *Public Health Rep* 2015; 130(5):426–430.

19. Public Health Leadership Forum. *The High Achieving Governmental Health Department in 2020 as the Community Chief Health Strategist.* RESOLVE Health Web site. http://www.resolv.org/site-healthleadershipforum/hd2020/. Published May 2014. Accessed March 25, 2016.

20. Institute of Medicine (U.S.). *For the Public's Health: Investing in a Healthier Future.* Washington, DC: The National Academies Press; 2012.

15

AMERICAN INDIAN PERSPECTIVES ON POPULATION HEALTH

Donald Warne and Melanie Nadeau

As indigenous peoples, the American Indian (AI) population has a unique legal, historical, and policy history in the United States. The complexity of health policy combined with poverty and other social determinants of AI health has led to significant population health challenges.

History of Federal Health Services for American Indians

AIs comprise the only population in the United States whose members are born with a *legal right* to health services. This right is based on the U.S. Constitution, treaties, and other legal bases. Unfortunately, the federal agency charged with the responsibility to provide health services, the Indian Health Service (IHS), is significantly underfunded (The Henry J. Kaiser Family Foundation 2013; National Tribal Budget Formulation Workgroup 2015). The subsequent lack of adequate public health and medical services has led to some of the worst health disparities in the nation.

U.S. Constitution

The Commerce Clause (Article I, Section 8) of the U.S. Constitution gives Congress the power "to regulate commerce with foreign nations, and among the several states, and with the Indian tribes" (Indian Health Service 2005). This is seen as the legal basis for tribal sovereignty in federal Indian law—tribes are placed on par with foreign nations. Of course, tribes have considered themselves to be sovereign nations long before European contact and the writing of the Constitution. Unlike other populations in the United States, federally recognized AI and Alaska Native tribes have a unique government-to-government relationship with the federal government, and this relationship has an impact on the delivery of health services ("Basis for Health Services" 2015). The Supremacy Clause (Article VI, Clause 2) of the U.S. Constitution states that "the Constitution, federal laws made pursuant to it, and treaties made under its authority, constitute the supreme law of the land" (Cornell University Law School 2016).

Treaties

Treaties that were signed by the U.S. Government and AI tribes often call for "all proper care and parental protection" as well as the provision of medical services, physicians, or the establishment of hospitals for the care of AI people. The Treaty Clause (Article II, Section 2) of the U.S. Constitution gives the President the authority to negotiate international agreements with other nations with "the advice and consent of a supermajority of the U.S. Senate" (Indian Health Service 2005). From the perspectives of many tribal leaders, underfunding of the IHS represents a violation of treaty rights.

Legal Basis for Health Services

Snyder Act (Public Law 67–85)

The Snyder Act of 1921 further acknowledged that health services for AIs are the responsibility of the federal government and called for Congress to appropriate funding "from time to time . . . For relief of distress and conservation of health" ("Basis for Health Services" 2015; "Public Law 67–85—The Snyder Act—25 U.S.C. 13 Section 13. Expenditure of Appropriations by Bureau" 1921) The Snyder Act provides legal authority for Congress to appropriate funding to the Bureau of Indian Affairs (BIA) ("Public Law 67–85—The Snyder Act—25 U.S.C. 13 Section 13. Expenditure of Appropriations by Bureau" 1921). The IHS was not established as a separate agency until 1955 ("Public Laws of the Eighty-Third Congress, Second Session, 1954. Public Law 568" 1954).

Merriam Report

The Merriam Report in 1928, also known as "The Problem of Indian Administration," was funded by the Institute for Government Research to assess health, education, economics, and other social circumstances among the AI population (Congress 2016). The Report showed significant economic, educational, and health disparities among AIs and called for policy changes to improve conditions.

Indian Reorganization Act (Public Law 73–383)

Following years of federal assimilation policies, the Indian Reorganization Act (IRA) was

> An Act to conserve and develop Indian lands and resources; to extend to Indians the right to form business and other organizations; to establish a credit system for Indians; to grant certain rights of home rule to Indians; to provide for vocational education for Indians; and for other purposes.
>
> *("Indian Reorganization Act" 1934)*

The goal of the IRA was to promote tribal sovereignty and self-sufficiency, and it established a model tribal constitution that is still used by many tribes in the 21st century ("Indian Reorganization Act" 1934).

Transfer Act (Public Law 83–568)

Following a history of poor management and bad health outcomes, the Indian health program in the BIA (Department of Interior) was moved to the Public Health Service by the Transfer Act of 1954 (Indian Health Service 2005). The act states

> That all functions, responsibilities, authorities, and duties of the Department of the Interior, the Bureau of Indian Affairs, Secretary of the Interior, and the Commissioner of Indian Affairs relating to the maintenance and operation of hospital and health facilities for Indians, and the conservation of the health of Indians, are hereby transferred to, and shall be administered by, the Surgeon General of the United States Public Health Service.
>
> *("Public Laws of the Eighty-Third Congress, Second Session, 1954. Public Law 568" 1954)*

The IHS was then formally established in 1955 as an agency within the Department of Health, Education, and Welfare, now the Department of Health and Human Services (Indian Health Service 2005).

Indian Self-Determination and Education Assistance Act (Public Law 93–638)

The Indian self-determination law was enacted in 1975, and it allows for tribes to contract or compact with the federal government to assume management and control of health services, including any program, function, service, or activity of the IHS (Indian Health Service 2005). As a result, most tribes operate at least some components of their health system, and the majority of the IHS budget is now managed by tribes under "638" contracts and compacts.

Indian Health Care Improvement Act (Public Law 94–437)

Originally passed in 1976, the Indian Health Care Improvement Act (IHCIA) created several new AI health programs, including Urban Indian Health Centers, IHS scholarships, and others (Heisler 2011). The goal of the IHCIA is to provide sufficient, high-quality health services that are needed to improve AI health status to the highest possible level, and to encourage tribal participation in the planning and management of health services (Heisler 2011). This law was permanently reauthorized as part of the Affordable Care Act in 2010 (Heisler 2011; National Council of Urban Indian Health 2011). The law reinforces that

> Federal health services to maintain and improve the health of the Indians are consonant with and required by the Federal Government's historical and unique legal relationship with, and resulting responsibility to, the American Indian people.
>
> *("Indian Health Care" 1985)*

"I/T/U" Health System

Due to this complex legal and policy history, provision of health services for AIs has evolved into three primary service delivery systems that are not typically well coordinated. The "I/T/U" health system includes the Indian Health Service, Tribal health programs, and Urban Indian Health Centers.

Indian Health Service

The IHS was established in 1955 following the Transfer Act (Indian Health Service 2005), and recurrent federal funding for Indian health programming was established by the Snyder Act in 1921 (Indian Health Service 2005). The IHS is divided into twelve operating regions or "Areas" (Figure 15.1) (Indian Health

FIGURE 15.1 Indian Health Service Areas

Service 2016a). Each area is different and contains varying numbers of tribes, states, and AIs. Tribes that use IHS-managed facilities are typically called "Direct Services Tribes" owing to the fact the IHS directly operates the service units (hospitals or clinics) (Indian Health Service 2012). Some areas of the IHS have no IHS-operated facilities (e.g. Alaska and California), whereas the service units in other areas are predominantly IHS managed (e.g. Great Plains) (Indian Health Service 2016a).

Tribal Health Programs

In the more than forty years since the passage of Public Law 93–638, the vast majority of tribes now operate health programs under 638 contracts and compacts. Some tribes have elected to "638" some health services (e.g. Community Health Representative programs, substance abuse treatment programs, etc.) while the IHS operates the clinic or hospital (Warne 2011). In these circumstances, public health programming is frequently a tribal function whereas medical services are an IHS function. The degree of integration and coordination is variable; however, in the authors' experiences, coordination between tribes and IHS could be significantly improved.

Urban Indian Health Centers

Title V of the IHCIA established the Urban Indian Health Centers. Currently, thirty-four urban programs (Indian Health Service 2016b) exist nationally that are funded through the IHCIA. However, funding from the IHS is quite low for these programs, and although 60% of AIs lived in cities as of 2010 (Office of Minority Health 2016), the urban programs received only 1% of IHS funding during the 2013 fiscal year (The Henry J. Kaiser Family Foundation 2013).

American Indian Health Disparities

The AI population suffers from significant health disparities. Rates of death due to unintentional injuries (Jacobs-Wingo et al. 2016; Wong et al. 2014), infant mortality (Wong et al. 2014), and chronic diseases (Jacobs-Wingo et al. 2016) are consistently higher among AIs than the general U.S. population. According to the North Dakota Department of Health, the average age at death between 2010 and 2014 for AIs was 56.8 years as compared to 76.6 years for the white population (North Dakota Department of Health 2014). AIs in many regions of the United States live in third-world health conditions, and a significant national effort is required to promote collaboration and to solve this health crisis. Described below are common risk factors, social determinants of health, and chronic disease and infectious disease disparities among the AI population.

Risk Factors and Social Determinants of Health

Historical Trauma

Historically traumatic events have been described as "cataclysmic" events in a population that has long-standing and inter-generational influences. For AIs, the loss of land, culture, language, traditional ceremonies, and self-sufficiency over the last several centuries has led to a collective sense of loss and social injustice. Several researchers have examined the impact of historical trauma and its negative impact on AI health (Gone 2009; Hartmann and Gone 2014).

Boarding School Experiences

The boarding school era in the 19th and 20th centuries included multiple generations of children being taken away from their homes, communities, and families, and being placed in residential schools that could be thousands of miles away (Cross, Day, and Byers 2010). Unfortunately, physical, emotional, and sexual abuse was not uncommon, and the negative consequences have an impact on subsequent health status (Cross, Day, and Byers 2010). In addition, the mortality rates among boarding school residents was high, and many of the schools are adjacent to large cemeteries in which dozens of AI children are buried (Marr 2016). The survivors of the boarding school experience endured abuse, neglect, and the loss of playmates and friends (Graves et al. 2007). In addition, traditional parenting and nurturing of children was disrupted, resulting in harmful impacts of boarding schools across generations (Graves et al. 2007).

Adverse Childhood Experiences

The groundbreaking Adverse Childhood Experiences (ACEs) study showed the cumulative negative health consequences of adverse experiences in childhood (Felitti et al. 1998). ACEs are categorized into ten domains of abuse and household dysfunction (Dube et al. 2003). The total number of ACEs one experiences is correlated with poor adult health outcomes, including depression (Campbell, Walker, and Egede 2016; Felitti et al. 1998; Roh et al. 2015), anxiety (McGuinness and Waldrop 2015), post-traumatic stress (McGuinness and Waldrop 2015), substance abuse (Campbell, Walker, and Egede 2016; Felitti et al. 1998), diabetes (Campbell, Walker, and Egede 2016; Felitti et al. 1998; Huffhines, Noser, and Patton 2016), cancer (Brown, Thacker, and Cohen 2013; Felitti et al. 1998), and heart disease (Anda et al. 2008; Campbell, Walker, and Egede 2016; Felitti et al. 1998), among other conditions (Campbell, Walker, and Egede 2016; Felitti et al. 1998). Unfortunately, the limited data available shows that ACEs are more prevalent in many AI communities (Ravello, Abeita, and Brown 2008; Roh et al. 2015).

Poverty

Poverty is correlated with poor health status. Nationally, 2.4 times as many AIs as whites live at or below the federal poverty level (Office of Minority Health 2016), and in some areas of the IHS, including the Great Plains, disparities in poverty are even more pronounced ("2013 American Indian Population and Labor Force Report" 2014).

Obesity

AI obesity rates are higher than almost all other racial and ethnic groups (Office of Minority Health 2013). Poverty combined with the history of federally sponsored food programs, such as the Food Distribution Program on Indian Reservations (FDPIR) operated by the U.S. Department of Agriculture, have led to diets that are high in calories and have poor nutritional value (Shanks et al. 2015). Foods historically available in the FDPIR (also known as the commodity food program) consisted of bleached flour, refined sugar, lard, vegetable shortening, sugar-sweetened beverages, pure corn syrup, canned meat, and cheese (Shanks et al. 2015). Loss of access to traditional food systems combined with limited financial opportunities on many AI reservations place the AI population at high risk for obesity and its associated chronic diseases.

Commercial Tobacco

Significant regional differences exist in the use of commercial tobacco among AIs. In the Northern Plains tobacco usage is the highest and, not surprisingly, Northern Plains AIs suffer from the highest cancer mortality rates in the nation (Centers for Disease Control and Prevention 2014). A potential root cause of this disparity could include the traditional usage of tobacco and other herbs (e.g. red willow, etc.) that were smoked for ceremonial purposes and prayer (Margalit et al. 2013). With a cultural connection to smoking, it is possible that AIs in the Northern Plains were more susceptible to cigarette smoking than other populations, and subsequent addiction to nicotine occurred (Kunitz 2016). Commercial tobacco usage increased following World War II (Proctor 2001), when AIs participated in the military at higher rates than other races and ethnicities (Department of Veterans Affairs 2015), and distribution of cigarettes to soldiers was commonplace.

Alcohol

Rates of binge drinking, alcohol misuse, and alcohol mortality rates have been higher among AIs (Cunningham, Solomon, and Muramoto 2016). However, numerous studies also show that AIs have the highest rates of alcohol abstinence, likely due to observations of alcohol's devastating effects among many family and community members (Bezdek and Spicer 2006; Cunningham, Solomon, and Muramoto 2016). The AI population has higher prevalence of both binge drinking and abstinence, and relatively lower prevalence of social drinking as compared to the non-AI population (Cunningham, Solomon, and Muramoto 2016). Perhaps future studies should determine resiliency factors that lead many individuals to abstinence in the face of challenging social circumstances.

Substance Abuse

The 2005–2008 National Survey on Drug Use and Health showed a higher prevalence of substance abuse in the AI adolescent population, including marijuana and opiates (Wu et al. 2011). Addiction to prescription opioids, tranquilizers, stimulants, and sedatives is increasing as well (Wu et al. 2011). Overdose-associated emergency room visits and hospitalizations are increasing costs, and deaths due to overdose are also on the rise (Herzig et al. 2014). Solving this population health challenge and improving outcomes will require expanded collaboration among IHS, tribes, medical systems, public health systems, and mental health/substance abuse stakeholder groups and providers.

Chronic Diseases

Diabetes

AIs have the highest prevalence of diabetes and the highest diabetes mortality rates in the nation (Cho et al. 2014). The basis for this disparity is multi-faceted, with poverty-related lack of access to healthy foods as many AI reservation communities are food deserts, less access to school- or community-based physical activity programs, and possibly genetic predisposition.

Heart Disease

As is the case in many populations, heart disease is the leading cause of death for AIs (Jacobs-Wingo et al. 2016). This is not surprising given the elevated prevalence of obesity and diabetes nationally, and high rates of smoking among Plains Indians and Alaska Natives (Jacobs-Wingo et al. 2016). Nationally, AI men and women have a 21% greater mortality rate from heart disease, and AIs in the Northern Plains have a 58% greater heart disease mortality rate, as compared to the white population (Veazie et al. 2014).

Cancer

Significant regional disparities in cancer mortality exist in the AI population (Wiggins et al. 2008). Not surprisingly, cancer incidence and mortality rates correlate closely with commercial tobacco use (Wiggins et al. 2008). Due to underfunding of the IHS and to lack of access to appropriate screening, AIs are the only population in the United States with increasing mortality due to colorectal cancer (CRC) (Perdue et al. 2014). Poverty, lack of insurance, limited IHS resources, and cultural factors have led to lower rates of CRC screening among AIs (Maly et al. 2014).

Infectious Diseases

HIV

Incidence of Human Immunodeficiency Virus (HIV) increased by 63% between 2004 and 2014 (Centers for Disease Control and Prevention 2016b). Of the estimated 44,073 new HIV diagnoses in the United States in 2014, 1% (222) were among AIs, and of those, 77% were men and 22% were women (Centers for Disease Control and Prevention 2016a). A major concern for AI population health is the potential significant number of AIs infected with HIV who are unaware of it, and although Sexually Transmitted Infection (STI) rates are high, screening rates for HIV are typically low (Centers for Disease Control and Prevention 2016a). In addition, due to underfunding of IHS, local access to HIV treatment and services is limited (Centers for Disease Control and Prevention 2016a).

Sexually Transmitted Infections

Nationally for AIs, incidence rates of chlamydia and gonorrhea are higher than the general population, and the rate of primary and secondary syphilis is lower (Centers for Disease Control and Prevention and Indian Health Service 2014). However, significant regional differences exist regarding STI diagnoses, with Alaska and Great Plains areas having the highest rates of chlamydia and gonorrhea (Centers for Disease Control and Prevention and Indian Health Service 2014).

Hepatitis C

Although data are limited, an emerging challenge in AI population health is the increasing incidence of Hepatitis C Virus (HCV) infections. HCV can lead to liver failure and, in some cases, liver cancer (De Mitri et al. 1995). Co-occurring alcohol abuse can increase risk for liver failure, and co-infection with HIV is common (Rempel and Uhanova 2012). Recent advances in HCV treatment bring opportunities for a cure; however, the cost of these newer medications is high, and access to them is limited by IHS underfunding (Rempel and Uhanova 2012).

Tuberculosis

Although the AI population in the United States is less than 2% of the overall population (Norris, Vines, and Hoeffel 2012), the rate of tuberculosis is approximately thirteen times higher among AIs compared to whites (Cheek et al. 2014). Between 2003 and 2008, AIs diagnosed with tuberculosis were more likely than other races or ethnicities to be homeless, abuse alcohol, live in poverty, and lack health insurance (Bloss et al. 2011).

Future Directions

Clearly, the AI population health challenges are significant. Improvements in primary, secondary, and tertiary prevention are needed to solve the substantial population health disparities. To be most effective, expanded partnerships among tribes and IHS, public health, medical, and academic professionals are needed to identify effective solutions to address the AI public health crisis. Moving forward, a multi-pronged approach in collaboration with numerous stakeholders is needed. In the discussion below, we address the role of Centers for Medicare and Medicaid Services, the impact of the Affordable Care Act, and the need for expanding AI-specific evidence-based practices.

Role of Centers for Medicare and Medicaid Services

Centers for Medicare and Medicaid Services (CMS) is the largest agency within the federal Department of Health and Human Services (HHS). CMS serves over 126 million people through Medicare, Medicaid, and the Children's Health Insurance Plan (CHIP), and the CMS budget in FY 2016 was over $640B of the $970B HHS budget (U.S. Department of Health and Human Services 2015a). The IHS appropriation was just over $5B. Figure 15.2 shows the per capita healthcare expenditures for Medicare, Veterans Administration (VA), Medicaid, Federal Employees Health Benefits, and IHS. Medicare is funded at nearly $12,000 per beneficiary per year, VA is funded at over $7,000 per year per qualifying veteran, Medicaid receives over $5,500 per person per year, and federal employee health benefits are funded at over $5,200 per employee per year (National Tribal Budget Formulation Workgroup 2015). By contrast, IHS receives approximately $3,100 per patient per year for medical services. In addition to much-needed increases in Congressional appropriations, the I/T/U system depends on third-party revenue generated by billing health insurance.

As tribal citizens, U.S. citizens, and state residents, AIs are eligible to enroll in CMS programs. Due to high rates of poverty, many AIs are enrolled in or eligible for Medicaid and CHIP. According to Medicaid enrollment data, AIs and Alaska Natives in the states of Alaska, South Dakota, Montana, and North

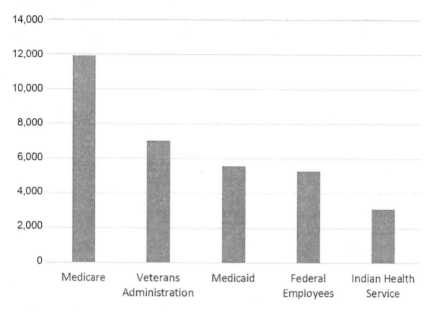

FIGURE 15.2 2013–2014 Per Capita Expenditures, U.S. Dollars

Dakota represent 21–36% of the Medicaid population, exceeding their overall population percentages (National Tribal Budget Formulation Workgroup 2015). AIs are over-represented in the Medicaid populations of several other states, including Arizona, New Mexico, Montana, and Oklahoma. Medicaid payments to IHS and tribal "638" programs are paid with 100% federal funds (National Tribal Budget Formulation Workgroup 2015). A CMS ruling in February 2016 now allows for the 100% federal funds to follow the patient to the private sector following a referral (Centers for Medicare & Medicaid Services Center for Medicaid & CHIP Services 2016). This ruling provides for improved care coordination across IHS, tribal, and private sectors, and potentially improved quality of care. In addition, the states will benefit through decreased Medicaid expenditures. As a result, future collaborations among tribes, IHS, states, and private sector providers should include expanded outreach, education, and enrollment of AIs into Medicaid and other CMS programs. Increased enrollment in health insurance programs will provide improved access to much-needed healthcare services and growth in third-party revenue. These additional funds can be used by IHS and tribes for public health, health promotion, and disease prevention initiatives, and these expanded efforts should result in decreased population health disparities.

Impact of the Affordable Care Act

The Affordable Care Act (ACA) has several provisions unique to the AI population, including a waiver of the individual mandate, no pre-defined enrollment periods, and no cost sharing up to 300% of the federal poverty level (FPL) (U.S. Department of Health and Human Services 2015b). As of 2016, numerous states with significant AI and Alaska Native populations have expanded Medicaid (Artiga and Damico 2016). Unfortunately, some states with large numbers of AIs, including South Dakota, Nebraska, Kansas, Oklahoma, and others, have not yet expanded Medicaid (The Kaiser Commission on Medicaid and the Uninsured 2016). In states with Medicaid expansion, the opportunity exists to enroll the vast majority of AIs into Medicaid, Medicaid expansion, Marketplace, and Medicare programs (The Kaiser Commission on Medicaid and the Uninsured 2016). In some states like North Dakota, essentially all AIs in the state would be eligible for health insurance at little to no cost to the tribes or to the individuals (The Kaiser Commission on Medicaid and the Uninsured 2016). In these circumstances, the budget limitations of IHS for Purchased and Referred Care (PRC) would be overcome.

PRC is used by IHS and tribes for services that cannot be provided locally, including many types of specialty care. Historically, the PRC budget was not adequate to meet health needs, and many referrals were denied due to lack of funding. If all AIs were enrolled in health insurance, there is virtually no need for PRC funds. Tribes could choose to contract for PRC dollars under the 638 mechanism, and they could use these resources to cover any potential cost sharing to individual tribal members. In this process, all health services would still be paid with 100% federal dollars, consistent with treaty rights and federal trust responsibility. Numerous tribes across multiple states are in the process of engaging ACA opportunities to expand access to health services, and this trend should continue into the future. The long-term impact could include significantly improved population health outcomes.

Creating an American Indian "Evidence Base"

Medicine, public health, and other disciplines have increased their focus on utilizing evidence-based practices (Greenhalgh, Howick, and Maskrey 2014; Harris et al. 2012). Unfortunately, many of these practices were tested and proven to be effective in non-AI communities. For public health in particular, one size does not fit all, and a health promotion program that is shown to be effective in a large metropolitan area may or may not be effective in a rural, impoverished tribal community. In addition to the multitude of cultural differences, many tribal communities face other challenges that do not occur in most cities. For example, many tribal communities are in food deserts in which a local super-market or grocery store does not exist within hundreds of miles, and there is no public transportation system. In this case, an evidence-based practice utilizing fresh fruits and vegetables to address health issues such as obesity, diabetes, or heart disease cannot be applied in the tribal community without additional resources to create the policies, systems, and environment to improve community access to these foods. As another example, many tribal reservation communities do not have sidewalks, safe neighborhoods, or local access to fitness centers. Again, an evidence-based practice that promotes physical activity would need to account for differences in community infrastructure.

Despite the challenges, in the authors' experiences, there are numerous examples of excellent population health programs across Indian Country. However, many of these programs have not been formally evaluated, and even fewer have been published in peer-reviewed journals. The need exists to develop an AI-specific inventory of evidence-based practices and to modify replicated best and promising practices in AI populations. Expanded partnerships with funding agencies such as the CDC, HHS, and foundations are needed to increase the focus on expanding *population-specific* evidence-based practices, including AI populations.

References

Anda, Robert F., David W. Brown, Shanta R. Dube, J. Douglas Bremner, Vincent J. Felitti, and Wayne H. Giles. 2008. "Adverse Childhood Experiences and Chronic Obstructive Pulmonary Disease in Adults." *American Journal of Preventive Medicine* 34 (5): 396–403. doi:10.1016/j.amepre.2008.02.002.

Artiga, Samantha, and Anthony Damico. 2016. "Medicaid and American Indians and Alaska Natives." *The Henry J. Kaiser Family Foundation. The Kaiser Commission on Medicaid and the Uninsured* March: 1–14.

"Basis for Health Services." 2015. *Indian Health Service.* ihs.gov/newsroom/factsheets/basisforhealthservices.

Bezdek, Marjorie, and Paul Spicer. 2006. "Maintaining Abstinence in a Northern Plains Tribe." *Medical Anthropology Quarterly* 20 (2): 160–81.

Bloss, Emily, Timothy H. Holtz, John Jereb, John T. Redd, Laura Jean Podewils, James E. Cheek, and Eugene McCray. 2011. "Tuberculosis in Indigenous Peoples in the U.S., 2003–2008." *Public Health Reports* 126 (September–October): 677–89.

Brown, Monique J., Leroy R. Thacker, and Steven A. Cohen. 2013. "Association between Adverse Childhood Experiences and Diagnosis of Cancer." *PLoS ONE* 8 (6): 1–6. doi:10.1371/journal.pone.0065524.

Campbell, Jennifer A., Rebekah J. Walker, and Leonard E. Egede. 2016. "Associations between Adverse Childhood Experiences, High-Risk Behaviors, and Morbidity in Adulthood." *American Journal of Preventive Medicine* 50 (3). Elsevier: 344–52. doi:10.1016/j.amepre.2015.07.022.

Centers for Disease Control and Prevention. 2014. "Best Practices for Comprehensive Tobacco Control Programs—2014." *U.S. Department of Health and Human Services, Centers for Disease Control and Prevention, National Center for Chronic Disease Prevention and Health Promotion, Office on Smoking and Health,* 1–52. http://www.cdc.gov/tobacco/

stateandcommunity/best_practices/pdfs/2014/comprehensive.pdf?utm_source=
rss&utm_medium=rss&utm_campaign=best-practices-for-comprehensive-tobacco-
control-programs-2014-pdf.

———. 2016a. "HIV among American Indians and Alaska Natives in the United States."
Atlanta, GA. http://www.cdc.gov/hiv/group/racialethnic/aian/.

———. 2016b. "HIV/AIDS." http://www.cdc.gov/hiv/group/racialethnic/aian/.

Centers for Disease Control and Prevention and Indian Health Service. 2014. "Indian
Health Surveillance Report—Sexually Transmitted Diseases 2011." Atlanta, GA.

Centers for Medicare & Medicaid Services Center for Medicaid & CHIP Services. 2016.
"Federal Funding for Services 'Received through' an IHS/Tribal Facility and Furnished
to Medicaid-Eligible American Indians and Alaska Natives." Baltimore, MD. http://
www.nihb.org/docs/02262016/SMD-16–002.pdf.

Cheek, James E., Robert C. Holman, John T. Redd, Dana Haberling, and Thomas W.
Hennessy. 2014. "Infectious Disease Mortality among American Indians and Alaska
Natives, 1999–2009." *American Journal of Public Health* April: 1–7. doi:10.2105/AJPH.
2013.301721.

Cho, Pyone, Linda S. Geiss, Nilka Rios Burrows, Diana L. Roberts, Ann K. Bullock, and
Michael E. Toedt. 2014. "Diabetes-Related Mortality among American Indians and
Alaska Natives, 1990–2009." *American Journal of Public Health* April: 1–8. doi:10.2105/
AJPH.2014.301968.

Congress. 2016. "S. Rept. 112–166—Amending the Act of June 18, 1934, to Reaffirm
the Authority of the Secretary of the Interior to Take Land into Trust for Indian
Tribes." Accessed May 18. https://www.congress.gov/congressional-report/112th-
congress/senate-report/166/1.

Cornell University Law School. 2016. "Article VI." Accessed May 18. https://www.law.
cornell.edu/constitution/articlevi.

Cross, Suzanne L., Angelique G. Day, and Lisa G. Byers. 2010. "American Indian Grand
Families: A Qualitative Study Conducted with Grandmothers and Grandfathers Who
Provide Sole Care for Their Grandchildren." *Journal of Cross-Cultural Gerontology* 25:
371–83. doi:10.1007/s10823–010–9127–5.

Cunningham, James K., Teshia A. Solomon, and Myra L. Muramoto. 2016. "Alcohol
Use among Native Americans Compared to Whites: Examining the Veracity of the
'Native American Elevated Alcohol Consumption' Belief." *Drug and Alcohol Dependence*
160. Elsevier Ireland Ltd.: 65–75. doi:10.1016/j.drugalcdep.2015.12.015.

De Mitri, M.S., K. Poussin, P. Baccarini, P. Pontisso, A. D'Errico, N. Simon, W. Grigioni,
A. Alberti, P. Pontisso, N. Simon, and M. Beaugrand. 1995. "HCV-Associated Liver
Cancer without Cirrhosis." *Lancet* 18 (February): 413–15.

Department of Veterans Affairs. 2015. "American Indian and Alaska Native Veterans:
2013 American Community Survey."

Dube, Shanta R., Vincent J. Felitti, Maxia Dong, Daniel P. Chapman, Wayne H. Giles,
and Robert F. Anda. 2003. "Childhood Abuse, Neglect, and Household Dysfunction
and the Risk of Illicit Drug Use: The Adverse Childhood Experiences Study." *Pediatrics*
111 (3): 564–72.

Felitti, Vincent J., Robert F. Anda, Dale Nordenberg, David F. Williamson, Alison M.
Spitz, Valerie Edwards, Mary P. Koss, and James S. Marks. 1998. "Relationship of
Childhood Abuse and Household Dysfunction to Many of the Leading Causes of
Death in Adults: The Adverse Childhood Experiences (ACE) Study." *American Journal
of Preventive Medicine* 14 (4): 245–58.

Gone, Joseph P. 2009. "A Community-Based Treatment for Native American Historical Trauma: Prospects for Evidence-Based Practice." *Journal of Consulting and Clinical Psychology* 77 (4): 751–62. doi:10.1037/a0015390.

Graves, Kathleen, Louise Shavings, Cookie Rose, Anda Saylor, Stacey Smith, Cheryl Easley, and George P. Charles. 2007. "Boarding School Project: Mental Health Outcome." *National Resource Center for American Indian, Alaska Native, and Native Hawaiian Elders* July: 1–29.

Greenhalgh, Trisha, Jeremy Howick, and Neal Maskrey. 2014. "Evidence Based Medicine: A Movement in Crisis?" *BMJ* 348 (June): 1–7. doi:10.1136/bmj.g3725.

Harris, Jeffrey R., Allen Cheadle, Peggy A. Hannon, Mark Forehand, Patricia Lichiello, Eustacia Mahoney, Susan Snyder, Judith Yarrow, and Judith Yarrow. 2012. "A Framework for Disseminating Evidence-Based Health Promotion Practices." *Preventing Chronic Disease* 9: 1–8.

Hartmann, William E., and Joseph P. Gone. 2014. "American Indian Historical Trauma: Community Perspectives from Two Great Plains Medicine Men." *American Journal of Community Psychology* 54: 274–88. doi:10.1007/s10464–014–9671–1.

Heisler, Elayne J. 2011. "The Indian Health Care Improvement Act Reauthorization and Extension as Enacted by the ACA: Detailed Summary and Timeline." http://www.ncsl.org/documents/health/indhlthcarereauth.pdf.

The Henry J. Kaiser Family Foundation. 2013. "Health Coverage and Care for American Indians and Alaska Natives." *The Henry J. Kaiser Family Foundation* October: 1–20.

Herzig, Shoshana J., Michael B. Rothberg, Michael Cheung, Long H. Ngo, and Edward R. Marcantonio. 2014. "Opioid Utilization and Opioid-Related Adverse Events in Nonsurgical Patients in US Hospitals." *Journal of Hospital Medicine* 9 (2): 73–81. doi:10.1002/jhm.2102.

Huffhines, Lindsay, Amy Noser, and Susana R. Patton. 2016. "The Link between Adverse Childhood Experiences and Diabetes." *Current Diabetes Reports* 16 (54): 1–9. doi:10.1007/s11892–016–0740–8.

"Indian Health Care." 1985. In *25 U.S. Code Title 25—Indians*, 432–545. https://www.ihs.gov/ihcia/includes/themes/newihstheme/display_objects/documents/home/USCode_Title25_Chapter 18.pdf.

Indian Health Service. 2005. "IHS Gold Book." *US Department of Health and Human Services* Rockville, MD, 1–31. https://www.ihs.gov/newsroom/factsheets/.

———. 2012. "Direct Service Tribes." https://www.ihs.gov/odsct/dst/.

———. 2016a. "Locations." Accessed May 18. https://www.ihs.gov//locations/.

———. 2016b. "Office of Urban Indian Health Programs." Accessed May 28. https://www.ihs.gov/urban/.

"Indian Reorganization Act." 1934. *National Archives and Records Administration. Office of the Federal Register.* https://research.archives.gov/id/7873515.

Jacobs-Wingo, Jasmine L., David K. Espey, Amy V. Groom, Leslie E. Phillips, Donald S. Haverkamp, and L. Stanley. 2016. "Causes and Disparities in Death Rates among Urban American Indian and Alaska Native Populations, 1999–2009." *AJPH Research* 106 (5): 906–14. doi:10.2105/AJPH.2015.303033.

The Kaiser Commission on Medicaid and the Uninsured. 2016. "Medicaid Enrollment & Spending Growth: FY 2015 & 2016." Washington, DC. http://kff.org/report-section/medicaid-enrollment-spending-growth-fy-2015-2016-issue-brief/.

Kunitz, Stephen J. 2016. "Historical Influences on Contemporary Tobacco Use by Northern Plains and Southwestern American Indians." *AJPH History* 106 (2): 246–55. doi:10.2105/AJPH.2015.302909.

Maly, Annika G., Tessa L. Steel, David A. Lieberman, and Thomas M. Becker. 2014. "Colorectal Cancer Screening among American Indians in a Pacific Northwest Tribe: Cowlitz Tribal BRFSS Project, 2009–2010." *Public Health Reports* 129 (May–June): 280–88.

Margalit, R., S. Wantanabe-Galloway, F. Kennedy, N. Lacy, K. Red Shirt, L. Vinson, and J. Kills Small. 2013. "Lakota Elders' Views on Traditional versus Commercial/Addictive Tobacco Use; Oral History Depicting a Fundamental Distinction." *Journal of Community Health* 38: 538–45. doi:10.1007/s10900–012–9648–7.

Marr, Carolyn J. 2016. "Assimilation through Education: Indian Boarding Schools in the Pacific Northwest." *University of Washington Libraries.* Accessed May 18. http://content.lib.washington.edu/aipnw/marr.html.

McGuinness, Teena M., and Jessica Waldrop. 2015. "Adverse Childhood Experiences and the Mental Health of Veterans." *Journal of Psychologocial Nursing* 53 (6): 23–6.

National Council of Urban Indian Health. 2011. "PPACA & IHCIA Training Report." *National Council of Urban Indian Health,* 1–24.

National Tribal Budget Formulation Workgroup. 2015. "Turning the Corner in Indian Health Treaty and Trust Obligations: Writing a New Future for American Indians and Alaska Natives. The National Tribal Budget Formulation Workgroup's Recommendations on the Indian Health Service Fiscal Year 2017 Budget May 201." *National Indian Health Board.* http://www.nihb.org/docs/06242015/Final FY 2017 IHS budget full report.pdf.

Norris, Tina, Paula L. Vines, and Elizabeth M. Hoeffel. 2012. "The American Indian and Alaska Native Population: 2010." *United States Census Bureau* January: 1–21.

North Dakota Department of Health. 2014. "Vital Records." http://ndhealth.gov/vital/.

Office of Minority Health. 2013. "Obesity and American Indians/Alaska Natives." http://minorityhealth.hhs.gov/omh/browse.aspx?lvl=4&lvlid=40.

———. 2016. "American Indian/Alaska Native Profile." Rockville, MD. http://minorityhealth.hhs.gov/omh/browse.aspx?lvl=3&lvlid=62.

Perdue, David G., Donald Haverkamp, Carin Perkins, Christine Makosky Daley, and Ellen Provost. 2014. "Geographic Variation in Colorectal Cancer Incidence and Mortality, Age of Onset, and Stage at Diagnosis among American Indian and Alaska Native People, 1990–2009." *American Journal of Public Health* 104 (S3): S404–14. doi:10.2105/AJPH.2013.301654.

Proctor, R. N. 2001. "Tobacco and the Global Epidemic of Lung Cancer." *Nature* 1 (October): 82–86. doi:10.1038/35094091.

"Public Law 67–85—The Snyder Act—25 U.S.C. 13 Section 13. Expenditure of Appropriations by Bureau." 1921. https://www.ihs.gov/chs/documents/SNYDER_ACT.pdf.

"Public Laws of the Eighty-Third Congress, Second Session, 1954. Public Law 568." 1954. *Indian Affairs: Laws and Treaties* VI. Washington, DC: Government Printing Office: 634–35. http://digital.library.okstate.edu/kappler/vol6/html_files/v6p0634b.html#mn11.

Ravello, Lori De, Jessica Abeita, and Pam Brown. 2008. "Breaking the Cycle/Mending the Hoop: Adverse Childhood Experiences among Incarcerated American Indian/Alaska Native Women in New Mexico." *Health Care for Women International ISSN* 29 (3): 300–15. doi:10.1080/07399330701738366.

Rempel, Julia D., and Julia Uhanova. 2012. "Hepatitis C Virus in American Indian/Alaskan Native and Aboriginal Peoples of North America." *Viruses* 4: 3912–31. doi:10.3390/v4123912.

Roh, Soonhee, Catherine E. Burnette, Kyoung Hag Lee, Yeon-Shim Lee, D. Easton, and Michael J. Lawler. 2015. "Risk and Protective Factors for Depressive Symptoms among American Indian Older Adults: Adverse Childhood Experiences and Social Support." *Aging & Mental Health* 19 (4): 371–80. doi:10.1080/13607863.2014.938603.

Shanks, Carmen Byker, Teresa Smith, Selena Ahmed, and Holly Hunts. 2015. "Assessing Foods Offered in the Food Distribution Program on Indian Reservations (FDPIR) Using the Healthy Eating Index 2010." *Public Health Nutrition* 19 (7): 1315–26. doi:10.1017/S1368980015002359.

U.S. Department of Health and Human Services. 2015a. "HHS FY2016 Budget in Brief." http://www.hhs.gov/about/budget/fy2016/budget-in-brief/index.html.

———. 2015b. "The ACA & American Indian & Alaska Native People." http://www.hhs.gov/healthcare/facts-and-features/fact-sheets/aca-and-american-indian-and-alaska-native-people/index.html.

U.S. Department of the Interior, Office of the Assistant Secretary—Indian Affairs. 2014, January 16. "2013 American Indian Population and Labor Force Report." https://www.nnidatabase.org/2013-american-indian-population-and-labor-force-report

Veazie, Mark, Carma Ayala, Linda Schieb, Shifan Dai, and Jeffrey A. Henderson. 2014. "Trends and Disparities in Heart Disease Mortality among American Indians/Alaska Natives, 1990–2009." *American Journal of Public Health* 104 (S3): 359–68. doi:10.2105/AJPH.2013.301715.

Warne, Donald. 2011. "Policy Issues in American Indian Health Governance." *Journal of Law, Medicine & Ethics* 39 (Suppl 1): 42–5.

Wiggins, Charles L., David K. Espey, Phyllis A. Wingo, Judith S. Kaur, Robin Taylor Wilson, Judith Swan, Barry A. Miller, Melissa A. Jim, Janet J. Kelly, and Anne P. Lanier. 2008. "Cancer among American Indians and Alaska Natives in the United States, 1999–2004." *Cancer* 113 (S5). Wiley Subscription Services, Inc., A Wiley Company: 1142–52. doi:10.1002/cncr.23734.

Wong, Charlene A., Francine C. Gachupin, Robert C. Holman, Marian F. Macdorman, James E. Cheek, Steve Holve, and Rosalyn J. Singleton. 2014. "American Indian and Alaska Native Infant and Pediatric Mortality, United States, 1999–2009." *American Journal of Public Health* April: 1–9. doi:10.2105/AJPH.2013.301598.

Wu, Li-Tzy, George E. Woody, Chongming Yang, Jeng-Jong Pan, and Dan G. Blazer. 2011. "Racial/Ethnic Variations in Substance-Related Disorders among Adolescents in the United States." *Archives of General Psychiatry* 68 (11): 1176–85.

16

THE MILLION HEARTS HYPERTENSION LEARNING COLLABORATIVE AS A MODEL FOR POPULATION HEALTH IMPROVEMENT

José Thier Montero and Sharon Moffat

Modified with permission from: Opportunities to improve population health by integrating governmental public health and health care delivery: lessons from the ASTHO million hearts quality improvement learning collaborative. Montero J.T., S.G. Moffat, and P.E. Jarris. 2015. Discussion paper. Institute of Medicine. Washington, DC.

Introduction

To achieve and maintain meaningful improvement in population health, we must work together, in functional partnerships, with a priority on learning from successes, difficulties, and maybe especially from failures. This learning needs to happen at all levels of the sociopolitical (national, state, county, local), organizational (hospital, health center, solo practice), and sectoral (health and partners on the social determinants of health) arenas of health care.

Partnerships toward population health must be grounded in a set of shared goals and be unequivocally committed to achieve effective collaboration at all levels of the continuum of health. It is important as well that we agree on the scope of the continuum of health as going beyond the continuum of care, because through effective collaborations we can make measurable progress in addressing inequities related to the social determinants of health.

There is a body of evidence of successful collaboration between hospitals and public health agencies. Less comprehensive is the literature of successful collaboration among public health organizations, health care delivery institutions, and organizations dedicated to work on different aspects of the social determinants of health. This may be a direct result of the lack of a shared agenda, goals, and direction. Such lack may impede a more active, meaningful, and targeted collaboration. As stated in a report by Larry Prybil and his collaborators:

> There now is an extraordinary opportunity for mutually beneficial coop-
> eration among hospitals, public health departments, and others who share
> commitment to improving community health. It is hoped that hospital
> and health department leaders seize this opportunity and collaborate in
> bringing about transformational change.
>
> *(Prybil et al., 2014, p. 1)*

As many cities, counties, and states engage to develop community health improvement plans, and the federal government provides guidance toward better integration on improved performance for selected clinical conditions (Hester et al., 2015) or new and innovative payment methodologies (CMS request for proposals for Accountable Health Communities, 2016), we can build on experiences such as the Association of State and Territorial Health Officials' (ASTHO) 10-state quality improvement learning collaborative on hypertension.

This project is a model on how to embrace the challenge of improving population health. In this chapter, we examine not only the components of success, but the barriers to sustaining and spreading successful models of population health improvement through the integration of public health and health care delivery and other partners on the social determinants of health arena. This project provides an adaptable format for sustainable population health improvement. And, even though this learning collaborative specifically focused on improving hypertension diagnosis and control, the lessons learned can work for multiple health conditions and apply to a variety of population health improvement projects.

To improve health at a population level and support lifestyle and other changes in homes and communities, we need to continue developing more effective and efficient models of care while engaging other sectors in the system affecting the social determinants of health. However, making these improvements one provider, one clinic, or one community at a time is not enough to stem the urgent need to effectively improve population health. As the Institute of Medicine noted in the report *Primary Care and Public Health: Exploring Integration to Improve Population Health*, "The integration of primary care and public health could enhance the capacity of both sectors to carry out their respective missions and link with other stakeholders to catalyze a collaborative, inter-sectoral movement toward improved population health" (National Research Council, 2012).

Million Hearts® is a national initiative, launched in September 2011 by the Department of Health and Human Services. Its aim is to prevent 1 million heart attacks and strokes in the United States over a five-year timeframe. Million Hearts aims to prevent heart attacks and strokes by:

- Improving access to effective care
- Improving quality of care for the ABCS of heart health:
    - Aspirin when appropriate
    - Blood pressure control

- ○ Cholesterol management
- ○ Smoking cessation
- Focusing clinical attention on the prevention of heart attack and stroke
- Activating the public to lead a heart-healthy lifestyle
- Improving the prescription and adherence to appropriate medications for the ABCS

ASTHO, with funding from the U.S. Centers for Disease Control and Prevention (CDC), led a 10-state multi-quality improvement (QI) learning collaborative to support Million Hearts. The collaborative used QI rapid-cycle clinical, community, and data system interventions to accelerate improvement in hypertension control. All 10 states have (1) incorporated NQF-18 reporting into clinics, (2) established registries to identify undiagnosed and uncontrolled hypertensive patients, (3) adopted clinical protocols to identify and follow up with hypertensive patients, and (4) created linkages to community resources, including patient self-management.

To address hypertension, state teams focused on solutions at both the state policy level and the clinical and community level. More than 250 QI cycles were tested in one-month periods, generating rapid successes and helping to quickly identify impediments. The collaborative established five key levers for improvement:

1. A commitment from leadership across the health system (at local, state, and national levels).
2. Identification of community and clinical resources and linkages, such as team-based care delivery systems, faith-based outreach programs, healthy lifestyle promotions, and skills development for chronic disease self-management.
3. Use of multiple data sources to inform action.
4. Use of standardized protocols in areas such as hypertension management, community screening and referral, and equipment calibration.
5. Identification of financing opportunities, including private and public payment and federal and state grants.

Participating states reported impacting 90,000 patients on the early implementation stages and estimated a potential reach of 1.5 million patients upon full statewide implementation. In the first nine months, several clinics demonstrated improvement by helping 11 percent of the patients achieve control of their hypertension. Participating states have been sharing their experiences with other states, demonstrating that collective national, state, and local leadership can have a positive impact on this cardiovascular epidemic. The collaborative's successful first year led it to expand to six additional states and one territory, for a collective national QI collaborative of 16 states (Moffat et al., 2015).

The Components of Success

National, State, and Local Leadership

The ASTHO Million Hearts Learning Collaborative drew on state health officials' leadership to identify new approaches to linking clinical and public health systems to improve population health. State health officials set the vision and priority direction for their states' projects and played a key role in identifying unique stakeholders and convening clinicians and organizations that had limited prior experience working together on health systems transformation. ASTHO provided each state team with a pre- and post-intervention evaluation tool and analyzed each state's partner communications at all levels to suggest areas for improvement.

The teams succeeded partly by leveraging local, state, and national partners' leadership, which included clinicians, clinical managers and staff, community organizers, academic institution experts, state and national public and private payers, and representatives of national organizations like the American Heart Association and quality improvement organizations. Leaders at the state agency level facilitated internal change from traditional program implementation to rapid-cycle, system-wide change with engagement from the provider and payer communities. These early successes spread and became sustainable thanks to such key team strategies as leveraging "siloed" (e.g., disease-specific) funding and identifying new funding opportunities. For example, several states in the collaborative have applied to a diverse array of funders, including the Centers for Medicare and Medicaid Services' State Innovation Model (SIM) grants aimed at improving population health.

Linking Patients with Community Resources

Purposefully and proactively integrating health systems, community partners, and engaged patients can create a much greater impact than any one entity's efforts alone. Building strong linkages between the clinical setting and community assets is key to improving the health of a community. Clinics can link patients to numerous community assets and resources, including culturally sensitive programs, volunteers, transportation, community activities, and events. Each ASTHO learning collaborative state has drawn from its communities' rich assets by engaging local leaders, workers, and volunteers (e.g., paramedics, barbers, faith-based community leaders, pharmacists, dental hygienists, and librarians) in its hypertension interventions.

In one of the states participating in the collaborative, the teams worked with some groups to help them become more self-sufficient through farming and healthier through improved access to fresh fruits, vegetables, and other healthy food. They brought local farmers to the clinic and organized farm stands, then innovative electronic benefits transfer/supplemental nutrition assistance program technology enabled customers to utilize their supplemental nutrition (food stamps) benefit. In addition, with the support of the food bank and other organizations, these patients' benefits were doubled to support purchases of additional fruits and vegetables.

Using Data to Drive Action

Important patient and community health data can be found in electronic and paper clinical records, payer claims, pharmacies, and local and state health agencies, among other locations. This data can be used to drive action for optimum population health improvements in the following ways:

- Clinicians and patients can use the data to make informed care decisions.
- Clinicians can use population health data to target individual patients from their clinic population for additional follow-up and engagement with appropriate community resources.
- Local and state health agencies can use population health data to target their limited resources to areas of highest need.
- Payers can use data to identify and reward areas that achieve success measures with payment incentives and replication opportunities.

Each state in the ASTHO learning collaborative identified a need to improve its ability to achieve data-driven action. The learning collaborative provided an opportunity for states to bring current and new partners together to test where data existed but was not being used or linked back to clinicians. State health leaders have played a key role in facilitating these partnerships to identify opportunities to use data more strategically to improve health outcomes. For example, several states worked with pharmacies to improve medication adherence using clinical and payer claims data to address the multiple barriers to adherence. Each state health department is also using population health data, such as information from the Behavior Risk Factor Surveillance Survey, to target areas for priority outreach and to replicate successful models.

Standardizing Protocols

Successful outcomes in clinical care settings are often dependent on establishing and standardizing treatment protocols. However, to achieve population health improvement, states need to identify and standardize protocols far beyond the clinical setting. Public health, clinical care, and community partners can work together to address this issue. In the ASTHO learning collaborative, these partners identified and developed innovative protocols to test change and improve hypertension outcomes using quality measures.

In one example, New Hampshire's learning collaborative team benefited from Cheshire Medical Center/Dartmouth-Hitchcock Keene's experience. This partner integrated community and clinical partners and increased patient engagement in two federally qualified health centers in different metropolitan areas. The Medical Center's integrated approach to hypertension control protocols, which reached 85 percent for more than 12,000 patients, helped the federally qualified health centers improve blood pressure control by 10 percentage points in less than nine months. This exemplifies the power of identifying a successful and standardized model and working with community and clinical partners in other municipalities to replicate success, while still drawing on each community's unique assets.

In another example, teams updated protocols for taking and reporting blood pressures in community settings, referral protocols between community partners and clinical settings, protocols for medication adherence follow-up, training protocols for community health workers, and protocols on data sharing.

Resources to Sustain and Spread Improvement

To sustain and spread successful population health improvement models, we need to strategically identify and plan for resources that support success at the local, state, and national levels. Needed resources include not only funding but an expert workforce, community assets, payment policies, and collaborative partnerships.

ASTHO established its learning collaborative through funding from CDC to leverage the national focus on the Million Hearts initiative. ASTHO used this funding to support states, national partners, and internal infrastructure for the collaborative. The participating states were required to identify and implement a plan to sustain and replicate successes. ASTHO provided states with funding to do the work along with a structured process for developing and measuring goals, engaging stakeholders, and obtaining access to national and federal experts.

This federal investment in a 10-state learning collaborative created a critical structure for state health agencies and their partners to strategically plan for resources to sustain and spread their success. For example, in all 10 states, this work has informed other CDC-funded state-directed chronic disease programs. In six states, the collaborative partnerships and successes have informed the states' applications for SIM grants. States also learned strategies to identify and maximize resources, such as using community health benefit funds to support registry managers in clinic settings. In addition, each state leveraged its state leaders' expertise: Alabama consulted with academic leaders on health disparities to inform their work; many states consulted with their quality improvement organizations; and several states partnered with state medical societies to help spread their successes.

Addressing Barriers to Sustaining and Spreading Successful Models of Population Health Improvement

Implementing a Quality Improvement Approach

Clinicians, payers, and local and state health leaders can identify successes in small or local settings, but often lack ways to systematically spread these successes across regions and states. Without a quality improvement approach, it is very difficult to understand impediments to success, make adjustments, and sustain and replicate successes, which in turn limits opportunities for improved population health.

In the early phases of the Million Hearts Learning Collaborative, partners worked together to identify examples of success and created plans to replicate it using the plan-do-study-act (PDSA) quality improvement process to rapidly test change improvements. The PDSA model provides a format whereby states and partners work closely to test plans multiple times before taking them to scale and provides a common quality improvement language platform where both, the public health and the clinical partners, felt comfortable. During this process, state health agencies engage partners at the highest decision-making level along with regional partners, community and clinical providers, and local public health agencies. As states implement action plans and learn from each other, this rapid-cycle model allows for all levels of the system to test the model for change, study its effects, test again until the process is fully refined, and then support meaningful dissemination. The 10 states identified problems and solutions and tested these solutions, generating rapid successes and helping to quickly define impediments.

Requiring state teams to report results to their partners and the other learning collaborative teams has assured ongoing quality improvement across this national collaborative. In addition, besides convening two in-person meetings of the 10 state teams, ASTHO draws on a unique organizational strength: its use of technology to provide virtual meetings. Virtually connecting all 10 states and their partners for real-time information sharing goes far beyond conference calls: ASTHO also facilitates visual presentations and simultaneously engages all partners. Through these meetings states have been able to share challenges and solutions as well as motivate and support each other (Moffat et al., 2015).

Linking Community Resources

Communities' unique needs and resources have long been valued as a major contributor to improved population health. However, if these community attributes are valued in isolation, the communities' impact may be limited, because clinical and public health partners may miss opportunities to link patients to these resources. Thus, the efforts of communities may not be fully realized or spread through the community, region, and state.

The Million Hearts Learning Collaborative brought community partners to the planning team to identify unique community needs, priorities, and resources. For example, one state used farmers' markets to educate patients on heart-healthy foods and provide blood pressure monitoring. In another state, multilingual translators worked with clinicians, the state medical society, and local and state health agencies to translate materials on blood pressure control. One state worked with librarians in different regions to provide blood pressure monitoring equipment to local residents. Other states used community paramedics, pharmacists, dental hygienists, barbershop employees, and librarians to provide blood pressure information, equipment, and monitoring. In several states community partners started to use the Stanford Chronic Disease Self-Management Program to help individuals act on their health care providers' recommendations.

As we think how to initiate, sustain, and scale up population health initiatives similar to this learning collaborative, we recognize the value of community engagement toward establishing linkages to varied community resources. Across the country, hospitals are engaged to improve the health of the communities they serve, and here we showed an effort that enables an innovative approach to the use of community benefits under a community health improvement perspective. The literature suggests that local and state public health officials engage the communities, partner with local hospitals' top leadership to share data, assessment methodologies, and evidence-based interventions, and connect hospitals with existing community coalitions to prevent inequities among disparate populations (Rosembaum, 2013). This collaborative demonstrated the value of this approach and achieved its goal to link the providers and patients to the community resources.

Using Data to Drive Action

Learning collaborative states repeatedly noted that the lack of a data feedback loop for clinicians, payers, and local and state leaders was a barrier to improving hypertension rates. All 10 states regularly gathered data by multiple methods, yet did not systematically collect this information to drive action. For example, states did not mine data from electronic health record reports and analysis to identify new and uncontrolled hypertensives in a clinic's population. Payers' and local and state public health agencies' data were typically not connected or interoperable. This created barriers to using data to inform community-, regional-, and state-level population health interventions. Without data feedback loops, states continued to miss opportunities to inform priority areas of need, target resources, and evaluate population health progress.

State teams address these data barriers in multiple ways. In a New Hampshire clinic, registry managers, supported by community health benefit funding from a regional hospital system, review clinical data and alert priority individuals for recall physician visits. Registry managers actively manage data and have a critical role in providing regular transparent feedback to clinicians on hypertension control and prioritizing patients that need follow-up. In Vermont, the state health agency works with public and private payers to identify data and target specific regions for interventions to improve hypertension. Other states are working with pharmacies to link care providers with information on patient medication use.

Building a Public Health Workforce Skilled in Health Systems Transformation

One of public health's greatest strengths is the diversity of its workforce, which includes epidemiologists, health educators, lawyers, nurses, physicians, social workers, and many other professionals. At the same time, this diversity of education and skill may not include understanding health systems change implementation. As ASTHO observed in the Million Hearts Learning Collaborative, although public health staff were eager to improve diagnosis and control of hypertension, they frequently sought programmatic interventions instead of taking a health systems approach drawn from multiple partners' expertise. Additionally, many public health staff had limited experience in leading quality improvement change using PSDA rapid cycles.

In 2013, a group of 67 public health organizations representing the full spectrum of public health practice identified systems thinking and change management as two of the top three areas in which the public health workforce needs to improve (Kaufman et al., 2014). To better help public health staff lead sustainable, replicable population-level improvements, it is critical to educate them on moving from program implementation to health systems change. This investment requires support from public health leaders at the local, state, and national levels. This training should include how to use a quality improvement approach with active PDSA cycles to develop and support the components of successful change. The National Board of Public Health Examiners offers a certification of public health professionals (CPH) program to enhance the public health workforce. Additionally, local and state health agencies can pursue Public Health Accreditation Board (PHAB) accreditation to build a public health workforce skilled in health systems change.

Identifying Resources to Sustain and Spread Models of Success

As noted above, a key component for sustaining and spreading successful models of population health improvement is having a strategic plan for maintaining resources, because combining efforts and resources have demonstrated improved success. This was a requirement of the ASTHO Million Hearts Learning Collaborative. Although it was challenging, each of the 10 states identified sustainability plans, including optimizing current CDC funding, working with federally qualified health centers through their HRSA-supported work, applying for SIM grants, and drawing on community, regional, and state partners.

As federal agencies and foundations develop additional funding opportunities, there are several lessons to take from ASTHO's Million Hearts Learning Collaborative. First, health systems collaboration requires support for sustained high-level leadership that can convene across sectors (e.g., state health officials). Learning collaboratives must also require teams to develop and implement plans to sustain and spread their successes. Additionally, statewide and national quality improvement learning collaboratives need funding if they want to replicate successes beyond one community or clinic setting at a time; private and public payers must also be actively engaged at state, regional, and national levels to develop payment models that support these collaboratives.

An issue that was not directly addressed by this collaborative was how to collect and utilize information on health and economic returns from the intervention. For example, what was the cost-effectiveness of the learning collaborative? We may need to address new partnerships, perhaps through academic organizations, to be able to provide this type of evaluation. As we move into new models of care and innovative payment methodologies that pay for value, we need to be able to capture the savings to reinvest properly on the community-based components of this initiative. This will be one of the more successful approaches for sustaining and spreading the success of models like the one described here.

Finally, it is important to support multilevel partnerships across communities, regions, states, and the nation to help identify opportunities to optimize unique resources and expertise to sustain and spread success. Toward this end there are different tools that help organizations address the building partnerships process. The Public Health Foundation developed a population health driver diagram framework that can be used to identify and address resources and areas for collaboration. This driver diagram identifies primary and secondary drivers of an identified community health objective and creates the framework for the proper selection and alignment of the multiple actions that are necessary to achieve the community objectives. Because it is a tool that encourages participation, it allows the community and different public and private organizations to identify and commit to roles, actions, and accountabilities that are within their expertise.

Conclusion

Lessons learned from nationally led quality improvement initiatives like ASTHO's Million Hearts Learning Collaborative can help inform and achieve other population health improvements. To start, population health improvement requires that we understand successful models of health systems change, clearly identify the components of and barriers to success, and develop methods for sustaining and expanding successful models beyond their initial locations or communities. In addition, by collaborating, public health partners can identify opportunities to move from isolation through the continuum of integration to weave expertise into a coherent and consistent approach to improving health outcomes (National Research Council, 2012). This initiative provides clear evidence of the possibilities for the success of national approaches such as the recently launched CDC's 6/18 initiative (Hester et al., 2015) or the conceptual approach described by Auerbach (2016) in "The 3 Buckets of Prevention." It is therefore crucial to recognize and build upon each partner's expertise and unique contributions. Finally, if our goal is to improve population health, we cannot afford to create success one clinic or one practice community at a time. It will take collaboration between public health, clinical, and community leaders to sustain and spread models of successful population health improvement and to strategically identify and plan for the resources that support success.

Bibliography

Auerbach, J. 2016. The three buckets of prevention. *Journal of Public Health Management* 22(3):1–4.

Bialek, R., J. Moran, and M. Kirshy. 2015. *Using a population health driver diagram to support health care and public health collaboration.* Discussion paper. Washington, DC. Institute of Medicine.

Centers for Medicaid and Medicare Services. Accountable Health Communities Model. https://innovation.cms.gov/initiatives/AHCM innovation

Hester, J.A., J. Auerbach, L. Seef, J. Wheaton, K. Brusuelas, and C. Singleton. 2015. *CDC's 6/18 initiative: Accelerating evidence into action.* Washington, DC. National Academy of Medicine.

Kaufman, N.J., M.A. Castrucci, J. Pearsol, et al. 2014. Thinking beyond the silos: Emerging priorities in workforce development for state and local public health agencies. *Journal of Public Health Management and Practice* 20(6):557–565. http://journals.lww.com/jphmp/pages/articleviewer.aspx?year=2014&issue=11000&article=00001&type=abstract (accessed January 21, 2015).

Million Hearts Fact Sheet. http://millionhearts.hhs.gov/files/MH_Fact_Sheet.pdf

Moffat, S., P. Jarris, E. Romero, and L. Waddell. 2015. Health system change: Supporting 10-state learning collaborative for rapid-cycle change. *Journal of Public Health Management and Practice* 21(1):100–102. http://journals.lww.com/jphmp/Fulltext/2015/01000/Health_System_Change___Supporting_10_State.18.aspx (accessed January 21, 2015).

Montero, J.T., M.V. Lupi, and P.E. Jarris. 2015. *Improved population health through more dynamic public health and health care systems collaboration.* Discussion paper. Washington, DC. Institute of Medicine.

National Research Council. 2012. *Primary care and public health: Exploring integration to improve population health.* Washington, DC: The National Academies Press. http://www.iom.edu/Reports/2012/Primary-Care-and-Public-Health.aspx (accessed January 21, 2015).

Persson, K. 2016. *Integrating clinical care with community health through New Hampshire's million hearts learning collaborative: A population health case report.* Discussion paper. Washington, DC. National Academy of Medicine.

Prybil, L., P.E. Jarris, and J.T. Montero. 2015. *A perspective on public-private collaboration in the health sector.* Washington, DC. National Academy of Medicine.

Prybil, L., F.D. Scutchfield, R. Killian, A. Kelly, and G. Mays. 2014. *Improving community health through hospital-public health collaboration.* Lexington, KY. Commonwealth Center for Governance Studies, Inc.

Rosembaum, S. 2013. *Principles to consider for the implementation of a community needs assessment process.* Washington, DC. Department of Health Policy, George Washington University. School of Public Health and Health Services.

17

DEVELOPING AND IMPLEMENTING A POPULATION HEALTH DRIVER DIAGRAM

Ron Bialek and John W. Moran

Introduction

In its report *The Future of the Public's Health in the 21st Century*, the Institute of Medicine calls for significant movement in "building a new generation of inter-sectoral partnerships that also draw on the perspectives and resources of diverse communities and actively engage them in health action."[1] Recognizing the large share of the U.S. gross domestic product that is going toward healthcare and the reality that investments in healthcare are not achieving the results desired by our communities and nation, there is an increasing demand to get greater value from the healthcare dollar. Given these realities as well as incentives created under the Affordable Care Act and other healthcare reforms, there is a growing recognition of the need for the healthcare, public health, and other sectors in individual communities and across the nation to collaborate and align their efforts to improve health outcomes.

As noted by Michael Stoto in his Academy Health brief, *Population Health in the Affordable Care Act Era*:

> The phrase "population health" is increasingly used by researchers, practitioners, and policy makers in healthcare, public health, and other fields. Although understanding of this phrase differs, many see attention to population health as a potent opportunity for healthcare delivery systems, public health agencies, community-based organizations, and many other entities to work together to improve health outcomes in the communities they serve.[2]

Public health and healthcare organizations are more effective when they combine their efforts to address a community population health issue than when they work separately and competitively. The population health driver diagram framework, which is the topic of this chapter, helps guide efforts for public health, healthcare, and other organizations to work collaboratively rather than competitively, offering far-reaching potential for both the sectors and the communities they serve.

What Is a Population Health Driver Diagram?

A population health driver diagram[3] captures a proposed community health change program into a single visual graphic diagram that shows a potential path for health improvement. It depicts a detailed theory of potential change, developed by subject matter experts within communities, about how to address a community health challenge by showing a potential improvement path. A population health driver diagram organizes information on proposed activities so the relationships between the aim of the improvement project and the changes to be tested and implemented are made clear. This makes it easier for the various community agencies and organizations to see where they fit into the improvement change process. A measurement framework can be developed for the actions and sub-goals to help monitor progress as actions are agreed upon and teams can be formed to start the implementation of the change.

Communities thrive when they can collectively respond swiftly and strategically to population health challenges. Communities develop a synergy when they collectively tackle health improvement opportunities that will improve the lives of the people in their communities. Done right, development work can lay a strong foundation for a better community future and the ability to tackle other pressing issues.

A population health driver diagram is best used as a systematic way to explore and address the cause and effect relationships of factors that exist related to a targeted community health challenge. When using this framework, communities should first achieve consensus about the AIM and goals of the improvement.

Components of a Population Health Driver Diagram

A driver diagram has four main components, as shown in Figure 17.1:
1. AIM of the improvement project
2. Improvement outcome(s)—goals
3. Primary drivers
4. Secondary drivers

Starting a Population Health Driver Diagram Project

To be successful, a community population driver diagram improvement project needs to have clearly defined roles and responsibilities for all the parties involved. Usually there is a lead organization (e.g., Community Chief Health Strategist) and an organization that will facilitate the process. The following are major activities that each needs to perform in this process.

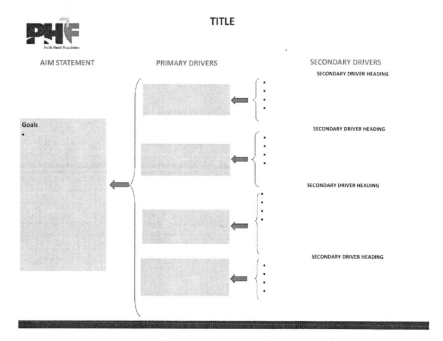

TITLE

FIGURE 17.1

The lead organization will:

- Take the lead in working with the facilitating organization to draft and refine a population health driver diagram to address a community health need
- Identify and convene community stakeholders to work towards reducing risks associated with the identified community health need
- Work with community stakeholders to develop and implement aligned interventions, measures, and targets
- Be the backbone organization for the initiative—plan and hold meetings, communicate between meetings, and provide logistical support for the initiative and the members of the coalition once formed
- Serve as the coordinator of activities throughout the initiative
- Help to identify and appoint team leaders
- Communicate and disseminate timely information on a regular basis:

  - Provide meeting summaries
  - Provide an updated population health driver diagram
  - Identify relevant research materials
  - Use evidence-based intervention
  - Report on initiative's progress

The facilitating organization assists the lead organization with major activities and will:

- Help draft and refine the population health driver diagram, select interventions, and develop measures and targets
- Facilitate meetings with internal staff and stakeholders in the coalition
- Use quality improvement methods and tools to facilitate improvement teams, develop an understanding of causes of the health issue, develop potential solutions, and test potential solutions
- Assure the overall timeliness and success of this initiative by applying project management tools and techniques
- Disseminate information about this initiative, lessons learned, and resources developed for other communities to use

The Process to Develop and Implement a Population Health Driver Diagram

In our work at the Public Health Foundation on developing and implementing population health driver diagrams focused on community health improvement, we have developed a 14-step process to guide our clients to success. These 14 steps are listed below:

1. **Pre-work:** It is necessary for the lead organization to complete pre-work tasks prior to forming and convening a coalition that will tackle a community health issue. Completing these tasks will help the process run smoothly. These pre-work tasks will also provide the lead organization with the data to develop the communication strategy that will be compelling for stakeholders to become engaged in a coalition and enthusiastically participate. The completion of each of these tasks will help the coalition get off to a smooth start. The pre-work tasks include:

    - Work with the facilitating organization to develop a draft population health driver diagram for the health improvement initiative.
    - Compile a profile assessment report that identifies prevalence of and factors associated with the health initiative in the community (e.g., scope, numbers involved, community map, regional and national statistics).
    - Start the development of an inventory of what the health department, other governmental agencies, community-based organizations, healthcare institutions, businesses, and others currently are doing related to this initiative. This inventory will be updated regularly at coalition meetings as new information is uncovered.
    - Identify internal resources and a lead person for the initiative.
    - Identify potential primary driver team leaders. These potential leaders can be within or outside the lead organization. They need to be subject matter experts in the primary drivers they will lead.

- Develop a listing of potential participants and select the core team members.
- Develop timeline of meetings and potential locations.
- Develop a communication strategy and timeline for internal participants and external coalition partners.

The lead organization can utilize the Planning Before You Communicate spreadsheet[4] available from the Public Health Foundation to develop consistent, clear, and crisp communications within and outside the community. The goal of this tool is to help the lead organization design communications that have the following characteristics:

- Keep It Simple—If you or someone on your team does not clearly understand, your audience will not either.
- Know Your Objectives—Each strategic communications activity should align directly with a main objective. If it does not, make the decision whether it is still worth doing and why.
- Know Your Audience—What tactics will be most helpful in reaching them with your messages? Where do they spend their time? How do they get their information?
- Be Direct—If you want action from your audience, clearly ask them for it within a given timeframe. Do not wait or hope or assume that they will get around to it sooner rather than later.

2. **Define the AIM[5] of the community health issue to be addressed:** The AIM of the community health initiative needs to be very clear because it sets the boundaries of what the coalition will and will not focus on. The coalition starts with the draft that the lead organization developed. There is a detailed discussion with coalition members about the AIM to build a consensus AIM that will guide future work. This AIM can be modified by the coalition as it continues to analyze the initiative and new information becomes available. There is an AIM Statement Template in Chapter 27 that can be used as a guide to get started.
    AIM Statements help to:

- Clearly articulate the goal or objective of the initiative
- Express the desired outcome of the initiative (may include sub-aims)
- Reinforce the initiative's desired outcome
- Identify the key leverage points, or "drivers," in the system
- Facilitate stakeholder buy-in and commitment to the changes that the initiative will require

The AIM Statement should be specific, measurable, and answer the questions "What are we trying to accomplish (the measurable AIM), by when, how much, and for whom (which population)?" If the AIM Statement is SMART

(Specific, Measurable, Attainable, Realistic or Relevant, and Time-bound), it helps to guide coalition members to define interventions that are within their control, are measurable, and can be successfully accomplished. When the tone of the AIM Statement is specific and not vague it guides the rest of the process to be specific.

3. **Identify a series of guiding principles for the initiative (optional step):** Some coalitions prefer to have stated guiding principles for the initiative. Guiding principles are defined by the participants regarding what is important to focus on during the improvement initiative. This helps to guide how choices are made, establish key behaviors for successfully working together, and keeps decision making consistent. Some examples of guiding principles can fall into the categories of cost, quality, equity, community engagement, among others.

   To develop these guiding principles, the coalition can complete an exercise where each member of the coalition lists their top three guiding principles for the initiative on a white board or flip chart paper. Similar principles that are posted have a check mark put next to them, and when all are listed they narrow the group down to the top ten using a consensus process. Then the coalition uses a voting method to prioritize the list to the top three to five principles (see Chapter 27 for the write-up on the Prioritization Matrix). These top five principles are used throughout the life of the coalition to ensure that there is a consistent process for decision making.

   Some coalitions imbed these guiding principles in the goal section of the population health driver diagram (see Figure 17.1) and refer back to them when decisions are being made.

4. **Understanding the cost of the population health issue:** Throughout the community health improvement initiative the coalition should develop and update a cost analysis of the effects of the community health issue to be improved. This should include the relevant costs to the community, employers, individuals, families, healthcare providers, and prevention programs. The coalition should keep updating the cost study as new facts are uncovered during the improvement initiative.

   The coalition needs to determine first what type of economic study should be performed and then stick to that model. Mixing different approaches to determining costs will cause confusion later when different approaches need to be compared and then the most effective one selected. There are numerous models for determining costs that can be used by the improvement team. Below is a sample of common costing methods being utilized:

   - Cost-effectiveness.
   - Cost-benefit—ROI. Chapter 19 in this book discusses ROI in more detail.
   - Scenario development—results and consequences—"What could happen if we take this or that action?"

5. **Identify the goals of the AIM:** The coalition will need to decide, after reviewing the evidence-based facts concerning the community health issue, the improvement goals that the community health improvement initiative plans to achieve. The coalition will discuss and describe in three to five goal statements what it plans to accomplish. Remember, a goal is an abstract and general umbrella statement under which specific objectives can be clustered. We want to develop goal statements that have associated actions and objectives that are very specific so that participants and others can understand what the coalition wants to achieve.

   It is a good idea to review with the coalition the difference between goals and objectives as shown in Figure 17.2. Objectives usually start to appear when secondary drivers are being developed.

6. **Identify primary and secondary drivers:** The primary and secondary drivers can be drafted before the coalition meets by convening an expert panel of individuals with subject matter expertise on the population health issue being considered for improvement. This should be a group of eight to ten experts who review relevant literature and then meet for a day to develop an initial draft of the population health driver diagram.

   Another approach is to have the coalition develop the population health driver diagram using an affinity process and interrelationship digraph when they first meet. This will require the lead agency to provide relevant literature before the meeting to all who will be attending because many coalition members may not be subject matter experts. The facilitating agency will need to provide a facilitator knowledgeable in both the affinity and interrelationship digraph methodology.

   Primary drivers are key drivers, system components, factors, or leverage points which contribute directly to achieving the AIM. They are the three to five main drivers the subject matter experts or coalition believe need to be addressed to achieve the desired outcome stated in the AIM Statement. Primary drivers are written as straightforward statements rather than as numeric targets. An example of a primary driver statement is *"Integration of Patient and Family into the Care Plan."* Secondary drivers are the activities and changes that will result in achieving the primary drivers. Secondary drivers are actions, interventions, or lower-level components necessary to achieve the primary

Goals are broad	Objectives are narrow
Goals are general intentions	Objectives are precise
Goals are intangible	Objectives are tangible
Goals are abstract	Objectives are concrete
Goals are generally difficult to measure	Objectives are measurable

FIGURE 17.2

drivers. They should be used to identify changes that can be tested in order to affect the primary drivers. Secondary drivers need to be tangible and actionable. Each secondary driver should be measurable.

7. **Appoint primary driver team leaders and team members:** The team leader and team members are key to the success of a population health driver diagram project. For a population health driver diagram team to be effective, it is essential to select the right leader and team members with the right skills. It is not the number of people, but rather how well they function and work together. Improvement team members must respect each other, and share common goals, visions, agendas, and timelines to be successful. Team leaders should be chosen for each primary driver identified to coordinate activities/actions of the team between meetings and to report at coalition meetings on progress achieved by the team. Their role is to lead and facilitate team meetings to help develop the focus of their primary driver and develop associated secondary drivers that will contribute to achieving the AIM of the improvement initiative.

   Selecting the right team leader and members is a difficult task for the coalition. The Team Member Selection Matrix[6] can be used by the coalition to help facilitate the process of selecting the right people for each improvement team.

8. **Develop partner contracts (optional):** Some coalitions like to have all the partners in the coalition make a commitment to the process which indicates their level of involvement, resources they will provide or need, the primary driver they will support, and members who will be on which teams. These partner contracts can be formal and in writing, informal agreements stated in front of the whole coalition, or a poster made that depicts the community health improvement initiative which all coalition members sign. Some have used the poster signing as a news event, with the commitment being captured live. Some coalitions that have worked together before do not feel the need for a formal or informal commitment because they trust that each other will be active and engaged participants. Each coalition will determine its approach to partner contracts.

9. **Refine each primary and secondary driver:** An Agree/Add/Change Matrix, shown in Figure 17.3, is a tool to use that provides all members of the coalition with an opportunity to comment on the other drivers they are not involved with. At this point the primary driver teams (i.e., improvement teams) have been focused on their assigned primary driver and are developing secondary drivers that support the accomplishment of that primary driver. It is suggested to hold a retreat where each team lead presents its assigned primary driver and associated secondary drivers to the coalition. Once this has been completed, the teams should display the primary and secondary drivers on the Agree/Add/Change Matrix.

   The members of the various improvement teams are then rotated to the other primary drivers and have a chance to show where they agree, where

Primary Driver	Secondary Drivers	Agree	Agree & Add	Change
		√	✚	—

FIGURE 17.3 Agree/Add/Change Matrix

would add, and where they disagree with the secondary drivers shown. The team lead for each primary driver does not rotate. This individual needs to explain the primary and secondary drivers if there is confusion and also captures the each rotating group's input. This round robin input enables everyone in the coalition to feel that they have contributed to the development of all the population health driver diagram drivers and gives everyone a clear understanding of each primary and secondary driver and how these drivers fit in or affect the overall work of the coalition.

In this step some things that may have been overlooked can be incorporated and similar secondary drivers that span other primary drivers can be noted before actions are taken. Similar actions across primary drivers can be coordinated or a separate team can be formed for those actions that may impact multiple primary drivers.

Once the round robin input has been completed, the primary driver teams meet and make any changes they deem appropriate from the input provided and finalize their piece of the population health driver diagram.

10. **Determine actions for secondary drivers:** Once the coalition members have given all primary driver teams their input and the teams have synthesized the input into the final population health driver diagram, it is time to begin action planning. Each primary driver team needs to begin to focus on the

concrete actions they are going to take to achieve the primary and secondary drivers they have been assigned. The teams focus first on evidence-based best practice approaches that have already been developed and tested by others and change packages that might be available and can be easily implemented. Some improvement teams have tried approaches using proven process improvement concepts, such as waste elimination, workflow improvements, quality improvement, and variation reduction. The teams should use quality improvement tools in planning the interventions they decide to undertake so that robust solutions are developed that address the root causes of the health issue.

11. **Analyze action areas for overlap with other secondary drivers using a matrix diagram:** Once all the primary driver teams have determined their interventions, it is recommended that all of the interventions be looked at in a matrix format as shown in Figure 17.4 to determine where overlap and duplication may exist. Coalition members can use this matrix by adding a check mark next to each secondary driver that potential action areas could address. Then the check marks can be totaled up for each column. The totals will indicate potential action areas that address more than one secondary driver.

    The coalition should focus on those potential action areas that address multiple secondary drivers because these actions will have greater impact on achieving the AIM. Another area in the matrix the coalition should explore is any secondary driver that does not have any action associated with it. It is important to understand why no actions were identified. Was something missed or is this secondary driver not important to achieving the AIM and should it be modified or eliminated?

List Potential Action Areas (AA)

List Secondary Drivers	AA1	AA2	AA3	AA4	AA5	AA6	AA7	Total
1. a								
b								
c								
2. a								
b								
3. a								
Total								

FIGURE 17.4

12. **Develop action area groupings to implement:** The coalition needs to review the individual action areas that will be implemented and check to be sure that the coalition has the right team lead and members for each primary driver. In addition, the coalition should decide on which primary driver team lead will lead the actions in action areas that impact multiple secondary drivers.

    Once the team leads and members are solidified, it is important to develop measures that will be used to assess the impact of the various parts of the health improvement plan actions/interventions. The coalition then develops baseline measures, achievement targets, and implementation timelines for each health improvement action/intervention. The use of quality improvement tools and techniques such as the Plan-Do-Check-Act (PDCA) cycle, Gantt Charts, or Critical to Tree (see Figure 17.5) will help the teams in these endeavors. Teams need to understand where they are starting from with a baseline measure for what they are trying to improve. These baseline measures can be compared to the desired achievement targets to determine the gap to be closed by the improvement initiative. Teams will then need to investigate what the causes of the gaps are before developing solutions to be tested.

13. **Trial implementation:** When improvement teams use the PDCA cycle, their project becomes a series of small sequential trials or experiments in which they are rapidly testing and then refining their solutions or ideas for how to achieve the desired outcomes. The PDCA cycle is shown in Figure 17.6.

    If a specific solution or combination of solutions does not have the desired impact, this can serve as evidence that aspects of the underlying assumptions may be flawed. If this happens, the next steps for the improvement team are to:

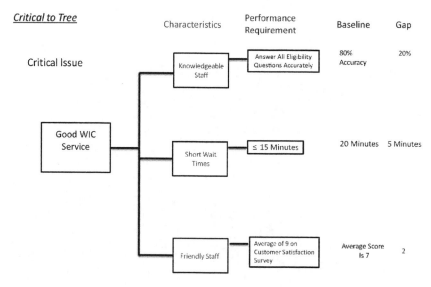

FIGURE 17.5

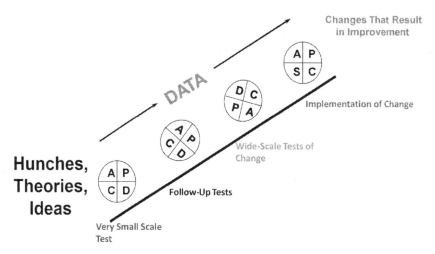

FIGURE 17.6

- Review and modify their assumptions, based on their learning from the trial implementation that did not work or have the desired impact
- Modify the existing potential change concept that was tried to incorporate some of the lessons learned
- Devise new potential change concepts

The improvement team then needs to evaluate the results of new or revised tests to determine if the new actions/interventions had the desired impacts. This sequence of actions is consistent with the PDCA cycle for managing improvements. The coalition continues this cycle until they have a solution or series of solutions that begin to close the gap between the baseline measures and the desired achievement targets.

14. **Finalize the change package:** Once the coalition is satisfied that tested changes work, they can finalize the change package and implement the actions/interventions more broadly.

Summary

It is important to remember that population health driver diagrams are "living" documents. They can and should be modified as theories of improvement are tested and as coalitions learn what drivers and interventions are important for achieving their desired results. As the coalition's population health driver diagram evolves, it helps to capture the learning that the participants have uncovered about the health issue and actions/interventions that are resulting in positive change. These learnings help to guide future improvements in other areas.

Population health improvement projects can lose momentum or derail because transformation at the community levels requires navigating often difficult economic, social, cultural, and political terrain. Using the population health driver diagram framework, by testing and retesting theories of improvement and by effectively engaging multiple stakeholders, can help overcome hurdles that can be entrenched or unpredictable in any project. The population health driver diagram provides an opportunity for multiple diverse stakeholders in a community to become involved and engaged and have their ideas of change considered and possibly tested to determine the impact towards achieving the coalition's population health AIM.

Notes

1. Institute of Medicine, *The Future of the Public's Health in the 21st Century*, National Academies Press, Washington, DC, 2002 (page 4).
2. Stoto, M., *Population Health in the Affordable Care Act Era*, Academy Health, Washington, DC, February 2013 (page 2).
3. Bialek, R., Moran, J., and Kirshy, M., *Using a Population Health Driver Diagram to Support Health Care and Public Health Collaboration*, Discussion Paper, Institute of Medicine, Washington, DC, February 4, 2015.
4. http://www.phf.org/resourcestools/Pages/Planning_Before_You_Communicate_Tool.aspx, accessed July 10, 2016.
5. Moran, J., and Duffy, G., *Public Health Quality Improvement Encyclopedia*, Public Health Foundation, Washington, DC, 2012 (pages 3–4).
6. http://www.phf.org/resourcestools/Pages/Team_Member_Selection_Tool.aspx, accessed July 10, 2016.

18

POPULATION HEALTH COMPETENCIES

Guiding Non-Clinical Hospital and Health System Workforce Development

Ron Bialek, Kathleen Amos,
Julie Sharp, and Janelle Nichols

Introduction

With the transformation of the U.S. health system due to expanded community benefit requirements, value-based purchasing, Accountable Care Organizations, global budgets, and other emerging developments in health reform, there is increasing need for hospitals, health systems, and other healthcare organizations to develop strategies for improving the health of populations. If successful, these strategies can drive down costs and, more importantly, improve the health of individuals and communities.

Whereas many public health professionals working in governmental health agencies have extensive experience and expertise in understanding the needs of populations and implementing strategies to improve population health, similar skills and competencies have not traditionally been as widespread within healthcare organizations. Hospitals, health systems, and others are now trying to identify and prioritize the relevant population health competencies most needed by employees engaged in the assessment of population health needs, and the development, delivery, and improvement of population health programs, services, and practices. This may include activities related to community health needs assessments, community health improvement plans, and implementation of community-based interventions.

Developing Population Health Competencies

The Public Health Foundation (PHF)[1] serves as staff to the Council on Linkages Between Academia and Public Health Practice (Council).[2] This Council, composed of 21 national public health practice and academic organizations,[3] developed and periodically revises a consensus set of Core Competencies for Public Health Professionals (Core Competencies).[4] These competencies guide public health workforce development and are included in Healthy People 2020;[5] the Public Health Accreditation Board (PHAB) Standards and Measures for health department accreditation;[6] job descriptions; employee performance reviews; competency gap analyses; workforce development plans; the TRAIN Learning Network;[7] and many other public health resources, systems, and strategies.

During the 2013 and 2014 annual meetings of the Association for Community Health Improvement (ACHI),[8] an arm of the American Hospital Association, copies of the Core Competencies were made available at PHF's exhibit booth. This resource was received positively by meeting attendees. PHF quickly ran out of copies to share during the 2013 meeting, and although a larger number of copies were offered in 2014, the same occurred.

PHF staff asked ACHI attendees (primarily individuals from nonprofit hospitals and health systems) why they were picking up the Core Competencies. The most common response was, "We have new population health responsibilities, and we don't know what we need to know. These public health competencies are a great starting point for us."

The idea that the Core Competencies, designed for the public health community, could serve as a starting point for population health professionals in non-clinical roles within healthcare organizations was an interesting notion. As a result of this interest, PHF held a workshop during the 2015 ACHI annual meeting to further explore the relevance and use of the Core Competencies in healthcare.

Over 40 individuals from hospitals and health systems attended this workshop. Attendees affirmed the relevance of the Core Competencies to their needs and their work with communities and hospital leadership and staff. Additionally, these hospital and health system professionals identified priority competencies from within the Core Competencies for population health activities. PHF summarized these findings on its PHF Pulse Blog[9] to enable additional discussion and feedback.

Following this workshop, an environmental scan was conducted in 2015 to look for other resources with similarities to the priority population health competencies that had been identified. Through this scan 16 public health publications were examined, revealing that the priority competencies demonstrated substantial alignment with most of these 16 resources.

In 2016, with support from the Centers for Disease Control and Prevention (CDC) and in partnership with ACHI, PHF revised the initial draft Priority Competencies for Population Health Professionals based on feedback received, and worked with ACHI to vet this new draft[10] during the 2016 Community Health Improvement Week[11] and through PHF's website, social media, and other communications channels. This new draft drew heavily from the public health Core Competencies, with minor changes to wording to more specifically focus on hospital and health system settings and needs.

The Current State of Population Health Competencies

Through an online feedback form and during presentations at meetings, more than 100 additional individuals provided feedback on the draft Priority Competencies for Population Health Professionals. Based on feedback received in 2015 and 2016, a broad consensus is developing on this priority set of competencies for population health professionals.

Figure 18.1 provides the 2016 draft of the Priority Competencies for Population Health Professionals that is being used for further vetting.

There is strong agreement that these competencies are indeed priorities for hospitals and health systems engaged in population health activities. In addition, comments during the vetting process have noted the following:

- The distinctions between population health, community health, and public health need to be better defined.
- It may be useful to note how these competencies may be used to address needs of vulnerable populations.
- This list of competencies is an important place to start for training and further discussions with the public health community.
- Additional competencies should be included related to:

  - Quality improvement
  - Informatics
  - Integration of population health concepts throughout hospitals/health systems
  - Engaging organizational leaders and elected officials to lead and advance policy decisions and initiatives that improve population health

The current list of Priority Competencies for Population Health Professionals can serve as a starting point for healthcare organizations looking to develop the skills and competencies of their workforce in population health. Whereas the list will likely continue to evolve, it provides guidance to educators, managers, leaders, and population health professionals in a multitude of healthcare settings who are responsible for training employees, creating job descriptions, conducting performance reviews, developing workforce development plans, and implementing population health strategies and interventions.

What's Next

Now that priority competencies are emerging for the population health workforce, it is important to identify ways to meet competency development needs. Fortunately, there already are strategies in place to do just that.

The TRAIN Learning Network, with over 1 million registered users from health departments, healthcare organizations, preparedness agencies, and other

Community Health Assessment

- Assesses community health status and factors influencing health in a community (e.g., quality, availability, accessibility, and use of health services; access to affordable housing)
- Develops community health assessments using information about health status, factors influencing health, and assets and resources
- Facilitates collaborations among stakeholders to improve health in a community (e.g., coalition building)
- Engages community members to improve health in a community (e.g., input in developing and implementing community health assessments, feedback about programs and services)

Community Health Improvement Planning and Action

- Implements population health policies, programs, and services that align with identified community health needs
- Influences policies, programs, and services external to the organization that affects the health of the community (e.g., zoning, safe housing, food access, transportation routes)
- Makes evidence-based decisions for policies, programs, and services (e.g., using recommendations from The Guide to Community Preventive Services in planning population health services)
- Contributes to the population health evidence base (e.g., community-based participatory research; authoring articles; making data available to researchers)
- Develops partnerships that will increase use of evidence in developing, implementing, and improving population health programs and services (e.g., between healthcare and public health organizations)
- Advocates for the use of evidence in decision making that affects the health of a community (e.g., helping decision makers understand community health needs, demonstrating the impact of programs)

Community Engagement and Cultural Awareness

- Recognizes the ways diversity influences policies, programs, services, and the health of a community
- Supports diverse perspectives in developing, implementing, and evaluating policies, programs, and services that affect the health of a community
- Ensures the diversity of individuals and populations is addressed in policies, programs, and services that affect the health of a community
- Communicates in writing and orally with linguistic and cultural proficiency (e.g., using age-appropriate materials, incorporating images)

Systems Thinking

- Describes healthcare and public health as part of a larger inter-related system of organizations that influence the health of populations at local, national, and global levels
- Describes factors affecting the health of a community (e.g., equity, income, education, environment)
- Explains the ways public health, healthcare, and other organizations can work together or individually to impact the health of a community

Organizational Planning and Management

- Contributes to development of organizational strategic plan (e.g., incorporates community health improvement plan, contains measurable objectives and targets)
- Manages programs within current and projected budgets and staffing levels (e.g., sustaining a program when funding and staff are cut, recruiting and retaining staff)
- Justifies programs for inclusion in organizational budgets
- Develops program budgets
- Defends program budgets
- Uses financial analysis methods in making decisions about policies, programs, and services (e.g., cost-effectiveness, cost-benefit, cost-utility analysis, return on investment)

FIGURE 18.1 Priority Competencies for Population Health Professionals

settings, contains a wide variety of online training in public health and population health. PHF is working with ACHI and CDC to develop online training plans that contain vetted training designed to address the Priority Competencies for Population Health Professionals. Even before these training plans are developed, any public health, healthcare, or population health professional can search for, access, and take training to help build skills and competencies in virtually all of the identified priority areas.

CDC is in the process of integrating population health competencies into many of its sponsored fellowship programs, such as through the Project SHINE fellowships in Applied Public Health Informatics, the Health Systems Integration Program, and the Informatics Training in Place Program.[12] These fellowship programs are becoming increasingly more available to individuals working in healthcare settings.

It also is important to recognize that many state, tribal, local, and territorial governmental public health agencies have staff with skills related to many of the competencies within the Priority Competencies for Population Health Professionals. An opportunity exists for hospitals, health systems, and other healthcare organizations to partner with these governmental agencies, providing needed staff and expertise to supplement the healthcare organizations' population health competency needs. Whereas this may require purchasing services from governmental agencies, the investment in these agencies and the assistance and learning that will occur working with these agencies will be money well spent. Not only will the healthcare organizations' needs be better met, but health department capacity and infrastructure can be expanded in ways that will improve the health of individuals and populations in the community. With health improvement also comes long-term cost savings. These governmental agencies also can provide needed skills and competencies that fall outside of the Priority Competencies for Population Health Professionals, but are important for successful hospital, health system, and overall healthcare strategies and programs to address community population health and institutional fiscal needs.

Notes

1. *Public Health Foundation.* Available from: http://www.phf.org/. Accessed: July 27, 2016.
2. *Council on Linkages Between Academia and Public Health Practice.* Available from: http://www.phf.org/programs/council. Accessed: July 27, 2016.
3. Member organizations of the Council include the American Association of Colleges of Nursing, American College of Preventive Medicine, American Public Health Association, Association of Accredited Public Health Programs, Association of Public Health Laboratories, Association of Schools and Programs of Public Health, Association of State and Territorial Health Officials, Association for Prevention Teaching and Research, Association of University Programs in Health Administration, Centers for Disease Control and Prevention, Community-Campus Partnerships for Health, Council

on Education for Public Health, Health Resources and Services Administration, National Association of County and City Health Officials, National Association of Local Boards of Health, National Environmental Health Association, National Library of Medicine, National Network of Public Health Institutes, National Public Health Leadership Development Network, Quad Council Coalition of Public Health Nursing Organizations, and Society for Public Health Education.

4. Council on Linkages Between Academia and Public Health Practice. (2014). *Core Competencies for Public Health Professionals*. Washington, DC: Public Health Foundation. Available from: http://www.phf.org/resourcestools/Documents/Core_Competencies_ for_Public_Health_Professionals_2014June.pdf. Accessed: July 27, 2016.
5. *Healthy People 2020*. Washington, DC: U.S. Department of Health and Human Services, Office of Disease Prevention and Health Promotion. Available from: https://www. healthypeople.gov/. Accessed: July 27, 2016.
6. Public Health Accreditation Board (PHAB). (2014). *Standards and Measures, Version 1.5*. Alexandria, VA: PHAB. Available from: http://www.phaboard.org/wp-content/ uploads/PHABSM_WEB_LR1.pdf. Accessed: July 27, 2016.
7. *TRAIN*. Available from: https://www.train.org. Accessed: July 27, 2016.
8. *Association for Community Health Improvement*. Available from: http://www.healthycommunities.org/. Accessed: July 27, 2016.
9. Amos, K. (2015 April 17). *PHF, ACHI Exploring Population Health Competencies*. PHF Pulse Blog. Available from: http://www.phf.org/phfpulse/Pages/PHF_ACHI_Exploring_ Population_Health_Competencies.aspx. Accessed: July 27, 2016.
10. *Priority Competencies for Population Health Professionals, Draft 2.0*. (2016). Available from: http://www.phf.org/resourcestools/Documents/Population_Health_Competencies_ Draft2.0.pdf. Accessed: July 27, 2016.
11. *Community Health Improvement Week*. Available from: http://www.healthycommunities. org/Education/CHIweek2016. Accessed: July 27, 2016.
12. Project SHINE Fellowships. Available from: http://www.shinefellows.org/. Accessed: July 28, 2016.

19

APPLYING ECONOMIC IMPACT ANALYSES TO POPULATION HEALTH IMPROVEMENT EFFORTS

Much to Be Learned, and Much to Be Gained

Greg Randolph, Lou Anne Crawley-Stout, and Kerri Ann Ward

Introduction

The United States spends almost double what other wealthy nations spend on healthcare, with little to no improvement in outcomes (Woolf 2013). Largely due to this fact, and an aging population, the healthcare industry is undergoing rapid and transformational change, including emphasis on finding solutions for persistent, costly population health challenges such as obesity and diabetes. Related, as the United States transitions to a value-based healthcare system, health-focused organizations (including public health) and communities are increasingly working collaboratively to improve population health with the desire of achieving lower healthcare costs as well as better health outcomes.

Additionally, public health practice is undergoing rapid change, often facing the need to deliver more with fewer resources due to governmental fiscal austerity and increasing demands to demonstrate the value and impact of the public funds.

Because reducing costs is arguably the major driver of the increasing focus on improving population health, it is not surprising that there is a growing interest in economic impact assessment (often generally referred to as return on investment (ROI) analysis, which is the term we will use in this chapter). ROI, one measure of population health improvement, provides two key advantages:

- ROI analyses can demonstrate impact across many varied types of projects and conditions.
- ROI can help prioritize action based on the "biggest bang for your buck" and can provide leaders with evidence to justify investments in population health improvement efforts that often require significant upfront investments.

In this chapter, we will review the basics of ROI analyses, discuss some of the challenges in applying ROI to population health efforts, explore how these tools have been applied to both public health settings and population health issues, share what we have learned to date, and propose a model for the ROI process when applying to population health efforts.

ROI Basics

History

ROI has been used in business and industry since the early 1900s to help analyze financial returns for strategic investments. Although ROI has spread to some healthcare organizations, it is not widely understood, nor frequently used, in public health. However, due to the focus on healthcare transformation and value-based care, it is becoming essential that public health practitioners link their work to tangible results to help prioritize investments (Crawley-Stout, Ward, See, and Randolph 2015). For this reason, ROI is receiving increasing attention among public health leaders and is beginning to be used more frequently to quantify the financial benefits of public health programs, aggregate public health spending, and quality improvement efforts (Ensign 2013).

The Calculations

There are two primary methods we use to express financial impact: economic impact and ROI. Economic impact shows the total financial return to an organization, whereas ROI shows the financial return for every dollar invested.

Economic Impact Formula

Economic impact (EI) is the total net financial benefits realized by an organization or community as the result of a specific investment. EI is expressed in absolute terms and the resulting dollar amount shows the total financial gain for the organization or community.

economic impact = total financial benefits − total costs

Return on Investment Formula

The ROI formula evaluates the *incremental* financial return (benefit or loss) experienced by an organization or community and is calculated by dividing economic impact by cost. Unlike EI, ROI is described in relative terms, and the resulting ratio shows how much benefit is realized for every dollar invested after covering expenses (Phillips and Phillips 2005, ROI Basics). For example, an ROI of $2 is interpreted as: For every $1 spent, $2's worth of benefit is realized in excess of costs. ROI can also be expressed as a percentage by multiplying the calculated ratio by 100. For example, an ROI of $2 for every $1 spent would be a 200% return. Because ROI is expressed in relative terms, it can be used to compare investment opportunities and guide decision-making.

$$ROI = \frac{economic\ impact}{total\ costs} = \frac{total\ financial\ benefits - total\ costs}{total\ costs}$$

Key Components for Calculating an ROI

There are two key components needed to calculate an ROI: benefits and costs. Before performing the calculations, these two key components are broken down further. For example, benefits are classified as either tangible (financial) or intangible (values unable to be quantified) and as internal or external (depending on who gains and the perspective from which the ROI will be calculated). Costs can also be separated into direct and indirect costs, based on whether the expenses result directly from the intervention being implemented or are a side-effect. Understanding these classifications is critical when deciding what specific numbers to include in the calculation and where to incorporate them.

Internal vs External Benefits

It is important to note that ROI can be calculated from an internal, external, or combined perspective. An internal ROI evaluates the financial benefit via process improvements to the investing organization, whereas an external ROI shows the financial benefit realized by others, often benefiting a larger population of people (such as other businesses, government, community members, or tax payers). A combined ROI evaluates overall financial benefit and includes both internal and external returns. ROIs are not commonly split into internal or external benefits, and instead the calculating organization usually agrees upon and clearly communicates the perspective from which the ROI is calculated and the inclusion criteria used.

YOU TRY

Problem 1: Internal ROI Example
XYZ clinic invested $8,000 to improve their patient flow in their Sexually Transmitted Diseases (STD) Clinic. Due to these changes, they can now see an additional 150 patients each year resulting in an additional $18,000 of profit. What is XYZ's year 1 internal ROI?

Problem 2: External ROI Example
It is estimated that an additional 20 cases of Pelvic Inflammatory Disease (PID) were prevented by treatment of STDs due to the clinic's increased

number of appointments. Each prevented case of PID is estimated to save the community $4,000. What is the year 1 external ROI?

Problem 3: Combined ROI Example
What is the year 1 combined ROI for the example above?

Answers

Problem 1: $\dfrac{\$18,000 - \$8,000}{\$8,000}$ = *$1.25. For every $1 invested, $1.25 was returned to XYZ clinic.*

Problem 2: $\dfrac{((20 * \$4,000) - \$8,000)}{\$8,000}$ = *$9.00. For every $1 invested, $9.00 was returned to the community.*

Problem 3: $\dfrac{\left[\$18,000 + (20 * \$4,000)\right] - \$8,000}{\$8,000}$ = *$11.25. For every $1 invested, $11.25 was returned to XYZ clinic and the community.*

Tangible vs Intangible Benefits

Tangible benefits, also called financial benefits, are those that can be converted into monetary terms and compared to intervention costs. Some tangible benefits (often internal benefits) are straightforward to calculate, such as reduced staff time or supply costs. However, with population health programs, tangible benefits, which are often external to an organization, are more complex. In order to monetize a benefit one must first attempt to isolate program impact to link an intervention to community gains. For example, if a clinical tobacco intervention is implemented during a year where a smoke-free policy is adopted in the community, the benefits realized need to be isolated from those attributable to this policy change. Likewise, before stating that an intervention is responsible for decreased STI expenses in a county, one must be able to justify how the program increased screening rates. The following methods should be considered when converting data to tangible benefits for population health interventions:

- Look for intervention-specific data and ROI tools (example: QuitlineNC ROI Tool)
- Look for topic-specific calculators (example: Alcohol Cost Calculator and CDC's Chronic Disease Cost Calculator)
- Use data sources to find national, state, and community-level statistics (example: Behavioral Risk Factor Surveillance System, Community Health Status Indicators, and State Centers for Health Statistics)
- Complete a brief literature search for academic papers related to your chosen intervention or topic area

When calculating ROI, not all benefits can be readily converted to a dollar amount. Intangible benefits are gains that cannot be easily expressed in financial terms. Intangible benefits may include items like increased staff satisfaction, increased teamwork, increased patient/client satisfaction, increased community knowledge, increased partner buy-in, increased community collaboration, and increased self-efficacy among chronic disease patients. Although these benefits may not be quantifiable, they should be qualitatively included in ROI analyses, as they are often very important to stakeholders and can carry substantial influence when presented effectively (Crawley-Stout, Ward, See, and Randolph 2015). There are methods for converting intangibles into financial benefits, such as intangible benefit multipliers (Moran and Riley 2012); however, it is a judgment call as to whether to employ them. Advantages are that these methods can elevate the importance of intangibles, whereas disadvantages include adding more complexity and being viewed as subjective by some stakeholders (Phillips and Phillips 2005, ROI at Work).

YOU TRY

Categorize each of the below benefits as tangible or intangible:
1. Decreased processing time
2. Decreased # of forms/paperwork
3. Increased staff satisfaction
4. Increased client satisfaction
5. Reduction in printing and postage costs
6. Increased teamwork
7. Increased appointment slots and patients seen
8. Decreased smoking rates in the community
9. Increased partner buy-in and participation
10. Increased breastfeeding rates in hospitals

Answers

1. Tangible, 2. Tangible, 3. Intangible, 4. Intangible, 5. Tangible, 6. Intangible, 7. Tangible, 8. Tangible (there are studies showing the increased healthcare and labor costs of smoking), 9. Intangible, 10. Tangible (there are studies linking increased breastfeeding rates to reduced future healthcare costs)

Direct and Indirect Intervention Costs

Direct costs are expenses that are directly associated with the intervention being implemented. These costs are easy to monetize and may include staff time, building expenses, equipment, or materials. Indirect costs are side-effects of an intervention. For example, an intervention promoting better air quality may result in the decreased profitability of a manufacturing plant leading to job losses in the community. Indirect costs are typically harder to isolate, connect to an intervention, and convert into dollar amounts (*A Guidebook* 2014). For instance, with the air quality and manufacturing plant example, other factors likely contributed to the plant's poor financial situation, making it difficult to say which portion of the unemployment costs should be attributed to the intervention being evaluated. In addition, quantifying the costs incurred as a result of the plant downsizing is difficult due to the large scope and complexity of activities affected by unemployment (such as an increased number of foreclosures, an increased number of residents leaving the community, and less community taxes being collected). Judgment is required to decide which indirect costs should be included in an ROI, as one must consider the strength of the connection between the intervention and cost as well as the effort required to monetize the expense.

Time Periods for Calculating ROI

When calculating ROI, it is important to choose the time period you will use to estimate costs and benefits. Typically, lengthening the time period will result in a higher ROI. This increase occurs because one-time costs are most often realized in the early years, whereas benefits can reoccur year after year.

A longer time horizon may be appropriate if project costs are spread out over many years, or if there is a substantial time lag between implementation of a project and realized benefits (as there often is in population health). Each project will need to be individually analyzed to determine the appropriate time period over which to consider costs and benefits. Although the time period used is at the discretion of each organization, it is recommended that organizations aim for internal consistency and use similar time horizons for similar projects. The time period chosen should be clearly communicated when reporting an ROI.

ROI Calculations and Complexity

There are varying degrees of complexity that can be used when calculating ROI. In the authors' experiences, simpler models can be effectively applied in many public health practice settings. Complex models (for example those including amortization, the time value of money, etc.) add rigor for scientific analyses and high stakes decision-making. However, greater complexity can make ROI analysis more difficult or impossible for public health practitioners and agencies, who often lack previous ROI experience and usually have limited resources and time available to work on ROI calculations (Crawley-Stout, Ward, See, and Randolph

2015). Complex models can also confuse the targeted community stakeholders, making the communication and interpretation of results difficult. The level of complexity must be chosen by the calculating organization after considering the purpose of the ROI and the target audience. The challenge is to apply the right amount of complexity to balance credibly with feasibility. This challenge can be better addressed by hospitals, health departments, and other partners working together to calculate ROI, as they can pool their resources and expertise. In addition, this collaboration can help create a common language and clearer expectations around their use of ROI.

CASE STUDY

A recent Granville Vance Public Health (GVPH) QI project is a good example of a ROI analysis with both internal and external/community benefits. The GVPH mission is to "protect and promote health in Granville and Vance Counties." Although the primary aim of their QI project was to increase revenue to support ongoing health services, their dedication to serving their community resulted in an additional population health goal of reducing unintended pregnancies.

The QI team targeted unintended pregnancies by instituting a standard process of enrolling qualified clients in the Family Planning Waiver (FPW) during the clients' visits. The FPW is a state program that provides family planning services if the applicant meets basic eligibility requirements. Thus, eligible participants can receive increased options for birth control. By enrolling more clients in FPW at GVPH, a reduction in unintended pregnancies and associated costs was realized.

To calculate their community benefits, the team searched the internet for unintended pregnancy cost data. The search led to Guttmacher Institute cost data on unintended pregnancies. The team learned that the average Medicaid cost per live birth in NC (pregnancy and infant up to one year of age) is $12,874 (Guttmacher Institute 2014). After their project was implemented, GVPH directly assisted additional clients in the program, preventing one enrollee per month from an unintended pregnancy. Thus, the program resulted in an estimated annual savings of $154,488 in Medicaid costs for unintended pregnancies (12 pregnancies prevented per year x $12,874).

Although the above description focused only on the community benefits, the EI and ROI analyses for both the internal and community benefits for GVPH are presented in Table 19.1.

TABLE 19.1 ROI Calculation

Project Aim: To increase revenue from billable services so that we can continue to serve our local community and health department customers.	
Benefits – Annualized Year 1	*Costs – Year 1*
Internal Financial Benefits $100,000	Project Costs $13,734
Community Benefits $154,488	
Total Benefits $254,488	
EI	$240,754 (Total Benefits – Costs)
ROI	$17 (EI/Costs)

For every $1 invested in the QI project, GVPH generated $17 in savings.
Intangible benefits included enhanced teamwork at GVPH and improved staff morale.

Application

A Proposed Model for Population Health ROI

The authors have created a population health ROI model that can be tested and refined in future population health initiatives. This model builds on the lessons learned from using the ROI Process Model for Public Health (refer to Lessons Learned section). It is designed to be easily applied and, at the same time, utilizes ample evidence to ensure a meaningful and believable result.

Figure 19.1 outlines the population health ROI model—its steps and components are described below:

- Step 1: Select the intervention(s) and consider the logic model or driver diagram and the evidence-based strategy with the ROI analysis in mind.
- Step 2: Determine key stakeholders and engage them. These stakeholders often provide valuable input regarding the design of the ROI plan and in identifying the data collection criteria, its availability, and its sources. Actively engage key stakeholders to ensure the ROI plan meets their needs and requirements. Solicit ROI expertise to provide support along the way.
- Step 3: Write an ROI measurement (data collection and analysis) plan to include cost categories and definitions, benefit categories and definitions, and a method to quantify the costs to develop and execute the intervention. Develop a timeline for data collection and analysis, and a data collection system. Determine if the ROI will be performed as prospective (an estimate prior to the intervention) and/or retrospective (post-intervention) analysis. For retrospective analysis, be sure to gather baseline data. Key stakeholders may be able to provide ideas and insights about these points of the ROI plan.

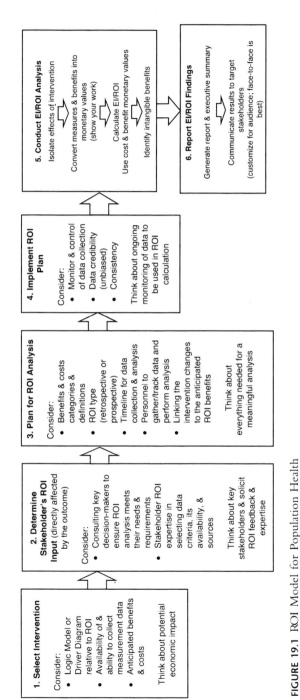

FIGURE 19.1 ROI Model for Population Health

Source: Data adapted from Crawley-Stout, Ward, See, and Randolph 2015.

- Step 4: Implement the ROI measurement plan along with the intervention. Classify the costs and benefits, and document intangible benefits. Analyze and document how benefits are linked to specific changes.
- Step 5: Conduct the ROI analysis by converting outcomes into monetary values, completing the EI and ROI calculations, and specifying intangible benefits.
- Step 6: Document EI/ROI calculations in detail, including sources of evidence. Prepare a detailed ROI report and an executive summary. Tailor reporting to the target audience(s).

Challenges in Using ROI for Population Health Efforts

Although ROI is receiving increasing attention in the field of public health, practitioners often struggle with its role in population health improvement initiatives. There are a number of challenges leading to this hesitancy to embrace ROI for population health. First, after interventions are implemented, population health improvement projects can take years before outcomes and the resulting benefits are realized. This time lag can make it challenging to link benefits to the interventions—a necessity for credibility (Mays 2012). Second, it is important to select interventions for ROI analysis where data is available or easily attainable, as this step "can make the calculation of the economic outcomes practical or impractical and credible or not" (*A Guidebook* 2014). In addition, many practitioners lack the skillset and experience to plan and manage ROI analysis and need step-by-step guidance from an expert (Crawley-Stout, Ward, See, and Randolph 2015). Overall, considering the resources and time needed for population health improvement initiatives, the cost of planning, executing, and calculating an ROI can often become an important factor to consider (*A Guidebook* 2014).

Despite these challenges, population health ROI analyses have been successfully applied in public health. For example, Population Health Improvement Partners (formerly known as the Center for Public Health Quality) included ROI analysis of QI projects undertaken in their quality improvement training program, Quality Improvement 101 (QI 101). Although most projects' ROI analyses related to internal benefits and costs of improvements specific to local and state public health agencies, some projects targeted external population health benefits. Examples of these projects are listed below and are detailed in a previous publication (Crawley-Stout, Ward, See, and Randolph 2015).

- The institution of a clinical evidence-based tobacco prevention program and the assessment of impact to employers in that community due to improved productivity of workers who ceased tobacco use. The community benefit was $57,840.
- Enhanced web-based applications in order to attract more physicians to rural settings and increase access to medical services. The community benefit was $266,000.

- The creation of an "express clinic" for sexually transmitted diseases (STD) resulted in an increase in STD screenings, and thus decreased pelvic inflammatory disease (PID) cases. The community benefit was $129,600.
- The re-engineering of hearing detection screening and related diagnostic process for infants. The community benefit was $329,000.

Lessons Learned

The authors have greatly increased their knowledge of ROI use by assisting teams with application in state and local public health agencies over the past five years (Crawley-Stout, Ward, See, and Randolph 2015). Some of the initial lessons learned include:

- Early planning is necessary for the analysis along with executing the data collection plan pre, post, and throughout the intervention.
- Ongoing technical assistance and coaching is essential support for public health professionals to ensure follow through with the work to conclusion of the ROI analysis.
- ROI analysis tools and templates are needed to promote a standardized method, and step-by-step guidance is essential.
- Public health professionals often need guidance on effectively communicating ROI results to key stakeholders.
- An effective ROI model to provide an overall understanding of the "big picture" of the ROI process is very helpful.

Based on collective experience and the literature, the authors have also developed the following basic principles for ROI analyses (*A Guidebook* 2014; Crawley-Stout, Ward, See, and Randolph 2015):

- Always take a conservative approach in estimating benefits, and base them on data; and avoid benefit data that may appear unbelievable by stakeholders.
- Include all costs associated with the intervention; in other words, avoid minimizing the costs.
- Develop a data collection strategy before beginning implementation, as data collection is usually the most complex part of the ROI process.
- Ensure there is ample documentation to support the line of reasoning and assumptions in ROI calculations—it will be very helpful in explaining results to stakeholders.
- Intangible benefits are extremely valuable in providing the total picture of benefits and should be captured and shared along with the tangible ROI results.
- Share findings with key stakeholders to demonstrate the value of the intervention and the competency of your organization as a partner in promoting better health outcomes.

Conclusions

In summary, the authors believe that while there is still much to be learned about how and when to apply ROI to population health efforts, these challenges are not insurmountable. Further, there are many opportunities that can be realized by applying ROI to population health improvement, such as prioritizing investments in health improvement, demonstrating the potential return on investments from prevention and population health efforts, and stimulating greater healthcare and public health collaboration by providing the business case for health systems to partner with public health organizations. And fortunately, due to efforts by CDC and many health economists, there is increasingly more data available to credibly perform population health ROI analyses.

As we learn more about how to apply ROI to maximize its impact, we will need to get this powerful tool in the hands of those working to improve health, especially at the community level. Thus, it will be critical to balance the need for rigor with a practical and feasible approach at the local/community level.

Acknowledgements

This article was supported by grants from the Duke Endowment, Blue Cross Blue Shield of North Carolina Foundation, and by funds made available from the Centers for Disease Control and Prevention, Office for State, Tribal, Local and Territorial Support under grant number 5U58CD001291–03. The content of this article are those of the authors and do not necessarily represent the official position of or endorsement by the Centers for Disease Control and Prevention.

Special gratitude to Granville Vance Public Health. Their steadfast work in quality improvement made the case study possible. We applaud Health Director Lisa Harrison, MPH, and the QI project's team lead, Leigh Anne Fowler, RN, PHN III, Maternal Health Coordinator/SIDS Counselor, for their ongoing pursuit of continuous quality improvement.

References

Crawley-Stout, L.A., Ward, K.A., See, C.H., and Randolph, G.D. 2015. Lessons Learned from Measuring Return on Investment in Public Health Quality Improvement Initiatives. *Journal of Public Health Management and Practices*, Published ahead of print.

Ensign, K. 2013. Estimating return on investment for public health improvements: Tutorial on using the new tool. http://www.astho.org/Accreditation-and-Performance/Estimating -Return-on-Investment-for-Public-Health-Improvements/.

A Guidebook: Economic Evaluation of Population-Based Prevention Interventions in an ACO Community. 2014. Carrboro, NC: NC Public Health incubator Collaboratives, North Carolina Institute for Public Health.

Guttmacher Institute. 2014. State Facts about Unintended Pregnancy: North Carolina. https://www.guttmacher.org/fact-sheet/state-facts-about-unintended-pregnancy-north-carolina.

Mays, Glen P. 2012. Estimating Value and ROI for Investments in Public Health. 2012 National Public Health Improvement Initiative Grantee Meeting. Atlanta, GA.

Moran, J., and Riley, B. 2012. Calculating the Real Value of Process Improvement: Factoring in Intangible Benefits. *Process Excellent Newsletter*, April 16. http://www.processexcellencenetwork.com/article.cfm?externalID=7153

Phillips, P., and Phillips, J. 2005. The Basics. In: *Return on Investment (ROI) Basics*. Alexandria, VA: ASTD.

Phillips, J., and Phillips, P. 2005. *ROI at Work: Best-Practice Case Studies from the Real World*. Alexandria, VA: ASTD.

Woolf, S., and Aron, L., eds. 2013. *US Health in International Perspective, Shorter Lives, Poorer Health. Panel on Understanding Cross-National Health Differences among High-Income Countries. Committee on Population, Division of Behavioral and Social Sciences and Education, and Board on Population Health and Public Health Practice, Institute of Medicine*. Washington, DC: The National Academies Press.

20

GRHOP [PCCP] HOW TO ORCHESTRATE IT

Working with Community and
Different Sectors to Achieve
Population Health Outcomes

*Tiffany Netters, Jamie Clesi Giepert,
and Eric Baumgartner*

The Event

From April 10, 2010, to July 15, 2010, approximately 4.9 million barrels of oil were discharged into the Gulf of Mexico as a result of the Deepwater Horizon oil rig explosion. BP and the U.S. Department of Justice settled criminal charges in November 2012, leading to criminal and civil settlements and other payments. One of the civil settlements, the Deepwater Horizon Medical Benefits Settlement, provided an opportunity to turn this unfortunate crisis into an investment for the health of Gulf Coast communities. It is important to highlight that while residents strive to understand how the Deepwater Horizon oil spill impacts health along the Gulf Coast, many also continue to face large health disparities across multiple chronic diseases, mental illness and environmental concerns.

A Unique Opportunity

Created as part of the Deepwater Horizon Medical Settlement, the Gulf Region Health Outreach Program (GRHOP) is a multi-year, $105 million initiative composed of five integrated projects designed to strengthen primary care, behavioral health and environmental health care services in oil spill impacted communities in Louisiana, Mississippi, Alabama and the Florida Panhandle. The program commenced in May 2012. The goal of the GRHOP is to inform residents of the targeted communities about their own health and provide access, now and in the future, to skilled frontline health care providers supported by networks of specialists knowledgeable in addressing physical, environmental, and behavioral and mental health needs, thereby improving the resilience of the targeted communities to future health challenges.

The target beneficiaries of the GRHOP are residents, especially the medically underserved, of 17 coastal counties and parishes in Alabama (Mobile, Baldwin), Florida (Escambia, Santa Rosa, Walton, Okaloosa, Bay), Louisiana (Orleans, Jefferson, St. Bernard, Plaquemines, Lafourche, Terrebonne, Cameron) and Mississippi (Hancock, Harrison, Jackson). The GRHOP is composed of four projects: the Primary Care Capacity Project, the Mental and Behavioral Health Capacity Project, the Environmental Health Capacity and Literacy Project, and the Community Health Workers Training Project. The GRHOP also incorporates a Community Involvement project that oversees community outreach efforts in coordination across all GRHOP projects. The Louisiana Public Health Institute (LPHI), located in New Orleans, Louisiana, was one of seven organizations selected to administer one of the projects—the Primary Care Capacity Project (PCCP).

Given LPHI's previous experience with program design, implementation and evaluation related to primary care access grants, LPHI was presented with the unique opportunity for administering this unprecedented project across four states. LPHI is a statewide, 501(c)(3) nonprofit organization founded in 1997 that serves as a partner and convener to improve population-level health outcomes. Its mission is to improve the health and quality of life of all Louisianans regardless of where they live, work, learn or play. LPHI coordinates and manages public health programs and initiatives in the areas of health systems development and community health improvement and provides an array of services to help meet the needs of local and national partner organizations.

LPHI was funded through $46.7 million of GRHOP funds to establish a regional health partnership across the four states to improve capacity and infrastructure for delivering high quality, high value health care. The project aims to help community health centers (clinics) to advance toward greater access to care, quality improvement, efficiency and financial sustainability through the use of evidence-based practices and innovative health information technology solutions. In May 2012, LPHI began to design the GRHOP—Primary Care Capacity Project (PCCP) with the purpose to expand access to integrated high quality, sustainable, community-based primary care in oil spill impacted communities within Louisiana, Mississippi, Alabama and Florida. This includes linkages to specialty mental and behavioral health services, as well as environmental and occupational health services.

Project Initiation and Planning

The first nine months of PCCP consisted of planning, design and development efforts that supported the advancement of the current primary care systems in the Gulf Region into high quality, more efficient and sustainable systems of care with integrated mental health, environmental and occupational health services and community linkages to increase health literacy and resilience.

LPHI took several key steps to initiate the PCCP. Such steps included the following:

- Naming project objectives and guiding principles
- Building a strong multi-disciplined team
- Identifying and engaging stakeholders across the region
- Understanding impacted communities' needs and priorities
- Developing actionable project goals

Project Objectives and Guiding Principles

As part of the PCCP initiation, it was important for the forming PCCP team to understand the project objectives and to develop guiding principles for carrying the work forward through the larger team. The PCCP scope of work outlined the following objectives:

- Regional Community Health Assessment

  - Comprehensive regional assessment of community health needs to inform priority-setting, policy-making, assets-cataloguing, health strategy development and the baseline for setting community health objectives and measuring change over time
- Community Health Clinic Capacity Building

  - Expanded access to integrated, sustainable community-based primary care and linkages to specialty mental and behavioral health, and environmental and occupational health services
  - Improved quality and effectiveness of health care services consistent with evidence-based practice and the Patient-Centered Medical Home (PCMH) model
  - Improved sustainability of community health clinics as business entities and increased organizational capacity based on the Federally Qualified Health Center (FQHC) and PCMH models
  - Establishment of a regional care collaborative that supports integration of services, sustainability of systematic changes and collaboration among providers as a group
  - Improved community disaster preparedness and resilience
- Community Engagement

  - Increased community engagement and resident participation in local community health planning efforts
  - Enhanced understanding by residents and leaders about the health of the community, services integration for "whole person" approach to health care and environmental health dynamics and services

PCCP program administrators understood the importance of developing and agreeing to shared, guiding principles for decision-making related to investments. Such guiding principles are integrated throughout project-planning and decision-making processes. The principles listed in Table 20.1 are weaved throughout program design, development, implementation, monitoring and evaluation.

TABLE 20.1

Guiding Principles	Specific Details
Commitment to Communities	• Stewardship • Transparency • Inclusion • Relevance • Respectfulness • Responsiveness • Investment in community solutions for high quality primary care and prevention services, health services integration especially with Behavioral Health and Occupational Medicine, health services gateway and community health promotion and resiliency • Focus: 1st—community; 2nd—primary care system; 3rd—Federally Qualified Health Centers • Communicate community benefit of high performing, sustainable primary care
Creating Lasting Community Benefit	• Systems approach that aims at policy change, environmental change, systems development or cultural norming • Strategic thinking • Sustainability, sustainability, sustainability • Leveraging • Create community independence, not dependency
Assets-Based	• Alignment and leveraging • Human capital • Cross-sector, not just health care
Evidence-Based	• Commitment to draw upon leading standards, guidelines, credible model practices
Collaborative Effort	• Mission first, avoid opportunism at expense of community • Among GRHOP entities • Community stakeholders • Cross-sector • Leadership, not control

The Team

A multi-disciplined team emerged within LPHI to design the project plan for the first year. The team consisted of project managers and technical experts across the various divisions of the organization that included health systems, evaluation, finance and operations, behavioral health, information services, planning and policy, media and communications, and community health (see Figure 20.1). A core management team was identified to serve on PCCP at full capacity while other staff members shared time among PCCP and other LPHI-funded health programs. Those who serve in a fulltime capacity were known as the Core Team and reported to the organization's Leadership Team. This group was responsible for managing all aspects of the project and organizing the larger team, as well as acquiring additional support through consulting experts. It became evident that leading this large complex team would be a critical component for project success.

While developing the roles of PCCP team members, LPHI experienced growth and identified an opportunity for organizational change and cultural development that would better support such a dynamic team structure. Also in the midst of role identification, this team experienced the team development process of "Storming, Forming, Norming and Performing." Several important roles emerged. The Core Team of managers was strengthened and received additional support

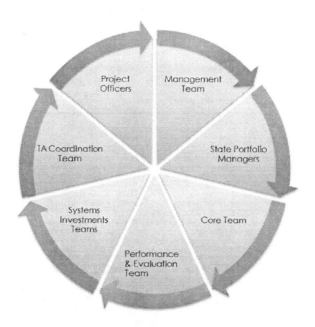

FIGURE 20.1 PCCP Team Structure Model

through newly hired program coordinators. Building upon promising practices outlined within the Project Management Institute, the team began to develop infrastructure, work processes and project management protocols for effectively managing and implementing PCCP objectives. Additionally, the role of Project Officer became crucial for streamlined effective communication with assigned stakeholders and partners. And the staff experts began to identify and develop a menu of possible technical assistance that could be provided.

Stakeholder Identification

The PCCP team established a priority to actively learn the new geographic footprint of the approved GRHOP jurisdiction. With PCCP being the first large program for LPHI to administer across state lines, the team deeply explored and assessed the communities, health centers (particularly FQHCs and Look-Alikes), current health systems, key stakeholders and potential local partners in the 17 counties and parishes. Building foundational and collaborative relationships with GRHOP partners and stakeholders throughout the coastal region was critical to developing and implementing an effective project to create sustainable change.

Early on, LPHI Leadership visited key stakeholders, given their long-standing relationships with public health officials. Those initial visits then provided additional contacts that were compiled to form the stakeholder management plan. Developing a stakeholder management plan was critical in effectively managing communications with stakeholders. It helped the team to quickly identify the below information on each individual:

- Stakeholder name and contact information
- Communications approach
- Key interests
- Current status—advocate, supporter, neutral, critic, barrier
- Desired support—high, medium or low
- Desired project role (if any)
- Actions and communications

Increasing access to high quality integrated health care services requires a collective action approach. With that approach in mind, the PCCP team understood the value in recruiting stakeholders from a variety of organizations and sectors, including health care, interfaith, schools, social services, business, local government and more.

Understanding Community Needs

The PCCP team strived to complement and advance already existing community resources so as to not duplicate or disrupt efforts. Data drove decisions, and PCCP utilized multiple ways of capturing meaningful data. One of the most effective ways to better understand those existing efforts as well as to identify gaps was to invite the authentic community voice to help inform the PCCP program design and investments.

Using evidence-based models, the PCCP assessment team developed a formal process for identifying and engaging additional key community informants, facilitating collection of community input, and data sharing to inform fast-track funding decisions. PCCP conducted Comprehensive Regional Community Health Assessments in order to engaged the impacted communities and gather their feedback. The objective was to use community knowledge to inform priority-setting, policy-making, assets-cataloguing, health strategy development and the baseline for setting community health objectives and measuring change over time. The team planned and convened Key Informant Meetings in certain communities of Louisiana, Mississippi, Alabama and Florida. Informant Meetings were also held in certain communities of Louisiana but not within the rapid assessment phase as two specific communities were pre-selected as priorities by the GRHOP Coordinating Committee.

The first phase of the assessment process, called a rapid assessment, was to identify a baseline of community health status, health care needs and assets, and barriers to care. The purpose of the **Rapid Community Health Needs Assessment** was to work with state partner organizations to further define and verify community health needs and gaps in health care services in order to inform specific funding priorities in those communities related to building primary care capacity. The two major components of the rapid assessment process were: (1) a review of existing data sources related to a subset of health and quality of life factors, and (2) a facilitated key informant community prioritization meeting per state to gather information from community members to validate, inform and prioritize findings from the data review. The findings from the Rapid Community Health Needs Assessments conducted in Mississippi, Alabama and Florida provided insight into the health priorities of the coastal counties of those states and subsequently informed decisions on Year 1 funding and technical assistance provided to eligible clinics in those regions.

The **Comprehensive Regional Community Health Assessment** is an extension of the Rapid Community Health Needs Assessments because it incorporates both the information derived from the initial data review and community stakeholders alongside a comprehensive review of existing data sources related to population and demographic trends, existing health outcomes and disparities data, community health care needs, environmental and occupational health issues, etc. Based on the priorities identified during the Key Informant Meetings, additional health and quality of life factors were included in the Comprehensive Regional Community Health Assessment reports, such as data related to veteran and military communities and data related to health disparities by ethnicity when available.

Creating a feedback loop was important to the team. Therefore, LPHI provided participants with Comprehensive Regional Community Health Assessment reports that included information collected from the Key Informant Meetings. PCCP developed these reports to present data and findings from the comprehensive quantitative data analysis and the qualitative data collection from key informants at the regional and community levels to supplement and validate the quantitative analysis.

Community Health Assessments (CHAs) involve a process of collecting, analyzing and using data to educate and mobilize communities, develop priorities, garner resources and plan actions to improve the public's health. It involves the systematic collection and analysis of data in order to provide health departments and the communities they serve with a sound basis for decision-making. A CHA should be part of ongoing broader community health improvement at a population level involving multi-sector stakeholders that can work collectively to improve community health. A community health improvement process uses CHA data to identify priority issues, develop and implement strategies for action, and establish accountability to ensure measurable health improvement, which are often outlined in the form of a community health improvement plan (CHIP). CHAs and CHIPs provide an opportunity to establish a baseline for setting community health objectives and measuring change over time as well as cataloguing community assets and barriers to improving health. Additionally, CHAs and CHIPs, along with an ASP, are the three prerequisites for voluntary accreditation of state and local health departments by the Public Health Accreditation Board.

Nationally recognized frameworks for comprehensive CHAs include but are not limited to the National Association of County and City Health Officials' Mobilizing for Action through Planning and Partnership (MAPP) model, the Catholic Health Association's assessment and community benefit planning, and the Association for Community Health Improvement's CHA Toolkit. All frameworks include collecting and analyzing data and convening community stakeholders to identify priorities and resources and develop action plans. The PCCP adapted best practices from these national frameworks to conduct comprehensive regional CHAs for the 17 named GRHOP parishes and counties.

Quantitative Data Analysis: Community Health Status

The comprehensive review of existing data sources in this report included an analysis of state, county and sub-county level data (where available) to characterize demographic, health and quality of life factors.

For the existing data review, the PCCP assessment team gathered and analyzed data for each of the 17 parishes and counties and for each state as a whole in order to obtain a baseline assessment of demographics, health status, health care access and barriers to care in each of the parishes/counties and relative to the state. Factors for which data were gathered and analyzed were chosen based on best practices of the Catholic Health Association and MAPP processes for selecting measurements that summarize the state of health and quality of life in a community. These factors then went through several rounds of review by GRHOP partners and community stakeholders to arrive at the final list of factors.

It should be noted that the Comprehensive Regional Community Health Assessment adds findings beyond what was included in the Rapid Community Health Needs Assessment from several data factors and sources including the Centers for Disease Control and Prevention's Gulf States Population Survey and Oxfam America's Social Vulnerability Index Project. Added data factors include indicators disaggregated by race and ethnicity when available, oil spill exposure and impact, mental health care coverage, veteran status, as well as a host of other data factors related to health risk behaviors and social environment.

Qualitative Data Collection and Analysis: Community Prioritization Meeting

Community prioritization meetings were held with key informants representing eligible counties. Key informants were comprised of representatives from state, regional and local community organizations and nonprofits, as well as local leaders from the health and education sectors. During the meetings, key informants were split into breakout groups by county for a facilitated discussion on community health needs and barriers to care. The top ten community health needs and barriers to care were identified by each group. The last part of the meeting was a community prioritization process and a description of next steps. Using electronic audience-response system polling, key informants prioritized community needs by voting.

Developing Actionable Project Goals

Throughout team development and planning, it was imperative to outline specific goals and objectives of the PCCP in order to better communicate with stakeholders and identify measurable outcomes and community impact. Utilizing national frameworks and "conventions" like HRSA, NCQA and NACHC, the team developed the following goals:

1.   Build capacity of community health clinics through direct funding via cooperative agreements and delivering customized group and individual technical assistance
2.   Support and advance health systems development through direct funding for health information exchanges, infrastructure investments and technical assistance
3.   Enhance the capacity of communities and build strategic partnerships to improve health through funding: state partners, the Community-Centered Health Home Demonstration Project, partnership engagement activities and technical assistance to non-clinical partners

The PCCP developed the below diagram to demonstrate the importance of investing in both primary care access and infrastructure but also into the systems of care so as to bridge health care services and public health.

CLINIC

- **PCMH**
- **Quality of Care**
- **EMR**
- **Meaningful Use**
- **Clinic**
- **Population Management**
- **Referrals**

SYSTEM

- **Shared services**
- **HIE**
- **Longitudinal Record**
- **Care Coordination**
- **Central Data Repository**
- **Analytics**
- **Population Metrics**
- **Reporting**
- **MU Stage 2-3**

FIGURE 20.2

Goal 1: Build capacity of community health clinics through direct funding via cooperative agreements and delivering customized group and individual technical assistance. Federally Qualified Health Centers (FQHCs) and Look-Alikes were chosen to receive direct clinic funding in each of the designated counties/parishes in Mississippi, Alabama, Florida and in certain communities of Louisiana. FQHCs and Look-Alikes were selected due to their mission of providing high quality primary care services utilizing evidence-based standards in underserved communities. An FQHC also represents the community in that more than 50% of its Board of Directors are consumers of the clinic's services. With regard to the current primary care environment in coastal Louisiana when compared to the GRHOP-designated coastal communities of Mississippi, Alabama and the panhandle of Florida, there are distinctions that are considered material with regard to the administration of PCCP. Among these distinctions are the urban concentrations of FQHCs in the greater New Orleans region and the pre-existing clinic funding and technical assistance (TA) from LPHI provided through prior funded programs.

The following inputs were considered in selecting clinics for participation in PCCP:

- Focus on sustainable infrastructure, ex. FQHC model
- Feedback from key community stakeholders
- Data gathered from community and clinical assessments
- Prioritization of certain, predetermined communities as outlined by GRHOP partners

The PCCP project team designed and implemented a unique approach to planning for clinic capacity building efforts. Highlights from key steps taken are listed below:

- Conduct clinical assessment to better understand the clinic's current capacity, including the following domains.
- Locations, population served, scope of services, scale of capacity, ability to capture and apply data for quality and efficiency assessment and continuous improvement, quality of care, efficiency of services, clinic infrastructure—specifically health information technology (HIT) and business operation systems, referral relationships, community standing.

- Customize funding support, scope of work, and technical assistance plans for each clinic utilizing data captured through the clinical assessment, community assessment, best practices for clinical operations and current clinic demands.

Developing Clinic Gold Standards

In alignment with several evidence-based models and national efforts to increase quality within primary care, PCCP developed a list of attributes of high performing clinics (see Table 20.2). This list became a critical touchstone of several processes, including the clinic contract negotiation process with clinic awardees and TA design.

TABLE 20.2

Attributes of a High Performing Clinic	Learn More Here:
Engaged Leadership	http://www.improvingchroniccare.org/downloads/engaged_leadership.pdf
Patient-Centered Medical Home Recognition	http://www.ncqa.org/Programs/Recognition/Practices/PatientCenteredMedicalHomePCMH.aspx
Meaningful Use of EMR	http://www.hrsa.gov/healthit/meaningfuluse/MU%20Stage1%20CQM/whatis.html
Empanelment	http://www.safetynetmedicalhome.org/change-concepts/empanelment
Clinical Decision Support	https://www.healthit.gov/policy-researchers-implementers/clinical-decision-support-cds
Transitions of Care	https://www.cms.gov/Regulations-and-Guidance/Legislation/EHRIncentivePrograms/downloads/8_Transition_of_Care_Summary.pdf
Patient Registries	http://www.cdc.gov/ehrmeaningfuluse/specialized_registry.html
Team-Based Care	http://www.ihi.org/communities/blogs/_layouts/ihi/community/blog/itemview.aspx?List=0f316db6-7f8a-430f-a63a-ed7602d1366a&ID=29
Health Information Exchange	https://www.healthit.gov/HIE
Eligibility Screening and Enrollment	http://www.nassembly.org/fspc/bridgingthegap/eligibilityenrollment.html
Community Centered	http://www.preventioninstitute.org/component/jlibrary/article/id-298/127.html
Pharmacy Assistance	http://www.hrsa.gov/opa/
UDS Data Use Optimization	http://www.bphc.hrsa.gov/datareporting/reporting/index.html
Operational Efficiency	http://www.nachc.com/PracticeOperationalManagement%20.cfm
Financial Management	https://www.nachc.com/Finance_and_Operations_Management.cfm
Chronic Disease Management	http://www.hrsa.gov/quality/toolbox/introduction/coreclinical/

Medication Reconciliation	https://innovations.ahrq.gov/taxonomy-terms/medication-reconciliation
Performance Improvement and Measurement	http://www.nachc.com/Quality%20Management.cfm
Mental and Behavioral Health Integration	http://www.thenationalcouncil.org/consulting-best-practices/center-for-integrated-health-solution/
Environmental and Occupational Health Integration	http://www.aoec.org

Clinic Assessments

Another PCCP input utilized in funding decisions was the clinic assessment tool. The assessment tool, collaboratively developed with GRHOP partners, consisted of 128 questions, which were completed during a face-to-face interview process with the appropriate clinic organizational staff members. The PCCP clinic assessment tool asked questions related to the operations and finances of the clinic, workforce capacity and access to care, health information technology, population management initiatives, occupational health, behavioral health and pharmacy services provided, and some additional questions related to community health and wellness initiatives and emergency preparedness procedures. PCCP conducted the on-site clinic assessments with each FQHC (and FQHC Look-Alike) in the designated GRHOP parishes/counties of Louisiana, Mississippi, Alabama and Florida.

Clinic Requests and the Negotiation

The final input to the clinic investment period was the negotiation. Following clinic leadership's review of data collected through the rapid assessment process, the clinic assessment and the attributes of high performing clinics, PCCP invited clinic operators to submit formal requests for funding. The PCCP team and GRHOP partners facilitated a face-to-face negotiation with the clinic in finalizing a scope of work and budget that aligned with the program goals and created lasting community benefit. PCCP encouraged clinics to invest in sustainable strategies for advancing the delivery of high quality health care.

Rapid phase funding was awarded to 11 eligible clinics based on a systematic methodology. For Louisiana, two communities were specifically identified in the settlement for fast-track funding: the New Orleans East Vietnamese community in Orleans Parish and the town of Jean Laffite in Jefferson Parish. In Mississippi, a sole large FQHC operator serves the three GRHOP counties and therefore was eligible for fast-track funding. LPHI also developed a formula to allocate fast-track funding in Alabama and Florida given the various operators. The methodology included a base payment for each operator, plus payment per number of sites, total patients and percentage of those patients that are uninsured. The payment methodology was reviewed with each state's primary care association.

Key Inputs for Translating Dollars into Community Benefit

PCCP utilized the key inputs mentioned above to determine funding decisions to clinics. From these inputs, the PCCP team developed recommendations, in alignment with GRHOP funded partners working within each state, for overall GRHOP coordination. See Figure 20.3 for input model.

The outcome of the process led to the executed cooperative agreement between the clinic awardee and LPHI. Awardees of PCCP funds must execute a cooperative agreement in order to receive funds to implement their projects. Once signed by LPHI and the Awardee, the cooperative agreement is legally binding and cannot be changed unless there is an official amendment approved and signed by LPHI. The activities described in the scope of work, which is included in the executed cooperative agreement, have been negotiated between LPHI and the Awardee.

Three key parties involved in the administration and management of the PCCP cooperative agreements are listed below, followed by Table 20.3, which provides a general summary of the primary roles for each.

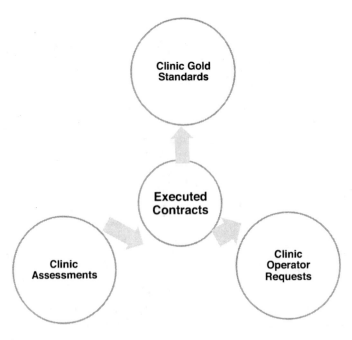

FIGURE 20.3

TABLE 20.3

Tasks, Roles and Responsibilities	Awardee	PCCP Project Officer	Finance and Compliance Manager
Develop Cooperative Agreement Funding Guidance			X
Clinic Budget Negotiations	X	X	X
Develop Scope of Work	Write	Review/Approve	Review/Approve
Communicate Funding Allocation		X	
Set Up Cooperative Agreement Packet		Review	Develop
Execute Cooperative Agreement	Review/Sign	Review	Develop/Issue
Attend Regular Meeting	X	X	
Finalize Work-Plan and Operations Plan	Write	Review	
Submit Quarterly/ Financial Expenditure Reports	Submit	Review/Approve	Review/Approve
Amend Budget Categories (for shifts over 10%)	Request	Review	Approve
Cooperative Agreement Extensions or Scope Revisions	Request	Review	Approve
Submit Reimbursement Requests	Submit	Review/Approve	Process
Process Payments			X

- Awardee: The clinic and recipient of a cooperative agreement award issued by LPHI, responsible for direct implementation of all elements associated with a project award as outlined in the cooperative agreement.
- PCCP Project Officer: The LPHI staff person assigned to manage the cooperative agreement and serve as the primary point of contact to the Awardees for questions related to the cooperative agreement and the project. The Project Officer should be copied on all emails and correspondences.
- Finance and Compliance Manager: The LPHI staff person who administers the cooperative agreement. This person issues program guidance, executes contracts, processes payments and generates reports.

After the initial payment (x% of total funding) is made upon signing the cooperative agreement, subsequent payments are provided quarterly on a cost reimbursement basis. This means each Awardee must pay the expenses per quarter first and then request reimbursement. The quarterly financial expenditure report serves as the invoice for the cooperative agreement reimbursement requests.

Goal 2: Support and advance health systems development through direct funding for health information exchanges, infrastructure investments and technical assistance.

As has been the framework affirmed by the GRHOP Coordinating Committee, PCCP allocated funding to invest in external systems that support clinics and/or community initiatives that advance access to integrated primary care; shared community-level quality and access improvement initiatives through care coordination; specialty referral systems; and/or community resiliency from a health perspective.

The guiding principles for this include: must be strategic in value, support a systems approach, encourage innovation, augment sustainability of other PCCP/GRHOP investments, support a regional approach, and be within PCCP project scope.

Goal 3: Enhance the capacity of communities and build strategic partnerships to improve health through funding: state partners, the Community-Centered Health Home Demonstration Project, partnership engagement activities and technical assistance to non-clinical partners.

Project Highlights of the Community

Community-Centered Health Home (CCHH) Demonstration Project and Greater New Orleans PCCP Quality Improvement Initiative (GNOPQII) have the following:

- Systems projects
- True integrated approach
- Leverages other community partners and work
- Regionalization through emergency management

The **PCCP Community-Centered Health Home (CCHH) Demonstration Project** aims to advance health equity and community resiliency by enhancing the capacity of selected community health centers to take the next step beyond the Patient-Centered Medical Home model and serve as trusted, effective partners in community prevention.

Prevention efforts that focus on altering unhealthy policies and inequitable resource distribution and improving community environments can substantially diminish health inequities. According to the best available estimates, environmental conditions, social circumstances and behavioral choices addressed through prevention have by far the greatest influence in determining health. As primary health authorities, medical professionals and institutions have significant opportunities to play a far greater role in advancing the health of the populations they serve through community prevention efforts that address behaviors and environments. Integrating the concept of health homes with a community prevention perspective produces multiple benefits: it's cost-effective; reduces demand for resources and services; and improves health, safety and equity outcomes on a community-wide and individual level. It provides a route for medical professionals to apply their assets, expertise and credibility to the challenge of creating environments that support health, equity and safety. The Community-Centered Health Home (CCHH) concept, developed by Prevention Institute, takes previous health home models a transformative step further by not only acknowledging that factors outside the health care system affect patients' health outcomes, but also actively participating in improving them. The defining attribute of the CCHH model is active involvement in community advocacy and change. As institutions focus on improving health at both the individual and population-wide level they will work toward solutions that solve multiple problems simultaneously. This project will allow for the health center processes toward adoption of CCHH elements and document progress toward implementation of CCHH.

In March 2015, under the CCHH Project, PCCP awarded grants to community health centers (CHCs) across the GRHOP jurisdiction that include: (Louisiana) Daughters of Charity and Crescent Care, (Mississippi) Coastal Family Health Center, (Alabama) Mobile County Health Department and (Florida) Escambia Community Clinic. In addition to the $250,000 two-year grant, PCCP and the Prevention Institute is providing comprehensive technical assistance (TA) and coaching on demonstrating the CCHH model. The CHCs receive individualized coaching on implementing the model and enhancing their partnerships in the community. In collaboration with the Prevention Institute, LPHI has been engaged with other national and regional partners like Kresge and Episcopal Foundations, as well as CCHH practitioners from around the country to discuss ways in which the model can continue to be implemented across communities.

The **GNOCHC-PCCP Quality Improvement Initiative (GNOPQII)** is a two-year, $1.95 million project that supports eligible clinical providers to reduce emergency department utilization and 30-day inpatient readmission among a high-risk population in the Greater New Orleans area to produce better health outcomes and appropriate utilization of health care services. GNOPQII leverages resources and expertise to support participating provider organizations with new patient recruitment services, transitional care management techniques, and evidence-based tools to define and target individuals with high-risk profiles.

The providers eligible to participate in GNOPQII include 11 FQHCs, comprising more than 40 clinical sites, within the Greater New Orleans area of Orleans, Jefferson, Plaquemines and St. Bernard parishes. These FQHCs are eligible to receive reimbursement for services provided to patients enrolled in the Greater New Orleans Community Health Connections (GNOCHC), which is the target population for the GNOPQII project.

GNOCHC is a Medicaid Waiver that covers primary care and behavioral health services in specific clinical settings and does not cover emergency department or inpatient hospital services. GNOCHC enrollees number approximately 60,000 and are working-age adults (18–64 years), at or below 100% of the Federal Poverty Limit (FPL), and who otherwise have no medical insurance. GNOCHC enrollees are of particular interest because they comprise a relatively high-risk, low-resource population, which is categorized as uninsured/self-pay by hospitals.

GNOPQII measures performance towards achieving the project goal of reducing avoidable hospitalizations and improving health outcomes based on several outcome measures:

1. Reduction in the rate of avoidable emergency department utilization and 30-day inpatient readmissions
2. Increase in the rate of primary care appointments that occur within 14 days of post-hospital discharge
3. Increase the rate of depression screening
4. Increase the proportion of GNOCHC enrollees who access high quality primary care services from an eligible-provider

An initial distribution of project funds is made on the basis of each provider agency's GNOCHC panel size and hospital utilization during the baseline period. Two subsequent disbursements made at one-year intervals incentivize improvements in the above outcomes relative to past performance—adjusted for the provider's GNOCHC patient panel size. This pool of funds represents more than half of the total project funds and supplements the resources to perform the GNOPQII interventions, which go beyond those services covered by the GNO-CHC payments made by the state Medicaid program.

The GNOPQII interventions are:

1. Targeted outreach to recruit new patients or rarely seen patients and navigate them to high quality primary care
2. Actionable data and analytics to define risk profiles associated with avoidable hospital utilization and identify high-risk individuals and subgroups for relevant interventions
3. Notifications and data sharing to alert providers of hospitalizations through real-time discharge notifications and access to longitudinal medical record that link patients across multiple providers
4. Transitional care management tools and models to support patients to manage health conditions after hospitalization

5. Targeted care navigation for high-risk patients that enlists patient naviga-
   tors with access to social services resources to provide intensive support to
   improve adherence to treatment regimens
6. Behavioral health-primary care integration through group TA offerings

For each intervention, GNOPQII provides models, evidence and resources but
is intentionally non-prescriptive to enable providers to innovate, experiment and
monitor their performance towards reaching the program's outcome goals. Success towards achieving the GNOPQII goals will demonstrate to health plans the
effectiveness of the network in managing the care of underserved populations
to contain costs and improve outcomes.

Section: Collaboration/Partnerships

LPHI's motto is "Bringing people, ideas and resources together." With that in mind,
the PCCP team has embraced several guiding principles on relationship development and management. New relationships and stronger relationships are key objectives in managing such projects. As noted within the Stakeholder Identification
Section, multiple sectors and levels of professionals were engaged. The PCCP team
prioritized the various groups and identified engagement and communication plans
for each. At the top of the list were the other funded project partners within the
GRHOP. The team utilized the below principles to guide these plans.

Principles include:

1. Having flexibility
2. Being transparent
3. Utilizing information provided
4. Identifying opportunities for leveraging
5. Identifying opportunities to sustain relationships
6. Agreed-upon expectations
7. Consistent communication
8. Peer learning with partners

Types of Relationships and the Value of Relationships

Various types of relationships and needed roles emerged.

Champions and Advocates

As outlined in the settlement language, LPHI is to partner with state organizations
whose mission, competencies and organizational relationships are aligned with the
goals of the GRHOP–PCCP. State partnerships allow for the maximization of the
investments in the impacted communities, provision of state-level policy education/
information for impacted communities and clinics, and provision of sustainable

partnerships for communities and their primary care service providers (specifically FQHCs and Look-Alikes). In Year 1, state partnerships were executed via cooperative agreements with Louisiana—the Louisiana Primary Care Association (LPCA), Mississippi—the Mississippi Public Health Institute (MSPHI) and Alabama—the Alabama Department of Public Health (ADOPH). Contract negotiations were under way with the Florida Department of Health and the Florida Institute for Health Innovation (FIHI, formerly referred to as Florida Public Health Institute). However, the Florida state partnership contract was not executed until Year 2 of the program. During Year 3, PCCP remained contracted with partners in each state, including LPCA, MSPHI, Alabama Primary Health Care Association (APHCA) and FIHI. PCCP continued to engage with additional unfunded strategic partners as well. Collaborating with GRHOP partners and other local entities is critical to the development and success of such an expansive project.

The state partners were local advocates for the project and provided necessary information and linkages to what was happening in the states. This relationship allowed for the transfer of knowledge, capacity and resources across LPHI and the partners. LPHI was able to use state-specific information from local partners to identify priorities for making investments and confirming project impact along the way, as shown in Table 20.4.

TABLE 20.4

State	State Partnership	Highlights of Accomplishments
Louisiana	LA Primary Care Association (LPCA)	LPCA helped serve the seven coastal parishes by supporting (1) community health assessment planning and implementation, (2) building community health clinic capacity, (3) development of Emergency Management Initiative through the Regional Care Collaborative and (4) partnerships and collaboration throughout the region.
Mississippi	MS Public Health Institute (MSPHI) and Mississippi Primary Health Care Association (MPHCA)	MSPHI serves as the fiduciary agent for the Mississippi Health Information Exchange to advance care coordination within Hancock, Harrison and Jackson counties. MPHCA serves the counties by supporting development of (1) Emergency Management Initiative, (2) building community health center capacity and (3) community engagement through collaboration.

| Alabama | AL Primary Health Care Association (APHCA) | APHCA enhanced the Health Care Controlled Network to advance systematic information exchange and quality improvement within the Alabama's Health Centers. APHCA also supported building clinic capacity, infrastructure and collaboration efforts. |
| Florida | Florida Institute for Health Innovation (FIHI) and Florida Association of Community Health Centers (FACHC) | FIHI supported the Panhandle Region through building community health capacity and partnerships. They served as a liaison with the county health departments and other national and state organizations. FACHC served as a development asset for the Emergency Management Initiative, training and partnership building. |

High Risk/High Priority

LPHI has built collaborations with other funded GRHOP partners in the managing of the clinical relationships and systems projects. Along the way, the PCCP team would confer with GRHOP partners, the PCCP-funded state partners and local public health agencies, as appropriate, to develop options in each state for funding consideration. Risks were associated with the coordination across the GRHOP Partners under the GRHOP Coordinating Committee. It was imperative for cohesive project implementation across partners. Because partners also had the ability to vote on important project components that were presented to the committee, they had high interest and influence on the project's success.

Section: Program Delivery

Translating Funding into Community Benefit

Project Implementation, Monitoring and Evaluation

Through progressive elaboration, the project evolved into several different phases that allowed for incremental implementation and additional project design. Three phases developed with specific components that include:

Phase 1 Principles

- Predetermined communities identified in settlement language
- Focus on FQHC and Look-Alike clinics
- "All get some" to engage into program
- No parish/county allocation concept
- No performance history of clinics
- No strong interest to focus on community system interventions

Phase 2 Principles

- Systems change and investment
- Higher functions of primary care access
- Community priorities and interventions
- Concept of parish/county allocation
- Performance history of clinics now exists
- Affordable Care Act

Phase 3 Principles—under development

- Higher functions of primary care access
- Systems change and investment
- Grant closeout and relationship continuity

Direct Clinic Funding with Customized and Complementary TA

By Year 4 of the GRHOP, PCCP successfully engaged all 17 counties and parishes in the GRHOP service area and built strong relationships with GRHOP partners and state and local organizations to increase access to primary care and build the capacity of community health centers and external community systems that support primary care. In the implementation of this project, the PCCP Management Team coordinated the components of contract monitoring, grantee management, communications, TA delivery and evaluation with the necessary team members. The team worked together according to the evolving program plan to ensure the funded clinics, partners and stakeholders.

Open communication systems between the clinic and Project Officer (PO) allowed for the flow of TA requests and coordination of TA delivery. The assigned PO is the clinic's point of contact for all matters related to PCCP; this includes requests for and coordination of technical assistance. The PO serves as a liaison between clinic staff and TA providers. This role includes, but is not limited to: scheduling meetings, assisting with site visits and sharing reports or other documentation and resources. The POs and TA providers meet regularly as a group for TA Coordination Meetings, which provide both parties the opportunity to discuss, plan, strategize and troubleshoot current and future TA delivery.

The PCMH model was used as a framework for developing and monitoring clinic project goals. A PCMH is a health care setting that provides patients with:

- Well-organized & on-time visits (optimal operational efficiency and care when needed)
- Enhanced access with their own provider & care team for continuity (same day appointment availability, 24/7 telephone access, alternatives to the 1:1 visit, information)
- Proactive care management (evidence-base clinical care, panel management, reminder systems, registries, behavioral health integration)
- Care coordination across settings (assistance with referrals, tracking for tests & referrals, care during transitions, information)
- Patient activation, engagement & participation in decisions on care (patient-centered customer driven, patient portal)
- Connections to community resources to extend resources for care
- Focus on health outcomes & goals for improvement
- Data-driven use of Health IT as tool to support the achievement of advanced primary care practice and optimal financial performance

LPHI's technical assistance model consisted of the following: customized individual TA and coaching, group peer learning collaborative, self-directed tools and a consultant approach. The LPHI experience from past project implementations, such as the Partnership for Achieving Total Health (PATH), Primary Care Access and Stabilization Grant, Crescent City Beacon Community and the New Orleans Charitable Health Fund, was used as a benchmark for TA delivery.

To deliver TA, PCCP POs and TA staff worked with each clinic in the successful completion of cooperative agreement/work-plan deliverables through regular conference calls and web-based project management tools. In order to provide TA in a more efficient and coordinated manner, the TA team conducted deep-dive reviews of the health centers' first cooperative agreement closeout assessments to prioritize TA needs and identify opportunities for synergy. Through this process, the TA providers and POs developed follow-up questions and proposed TA offerings for each clinic, which were explored and further refined through calls with key clinic staff. Together, the PCCP team and leadership of PCCP-funded clinics updated their respective TA plans to meet current clinic priorities and complement the cooperative agreement work-plans.

Priority topics for TA include, but are not limited to:

1. Patient-Centered Medical Home (PCMH) recognition, through enhancements to access, quality, reporting and patient experience

2. Adoption of electronic health records (EHRs) and achievement of Meaningful Use (MU) of electronic health data
3. With leadership by respective GRHOP partners, integration of behavioral health and environmental/occupational health into clinic services and EHR systems
4. Change management for improvements to clinic quality and efficiency
5. Business cycle improvement to support compliance and sustainability

The PCCP Wiki Space was developed for e-learning for participants and contains a resource library to complement the TA offerings for PCCP-funded clinics and partners. The TA team has collected guidance and resources from national experts and PCCP's own TA providers to provide tools, templates and literature to support the success of health centers. POs are able to refer clinics to the Wiki to find useful materials that can be reviewed on their own time.

The PCCP e-letter is dedicated to informing PCCP-funded clinics and partners on updated tools available through the PCCP Wiki Space, and pertinent updates about the program. The e-letter also serves as a space to share accomplishments and information among community health center partners.

Group TA Delivery through the Regional Care Collaborative

In accordance with the Deepwater Horizon Settlement, LPHI was to develop a regional network, later called the Regional Care Collaborative (RCC), that supports the organization and facilitation of regular communications among PCCP clinics through developing communication tools, hosting periodic meetings and joint training and continuing education sessions, and encouraging other opportunities to interact and collaborate with each other. The RCC, convened by LPHI, includes the GRHOP-funded program participants, and a resource team of experts working together to exchange information and experiences with the goal of improving processes, policies and/or practices. It is designed to improve quality and achieve measurable outcomes that are integral to the clinic's mission.

Via the RCC, the PCCP team, along with GRHOP partners, is facilitating collective TA events and fostering peer-to-peer learning opportunities to improve quality and effectiveness of health care services, to increase organizational capacity and to improve sustainability of CHCs in the Gulf Region. RCC topics include clinical transformation, PCMH, emergency preparedness and additional priority topics identified by the clinics.

The PCCP team created the RCC Steering Committee to inform the content and delivery methods for group TA offerings. Steering committee members represent PCCP staff, GRHOP partners, strategic partners (including state primary care associations) and PCCP-funded clinics. The RCC Steering Committee convenes to provide feedback on upcoming webinars and in-person forums.

Project Evaluation

The PCCP assessment and evaluation team provided evaluation expertise in developing the overall GRHOP Evaluation Framework and the PCCP Evaluation Plan. The team also provided technical assistance to clinical partners and other stakeholders on identified data needs, data visualization, data monitoring and reporting, and evaluation.

As mentioned early, the team planned and conducted the Rapid Community Health Assessment. They have been committed to acknowledging and amplifying existing assessments, activities and data. A principle instituted was that any community assessment that PCCP supported or administered would be "owned" by the community, not another study done to them.

Utilizing the CDC Evaluation Framework, the PCCP evaluation team has developed evaluation goals that include the following evaluation components: performance and outcome monitoring, process evaluation and outcome evaluation. The purposes of the PCCP evaluation are: (1) to determine if PCCP activities led to outcomes related to conducting and supporting regional Community Health Assessments (CHAs), building clinic capacity and engaging communities; and (2) to understand the impact of PCCP activities on the overall GRHOP goal of ensuring that residents of the Gulf Region are fully informed about their own health and have access, now and in the future, to skilled frontline health care providers supported by networks of specialists knowledgeable in addressing the physical, behavioral and mental health needs.

Performance monitoring activities were implemented to gather both process and outcome data from clinics on a regular basis for the purpose of oversight of PCCP funding and to inform areas for provision of technical assistance. Evaluation activities utilized quantitative data gathered through programmatic reporting activities and will include the collection of process and outcome data through surveys at the end of each program year. Additionally, qualitative data was gathered through interviews with key project participants and implementers, and case studies of project grantees. PCCP identified and used the "sentinel" output and outcome measures below that were analyzed frequently to ensure programmatic impact.

Sentinel Measures: Outputs

- # of unduplicated patients per year
- # sites pursuing or achieving PCMH recognition
- # sites achieved Stage 1 Meaningful Use/pursuing Stage 2
- # sites using electronic systems for Transitions of Care, care coordination, referral tracking
- # new FTEs since PCCP funding

Sentinel Measures: Outcomes

- Reduced time to third next available appointment
- Increased/improved access to clinic by target communities/populations
- Increased/improved "patient-centeredness" of clinic practice
- Increased efficiency and quality of care coordination
- Improved use of EMRs/HIT for care management, care coordination, performance management and quality improvement
- Improved financial and operational sustainability of clinic

PCCP continues to provide grants management and contract monitoring for funded organizations and continues to strive to better assist clinics with their multiple grant reporting processes while avoiding duplication in a manner that also aligns with the data needs of the other GRHOP partners and the overall GRHOP evaluation. In 2015, PCCP received and analyzed organizations' clinical data from PCCP-funded Year 2, Quarter 4 and the Year 2 Closeout Survey. The analysis made it evident that many clinics continue to have constraints in their ability to report systematically on some elements of their performance.

With implications on the clinics' abilities to engage in robust continuous quality improvement, report on the achievement of PCCP/GRHOP goals and inform evaluation, the evaluation team has begun to revise the clinic programmatic reporting process. PCCP has held discussions to review and revise the clinic reporting plan in alignment with the GRHOP Evaluation Subcommittee and will update the plan as indicated to better serve the clinics and to support PCCP, the GRHOP partners and to best inform the evaluation. In 2016, PCCP will introduce an updated process that has sufficient value to project evaluation and clinics' continuous quality improvement, is in sync with clinics' other reporting requirements (specifically UDS) and is less burdensome for the clinics.

The PCCP evaluation team also worked collaboratively with GRHOP partners under the guidance of Thomas Chapel, Chief Evaluation Officer, CDC, to develop a GRHOP enterprise evaluation framework identifying individual project activities, outputs and short-term outcomes, as well as mid-term and long-term outcomes shared across GRHOP projects.

Planning for Closeout

The closeout process for PCCP has been a priority for LPHI Leadership. In addition to assisting the funded clinics and partners in developing sustainability plans for their community efforts, LPHI is interested in sustaining the capacity to deliver similar services to other primary care systems and increasing prospects for future projects under its Clinical Transformation Portfolio. With sustainability at the forefront of many project decisions and activities, the PCCP team focused on building strong trusting relationships across the Gulf Coast. This included the capacity for high quality customer relations and effectively meeting expectations of stakeholders.

The PCCP project is scheduled to end in April 2018. With two years remaining, the team has developed processes to monitor deliverables, report on project impacts and lessons learned, and closeout contracts. The closeout outputs will include a final project report, lessons learned and recommendations to the organization for future project implementation and the recognition of the team's success.

21

RURAL PUBLIC HEALTH

Gail R. Bellamy and Michael Meit

As health conditions in a rural community in one State influence those in other communities in that State and in other States, it seems that all of the State governments and the Federal Government may be properly concerned with the development and maintenance of efficient local health service throughout our extensive rural area.
L. L. Lumsden, Senior Surgeon, U.S. Public Health Service, 1929[1]

According to Kindig, when we talk about *population health* we are talking about "the health outcomes of a group of individuals, including the distribution of such outcomes within the group."[2] Within the context of public health, *groups of individuals* have often been taken to be those in large population centers (> 500,000 people). Whereas there has been a more recent focus on population health issues at the zip code level, this effort has rarely focused on smaller population centers, or rural communities.

Definitions

Rural

Rural is not as easily defined as one might imagine. The federal government, for example, uses more than 15 definitions of rural which vary by federal agency. In general, however, definitions of rural are most often defined by exclusion. That is, metropolitan areas (i.e., urban areas) are defined and anything else, by virtue of not being metropolitan (i.e., nonmetro), is considered rural. The U.S. Census Bureau defines rural by exclusion. Specifically, the Census Bureau uses the terms "urbanized area (UA)" and "urban clusters (UC)." UAs are defined as consisting of

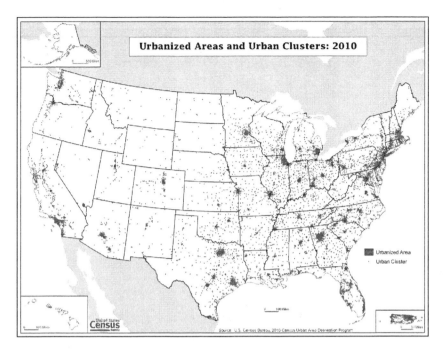

Urbanized Areas and Urban Clusters: 2010

Urbanized Area
Urban Cluster

Source: U.S. Census Bureau, 2010 Census Urban Area Designation Program

MAP 21.1 Urbanized Areas and Urban Clusters, U.S. Census Bureau[3]

adjacent, densely settled census block groups and census blocks that meet minimum population density requirements along with adjacent densely settled census blocks where together they encompass a population of at least 50,000 people. UCs are similarly defined, on the basis of both proximity and population density, however the overall population can be from 2,500 to less than 50,000. Essentially, UAs can be thought of as large cities, and UCs as smaller cities and towns. The Census Bureau defines all other areas not captured in UAs and UCs as rural. Map 21.1 shows UAs and UCs in the lower 48 states; areas not shaded are considered rural according to this Census definition. The areas outside of UAs and UCs encompass 59,061,367 individuals, or 21% of the U.S. population.

Other commonly used rural definitions are shown in Table 21.1.

Frontier refers to the most remote and isolated rural areas. As with the definition of rural, definitions of frontier vary by federal agency. The use of a particular definition depends on the purpose of the project being funded. Most commonly, definitions of frontier are based on population density (often 6 or fewer persons per square mile), although other factors may include distance from a population center or specific service, travel time to reach a population center or service, functional association with other places, availability of paved roads, and seasonal changes in access to services. The shaded areas of Map 21.2 represent frontier areas which are prevalent in the western parts of the country; these areas, not surprisingly, also incorporate many national parks, national forests, recreational areas, and Indian reservations.

TABLE 21.1 Commonly Used Rural Definitions[4]

Definition	Definition Description	Geographic Unit Used
U.S. Census Bureau: Urban and Rural Areas	The Census Bureau's classification of rural consists of all territory, population, and housing units located outside of urbanized areas and urban clusters. Urbanized areas include populations of at least 50,000, and urban clusters include populations between 2,500 and 50,000. The core areas of both urbanized areas and urban clusters are defined based on population density of 1,000 per square mile and then certain blocks adjacent to them are added that have at least 500 persons per square mile.	Census Block and Block Groups
Economic Research Service, U.S. Department of Agriculture & WWAMI Rural Health Research Center: Rural-Urban Commuting Areas (RUCAs)	This classification scheme utilizes the U.S. Census Bureau's urbanized area and cluster definitions and work community information. The RUCA categories are based on the size of settlements and towns as delineated by the Census Bureau and the functional relationships between places as measured by tract-level work community data. This taxonomy defines 33 categories of rural and urban census tracts.	Census Tract, ZIP Code Approximation Available
U.S. Office of Management and Budget (OMB): Core Based Statistical Areas (i.e., Metropolitan and Nonmetropolitan Areas)	A metropolitan area must contain one or more central counties with urbanized areas. Nonmetropolitan counties are outside the boundaries of metropolitan areas and are subdivided into two types, micropolitan areas and noncore counties. Micropolitan areas are urban clusters of 10,000–49,999 persons.	County

Economic Research Service, U.S. Department of Agriculture: Rural-Urban Continuum Codes (Beale Codes)	This classification system distinguishes metropolitan counties by the population size of their metropolitan area, and nonmetropolitan counties by degree of urbanization and adjacency to a metropolitan area or areas. All counties and county equivalents are grouped according to their official OMB metropolitan-nonmetropolitan status and further subdivided into three metropolitan and six nonmetropolitan groupings.	County
Economic Research Service, U.S. Department of Agriculture: Urban Influence Codes	This classification scheme subdivides the OMB metropolitan and nonmetropolitan categories into two metropolitan and ten nonmetropolitan categories. Metropolitan counties are divided into two groups by the size of the metropolitan area. Nonmetropolitan-micropolitan counties are divided into three groups by their adjacency to metropolitan areas. Nonmetropolitan-noncore counties are divided into seven groups by their adjacency to metropolitan or micropolitan areas and whether they have their "own town" of at least 2,500 residents.	County
Office of Rural Health Policy, U.S. Department of Health and Human Services: RUCA Adjustment to OMB Metropolitan and Nonmetropolitan Definition	This method uses RUCAs 4–10 to identify small towns and rural areas within large metropolitan counties. In addition, census tracts within metropolitan areas with RUCA codes 2 and 3 that are larger than 400 square miles and have population density of less than 30 people per square mile are also considered rural.	Census Tract within OMB Metropolitan Counties

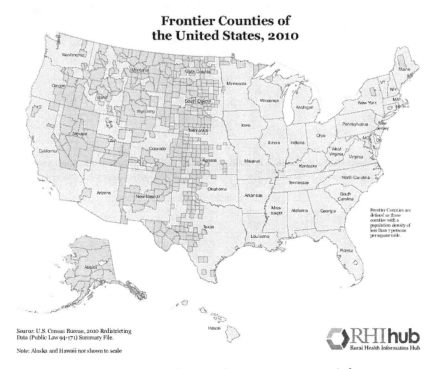

Frontier Counties of the United States, 2010

MAP 21.2 Frontier Counties in the United States (AK not to scale)[5]

Definitions aside, rural communities are far from homogeneous. Whereas rural America is still predominantly white, there are regional differences in population make-up. Not surprisingly, you see larger concentrations of Hispanic populations in nonmetro counties in the Southwest, but also along the various migrant streams that cut across the country. Larger concentrations of Black populations occur in the nonmetro counties of the South (including the Delta Region along the Mississippi River), and larger concentrations of Native Americans in the nonmetro counties of the central and western states.[6] Appalachia continues to be overwhelmingly white. Differences aside, all of these communities tend to share characteristics that often underlie health inequities, such as higher rates of poverty, isolation, and lower educational attainment.

Public Health

The next challenge, albeit not quite so daunting as defining rural, is to define public health. At its simplest, public health is focused on health at the community level. Whereas doctors, nurses, and other healthcare providers concern themselves with the health of individuals, public health practitioners are generally concerned with the health of populations. This distinction is significant, particularly as it relates to rural health, which has typically been thought of in terms of access to healthcare services—that is, recruiting physicians to underserved rural areas, building and sustaining individual hospitals and clinics, etc. Access to healthcare services, while critical to improving the health of both individuals and populations, is only one of public health's core functions, and only one aspect of assuring a healthier population.

Ultimately, a healthy population needs clean water and air, safe food and housing, access to accurate information regarding health and safety, and an adequate supply and distribution of competent health professionals. These conditions for health depend upon a strong public health infrastructure, which includes a well-trained and accessible public health workforce as well as a wide array of community-level partners. The public health workforce is most often composed of a complex network of individuals from a variety of technical backgrounds including nursing, health education, sanitation, laboratory science, medicine, and epidemiology, among others. The common thread that ties these individuals to the public health workforce is their commitment to addressing the health needs of the population, as opposed to individual health needs.

In bringing together the concepts of rural and of public health, *rural public health* can be thought of as the application of public health principles and methods to address the unique needs of rural populations.

The Challenges

Rural Health Disparities/Equity

It should come as no surprise in the 21st century that where a population lives can impact their health, even their ability to maintain their health. *Place matters.* In 2004, the American Journal of Public Health dedicated its October issue to *place*, specifically rural. An editorial by Philips and McLeroy[7] described the many lenses through which public health is viewed, adding one of particular relevance for public health professionals interested in rural:

> that lens through which one sees an important part of the history of public health's development as oscillation between a focus on health issues facing populations defined by their demographic characteristics and health issues in populations defined by their geographic location.
>
> *(p. 1661)*

The focus of research and intervention over the last 50 plus years has employed the former, focusing on issues facing populations defined by their demographic characteristics. Fast forward from the 2004 AJPH publication to 2008, when the Robert Wood Johnson Foundation, as part of their Commission to Build a Healthier America, also focuses on *place* for an issue brief[8] looking at neighborhoods and health, recognizing that where we live supports or challenges our health and our ability to be healthy: "Physical, social, and service environments can promote health or put health in jeopardy." Yet, in this brief rural, which is not a neighborhood per se, goes unmentioned.

Historically, a common misperception has held that rural citizens live in communities that promote healthy lifestyles through clean air and water, ample recreational activities, and healthy physical activity associated with working the land. These perceptions are long-standing, and have never been particularly accurate. As early as 1899, Pennsylvania Governor Daniel H. Hastings reported to the Pennsylvania legislature that it was fiction to assume "that the country districts are naturally so healthy that there is no need for laws to prevent disease."[9] Whereas it is certainly true that there are many healthful aspects of rural living, there are also many inhibitors to good health that are prevalent across much of rural America. Furthermore, these inhibitors vary widely based on regional and community economic status, issues such as a higher proportion of occupations associated with increased injury risk, persistent poverty, inadequate access to quality healthcare delivery systems, and many others.

Among the factors that contribute to the health status in rural areas is the shifting nature of rural populations, both in terms of their numbers and composition. Throughout much of the 20th century rural America lost population as millions of residents migrated to the cities[10]—although the total population remained relatively stable as births compensated for these losses. The trend of out-migration began in the 1920s, was most prominent in the 1940s and '50s, and continued through the 1960s. Interestingly, the 1970s saw a significant increase of in-migration, i.e., migration back *into* rural areas, but this was short lived and remains something of a mystery among demographers.[11] The remaining decades of the 20th century saw inconsistent population growth and decline across rural sub-regions due to changing economies.

As the numbers of rural residents have changed, so has the composition of rural populations. Although still predominantly white, with racial and ethnic minorities representing just 21% of the nonmetro population, minority populations accounted for 82.7% of the nonmetropolitan population gain between 2000 and 2010. In addition, the economic base of rural America has also changed. Agriculture provides just one example. In 1959, 4 in 10 rural Americans lived on a farm; today that has dropped to less than 1 in 10[12] with only 6.5% of the rural workforce engaged in farming.[13]

Four distinct efforts have helped to focus attention on rural health in America in the 21st century. Two of these, Urban and Rural Health Chartbook: Health, United States, 2001, and Rural Healthy People 2010, provided the most extensive documentation of rural health disparities to that point.[14] These efforts have each been updated with The 2014 Update of the Rural-Urban Chartbook and Rural Healthy People 2020, respectively. Additional efforts have analyzed mortality and longevity covering the 1990s into the first decade of the 21st century.[15] Each of these efforts and select findings are described below starting with Kindig and Singh.

The work of Kindig and Cheng (2013), published in *Health Affairs*, examined trends in male and female mortality for two periods, 1992–96 and 2002–06, in 3,140 U.S. counties. They found that although mortality rates fell in most U.S. counties, in 42.8% of counties female mortality rose. Although this study did not identify counties as rural versus urban, the study found that population density and median income are inversely correlated with mortality rates, i.e., as population density and median income go down, the case for most rural counties, the mortality rates go up. The work of Singh and Siahpush (2014), published in the *American Journal of Preventive Medicine*, focused on life expectancy at birth and specifically compared urban versus rural, both overall and by gender group for the period from 1969 through 2009. Not only did they find a gap, favoring urban residents overall, they documented a change for rural women, from greater longevity than urban women for the period 1969 through 1989, to a steadily decreasing longevity. Whereas these studies made it into the print press, they were limited in their focus (mortality, longevity) and did little to promote understanding of explanatory factors.

A broader focus on differences in health between residents of rural and urban America was provided by the Centers for Disease Control in the 2001 edition of its annual Health, United States publication, entitled Urban and Rural Health Chartbook: Health, United States, 2001. This work was revisited in 2014 with funding support from the Federal Office of Rural Health Policy. The 2014 Chartbook found that all-cause mortality rates across all age groups are highest in the most rural counties. That is, the most rural (nonmetro) areas have the highest rates and the most urban (Large Fringe metro) areas have the lowest rates of mortality. In 2015, the 2014 Chartbook authors[16] also took a look at mortality a la Kindig and Cheng (2013), focusing on the ten leading causes of death and analyzing findings along the rural/urban continuum. They found rural disparities for most of the ten leading causes of death, with greater disparities in the Appalachian and Delta regions and in the rural South.

When looking at disparities related to specific diseases and conditions, several findings are noteworthy:

- *Ischemic Heart Disease:* Heart disease is the leading cause of death in the United States and Ischemic Heart Disease (IHD) is responsible for 60% of all heart disease deaths. The rural heart disease mortality rate for persons 20 years of age or greater is over 9% higher than the national U.S. rate.[17]
- *Chronic Obstructive Pulmonary Disease (COPD):* COPD is the third-leading cause of death in the United States. The rural COPD mortality rate for persons 20 years of age or older is 21% higher than the U.S. rate.[18] This rate is particularly high in the Rural South, where the mortality rate for COPD and other similar chronic lower respiratory diseases is 39% greater than the national average.[19]

- *Deaths Attributable to Unintentional Injuries and Motor Vehicle Traffic-Related Injuries:* The fourth-leading cause of death in the United States, the rural mortality rate for this indicator is 38% higher than the overall U.S. rate, down from a 50% difference in 2001.[20]
- *Suicide:* Suicide rates for males 15 years and older are lowest in large metro counties and increase steadily as counties become less urban. For example, the suicide rate among rural men (26.3 deaths per 100,000 population) is significantly higher than in urban areas (19.2 deaths per 100,000). The suicide rate for males in the rural Northwest is particularly high (nearly 60% higher than the national average). The suicide rate among rural women is still much lower than that of men.[21]
- *Oral Health:* Research findings indicate that edentulism (total tooth loss) affects not only nutrition, but many other systemic disease processes. The percent of rural people 65 years of age and older with total tooth loss is 29% higher than the overall U.S. rate.[22]
- *Effects of Chronic Disease:* For the United States as a whole, limitation in activity due to chronic health conditions among adults is significantly more common in rural counties than in large metro counties.[23]

Rural Disparities in Health Behaviors/Risk Factors

Not unexpectedly, given the health outcomes noted above, many of the health behaviors that contribute to poor health status also appear disproportionately among rural citizens:

- Smoking is the single most preventable cause of disease in the United States. In 1999, the percentage of 12–17-year-old rural adolescents who smoked cigarettes in the past month was 15% higher than the percent for the entire United States. This gap between the smoking rates for rural and urban adolescents increased to 32% in 2011.[24]
- Similarly, the 1997–98 percent of rural adults (18 years and older) who smoke cigarettes was 13% higher than the U.S. total, and increased to 40% higher by 2011. The increased level of smoking in rural areas has a substantial negative impact on rural health status and mortality.[25]
- In 1999, adults in rural areas were more likely to consume alcohol than those living in other areas.[26] By 2011, the rates of binge alcohol drinking in rural and urban areas had become very similar, no longer indicating a greater impact on rural populations, but no less a problem.
- Sedentary lifestyle or lack of physical activity is another behavior that has a negative impact on health status. The percent of rural residents 18 years of age and older who are physically inactive in their leisure time is 20% higher than the U.S. average.[27]

- Both men and women in rural areas have higher rates of obesity than men and women in other areas. Females living in the rural South have particularly high rates of obesity compared to the national average, to women living in urban areas of the South, and to other rural regions.[28]
- Finally, rural residents are less likely to receive recommended preventive services and report, on average, fewer visits to healthcare providers.[29] This is in part due to the low number of physicians in rural areas.[30] While highly variable, the overall rates of general practitioners in rural areas is comparable to those in urban areas; the prevalence of specialists and general pediatricians is 72% less than the national average.

Based on the patterns of risk behaviors seen among rural residents, some have suggested that a unique "rural culture" should be considered among possible health determinants.[31]

Rural Priorities

As the Centers for Disease Control and Prevention were preparing the 2001 Health, United States with Urban-Rural Chartbook report, another Federal Agency, the Health Resources and Services Administration, was contracting with the Southwest Rural Health Research Center at Texas A&M University Health Science Center's School of Rural Public Health (today, School of Public Health) to create Rural Healthy People 2010, a companion to Healthy People, to identify health goals and objectives for rural America. This project began by soliciting input from rural stakeholders across the nation about rural health priorities from among the Healthy People topics. This was followed by reviews of the research and grey literature to identify what was known about those topics and a series of case studies to identify promising practices to address priority issues. Ten years later, work on Rural Healthy People 2020 began. Once again, rural stakeholders (n = 1254), including but not limited to healthcare providers, academics, directors and personnel of state offices of rural health, and directors of state AHECs, identified the ten topics from among the 42 Healthy People topics as priorities for rural America. Table 21.2 compares the top ten issues identified for 2010 to those identified for 2020. Access to quality health services remains solidly in first place, representing multiple issues (health insurance, quality health services, and emergency medical services). Many topics simply shifted priority status, while some new topics were identified for RHP2020 that displaced RHP2010 priorities (Oral Health and Cancer dropped out of the top ten and were replaced by Physical Activity and Health, Older Adults).

The RHP2020 priority areas are themselves diverse, representing diseases (heart disease, stroke, diabetes), health behaviors (smoking, tobacco use, physical activity, nutrition and weight), and populations (older adults, maternal, infant and child), as well as access (health insurance and health services). Not surprisingly, the

TABLE 21.2 Comparison of Rural Priorities for RHP2010 and RHP2020

Rural Healthy People 2010 Priorities	Rural Healthy People 2020 Priorities
Access to Quality Health Services #1	Access to Quality Health Services
Heart Disease and Stroke #2	Nutrition and Weight Status (up from #10)
Diabetes #3	Diabetes
Mental Health and Mental Disorders #4	Mental Health and Mental Disorders
Oral Health #5	Substance Abuse (up from #6)
Tobacco Use #6	Heart Disease and Stroke (down from #2)
Substance Abuse #6	Physical Activity and Health (new)
Educational and Community-Based Programs #6	Older Adults (new)
Maternal, Infant, and Child Health #6	Maternal, Infant, and Child Health (down from #6)
Nutrition and Overweight #10	Tobacco (down from #6)
Cancer #10	Not in the Top 10

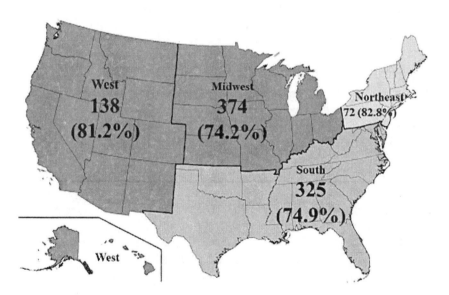

FIGURE 21.1 Response Rate by Census Regions for "Access to Quality Health Services" as a Top Ten Priority (Overall = 76.3%)

order of the ten priorities changes when examined from the perspective of Census Region. For example, although Access received the most votes overall, 76.3%, in Figure 21.1 you see how the voting varied by Census Region, from a high of 82.8% in the Northeast, to a low of 74.2% in the Midwest.

The reviews of literature conducted for each of the top 20 rural priority topics provide additional evidence of the continuing disparities between rural and urban populations, and, further, disparities within rural communities between Caucasian and racial/ethnic minority populations.[32]

Unfortunately, just documenting the continued existence of health disparities, while necessary, has proven to be insufficient to affect policy for rural as it was/ is for racial/ethnic minorities. To eliminate disparities you must also do something. Similarly, just documenting the need does not translate into the required resources to address the need.

Rural Health Infrastructure

Several significant issues emerge when considering the delivery of public health services in rural areas. Foremost among these is the diverse nature of the public health infrastructure across the nation. Each state has a different public health structure, and the local authority and capacity to deliver public health services varies widely. Consider the following: the Commonwealth of Massachusetts establishes local public health authority at the township level, resulting in over 300 local health departments (LHDs); Maine has 2 established LHDs, both in urban areas, and none in the remainder of the state; Idaho has a regionalized structure with 7 LHDs that cover each of the state's counties; Pennsylvania has 10 LHDs (6 county; 4 municipal), and the remainder of the state lacks direct local public health authority; New York has 58 independent county-level health departments covering each of its counties; and Florida has 67 state-run county-level health departments covering each of its counties.

The fact that as a nation we have 50 public health infrastructure models has significant implications for the delivery of public health services, especially in the rural communities of each of those states. Furthermore, and often neglected, many rural citizens reside in communities not served by a local governmental public health agency. Whether this is detrimental to population health largely depends upon how well other partners work to fill this governmental public health void. Importantly, public health infrastructure is not composed of just the governmental entities that work to assure population health, but also includes a wide array of partners such as hospitals, healthcare providers, non-profit organizations, cooperative extension agents, volunteers, and many others. In fact, many states that lack local governmental public health agencies have sought to establish county-level advisory groups to convene all of these important public health partners. Little research has been conducted to assess the effectiveness of these models, however, and concerns often arise when public health "isn't someone's job," but is rather dependent upon the dynamic leadership of one or two community volunteers. The bottom line is that public health is inherently a local pursuit and accordingly it tends to work best when it is responsive to local needs. Inasmuch as many rural communities lack this local-level component of the public health system, assuring this level of responsiveness is a much greater challenge.

Collaborating for Rural Population Health

Thanks to public (government) and private (foundations) funders, there are many resources that highlight promising projects and best practices that have been implemented by communities to address a variety of health issues. The Federal Office of Rural Health Policy (FORHP) in HRSA supports the Rural Health Information Hub, a source of information about programs, funding, and all things rural. Housed within the Rural Health Information Hub, FORHP has also supported the NORC Walsh Center for Rural Health Analysis and the University of Minnesota Rural Health Research Center to establish the Rural Community Health Gateway, a resource for rural evidence-based practices and promising approaches to addressing a wide variety of rural health issues including the development of Community Health Worker programs, obesity prevention, health promotion and disease prevention, and many others. The Robert Wood Johnson Foundation supports County Health Rankings, a source of information to help communities "select and implement" policies and programs that are evidence-based. (The latter, it should be noted, is not exclusively rural.) Another source, also funded by RWJF, is the Public Health Quality Improvement Exchange (PHQIX), intended to be a communication hub for those interested in learning about and sharing information related to quality improvement in public health. This site is also a source for QI projects that have been done across the country; again, this site is not exclusively rural. This brief list is not intended to be exhaustive, rather illustrative of the growing number of sources from which people can learn about what is being done, by whom, where, the nature of collaborations and collaborators, and contact people for more information.

The balance of this chapter will focus on five examples illustrating two separate scenarios to explore how rural communities can solve population health challenges through collaboration. In the first scenario, the community has a LHD; in the second scenario there is no LHD. As Hale (2015) indicates in a recent report published by Academy Health, local health departments are subject to the same challenges as the larger healthcare delivery system in the rural community: budget and staffing.[33] LHDs in rural areas have smaller staffs and rely on more part-time public health workers. With fewer staff and limited budgets, LHDs provide a narrower range of services and feel much less confident in their ability to perform some key public health functions, e.g., community needs assessment and improvement planning. Given these constraints, some LHDs have reached out to partners and have been able to narrow if not close some of the service gaps.

The following examples were chosen for inclusion here because they met four criteria: (1) the project occurred in a rural area, (2) it addressed one of the RHP2020 priority topics, (3) two or more partners were involved (scenario 1 specifically includes a public health department as one of the partners), and (4) there is evidence of success in achieving health outcomes.

Scenario 1 (Local Health Department)

Title: **Pleasant Street School 5–2–1–0: Fruits and Vegetables for School Snack Time** (PHQIX).

- RHP2020 Priority: **Nutrition and Physical Activity**.
- Partners: State and local health departments, a community-based organization, hospital, and a school.
- Project Aim: Second grade students will bring fruits and/or vegetables for snack at least 60% of the time by June 2009.
- Program: Taste-testing at snack time, visit grocery store, have "book buddies" with fifth graders, design bulletin board, integrate project into School Wellness Committee, and integrate into curriculum.
- Results: Second graders increased knowledge of nutritional benefits of fruits and vegetables. School received grant to provide fruits and vegetables to all students at snack time.

Title: **Project Lazarus** (RHIhub).

- RHP2020 Priority: **Substance Abuse**.
- Partners: The Wilkes County Health Department, Community Care of North Carolina, the Eastern Band of Cherokee Indians, the Mountain Area Health Education Center, the Governor's Institute on Substance Abuse, the UNC Injury Prevention Research Center, the NC Division of Public Health Injury Section, and the U.S. Army.
- Project Aim: Community partners responded to deaths from overdoses of opioids and pain relief medications by starting an overdose prevention program to: (1) prevent prescription medication overdoses, (2) present responsible pain-management practices, (3) promote substance abuse treatment and support services.
- Program: In-person trainings and continuing medical education for prescribers; toolkits that offer guidance to providers in the primary care, emergency, and care management settings, as well as provide information on community coalition building; treatment and recovery resources and assistance on local levels; harm reduction through access to naloxone, an antidote for opioid and heroin overdose; educating and mentoring youth at school and community events; resources for patients and families; training and technical assistance to community groups, coalitions, and clinicians.
- Results: Since program began overdose-related deaths have decreased, number of physicians using pain agreements and prescription monitoring has increased, and there has been a reduction in ED visits.

Title: **Healthy People, Healthy Communities** (RHIhub Community Health Gateway).

- RHP2020 Priority: **Nutrition and Weight Status; Diabetes; Heart Disease and Stroke.**

- Partners: Ephraim McDowell Health Care Foundation, Inc., in Danville, Kentucky, four county health departments, one extension office.
- Project Aim: Increase access to screening and risk-reduction education in Danville, Kentucky, area.
- Program: The project offers community-wide awareness education, screening activities, and follow-up for risk reduction related to cardiovascular risk factors with a focus on at-risk populations. Screenings include cholesterol, glucose, blood pressure, body mass index, Stroke Risk Score Card and on-site consultation with a registered nurse for review of the biometric information and scoring of risk factors. There is also an option for clients to participate in telephone case management to address risk reduction.
- Results: Decreased the risk of stroke and heart disease among participants.

Scenario 2 (without Local Health Department)

Title: **Videoconferencing Enhances Access to Psychiatric Care for Children and Adults with Mental Illness in Rural Settings** (AHRQ Health Care Innovations Exchange).

- RHP2020 Priority: **Mental Health and Mental Disorders**.
- Partners: University of VA Health System (UVHS), local mental health centers (for children), primary care and geriatric clinics (for adults).
- Project Aim: To enable children and adults in rural communities with mental illness to receive psychiatric care.
- Program: Psychiatric fellows and residents at the UVHS use videoconferencing to serve children and adult patients. Children gain access by visiting one of three mental health centers; adults gain access by visiting local primary care or geriatric clinics. Office of Telehealth provides support services and tools to facilitate care.
- Results: High satisfaction of participants with the services (parents, adults). Enhanced access, child psychiatry fellows held 12,000 sessions with children and adolescents from 2007 to 2012. https://innovations.ahrq.gov/profiles/videoconferencing-enhances-access-psychiatric-care-children-and-adults-mental-illness-rural

Title: **Franklin Cardiovascular Health Program (FCHP)** (RHIhub Community Health Gateway)

- RHP2020 Priority: **Nutrition and Weight Status; Diabetes; Heart Disease and Stroke**.
- Partners: Franklin Community Health Network includes Ben Franklin Center, Evergreen Behavioral Services, Franklin Memorial Hospital, NorthStar, Healthy Community Coalition, and Office Practices.

- Project Aim: To develop sustainable, community-wide prevention methods for cardiovascular diseases in order to change behaviors and healthcare outcomes in rural Maine.
- Program: Local community groups in Farmington, Maine, along with staff at the Franklin Memorial Hospital, studied mortality and hospitalization rates for 40 years in this rural, low-income area to seek intervention methods that could address cardiovascular diseases.
- Results: A decline in cardiovascular-related mortality rates and improved prevention methods for hypertension, high cholesterol, and smoking. https://www.ruralhealthinfo.org/community-health/project-examples/790

Challenges

Collaboration for population health in rural America is NOT without its challenges:

Improving Overall Population Health Does Not Reduce Gaps by Geography, as Evidenced by the Research Referenced Above

According to the 2014 Urban and Rural Chartbook and Kindig (2013), improving overall population health reduces mortality, but not necessarily geographic disparities in mortality. There are a few exceptions where gaps have actually increased (e.g., COPD, suicide). Similarly, within a given geographic locale, population health does not necessarily reduce health gaps between sub-groups.

Data for Benchmarking Is Very Limited, Making It Difficult to Monitor or Measure Improvements Achieved through Interventions

A majority of national databases do not have a large enough sample of rural residents to discern statistically significant differences. Further, rural research, particularly but not exclusively at the local (i.e., small community, small county) level, is limited by the issue of small numbers. Data resources that provide county-level data related across a variety of health measures often rely on data modeling techniques pulled from and aggregated across multiple similar counties. Whereas the counties may be similar in size, they are not necessarily similar in culture or other important demographic characteristics. Further, the pooling of data and modeling across counties limits our ability to identify positive outliers that may help to inform promising approaches to addressing community health issues.

Sustaining Population Efforts Is Difficult in Small Under-Resourced Communities

Grants from funding agencies, either public or private, enable communities to implement programs; unfortunately, the program often ends when the funding ends. Given that rural health departments are proportionally more reliant on state and federal resources, as opposed to local resources, they tend to have less flexibility to address locally identified needs.

Promoting Rural Population Health Collaborations Involves Breaking Down Silos

The passage of the Affordable Care Act in 2010 has had a variety of effects on rural communities and rural providers, not all that could have been predicted.

The ACA created a requirement for not-for-profit hospitals to conduct community needs assessments as the basis for community benefits work. In some communities, hospitals and public health departments began working together immediately, drawing on each other's skills, a win-win. In as many and possibly more communities, however, hospitals have paid consultants from out-of-town or out-of-state to do their needs assessments, while the health department has separately conducted its own needs assessment. Similarly, the ACA requires health insurers to cover preventive services at no cost to the patient. The decision by the state regarding whether or not to expand Medicaid can have differential impact on the community in this regard. For example, in rural communities with provider shortages where the health department is more engaged in clinical service delivery, ACA may provide new sources of revenue to support health department services. In other communities, however, the result may be shifts in service provision that can destabilize an already under-resourced public health system.

Discussion, Conclusions

There is no one definition of what constitutes rural. There is no one model of public health infrastructure for rural. There is no one demographic profile of rural residents. These are givens. Yet despite this heterogeneity, there are other givens. By and large the populations residing in rural America are older, poorer, and sicker. By and large rural communities have fewer public health and healthcare resources. In sum, place matters, however it is defined. If we had forgotten, then a few recent stories taken from the front pages of major newspapers remind us again: stories relating to the unexpected numbers of new cases of HIV/AIDS in rural Indiana; the unexpected numbers of new cases of tuberculosis in Alabama; the numbers of people addicted to and dying from opioids in New England and Appalachia; threats to community drinking water (West Virginia, Louisiana, Michigan). Each of these are preventable problems that require a strong public health infrastructure.

Addressing population health in rural America requires collaboration; indeed the successful examples of programs listed earlier reflect a variety of partners coming together. Not every community will have a strong local public health presence, but that does not preclude the coming together of other community-level partners, possibly together with the state department of public health and/or academic partners to address issues. The Internet provides an invaluable resource to stimulate the thinking of rural community organizations, faith-based organizations, academic institutions, local health departments, hospitals, and others, informing the plethora of rural stakeholders on what can be done to improve population health complete with toolkits, measures, and key informants. Unfortunately, "stone soup" only takes us so far, and most if not all of these wonderful programs and efforts will involve some form of financial cost both to implement and subsequently sustain. Although there are funding sources, they come with their own challenges. The downside of extramural funding resources is that they are often focused on new and innovative programs, do not cover operating costs, are for limited periods of time, and expect that somehow the community or organization will pick-up the cost or charge for it so as to make the program sustainable. Given that rural public health agencies are more reliant on state and federal resources for a proportion of their overall revenue, as opposed to local resources, the funding challenge is compounded by their having less flexibility to address locally identified issues. This challenge is further exacerbated when the multiple partners raise issues of ownership, organizational interests, and trust (Tuskegee from the past, Flint from the present).

Finally, population health will always be a challenge when applied in small communities. There is the challenge to the community of deciding where and how to deploy their limited resources; of overcoming a history of competition among potential partners within the community; and of deciding whether and how to partner—to marshal scarce resources—across county lines, with large urban providers, or with academic researchers, to name just a few. However, none of these challenges is insurmountable; the evidence is out there.

Notes

1. Lumsden, L.L. (1929). Extent of Rural Health Service in the United States, 1925–29. *Public Health Reports*, part 1, 44: 1204.
2. Kindig, D. (April 6, 2015). What Are We Talking About When We Talk about Population Health? *Health Affairs Blog*. http://healthaffairs.org/blog/2015/04/06/what-are-we-talking-about-when-we-talk-about-population-health/ Accessed 8/10/2015.
3. http://www2.census.gov/geo/pdfs/maps-data/maps/thematic/2010ua/UA2010_UAs_and_UCs_Map.pdf
4. Coburn, A.F., MacKinney, A.C., McBride, T.D., Mueller, K.J., Slifkin, R.T., and Wakefield, M.K. (March 2007). Choosing Rural Definitions: Implications for Health Policy. Issue Brief #2. Rural Policy Research Institute Health Panel. http://www.rupri.org/Forms/RuralDefinitionsBrief.pdf Accessed 3/3/2016.
5. U.S. Census Bureau, 2010 Redistricting Data (Public Law 94-171) Summary File.
6. Rural Health Reform Policy Research Center. (2014). *The 2014 Update of the Rural-Urban Chartbook*. Bethesda, MD: NORC Walsh Center for Rural Health Analysis.
7. Phillips, C.D., and McLeroy, K.R. (October 2004). Health in Rural America: Remembering the Importance of Place. *American Journal of Public Health*, 94(10): 1661–1663.
8. RWJF Commission to Build Healthy America: Issue Brief 3: Neighborhoods and Health. September 2008. Where We Live Matters for Our Health: Neighborhoods and Health.

9. "Biennial Message, Governor Daniel Hartman Hastings, January 1, 1899," *Pennsylvania Archives*, 4th ser., 12 (Harrisburg, PA, 1902), 315.

10. Ibid.; U.S. Census Bureau, 1920–2000.

11. Johnson, K. (2006). Demographic Trends in Rural and Small Town America. *The Carsey Institute Reports on Rural America*, 1(1): 8.

12. Whitener, L.A. and Parker, T. (April 2005). Policy Options for a Changing Rural America. *Amber Waves*, 3(2): 1. Updated May 2007.

13. Johnson, K. (2006). Demographic Trends in Rural and Small Town America. *The Carsey Institute Reports on Rural America*, 1(1): 7.

14. Eberhardt, M.S., Ingram, D.D., Makuc, D.M., et al. (2001). *Urban and Rural Health Chartbook: Health, United States, 2001*. Hyattsville, MD: National Center for Health Statistics.

15. Kindig, D.A., Cheng, E.R. (2013). Even as Mortality Fell in Most US Counties, Female Mortality Nonetheless Rose in 42.8 Percent of Counties from 1992 To 2006. *Health Affairs*, 32(3): 451–458; Singh, G.K., Siahpush, M. (2014). Widening Rural-Urban Disparities in Life Expectancy, U.S., 1969-2009. *American Journal of Preventative Medicine*, 46(2): e19–e29.

16. Knudson, A., Meit, M., Tanenbaum, E., Brady, J., Gilbert, T., Klug, M., Arsen, E., Popat, S., Schroeder, S. (2015). *Exploring Rural and Urban Mortality Differences*. Bethesda, MD: NORC Walsh Center for Rural Health Analysis. http://www.norc.org/Research/ Projects/Pages/exploring-rural-and-urban-mortality-differences.aspx Accessed 12/16/2016.

17. Rural Health Reform Policy Research Center. (2014). *The 2014 Update of the Rural-Urban Chartbook*. Bethesda, MD: NORC Walsh Center for Rural Health Analysis; Eberhardt, M.S., Ingram, D.D., Makuc, D.M., et al. (2001). *Urban and Rural Health Chartbook: Health, United States, 2001*. Hyattsville, MD: National Center for Health Statistics.

18. Eberhardt, M.S., Ingram, D.D., Makuc, D.M., et al. (2001). *Urban and Rural Health Chartbook: Health, United States, 2001*. Hyattsville, MD: National Center for Health Statistics.

19. Knudson, A., Meit, M., Tanenbaum, E., Brady, J., Gilbert, T., Klug, M., Arsen, E., Popat, S., Schroeder, S. (2015). *Exploring Rural and Urban Mortality Differences*. Bethesda, MD: NORC Walsh Center for Rural Health Analysis. http://www.norc.org/Research/ Projects/Pages/exploring-rural-and-urban-mortality-differences.aspx Accessed 12/16/2016.

20. Eberhardt, M.S., Ingram, D.D., Makuc, D.M., et al. (2001). *Urban and Rural Health Chartbook: Health, United States, 2001*. Hyattsville, MD: National Center for Health Statistics.

21. Knudson, A., Meit, M., Tanenbaum, E., Brady, J., Gilbert, T., Klug, M., Arsen, E., Popat, S., Schroeder, S. (2015). *Exploring Rural and Urban Mortality Differences*. Bethesda, MD: NORC Walsh Center for Rural Health Analysis. http://www.norc.org/Research/ Projects/Pages/exploring-rural-and-urban-mortality-differences.aspx Accessed 12/16/2016.

22. Rural Health Reform Policy Research Center. (2014). *The 2014 Update of the Rural-Urban Chartbook*. Bethesda, MD: NORC Walsh Center for Rural Health Analysis.

23. Ibid.

24. Ibid.

25. Ibid.

26. Ibid.

27. Ibid.
28. Ibid.
29. National Health Care Disparities Report, 2004. [OnlineAHRQ] http://www.ahrq.gov
30. Rural Health Reform Policy Research Center. (2014). *The 2014 Update of the Rural-Urban Chartbook.* Bethesda, MD: NORC Walsh Center for Rural Health Analysis.
31. Hartley, D. (October 2004). Rural Health Disparities, Population Health, and Rural Culture. *American Journal of Public Health*, 94(10): 1675–1678.
32. Rural Healthy People 2020. http://sph.tamhsc.edu/srhrc/rhp2020.html Accessed 12/9/2015.
33. Hale, N.L. (October 2015). Rural Public Health Systems: Challenges and Opportunities for Improving Population Health. *Academy Health.*

22

IMPLEMENTING POPULATION HEALTH STRATEGIES

Bill Barberg

Differentiating between Population *Healthcare* and Population *Health*

When the topic of population health is discussed, it is commonly understood that different stakeholders will have different definitions of "population." For example, hospitals will focus on specific subsets of their patient population, insurance companies will focus on the lives they are covering, and Public Health practitioners will focus on the population of an entire community. Much more significant than these differences in the definition of targeted populations, however, is the less-appreciated question of how a coalition is defining their approach to "health." The latter definition will determine whether an endeavor is focused primarily on improving *the healthcare of individuals in a population through clinical interventions* or whether it is focused on improving *a population's overall health primarily through community-oriented strategies.*

Currently, the majority of readily available articles and guidelines[1] for implementing population health focus on improving the *healthcare* of a population through clinical care delivered to individuals. The typical steps of a healthcare-based approach are:

1. Assess the health of the population.
2. Stratify the patients into categories in order to target interventions on the individuals with the greatest needs.
3. Engage the selected patients by:

    - Organizing interdisciplinary teams of physicians, nurses, and other care providers

- Creating a patient-specific care plan
- Implementing patient-centered care interventions

4. Evaluate the impact.

This clinically oriented approach strives to improve community collaboration by streamlining the transitions between care providers, the sharing of clinical data, and the coordination of patient-centered interventions across the continuum of care. David Kindig—who was influential in defining the term "population health" with Greg Stoddart in 2002[2]—suggests in a recent article in *Health Affairs* that a better term to refer to the healthcare-based approach would be "population medicine" or "population health management" instead of Population Health.

In contrast, approaches that are focused on improving the overall *health* of populations bear a greater resemblance to the efforts of Public Health practitioners working to improve Community Health. Community Health improvement strategies generally focus on creating policy-based, systemic, and environmental changes and addressing the social and economic factors that impact health such as access to full employment, housing, transportation, and education. Focused less on clinical care protocols or coordination, Community Health efforts emphasize access to "complete streets" (to encourage walking and biking), healthy food, active transportation, and insurance coverage, while also addressing the social determinants of health. This community-focused interpretation of Population Health is consistent with Kindig and Stoddart's original definition of Population Health as "the health outcomes of a group of individuals, including the distribution of such outcomes within the group."[3] It also is consistent with what the Robert Wood Johnson Foundation calls "a culture of health."[4]

Reasons to Emphasize a Group Orientation to Population Health

When considering the most effective way to improve Population Health, three points suggest that we can achieve greater impact by implementing strategies that extend beyond clinical interventions on individuals, broadening our focus to include *groups and communities* and the *social factors* of health:

1. **Eighty percent of the factors that impact health outcomes lie outside the realm of clinical care.**
   The widely recognized model used by the University of Wisconsin as the foundation for their County Health Rankings indicates that Clinical Care only accounts for 20% of the controllable factors that lead to health outcomes. In contrast, social and economic factors account for 40%; health behaviors like tobacco use, diet, and exercise account for 30%; and the Physical

Environment (which includes air quality, water quality, housing, and transit) accounts for 10%.[5] This model indicates that the greatest opportunities for making a sustainable impact on the health of a population lie in the 80% of factors outside the realm of clinical care.

2. **Four in five physicians acknowledge the importance of addressing the social needs of patients.**

Eighty-five percent of the 1,000 American physicians who participated in a national survey for the Robert Wood Johnson Foundation believe that their patients' social needs are as important to address as their medical conditions.[6] In the same survey, which was cited in a 2011 report entitled "Health Care's Blind Side," 80% of the physicians also indicated that they were not confident in their capacity to address their patients' social needs. Some of the most important needs that the physicians wished they could write prescriptions for were fitness programs, nutritious food, and transportation assistance. These types of social needs are most effectively met in collaboration with a community or neighborhood, not just by coordinating the medical care of specific individuals.

3. **Examples of improved health among large numbers of people almost always involve significant group dynamics.**

Success stories of community-wide health improvement involve important changes that cannot be achieved by individuals, even those working with a coordinated team of healthcare professionals. For example, Oklahoma City and Saddleback Church both achieved monumental goals in community-wide weight loss—in Oklahoma City, the mayor led a successful effort in which inhabitants lost a cumulative million pounds[7] and at Saddleback Church, minister Rick Warren led a successful effort in which members lost 250,000 pounds in one year.[8] In both of these communities, changes to the built environment, new policies, and social-level behavioral shifts (such as restaurants working to create and promote healthier meals) impacted large numbers of people.

In the case of Saddleback Church, simple changes like the shift from serving donuts to serving fruit in the fellowship breaks after the worship service were combined with endeavors to educate large numbers of the congregation on the importance of improved nutrition and exercise. The church took positive advantage of the powerful dynamic of small groups to provide social support and transportation assistance that made the life changes more practical and attainable. Pastor Warren describes the added elements that helped make their program successful as "faith, focus and friends." Dr. Mark Hyman, who helped craft the program, stated:

People who actually did the program together lost twice as much weight as people who did it alone. . . . [T]he community was the medicine. It's powerful to show how you can help each other. They shopped together, cooked together, and ate together. They exercised together. That accountability, the "Love Factor," was what helped people change. It's positive peer pressure.[9]

> The group dynamics harnessed by Saddleback Church were able to change people's behavior more effectively than medical care plans narrowly focused on individuals.

All three of these reasons suggest that even if a particular hospital or insurance company is only interested in improving the health of their patient population or the lives that they cover, the most effective strategies to improve population health are those focused on communities, neighborhoods, or other socially cohesive clusters of people. Some of the time and money that is currently invested in the population *healthcare* implementation should be re-allocated to investments that support improved *Community Health* by targeting groups that are in a good position to get healthy together.

There are many more compelling examples for the success of community-based health initiatives:

- A large apartment complex in Detroit is demonstrating how neighborhood-centered strategies can bring about lifestyle changes that would be hard to accomplish with individual-centered plans. Under the banner of "Communities of HOPE," with support from a small 501c3 organization and numerous volunteers, the residents have started a walking club, a social dance group, community straw bale gardening,[10] and a weekly potluck salad bar lunch. With some initial help from volunteers, residents are now able to shop at the mobile farmers' market that comes to their community room and buy just one item to add to a buffet where they can all enjoy salads made from a wide range of healthy items.[11]
- Walla Walla, Washington, has demonstrated the impact of a city-wide Children's Resilience Initiative to help youth overcome Adverse Childhood Experiences (ACEs). Some experts consider ACEs to be the nation's top Public Health issue and a root cause of a wide range of health problems.[12]
- North Karelia, Finland, a community of 170,000, dramatically reduced local cases of cardiovascular disease after it was identified by an international health organization as having the highest rate of heart attacks of any community in the world in the early 1970s.[13] By taking an innovative community-based approach, they were able to lower male cardiovascular mortality by over 70%—an unparalleled accomplishment.[14]

As Dan Buettner, author of the Blue Zone books, stated recently, "People may get sick as individuals, but they get healthy as a group."[15] Or, as Dr. George

Albee put it, "No epidemic has ever been resolved by paying attention to the treatment of the affected individual."[16] This would suggest that instead of spending so much effort identifying the *individuals* in the group who need the focused attention of a coordinated clinical care plan, Population Health efforts should focus on improving the overall health of the *whole group*.

Integrating Population Health Implementation with Community Benefit Requirements

Bringing about significant health improvement changes in a *community or neighborhood* is best accomplished by the combined efforts of a diverse set of cross-sector stakeholders such as non-profit organizations, schools, businesses, government departments, faith communities, libraries, and civic organizations. Although this type of collaboration can be uncomfortable territory for many hospital leaders and staff unfamiliar with approaches that go beyond patient-centered care coordination, when hospitals embrace a community-focused approach to Population Health, they are positioned to be leaders, or at least strong supporters, in community-wide efforts. A good place to begin these efforts is through existing Community Benefit requirements. Population Health leaders in the hospital can team up with those in the Community Benefit department who are working to meet the IRS requirements added by the Affordable Care Act, which require non-profit hospitals to conduct a Community Health Needs Assessment and develop an implementation plan every three years. It is surprising that in many healthcare systems, the work on Population Health is being done with little coordination or collaboration with those working to address the health priorities in the community. Once the key people within the Public Health and Community Benefits departments of the hospital or healthcare system agree to work together, they can begin the process of engaging the rest of the community in the journey toward improved Population Health.

Six Practical Steps to Engage a Community in Developing and Implementing a Collaborative Strategy

A multi-stakeholder strategy management approach to Population Health can improve the health of a community through six important steps:

1. Establish the Urgency and Commitment to Collaborate on Selected Health Issues.
2. Introduce the New Concepts, Techniques, and Tools for Managing a Community Strategy.
3. Engage the Coalition in Co-Creating a Strategy Map.
4. Distribute the Work of Strategy Execution.
5. Adopt Shared Strategy Measures and a Shared Measurement System.
6. Harness, Align, and Monitor the Actions.

These six steps, although not an exhaustive plan, provide important techniques and shifts that will significantly enhance the success of a community's health improvement efforts.

1. Establish the Urgency and Commitment to Collaborate on Selected Health Issues

A well-established prerequisite for any successful large-scale change is *urgency*. Most people and organizations are busy, so it is unlikely that they will make the necessary investment of effort if they don't see both the importance and urgency of action. It is important to clearly establish the "burning platform" that will make people realize that failing to act is more dangerous than the uncertainty and effort of working towards a solution.

In many communities, short lists of priority issues are defined in the Community Health Needs Assessments (CHNAs) conducted by non-profit hospitals and the Community Health Assessments (CHAs) led by Public Health departments. CHNAs and CHAs often engage many different stakeholders and create consensus on three to six priority health issues; they also provide data that support their decision to pick these issues. Population Health improvements could be more successfully implemented if the typical CHNA and CHA efforts were enhanced to include a focus on *collaboration* and *cost*:

Collaboration

The multiple organizations doing the CHNAs and CHAs in a community should agree to work together in the development of an approach and the gathering and analysis of data. It is clear that the groups will be more successful in assessing the health needs of a community—as well as its available assets, opportunities, and related information—if they collaborate in the process of gathering and sharing different types of data, conducting stakeholder interviews, and defining sub-geographies and doing analysis. Such a collaboration can also engage academic organizations and foundations whose expertise and data can improve the quality and depth of the assessments. The collaboration can save everyone time and money, produce more valuable analysis, and build the foundation for collaborative problem solving.

Cost

Analysis of the priority issues should extend beyond just the statistics of the health issue (e.g. the rate of obesity, tobacco use, or the levels of chronic disease) and make reasonable estimates of the specific costs of inaction for different groups in the community. The costs of population health problems—like diabetes, misuse of opioids, and child maltreatment—impact a broad range of community stakeholders. However, many of the leaders of these organizations don't sufficiently understand the connection between the Community Health issues and the direct costs and indirect negative consequences that their organizations will experience as a result. The more these stakeholders understand that *they* will be paying a heavy price if the current trends continue, the more likely they will be motivated to become part of the community coalition working on solutions.

With a modest amount of extra effort, the work of completing the CHNA and CHA can be leveraged to create the urgency to motivate a greater number of community stakeholders to move into action. For example, instead of just recognizing the statistics about the rising rate of prescription drug and opioid misuse in a community, the analysis should look at the many direct and indirect costs *and who is paying for them*. The average cost of care for a baby born to a mother with an opioid addiction is over $50,000 higher than for a typical baby.[17] The more the leaders of organizations that are paying those costs become aware of them, the more likely they will commit resources and efforts to be part of a collaborative strategy to address the issue.

It is also important to create a sense of community ownership around priority health issues by acknowledging that they cannot be solved by any one organization, policy, program, or sector. Communities like Weld County, Colorado (www.thrivingweld.com), and San Diego, California (www.livewellsd. org), are emerging as inspiring examples of collaboration in health improvement. Both communities have achieved a high degree of consensus and alignment on priority health issues among many different stakeholders. By appropriately engaging a broad spectrum of community stakeholders, the process of selecting priority health issues can create valuable buy-in from the community, not just from the organization making a report to meet a compliance requirement. If the leaders of a wide range of organizations come together and clearly communicate the need for teamwork—declaring their commitment to work as a team even if they compete with others in the community in some areas—then the next steps for achieving Population Health improvement become much easier.

2. Introduce the New Concepts, Techniques, and Tools for Managing a Community Strategy

Once there is a shared understanding of the need for urgency and unprecedented levels of teamwork to address specific priority health issues in a community, the next step is to establish support for the adoption of the concepts, techniques, and tools necessary for this higher level of collaboration. Over the past decade, even if they have reached a consensus on the specific priorities—such as reducing obesity, teen pregnancies, or diabetes—many communities have been unsuccessful at developing and implementing strategies to address those priorities. Few communities achieve anything close to the broad teamwork that is needed for

FIGURE 22.1

major progress. Too often, their efforts resemble Figure 22.1 above, in which the big dark-gray arrow represents stakeholders' theoretical agreement on the priority health issues and the smaller black arrows represent the fragmentation and lack of alignment of the many isolated efforts in the community.

Whereas some progress can be made if many different organizations are each devoting their individual efforts to positively impact a shared community goal, the real power of collaboration is harnessed when those organizations are able to combine their efforts and resources in mutually beneficial and mutually reinforcing ways that go beyond the sum of their previous isolated efforts (see Figure 22.2).

When there is an intentional shift from striving to find an evidence-based *program* to implement (looking for the silver bullet) towards focusing on *enhancing community teamwork and collaboration*, the community should also recognize that it may need to learn new tools and ways of working. The following are several

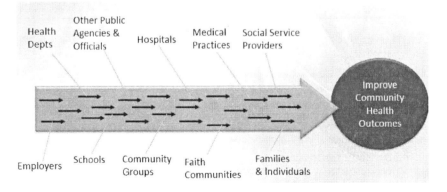

FIGURE 22.2

of the most important elements of community-oriented collaborative population health improvement plans:

Collective Impact

Organizations that aspire to work together in community-wide Population Health improvement efforts can benefit from understanding and adopting key points of the Collective Impact approach. This approach, which was described in Chapter 13 of this book, has gained a lot of momentum and growing awareness in recent years, shifting the thinking of many people and funders. Because it is still relatively new, the Collective Impact concept continues to be refined, and the techniques are maturing as more and more communities attempt to make it work. Because so many different sectors—healthcare, government, philanthropic, faith-based, non-profit, Public Health, and social entrepreneurs—have gained familiarity with the main concepts of Collective Impact, a common language is emerging. This language includes terms such as a common agenda, shared measurement, mutually reinforcing activities, continuous communication, and backbone support.

In addition to a growing body of knowledge on Collective Impact, other approaches such as Asset-Based Community Development and the Community Balanced Scorecard methodology offer techniques and insights to draw from. In their Winter 2015 article in the *Stanford Social Innovation Review* on "The Dawn of System Leadership," Peter Senge, John Kania, and Hal Hamilton stated that we are "at the beginning of the beginning in learning how to catalyze and guide systemic change at a scale commensurate with the scale of problems we face."[18] Leaders of these efforts should seek to adopt promising approaches to improve collaboration by building on the Collective Impact concept with new techniques and tools from other success stories or methodologies.

A Shared Strategy Map Framework

When working to harness the collaborative power of a diverse coalition, it is essential to have a common agenda around which to align the various organizations and programs. An effective common agenda should go well beyond an agreement on a few priority issues. Stakeholders should collaborate to develop a robust strategic framework within which the many different community stakeholders can then organize themselves according to their unique strengths.

Instead of using techniques such as linear logic models and specific work plans, which were designed for evaluating isolated programs, community coalitions should start by co-creating a strategic framework which will provide structure for the rest of the journey. This can be done by either using a Strategy Map or a framework based on Driver Diagrams. Several characteristics of Strategy Maps are especially valuable for building community consensus and supporting the communication and monitoring of a large-scale, multi-faceted strategy:

- Their flexible cause and effect logic provides structure and helps tell the story of the strategy and how the desired outcomes will be achieved.
- They contain higher-level "Objectives" that transcend any individual organization or program, describing the community strategy in a way that enhances teamwork.
- Their useful and enduring framework can be used by many different community stakeholders for more efficient and effective communication and planning.
- They do not attempt to describe specific inputs, participating organizations, short-term actions, or measures and targets (although the Strategy Map establishes the framework used to organize a shared set of measures and targets).

A well-designed Driver Diagram may have many of the same characteristics that make Strategy Maps useful. But one of the main differences between Strategy Maps and Driver Diagrams is that Strategy Maps don't attempt to structure the strategy using "primary" drivers and "secondary" drivers. As the framework becomes more robust and "zoomable," attempting to characterize drivers as being "primary" or "secondary" becomes increasingly awkward. Instead of this two-tier structure, Strategy Maps allow for more flexible relationships. Strategy Maps for population health issues are often structured with multiple levels of detail and the ability to "zoom in" on an appropriate level of detail for a specific topic.

The practices related to designing and using Strategy Maps are based on techniques for strategy management that have been used and refined for over 20 years. These techniques have their roots in the Balanced Scorecard methodology developed by Robert Kaplan and David Norton.[19] Countless practitioners and consultants have wrestled with this technique over the years, and the result is a robust body of knowledge that makes this approach powerful and effective.

Given the length of time it takes to build consensus and to implement changes that significantly improve health outcomes in a community, a well-designed strategy must be described in a way that will not change every year. If the specific short-term actions become the primary content of the strategy, then the strategy will likely need to be re-created annually, wasting a lot of time and disrupting efforts to build more advanced collaboration for bigger and more lasting changes.

Population Health Strategy Maps are built using an enduring but flexible framework that separates the Objectives—which are the building blocks of the Strategy Map—from the measures, targets, and actions that are also part of the strategy and strategy management system. The Objectives describe specific changes, but they don't specify how those changes will be measured. Rather than trying to quantify each of the multitude of actions that go into the strategy, the measures within Population Health Strategy Maps are used to *monitor the progress of accomplishing the strategic Objectives*, allowing for management that is both simpler and more powerful.

New Technologies That Enable Efficient and Effective Collaboration

Because of the complexity of addressing major Community Health issues through community collaboration, the amount of information can be overwhelming, even for highly motivated coalition members. While the details of each new type of technology go beyond the scope of this chapter, there are three underutilized types of technologies that can significantly enhance these efforts:

*   *A Strategy Management and Measurement system* can simplify the process of providing backbone support and continuous communication within a large coalition. By shifting away from big documents and cumbersome spreadsheets to a dynamic online platform, information can be managed much more efficiently at each step of the journey. An information system should not just be about collecting data and generating reports, but should support the communication of the strategy, the ways in which different organizations will work together, and the progress being made each month or quarter. A growing number of communities are using the InsightVision platform[20] to manage and monitor the multitude of details of a cross-sector, multi-stakeholder strategy. San Diego County received a 2016 Achievement Award from the National Association of Counties for the deployment of the InsightVision application to support their Collective Impact efforts.[21] In addition, the combined use of zoomable Strategy Maps and an online strategy management and measurement system was named a 2015 *Promising Practice* by the National Association of City and County Health Officials.[22]
*   *A Community Care Coordination platform* enables collaboration around a multi-faceted success plan for an individual or household. Unlike the strategy management and measurement systems, a Community Care Coordination platform manages individual and household-level data that must be HIPPA compliant. This technology focuses on coordinated care for individuals, but it will be more powerful if deployed as part of a strategy that also focuses on the health of a neighborhood or community. At a minimum, a Community Care Coordination platform can integrate with a variety of clinical and mental healthcare providers to allow for shared information, referrals, and a coordinated care plan. Ideally, the platform would also extend beyond clinical information and care providers to include resources and information for addressing social factors that impact health—like access to transportation, housing, education, job skills, and healthy food. If a broad spectrum of organizations pursues a shared strategy, aligning their efforts to achieve a priority health outcome, they will be better positioned to invest in and make use of this platform to coordinate care for individuals.
*   *Shared Knowledge platforms* can be used across the entire country to make it easy for local coalitions to have the most relevant information at their fingertips. Currently, no single software or website provides all this information, but

increasingly robust sites are emerging that can equip teams in communities to more efficiently and effectively get results. For example, a team that is focusing on advancing "Farm to School" efforts in a community should be leveraging the resources of http://www.farmtoschool.org/ to learn from others and avoid re-inventing the wheel. Shared Knowledge platforms do not have information about the specific strategy implementation details for any community, and they are not used to monitor real-time progress at either the community or individual level. Instead, Shared Knowledge platforms can serve as rich and well-organized encyclopedias of current information for local action teams, enabling them to easily access and share information about particular topics or strategies. Instead of a list of evidence-based actions (which tend to be isolated interventions that are relatively easy to research and evaluate), the Shared Knowledge platform should be designed to provide insights, examples of success (and failure), templates, and answers to questions that might be expected as communities strive to move from a high-level strategy into the details of implementation.[23] If every team that was working on their subset of a community-wide Population Health strategy were actively using and collaborating in the creation of online knowledge-sharing platforms, their work could move forward more rapidly, confidently, and effectively.

Communities who simultaneously make use of the Collective Impact approach, a shared Strategy Map framework, and other valuable supporting technologies will be positioned to develop and implement health improvement strategies that get results.

3. Engage the Coalition in Co-Creating a Strategy Map

Once there is a consensus on the need for a common agenda, the coalition leaders should engage a diverse team in the development of a Strategy Map. There is no one "right" way to collaboratively develop a Strategy Map, but many principles can be embraced to enhance the success of the effort.

Structure and Process

Community Health Strategy Maps (see Figure 22.3) are often organized into three layers (called "Perspectives") with a general cause-and-effect logic flowing from the bottom to the top:

- Outcomes
- Strategy
- Asset and Capacity Development

Each of these layers has a series of Objectives. The Objectives in the Outcome Perspective might include "Reduce Obesity" or "Minimize the Prevalence of

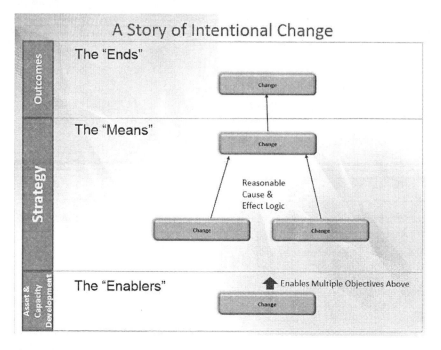

FIGURE 22.3

Diabetes." The Objectives in the Strategy Perspective might include "Expand Community Gardening" or "Improve Infrastructure for Biking and Walking." Achieving the Objectives in the Strategy Perspective should lead to achieving the Objectives in the Outcome Perspective. The Asset and Capacity Development Objectives might include "Strengthen the Community Health Improvement Coalition" or other changes that will improve the community's capacity to implement the Objectives in the Strategy Perspective.

As described above, the Strategy Map should focus on the *changes* that the community will be working to achieve, not the current actions or ongoing operations.

The sequential order in which a shared population health strategy is created and implemented is very important. It is best to build a consensus on the framework of Objectives (the Strategy Map) *before* wrestling with the details of the measures, targets, and actions. Establishing a consensus on the Objectives makes it easier to gain an agreement on the shared measures, targets, and actions that organizations will use to implement the strategy. Additionally, once there is agreement on a draft set of Objectives, subsequent steps in the process can be delegated to different smaller groups working in parallel on the next level of details (e.g. a more detailed definition, lists of current activities, the desired changes, evidence that supports pursuing the Objective, or possible measures).

Whereas the creation of an early draft should be facilitated by someone with experience in the design and development of Strategy Maps, additional input should be sought from other sources to help refine the map. For example, it can be helpful to look at recommendations from others around the country who are striving to address the same topic, to engage people working on the front lines of this issue in the affected community, and to involve those who are living with the health or social issues that the strategy is intended to address. Input from these sources can be used to refine a Strategy Map framework, ensuring that it fits the local situation and has buy-in from the broader community.

Tame the Complexity with "Zoomability"

The strategic framework can be made less overwhelming by creating "zoomable" Strategy Maps. Online maps and GPS systems enable people to work with massive amounts of information by allowing them to zoom in and out to different levels of detail. This zoomability allows people to focus on the areas and level of detail they are interested in, without being distracted by extraneous information. Similarly, Strategy Maps should be designed—either using advanced features of PowerPoint® or a platform like InsightVision—to be zoomable so that different people can focus on subsets of the overall population health strategy, without being overwhelmed with all the details. It is not practical to attempt to fully inform all the members of a coalition about all the details of all parts of the strategy. Doing so would quickly overwhelm people and is likely to result in a desire to focus on a few smaller issues, which by themselves will not be sufficient to achieve the desired outcomes at the broader population level.

The following pair of Strategy Maps for Weld County, Colorado, were developed by the North Colorado Health Alliance with help from Insightformation consultants. The first map focuses on their "Healthy Eating" strategy (Figure 22.4), and the second map zooms in on the strategy detail for improving nutrition in schools (Figure 22.5).

In the above Strategy Map, each Objective with a plus in the lower right corner indicates that there is a map with more details. In the zoomed-in Strategy Map below, the Objectives that are repeated from the higher-level map are shown in the same color as the "parent" map (light gray). The more detailed Objectives in the "child map" are in a different color (dark gray).

Like Google Maps, a zoomable Strategy Map framework allows people to easily navigate to the area they care about and see a single screen of information that is not overwhelming. More examples of zoomable Strategy Maps can be found at www.insightformation.com/zoomability.

4.   Distribute the Work of Strategy Execution

To achieve the necessary progress on the broad range of mutually-reinforcing changes that make up the strategy, it is important to *distribute the workload* among multiple *working groups* that can focus on subsets of the overall strategy. The use of well-designed Strategy Maps and strategy management techniques can help

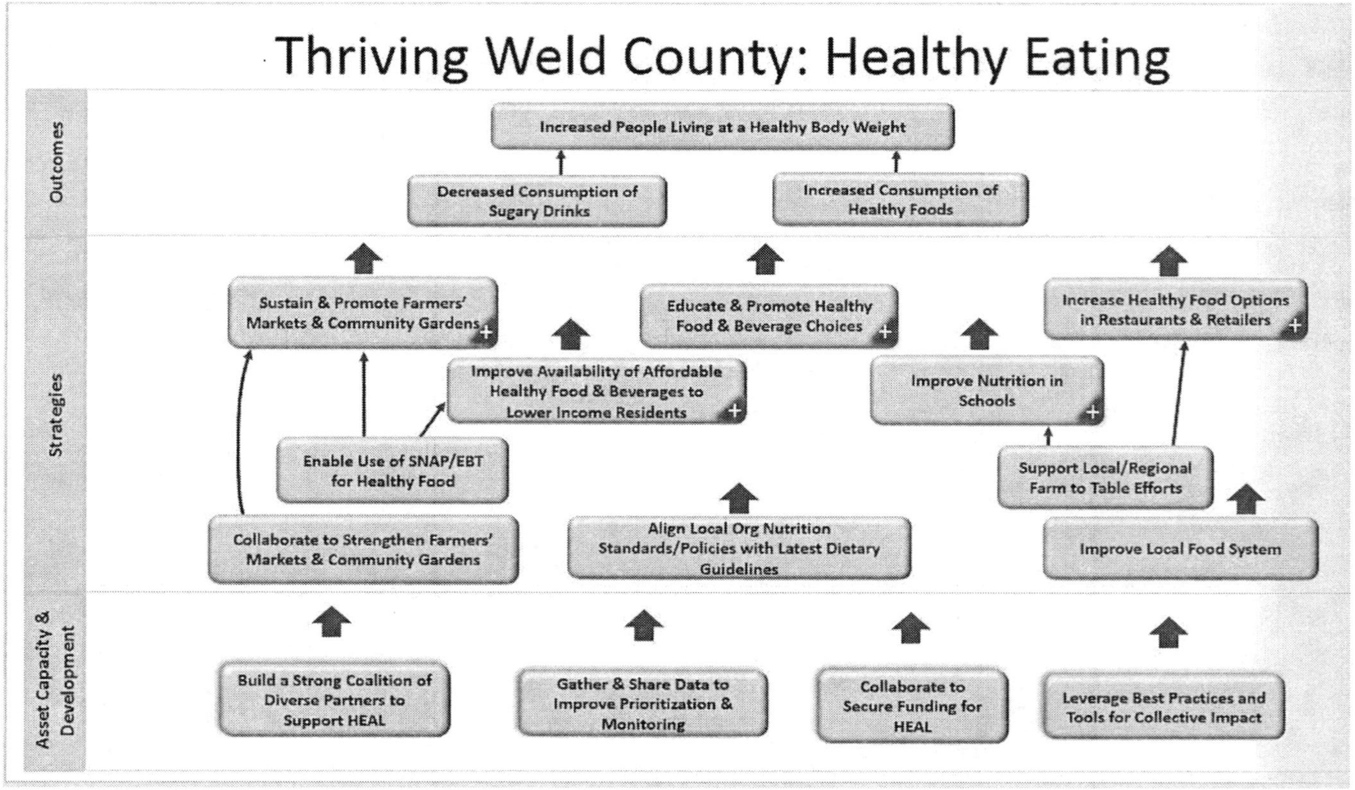

Thriving Weld County: Healthy Eating

Outcomes
- Increased People Living at a Healthy Body Weight
- Increased Consumption of Healthy Foods
- Decreased Consumption of Sugary Drinks

Strategies
- Increase Healthy Food Options in Restaurants & Retailers +
- Support Local/Regional Farm to Table Efforts
- Improve Nutrition in Schools +
- Educate & Promote Healthy Food & Beverage Choices +
- Align Local Org Nutrition Standards/Policies with Latest Dietary Guidelines
- Improve Availability of Affordable Healthy Food & Beverages to Lower Income Residents +
- Enable Use of SNAP/EBT for Healthy Food
- Sustain & Promote Farmers' Markets & Community Gardens +
- Collaborate to Strengthen Farmers' Markets & Community Gardens

Asset Capacity & Development
- Improve Local Food System
- Leverage Best Practices and Tools for Collective Impact
- Collaborate to Secure Funding for HEAL
- Gather & Share Data to Improve Prioritization & Monitoring
- Build a Strong Coalition of Diverse Partners to Support HEAL

FIGURE 22.4

Zoom: Improve Nutrition in Schools

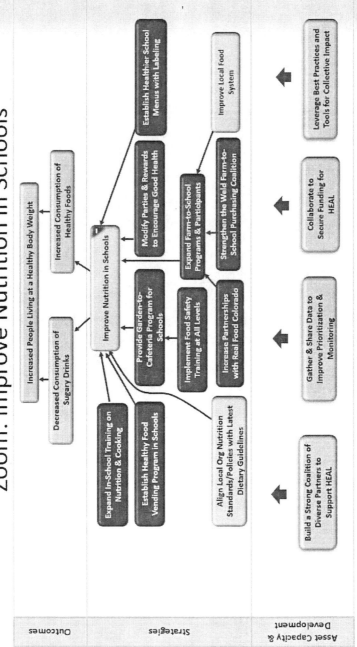

FIGURE 22.5

people avoid being overwhelmed by complex Population Health issues. It is not necessary for all the partnering organizations to become experts in the theory and techniques of strategy management. As long as the people who are providing "backbone support" understand how to structure and manage the details of a large integrated strategy, everyone else can benefit from that structure. Once people appreciate the basic concept of the Strategy Map, they can focus their efforts on working on their smaller parts of the larger puzzle and be confident about how they are contributing to the overall strategy.

As soon as there is a reasonable consensus on the Strategy Map framework, the various working groups can begin working, in parallel, on strategy implementation, starting with the following:

- *Encourage other organizations in the community to organize and align their work around the same framework.* If the hospitals, health department, Federally Qualified Health Centers, key funders, and organizations like the United Way are aligned around the same Strategy Map, the acceleration of progress should be very significant. The more people become familiar with the same strategic framework, the more they can focus on implementing the strategy, not just trying to understand or create it.
- *Establish a "lead advocate" for each Objective.* This person is not responsible for *doing* the work to accomplish the Objective, but they can be an ambassador and spokesperson for that Objective, allowing more efficient delegation and communication. In some communities where there has been a lot of competition among organizations working to address an issue, the "lead advocate" role can be a small team of peers rather than an individual.
- *Define a "From–To Gap" that clarifies the current state, the desired state, and the gap between those states.* This is a valuable step in enhancing the clarity and consensus that helps accelerate strategy implementation. Defining the "From–To Gap" also helps spur creativity regarding how that gap could be closed, how to measure progress, and who might collaborate to help close the gap.
- *Identify the current efforts that are under way to help close the gap.* Explore how those efforts could be enhanced by better teamwork, "assists" from other organizations that might not currently be involved, and the use of new technologies or processes.

It is helpful for each team to follow a similar process, using shared tools and aligning with the same overall Strategy Map framework so that they can easily access and understand the information being used by other working groups when they need to. Without an efficient way to manage the complexity and information of a robust strategy, funders or leaders sometimes struggle to understand all of the details of the entire strategy, and they may slow down and narrow the scope of the strategy to something they can keep track of in their heads. This creates an unnecessary bottleneck that limits the community's ability to implement a comprehensive strategy that is supported by a broad group of organizations and is capable of achieving the priority outcomes. With a high-level Strategy Map that gives the big picture, accompanied by a software-enabled way to zoom in and see the supporting details, funders and leaders can have greater confidence that the strategy will be successfully implemented.

5. Adopt Shared Strategy Measures and a Shared Measurement System

Most funders and boards have placed a great emphasis on measurement in recent years. Yet, as more and more time gets consumed by developing measures and gathering data, it is questionable whether the emphasis on measurement is proving to be as helpful as was once thought. Our recent experience suggests that to effectively support the successful implementation of population health, communities should adopt important changes in the way measures are typically developed and used. The following four changes are particularly important for implementing a Population Health strategy.

Shifting from Measuring Actions to Aligning Actions to Impact a "Driver Measure"

In communities that struggle to implement their health improvement plans, it is quite common to have a table in Word or Excel that identifies the goals or objectives. This table has a column listing the actions (sometimes called "tactics" or some other term) and then a column to identify the *success measures* for those actions (see Figure 22.6).

Because significant improvements in population health outcomes will generally require a large number of different actions by different organizations, this template tends to lead to a huge number of very different measures. The practice of requiring measures of success for each action is based on an *evaluation mindset* and an emphasis on accountability as the key to achieving big outcomes.

Whereas this mindset might be appropriate for a narrowly focused project, it does not work well for large strategies striving to improve the health of a community. It imposes a significant burden on the coalition to precisely define and gather the data for a large number of measures, and then to generate reports. Even when precious resources are expended to get the data and generate the reports, the results are usually not very useful. The sheer number of measures tends to overwhelm everyone (including those who request the reports). Frequently, people end up so frustrated with the whole measurement process that they never actually report on the success measures. Even if the report is created and used to evaluate each action, it does little to improve the alignment—the intentional crafting of the mutually reinforcing activities—which is so important for achieving the desired outcomes.

Goal:	Put SMART Goal Statement Here		
Describe Strategy Here:			
Actions	Success Measures	Partnering Organizations	Status Update

FIGURE 22.6 Example of a Typical (but Problematic) Template to Define Measures

Picking programs or actions and then defining success measures for evaluation and accountability creates a serious barrier to a more streamlined, elegant, and powerful approach to shared measurement. When many different organizations that are pursuing funding (or who have been awarded grants) each try to develop measures that they can accomplish on their own, the result is typically a very fragmented collection of inconsistent measures. The more those fragmented measures are used to evaluate and hold organizations accountable (and determine their future funding) the less willing the organizations tend to be to step back and think about shared measurement and collaboration.

In most communities, hundreds of organizations are each declaring how their measures demonstrate their success, yet community-wide progress on the bigger issues proves to be minimal. What's missing? In recent years, we've seen funders pressure grantees to demonstrate through their evaluation process that their program is impacting the big outcome measure—like reducing the community prevalence of diabetes or child maltreatment. Whereas this is understandable, because funders have been giving grants for decades without seeing the com-munity outcome measures significantly improve, this pressure to impact big outcomes puts grantees and those seeking funding in a difficult predicament. How can they show that *their program* is causing improvements in the community outcome measure when their success is only one part of the much larger system of change that is needed to achieve the community outcome?

Instead of emphasizing success measures for each of the individual actions or programs, it is more effective to focus on *community strategy measures* that monitor the key drivers, each of which are *bigger than the work of any one organization or program*. For each of the high-level outcome measures, there are typically two to four of these community strategy (driver) measures, each of which can be impacted quicker and more easily than the high-level outcome measures. The coalition should then set target levels for these measures that, if achieved, would likely result in success in hitting the target for the high-level outcome measure. *It is the intentional, proactive, and collaborative efforts to move these shared driver measures toward their targets that makes community strategy management so powerful*. One of the main advantages of developing and aligning around a Strategy Map (or a Driver Diagram) is that it provides a set of strategic Objectives (drivers) that are seen by the coalition as sufficient to achieve the ultimate outcome of the strategy. The measures for these Objectives become valuable tools for managing the community-wide collaboration to achieve the outcomes.

Switching from measures used primarily for *evaluating actions or programs* to measures used for *managing strategy implementation* has important implications and benefits. Instead of asking for the action and *then* asking for the measure of success (for evaluation), this switch changes the process to determining the measure that needs to be moved and then asking *what actions* will be needed—by many organizations in a mutually reinforcing way—to move that measure to the target level. The switch creates a much smaller set of strategic measures to manage, so more time can be spent on getting things done and less time spent in developing and managing the overhead of a large, cumbersome set of success measures (regardless of whether you are using a measurement software platform). Finally, this switch to strategic measurement changes adds a creative problem-solving approach to the evaluation of measures, provoking questions like:

- If there is insufficient progress being made with a community strategy (driver) measure, then what else can be done?
- What other community organizations can be engaged to assist in the success of the efforts under way?
- Are there other ways to improve community teamwork?
- Are the intended actions being accomplished, or have they been neglected?

Consider the case in Weld County, Colorado. The first Strategy Map pictured in this chapter shows a strategic Objective to "Sustain & Promote Farmers' Markets & Community Gardens." One of the strategic measures counted the vendor sales in the county's largest farmers' market. When the health improvement collaborative stopped looking at this number as an evaluation measure for the success of the Greeley Farmers' Market and began to see it as an indicator of success for their overall strategy, they realized it was necessary to develop creative ways for the community to work together to increase participation and sales in the farmers' market:

- Once the farmers' market was able to accept SNAP payments, a community funder helped support a double-up program to provide an added incentive for people with SNAP cards to use them at the farmers' market to purchase fresh vegetables.
- In the *Chef at the Market* program, chefs from local restaurants put on demonstrations of cooking with the fresh produce being sold there.
- The health department supported cooking classes that developed cooking skills and encouraged people to buy produce at the farmers' market.
- A local non-profit, Make Today Count!, partnered with the Healthy Kids Club to offer a "Growing Kids" program with a free Kid's Zone at the farmers' market that offered fun and creative activities to encourage healthy eating.

Some of these efforts—such as the double-up program—had a solid base of evidence behind them, whereas other efforts tapped into the ideas and energy of community members and organizations to advance a strategy that they agreed with. A lot of time could be spent trying to evaluate which action was responsible for the improvement, but each effort contributed in different and mutually reinforcing ways. There was no single "silver bullet." Instead, the positive impact emerged through diverse stakeholders working together to move a measure more effectively as a team than any could have accomplished acting in isolation.

FIGURE 22.7 Screenshot from www.thrivingweld.com

Figure 22.7 is a chart from www.thrivingweld.com (powered by InsightVision) that shows how the county stakeholders reversed the four-year downward trend by taking shared responsibility for working together on a strategy that they had helped to define.

When the use of measurement shifts in this way, the costs and burdens of maintaining the measurement system drop dramatically. Organizations in the community are then able to see measurement as a *positive tool for teamwork* instead of something that will be used to punish them for things that are beyond their control.

Strategy Measures versus Operational Measurement and Performance Improvement

The work by Kaplan and Norton around the Balanced Scorecard methodology is the most advanced, researched, and effective body of work that exists on strategy execution and measurement. These two experts begin their fifth book, *The Execution Premium*, with a very important statement: "Managing strategy differs from managing operations."[24] They likely opened the book with this statement because experts in operational performance management were *misapplying the measurement techniques of operational performance improvement to strategy management*. In operational performance management methodologies (such as Six Sigma), data is gathered to monitor an ongoing process, such as a manufacturing line. The data is analyzed to get a baseline of performance, and then a series of steps are taken to analyze and improve the process. This "science of improvement" has a long track record of success and a rich set of tools and techniques. Most of these techniques, however, are primarily designed for incremental improvement of established operational processes—not for transformational change such as those of a coalition attempting to reverse obesity and diabetes for an entire community.

Applying an operational approach to measurement will create a variety of problems when trying to develop a measurement strategy for implementing Population Health. For example, if the methodology began by gathering existing operational data on a population health issue such as "reduce the Negative Impact of Adverse Childhood Experiences" for which data is not widely available or legally shared, things will be bogged down quickly. Countless efforts to improve Community Health have stalled out because people believed the first step was to gather the data to start the analysis process, but the community was unable to figure out how to get the needed data.

An operational approach to measurement also tends to focus on collecting a lot of data on what is currently being done—how many patients were served, how many referrals were made, how many people attended the training sessions—without regard to the changes the strategy is attempting to make. Even if this operational data is available, it has little to do with managing the implementation of a strategy that, through breakthroughs in community teamwork, aims to bring about dramatic improvements to a complex health issue. This operational data clutters up a strategy measurement system and leads to thinking about minor incremental improvements instead of the bigger changes that are typically needed to achieve meaningful population health improvements.

When people realize that the measurement techniques they have been trained in were developed for *operational measurement* and incremental *performance improvement*, they can more easily embrace the different strategy management approaches to measurement that contribute to successful *strategy implementation* on a big picture level. Instead of starting with data and analysis, strategy measurement starts with clarifying a vision for change. The Strategy Map then clarifies the pathways for achieving that big change with a series of mutually reinforcing Objectives. The measures in this case are simply the best available, pragmatic, quantitative indicators of progress in achieving those Objectives.

Shifting from an Emphasis on Evaluation and Accountability to an Emphasis on Strategy and Teamwork

It is not enough to merely change the measurement approach in order to *define* a better set of measures. The leadership mindset in how the measures are *used* should also be changed. One of the major lessons of the first 25 years of the strategy management field has been the realization that overemphasizing measures and accountability can contribute to dysfunctional behavior and unintended consequences. This is especially true when working with the type of large, multi-sector, voluntary coalitions that are so important for Population Health improvement.

An overemphasis on measures and accountability can make potential partners hesitant to collaborate because of the burden of data collection and the risk of being held accountable for something that they didn't feel they could control. The overemphasis also creates a motivation to design measures and targets that can be more easily attained, reducing the appearance of failure. There are almost always ways to move the measure in the desired direction without actually accomplishing the underlying change that was intended. And when "gaming" the measure is easier than achieving the desired change, a narrow focus on measures will often encourage actions that create a false sense of success, falling short of what could have been attained in true population health improvement.

In contrast, emphasizing a co-created strategy creates a positive motivation for others to become part of the team and make improvements in areas that they care about as an organization. If developing measures and gathering data are viewed as elements of a communication strategy that enables better teamwork, stakeholders will be more motivated to design the measures and participate in the collection of data. If all the stakeholders endeavor to understand the strategy, clearly define the desired changes for each Objective, and recognize that the measures are a quantitative tool to gain insights on the progress being made, each organization will be less likely to try to game the measures in order to look good.

Shifting from Fragmented and Isolated Measurement Systems to a Shared Measurement System

Without a collaborative approach to measurement, organizations commonly spend a lot of resources gathering data in their own isolated and fragmented ways. Each organization is likely to take the shortest path to get the data required by their funders or researchers. When considered in isolation, each organization sees the added cost of aligning and coordinating their measures with others as being more work than it is worth. In contrast, if measure and data collection practices are viewed from a community-wide perspective, all the fragmented and isolated gathering of data and reporting on measures is terribly wasteful and inefficient. This fragmentation also makes it difficult to get a more comprehensive view of the community because when stakeholders attempt to aggregate isolated data, the inconsistency in measure definition, data collection methodology, and the incompatible structures creates frustration and confusion for funders, organizations, and, ultimately, the communities they are attempting to serve.

Significant increases in efficiency are possible if the many stakeholders who are collecting data and developing measurements can step back and consider how to take a more systematic approach to collecting, sharing, and analyzing data using a shared system. Whereas some organizations might use data privacy regulations as an excuse for not collaborating, the type of data that is valuable for managing the Population Health improvement efforts described in this chapter is rarely restricted by privacy requirements because the monitoring of strategy execution does not necessitate individual-level data. Data may be integrated in a regional Health Information Exchange to simplify the de-duplication of individuals and avoid double-counting, but *only aggregated data will flow into a shared strategy measurement system.*

In addition to streamlining data collection and measure definition, a shared measurement system can include a technology platform that supports many different users for different purposes. Most communities have an overwhelming number of informal and largely manual data collection and reporting systems. Numbers exist in countless spreadsheets, manually maintained websites, and custom-built reports and databases that usually serve a narrow purpose. These fragmented systems are often abandoned when their short-term purpose is completed, resulting in the loss of valuable data and making it difficult to track historical changes. Given that true Population Health improvement generally takes several years, the scattering of information into different "data silos"—many of which are abandoned and hard to identify later—is very problematic. Without any "go to" data source for the important measurements of Population Health, as well as related factors and information on the progress of long-term strategies, each funder, researcher, or community leader will likely just create another manual and isolated "system" to accomplish a narrow goal.

In contrast, when a community works as a team to align around a robust, long-term Population Health strategy, they can easily create and use a shared data and measurement system. Ideally, that system is organized around the Strategy Maps co-created by the stakeholder organizations. In Weld County, Colorado, for example, the United Way organization decided to align its funding around the Strategy Maps it helped to co-create, and they are requiring their grantees to report their information into the shared InsightVision system. This alignment not only saves United Way (and their grantees) the work of creating a separate data and measurement system just for a single purpose, but it also enhances the value of the shared measurement system for the entire community. United Way grantees now have a greater motivation to understand and support the community's strategy for health improvement, and the data that the grantees report helps make the shared system more complete and robust.

When community stakeholders embrace these four shifts, then measurement can become a powerful contributor to successfully implementing a Population Health strategy.

6.   Harness, Align, and Monitor the Actions

The previously described techniques are intended to improve the success of the *aligned actions* that lead to the desired changes and outcomes. Without the actions, strategy implementation remains a hollow hope even if you are measuring and evaluating every part of a well-crafted strategy. In previous steps, we've intentionally separated the actions from the Objectives and measures. But once the strategic framework is in place and there is a preliminary plan for measurement, the work on actions can begin. The following techniques can help improve the management of the actions, allowing a Population Health strategy to be successfully implemented.

Define Actions That Can Be Completed in a Relatively Short Time

Achieving Population Health goals typically takes several years. Priority health issues such as diabetes, heart disease, mental health, or substance abuse are not going to be successfully addressed in one or two years. Most major changes to Population Health outcomes will take between five and ten years to accomplish. However, if high-level actions are defined with a five- to ten-year duration, short-term accountability is often lacking to keep organizations moving forward at the necessary pace to achieve that long-term success. Let's be honest—it will take a LOT of actions by many different organizations to achieve the type of changes that are usually part of the aspirational goals in Population Health strategies. If individual actions are too big, no organization will feel an appropriate level of accountability or be willing to accept ownership of an action. But even narrowly defined, organization-specific actions won't create much urgency if they are vaguely defined with five-year timelines.

Because of their other urgent priorities, few organizations will do much to advance an action that has a deadline that is five years out. The plan will likely be lost and forgotten by the time they feel any accountability to accomplish the action. For these reasons, actions on Population Health Logic Models are almost impossible to manage. Because, by definition, a Logic Model includes actions, a coalition using a Logic Model as a primary tool for implementing Population Health is stuck with two bad choices: (1) set vague high-level actions that can't be realistically managed, or (2) clutter your Logic Model with a large number of actions that make the model very difficult to comprehend.

In contrast, if the coalition is using a zoomable Strategy Map, which doesn't include actions, they can zoom in to an appropriate level of detail of the Strategy Map and *then* build out the plan for the actions. The working group for that Objective (or cluster of Objectives) can agree on the specific actions to be accomplished in the short-term by specific members of the coalition working to make progress on the larger Objectives for that part of the strategy. If specific parts of the strategy are delegated to many different working groups (or action teams), each of those teams can define a reasonable number of actions that can be assigned to specific organizations and realistically accomplished in a relatively short period of time. People working on the actions in one zoomed-in subset of the overall strategy don't need to be bothered with the specifics of the many detailed actions being accomplished on other parts of the strategy. This process is significantly simplified by the use of an online strategy management platform.

By defining focused actions that, in most cases, can be completed in less than a year, with significant progress possible each month or quarter, organizations responsible for specific actions will experience an urgency to do things sooner. With well-defined and relatively short-term actions, progress can be managed much more effectively to achieve the long-term results.

Blending Emergence with Intentionality

Hoping to create shorter-term accountability for long-term actions or goals, some funders are asking for detailed work plans with annual or quarterly tasks. Developing these work plans can be a big burden on grant applicants or recipients as it is not realistic to anticipate all the ways that community organizations could collaborate to accomplish something over the next five years. Even when these work plans are created, they often become a constraint that limits stakeholders' flexibility to innovate and take advantage of opportunities (or adjustments) that could enhance the effectiveness of the effort to achieve a long-term goal. Instead of work plans, funders and coalition leaders should rely on the strategy framework and strategy measures to manage the big, long-term picture, while allowing for "emergence" in how the community innovates and continually adds aligned actions to accomplish the well-defined Objectives in their part of the Strategy Map.

Mark Kramer and John Kania, authors of a 2011 article on Collective Impact, wrote an excellent follow-up article in 2013 on "Embracing Emergence: How Collective Impact Addresses Complexity." In the 2013 article, they contrast more premeditated approaches with their recommended approach for emergent Collective Impact:

> The problem is that such predetermined solutions rarely work under conditions of complexity—conditions that apply to most major social problems—when the unpredictable interactions of multiple players determine the outcomes. And even when successful interventions are found, adoption spreads very gradually, if it spreads at all.
>
> Collective impact works differently. The process and results of collective impact are emergent rather than predetermined, the necessary resources and innovations often already exist but have not yet been recognized, learning is continuous, and adoption happens simultaneously among many different organizations.
>
> In other words, collective impact is not merely a new process that supports the same social sector solutions but an entirely different model of social progress. The power of collective impact lies in the heightened vigilance that comes from multiple organizations looking for resources and innovations through the same lens, the rapid learning that comes from

continuous feedback loops, and the immediacy of action that comes from a unified and simultaneous response among all participants.[25]

When combined with the details of a robust Strategy Map framework and a technology platform to manage the supporting information, an approach that embraces emergence becomes even more powerful for successfully improving Population Health.

Recruit Others in the Community Who Can Provide "Assists"

Whereas each action should have an owner responsible for taking the lead in getting the action done, Collective Impact is greatly enhanced if the coalition—specifically the working groups (action teams) that are working on their subset of the overall strategy—is consistently looking for ways to engage other community organizations or individuals in providing "assists." While this sports analogy is getting to be a bit dated, it can be helpful to think of how the Utah Jazz point guard, John Stockton, helped Karl Malone score almost 37,000 points during a time when Michael Jordan scored just over 32,000 points. For nine years, John Stockton led the NBA in assists. He was not personally focused on scoring points, but rather on being a strong team player who could pass the ball to Karl "the Mailman" Malone, who would "deliver" the score. In communities, there are often John Stockton-like stakeholders that are not, *by themselves*, able to implement an evidence-based intervention to solve a Population Health problem. These stakeholders don't see themselves as being able to make a measurable difference in Community Health issues, even if they care a lot about these issues. Instead of leaving these valuable stakeholders on the sidelines without a chance to contribute to a team victory, the working groups should look for ways to recruit them to provide assists to the organizations that are working on the actions needed to implement the strategy.

Assists can come from many types of organizations and individuals. For example, in Weld County, Colorado, a college intern who volunteered for three months played a major role in helping the coalition adopt the InsightVision platform. And in Detroit, the Communities of Hope endeavor assembled a variety of organizations who each contributed in small but valuable ways to promote healthy eating and active living. One of these organizations was the Motown band, The Contours, who provided a free concert for apartment residents to motivate them to come out and learn about the vision and programs that were being offered to improve their health and quality of life. At another Communities of Hope event, one of the band members delivered an inspiring call to action for residents. The Contours volunteered to perform because they were inspired by the overall Communities of Hope strategy and were eager to contribute to something important by sharing the unique gifts that they had to offer.

FIGURE 22.8 Photo Shared by "More than Pink" of Waconia, MN

In Waconia, Minnesota, the seniors in the town's nursing home provided one of the most memorable assists to a program called "More than Pink." This program was launched by a group of moms to help build the confidence and skills of their elementary-school-aged girls, and a wide variety of local volunteers contributed to the success of More than Pink. The seniors in the nursing home made signs, waved pompons, and banged on pots with spoons as the girls and their parents ran by the nursing home in the 5K run that was the culmination of the summer fitness program (see Figure 22.8).

With a little creativity, many people's untapped talents and organizations' unused resources can become part of a true community strategy for improving Population Health. When the principles and techniques of Asset-Based Community Development are combined with a well-defined strategy framework, underutilized assets in a community can be engaged in creative ways to achieve a multiplied impact.

Finding Mutually Reinforcing and Mutually Beneficial Actions

Whereas the concept of Mutually Reinforcing Activities is a central tenet of the Collective Impact approach, communities often struggle to put this concept into practice. One of the key steps in creating Mutually Reinforcing Activities is to engage the community around a robust Strategy Map and then look for "assists" for improving the success of the priority actions. The number of assists can be increased by looking for organizations that would benefit from working together rather than working independently. If organizations can each benefit from the collaboration, then together their actions become both mutually reinforcing and mutually *beneficial*. Organizations naturally seek to do things that lead to their own benefit.

The backbone organization working to enhance Collective Impact looks for stakeholders that would gain significant benefits from accomplishing the outcome Objectives and works to align these organizations and get them to commit resources to the larger community team. The more immediate the mutual benefit, the easier it is for an organization to commit to taking action that will be part of the overall strategy.

Simplify Action Monitoring

If actions are defined to be narrow and relatively short-term, then they can often be measured by simply estimating the percentage complete. A status update note may include other quantitative indicators of how much has been accomplished, but these numbers don't need to be tracked like the other measures. The organization responsible for each action should make a monthly or quarterly estimate of the percentage of their action that is already completed, along with a brief comment giving some explanation of what they did since the prior estimate. This approach to monitoring progress takes very little time (especially compared to the success measures that are often developed for actions) and provides effective information, motivation, and accountability.

If action owners were asked at random times to estimate the percentage completed for their action without a context of prior estimates or anticipated timelines, this would be a weak approach to monitoring progress. But, if the estimated percentage complete is reported each month (or quarter) and all prior estimates are easily visible, this approach can be highly effective. For example, if a person reports 10% progress for three consecutive months and the action is supposed to be completed in nine months, then the person responsible for that action should feel pressure to get moving (or get help). Or, if a person's estimate of percentage complete goes from 30% to 90% complete in one month, they would be expected to provide a comment on what was accomplished, which could include different descriptions (including different quantitative indicators) from month to month. The flexibility of these comments provides a valuable form of communication that is much simpler than reporting on a pre-defined success measure. Whereas some might argue that estimating the percent complete is too subjective, if the action is well defined, it would take a glaring act of deceit to state that it was 100% complete if it had not been completed to at least a reasonable degree.

If an action has a budget and money is being spent to get specific things done, then it might be appropriate to also monitor the amount of that budget that has been spent to date, ideally comparing this amount with a plan such as an estimated budget by quarter. Often, the details of what amounts are being spent for actions are not broadly communicated. This information doesn't need to be shared with everyone, as it could be overwhelming and lead to micromanagement, distracting debates, and other behaviors that might interfere with successful strategy implementation. But sharing high-level summaries provides helpful transparency, and the people who are responsible for completing the actions should have good information on their available resources so they can be proactive about addressing resource gaps that could hinder their success for that action. After all, the whole community team is depending on them. Community strategy management is about working together to anticipate and solve problems, rather than trying to place the blame of failure when an individual endeavor does not succeed.

While not exactly the same, this simplified form of progress monitoring is similar to how well-performing large organizations successfully monitor the multitude of details that go into implementing a big strategy. These larger organizations don't create a big spreadsheet and try to develop success metrics to evaluate every little part of the strategy. Instead, once the strategy is defined, they mainly want to know if all the actions that go into the strategy are *on time* (percentage complete consistent with what was planned for) and *on budget*. If important actions are not moving forward as planned, then wise leaders must know as quickly as possible so they can engage the appropriate stakeholders in problem-solving to get those specific actions back on track. In addition to monitoring a large number of actions, a relatively small number of strategic measures help leaders stay informed as to whether or not the combined progress of all those actions is having the desired impact. If not, they look to make adjustments at that higher level by modifying the strategy or changing the actions that are supposed to be driving the progress. Communities can emulate this approach.

Create a Cadence of Expectation and Accountability

One frustrating characteristic of most Community Health improvement efforts is that, after the initial meetings in which participants talk about the problem and potential solutions, subsequent meetings are often less interesting and productive as the group begins to struggle with engaging a large number of stakeholders to make an impact. Too often, after the early enthusiasm fades, many participants don't see much value in coming to a big meeting just to listen to uninspiring status updates. As participation wanes, the coalition may begin to struggle to maintain progress on much of what they set out to accomplish. After being bogged down for a while, there is often a shared feeling that they need a new start. To avoid that fate, it is important to establish a *cadence*, like the drumbeat for a marching band, that keeps the group moving forward as a team. Rather than focusing on compliance or any form of punitive accountability, Population Health coalition leaders should adopt practices to create enthusiasm about making progress and that actively engage participants at the meetings so they see the value of showing up.

Many of the techniques and tools described in this chapter should contribute to building that enthusiasm and momentum. The Strategy Map framework allows the strategy to be organized into many smaller groups, and the "digital backbone" of an online strategy management platform allows for "continuous communication," which is one of the five conditions for Collective Impact. This infrastructure allows a coalition to replace most of their large group meetings with a parallel set of smaller, action-oriented meetings, while simultaneously improving people's understanding of the details that matter to them.

One of the most important ways to avoid getting bogged down is to establish the expectation that the coalition needs everyone to pitch in to help move the priority actions forward. Then, if actions are created that are small enough for an organization to take on and demonstrate progress towards successful accomplishment by the next monthly or quarterly meeting, then there should be a positive peer pressure that creates healthy accountability. If most of the actions are part of a mutually reinforcing and mutually beneficial approach to addressing a larger issue, then each of the organizations has a positive form of motivation to contribute to building positive momentum and success.

A key element in creating cadence and building momentum is regular, usually monthly, meetings of the working groups. Leaders of those groups should encourage a pre-meeting practice where people review the status of actions that are most relevant to their interests and look at any of the "driver measures" that have changed (because driver measures should be updated more frequently than the outcome measures). Participants should then recommend (often via email) one or two topics where success can be recognized and *celebrated*. They can also suggest one or two topics where the group needs to *clarify* details on a strategic Objective, measure, or action. Finally, they should suggest one or two areas in which the team could engage in some *creative problem solving* to help move forward an action or Objective that is not going as well as expected.

If the coalition members have an easy way to share information online, then this practice can be an incentive for the owners of actions to keep their progress information updated. It also motivates people to stay informed about the things they care about—and it doesn't require them to sit in a long meeting hearing about things they have less interest in. Finally, gathering this specific input is a dynamic, collaborative way to structure the agenda for high-impact meetings. The working group leaders can review the input from the group members and spend the majority of the meeting picking specific topics to *celebrate* or *clarify*, or engage participants in *creative problem solving*.

Engage Funders in Supporting Priority Actions

The final recommendation for harnessing, aligning, and monitoring actions involves the funders who give grants to support health improvements in the community. The practices of funders have a strong impact on how a community works to address any issue. In order to best support the kind of community teamwork described in this chapter, funders should consider adopting two practices that are not currently common in most communities.

Funders Should Be Actively Involved with Developing the Strategy Map Framework

This goes beyond funding those efforts (although that is an investment they should make). Their involvement will be most effective if they participate as peers bringing community assets to the table to work with others to address an issue that is important to the community. Ideally, multiple funders will be part of the process and will share a commitment to work together to fund the *strategy* in a collaborative way. If the funders work together with the group that is developing the Strategy Map, they will have an understanding of the Strategy Map and can align at least some of their funding efforts to support the implementation of the strategy.

Funders Should Have a Process to Rapidly Fund Priority Actions That Are Identified by the Working Groups as Being Important to Strategy Implementation

The strategy-centered approach described in this chapter should result in a significant number of short-term actions that can be promptly executed by the organizations with ownership of specific actions. If a community organization is working as part of a team to implement an action that is one of the Mutually Reinforcing Activities for achieving an Objective on the Strategy Map, then they should have a streamlined process to request the needed funds. The requesting organization should not have to go through a long process or be made to demonstrate how their action will, by itself, lead to some specific outcome. There should not need to be a competitive funding process or an isolated approach to evaluation that tries to assign the credit for the top-level outcomes to the specific action which the funder supported. Instead, the funders should understand that the strategy involves many intertwined actions that are aligned to accomplish the Objectives on the Strategy Map. Many of the actions that are undertaken to implement the Population Health strategy should not require funding from a philanthropic source, but when philanthropic funding *is* required, the overall success of the strategy implementation will be enhanced if the community funders are aligned with the strategy and committed to their role in the team.

Conclusion

Whereas there are abundant articles and discussions about Population Health, there has not been a clear consensus on how to implement Population Health strategies. Many of the recommendations focus on optimizing clinical care for individuals in a population. In contrast, this chapter emphasizes a multi-stakeholder strategy management approach that focuses on improving the health of a group (such as a neighborhood or community) through the six important steps above.

Notes

1. https://www.google.com/search?q=implementing+population+health&ie=utf-8&oe=utf-8
2. http://ajph.aphapublications.org/doi/abs/10.2105/AJPH.93.3.380
3. David Kindig and Greg Stoddart. What Is Population Health? *American Journal of Public Health*, March 2003: Vol. 93, No. 3, pp. 380–383. doi: 10.2105/AJPH.93.3.380
4. http://www.rwjf.org/en/library/annual-reports/presidents-message-2014.html
5. http://www.countyhealthrankings.org/our-approach
6. http://www.rwjf.org/en/library/research/2011/12/health-care-s-blind-side.html
7. http://www.bloomberg.com/bw/articles/2012–08–23/the-city-that-shed-a-million-pounds
8. https://www.youtube.com/watch?v=7kpblJZFaio
9. https://www.youtube.com/watch?v=7kpblJZFaio
10. http://communitystrawbalegardening.weebly.com/
11. www.insightformation.com/communitiesofhope
12. http://magellanhealth.com/media/739590/wallawalla.pdf
13. http://www.who.int/chp/media/en/north_karelia_successful_ncd_prevention.pdf
14. https://www.idf.org/sites/default/files/attachments/article_593_en.pdf
15. http://www.mprnews.org/story/2015/10/05/mpr_news_presents
16. http://www.preventioninstitute.org/component/jlibrary/article/id-372/127.html (page 8)
17. http://wolterskluwer.com/company/newsroom/news/2015/05/treating-infants-of-mothers-with-opioid-dependence.html
18. http://ssir.org/articles/entry/the_dawn_of_system_leadership
19. https://www.amazon.com/Strategy-Focused-Organization-Scorecard-Companies-Environment-ebook/dp/B004OEILJA?ie=UTF8
20. http://insightformation.com/insightvision/
21. http://www.insightformation.com/livewellsandiego
22. http://archived.naccho.org/topics/modelpractices/displaymp.cfm?id=1108
23. An example would be https://ifi-opioidcrisis.wikispaces.com/ Request permission to join at www.insightformation.com/opioidcrisis
24. Robert S. Kaplan and David Norton, *The Execution Premium*. Cambridge, MA: Harvard Business Review Press, 2008, p. 1.
25. http://ssir.org/articles/entry/embracing_emergence_how_collective_impact_addresses_complexity

23

PROMOTING MULTISTAKEHOLDER CONSENSUS AND A COLLABORATIVE APPROACH TO POPULATION HEALTH

Allen Leavens, Elisa Munthali, and Marcia Wilson

Introduction

The attention of national, state, and local policy and practice across the public and private sectors is increasingly turning to the question of how to achieve better health outcomes and health status of entire communities. However, the task of improving health at a population level is a challenging imperative. Guided by the National Quality Strategy,[1] the U.S. Department of Health and Human Services (HHS) enlisted the resources of the National Quality Forum (NQF) to help promote population health more actively. As a neutral convener of individuals and groups interested in improving health outcomes and healthcare quality, NQF was uniquely positioned to engage a variety of national experts to guide this effort.

Background

Funded by the HHS in 2013, NQF initiated a project to coordinate development of an evidence-based framework that could provide a roadmap for communities interested in making an impact on population health. NQF convened a multistakeholder panel of experts[2]—including population and community health experts, public health practitioners, healthcare providers, coordinators of home and community-based services, consumers, and employers—to provide input and guidance in developing the framework. What made the project particularly unique, however, was the opportunity to gain practical, real-world feedback on the evolving framework from actual communities doing multisector population health improvement work across the country. The experiences and feedback from these communities provided critical insights that shaped and strengthened the final results of the framework.

Foundational Principles

The NQF project team built upon groundwork established in a prior NQF-commissioned paper[3] and also completed an updated environmental scan[4] of existing population health frameworks and initiatives. From this foundation, the team created a compilation of past and current approaches to population health improvement at a local, state, regional, and national level. The NQF expert committee then reviewed these findings, identified common components across initiatives, and provided guidance on creating a document called the *Action Guide*—a handbook of significant resources, useful tools, and illustrative examples organized around ten elements deemed critical for success in collaborative population health improvement efforts. The *Action Guide* was developed in order to organize and consolidate content from the best existing sources—in a sense acting as a high-level "guide to the guides" on population health improvement.

Given differences in definitions, cultural perspectives, and viewpoints among individuals and groups working on population health improvement, developing key definitions and principles was critical to establishing clarity and shared understanding. For instance, a population was defined as all individuals within a geopolitical area, which can help focus attention on improving health for everyone through multiple avenues and settings (e.g., working with schools, employers, and other organizations to address health-related issues) rather than waiting until someone needs to visit a healthcare facility. A strong emphasis was placed on upstream determinants of health, such as behaviors and social factors, while recognizing that these can often be very difficult to change across an entire population. The ten Action Guide elements were utilized to identify concrete issues and processes that should be addressed to improve population health within the larger overall framework. Table 23.1 describes the ten Action Guide elements.

Within each section of the Action Guide dedicated to one of the ten elements, additional context and examples were incorporated with the intent of illustrating the basic underlying concepts. Links to more in-depth resources were used in order to keep the Action Guide fairly concise and minimally duplicative of existing content identified during the environmental scan. The Action Guide was developed with a recognition that there would likely be wide diversity among intended users of its content, including groups and organizations at very different stages of work (e.g., nascent versus mature efforts to improve health of a community). In addition, attention was given to noting that the Action Guide elements do not need to be addressed in a linear sequence, again accounting for variety in collaborative groups. Despite the concerted efforts to make the Action Guide practical and useful, however, a reality check was also needed on whether it would meet the needs of stakeholders in the field who are actually attempting this type of work.

TABLE 23.1 Ten Core Action Guide Elements

Collaborative Self-Assessment	Determining·strengths/weaknesses in the current state of health for a community, and outlining the desired future state that might be achieved through collaborating across sectors to make improvements
Leadership across the Region and within Organizations	Identifying individuals with the capabilities to guide or influence others to achieve common goals
Audience-Specific Strategic Communication	Taking a customized approach to interacting with and engaging diverse stakeholders
A Community Health Needs Assessment and Asset-Mapping Process	Completing a comprehensive review of health-related gaps or needs in a community, as well as existing resources and assets
An Organizational Planning and Priority-Setting Process	Establishing a clearly defined approach to developing consensus on collaborative priorities and plans
An Agreed-Upon, Prioritized Set of Health Improvement Activities	Identifying specific strategies and actions that can have the most positive impact for a given set of objectives and circumstances
Selection and Use of Measures and Performance Targets	Choosing an approach to assessing and monitoring progress on objectives
Joint Reporting on Progress toward Achieving Intended Results	Developing a process for disseminating assessment results, and sharing successes as well as accountability for reaching goals
Indicators of Scalability	Striving to spread promising processes and outcomes as far and wide as possible
A Plan for Sustainability	Planning ahead to account for the long-term needs and goals of an effort

Steps on the Road to Collaboration

At the beginning of the second year of the project, ten diverse groups working on multisector population health improvement initiatives were selected from across the nation to become active users of the Action Guide. Groups of different size, composition, location, scope/focus of work, and other such aspects had been considered in the selection process so that a broad array of perspectives would be brought to the task. Each of the ten "field testing groups" (FTGs)[5] that were ultimately chosen agreed to help evaluate and refine Action Guide content through a series of interactive activities.

FTG representatives were given an opportunity to meet and share their work to date with one another. The FTGs raised a variety of interesting issues and shared problems for discussion. For example, several representatives pointed out the challenges and opportunities of policy interventions for population health.

FTGs noted that, while opposing political forces can make changing policy difficult, successful policy changes that make a positive difference on health outcomes can have lasting impacts on a community long after grant funding or other temporary financing runs out. One FTG related how a successful change in policy increasing access to healthcare services would benefit many of their community members going forward into the future. FTGs described varied examples of health disparities, social and economic inequities, and other challenges facing their communities, but all acknowledged the importance of considering broad determinants of health and the potential benefits of cross-sector collaboration to address them.

FTGs listed areas of interest for which they would like to have access to expert guidance as they worked on their respective initiatives. This input was used to match FTGs with members of the NQF expert committee for site visits at each of the FTG locations. Site visits provided an opportunity for committee members to more fully explore the issues facing the communities in the field, and to obtain open and honest feedback on what might need to be added, modified, or removed from the Action Guide. To promote shared learning among the FTGs, the NQF project team periodically sent the FTGs "homework" questions related to the Action Guide elements and then held teleconferences to discuss responses and common themes across the groups.

Lessons Learned from the Field Testing Groups

The ten FTGs used the ten core elements from the Action Guide to reshape and strengthen activities related to their community-specific goals. Linkages among the FTGs, the committee experts, and NQF staff also created a learning community that facilitated sharing and allowed for the transfer of knowledge and resources. For example—site visits conducted with the FTGs provided benefits to the communities. Besides the insights provided by national experts from the project committee on issues such as use of population-level data and quality measurement, the mere presence of the site visitors was leveraged by several FTGs as an avenue for organizing broader stakeholder engagement. Several FTGs scheduled gatherings of additional community partners to share updates on their work or to discuss future plans that coincided with the site visits.

The FTGs identified several core elements from the Action Guide as being particularly challenging within their communities, highlighting areas where special emphasis may be needed for population health improvement efforts to succeed. Many FTGs indicated that obtaining more guidance about how to establish and maintain effective collaboration among diverse partners was their number one challenge. Although there was widespread agreement that collaborating across sectors—particularly between traditional healthcare entities and stakeholders outside of healthcare—is important and necessary for long-term progress, most FTGs also readily acknowledged that competing priorities and incentives can hamper such efforts if there is insufficient attention given to ensuring that each partner perceives value in participating.

Some FTGs recommended use of specific assessment tools to determine the extent of success (and opportunities for improvement) toward forging truly collaborative relationships. Others suggested specific approaches that could be used to optimize work with multiple stakeholders across sectors, such as utilizing a collective impact model[6] and relying on a "backbone organization" to help coordinate the different groups involved. Given the rapidly expanding interest in this type of collaborative activity, there were also a wide range of parallel efforts in the field noted to be potential resources for identifying best practices that the FTGs and other community groups could learn from.

FTGs recommended clarifying how the various Action Guide elements relate to each other—particularly under the umbrella of the first element, "collaborative self-assessment." This prompted creation of a graphic representation of the ten elements within the Action Guide. Collaborative self-assessment is at the top with a clustering of the elements that tend to be more iterative and sequential in an outer cycle underneath. The core elements that are important to consider throughout the duration of a collaborative effort are listed at the center (see Figure 23.1).

Another important lesson learned from the FTGs was that examples and stories can often convey the key points behind an issue much more efficiently and meaningfully than a mere technical description. For instance, rather than providing a detailed accounting of the potential healthcare costs saved through provision of

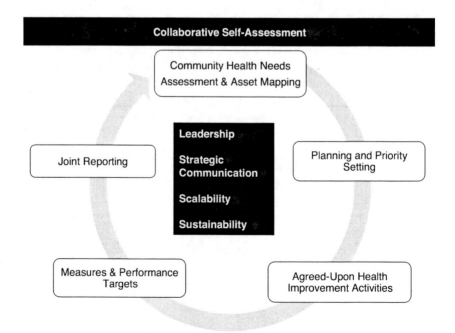

FIGURE 23.1 Relationships among the Action Guide Elements

supporting housing to those in need, telling the story of a specific individual who is able to live healthier, happier, and with reduced use of emergency room visits after obtaining a safe, affordable place to live, is much more impactful. This type of communication is particularly important when individuals or groups can readily identify with others who may be facing similar challenges. For this reason, additional examples were added within the Action Guide element sections, and a new resource link was also added related to effective use of stories in communicating with stakeholders. Profiles of each FTG (including question and answer summaries) also were posted on the section of the NQF website devoted to the project, intended to reach a wider audience and better connect with the readers.

Measurement of progress on mutual objectives can be an important way to unite diverse partners around common goals. FTGs supported this notion, but indicated that the use of measures and data was an area where more information was needed. There was consensus among the FTGs and the expert committee that planning efforts and priority-setting should drive measure selection, at least in theory. However, many FTGs noted that from a practical standpoint they were often focused on using measures required for other preexisting reporting initiatives, or for which data happened to be readily available. Some groups pointed out the challenge of shared accountability for improving measure results. Several FTGs were still at a relatively early stage of their initiative and had a high degree of uncertainty over what and how to measure their progress over time. All of these issues pointed to the need for further development of resources and guidance about selection of measures and data sources for population health improvement.

Concern about sustaining population health initiatives was also an issue that many FTGs acknowledged was very relevant to them. FTG feedback indicated that more accessible information is needed about different financing mechanisms for population health improvement efforts, and consideration needs to be given as to how to adapt or transition in order to stay relevant over time. One specific suggestion was to highlight the need for individuals or organizations with financial acumen to be at the table when multisector groups come together to plan their initiatives.

After considering all the feedback provided during the second project year, the Action Guide 2.0[7] was finalized in the summer of 2015. Including revised content, a number of new linked resources, and a variety of fine-tuned language, this second version retained much of the core emphasis from the first version, while also addressing many of the important issues raised by the FTGs. However, even as this second phase of the project wrapped up, the constantly evolving nature of the field made it clear that planning for next steps had to begin immediately.

Future Implications

The NQF expert committee, FTGs, and other stakeholders continue providing additional input and feedback on this work at press time, ultimately leading to the Action Guide 3.0 completion in the summer of 2016. A broader lens indicates that efforts to collaboratively improve population health will be an ongoing goal actively pursued by many groups for years to come. For example, recent high-profile efforts to define specific measure sets to assess the health and health-care of the nation, such as the IOM Vital Signs core measures and Robert Wood Johnson Culture of Health measures, underscore the desire of many stakeholders to identify key indicators of health in the United States. But there is also a continued need to identify and refine measures that can be most useful for Community Health Needs Assessment (CHNA) and monitoring improvement at the local level.

Looking ahead, improving population health through collaboration appears to be a promising but often challenging endeavor. Besides the current NQF project discussed, a variety of other initiatives are under way that are testing out best practices for multisector collaboration on population health improvement, such as HICCup: The Way to Wellville; the BUILD Health Challenge; and the IHI 100 Million Healthier Lives Campaign. The Federal government is also funding innovative models that may promote more upstream focus on population health, such as the Maryland All-Payer Model that essentially rewards hospitals for keeping patients healthy in the community.

In this rapidly changing environment, there is much opportunity for all stakeholders to continue learning and improving. The NQF Action Guide and companion measurement pieces represent one attempt at integrating find-ings from a large and growing body of exciting work focused on improving population health through working in partnerships with others. By continually seeking to refine and enhance our approach to collaborative multisector efforts at the local, state, and national levels, we can hopefully achieve our goal of better population health much more quickly and fully than previously thought to be possible.

Notes

1. U.S. Department of Health and Human Services. National Quality Strategy. Available at: http://www.ahrq.gov/workingforquality/. Last accessed February 2016.
2. http://www.qualityforum.org/WorkArea/linkit.aspx?LinkIdentifier=id&ItemID=78048.
3. Jacobson, DM and Teutsch S. An Environmental Scan of Integrated Approaches for Defining and Measuring Total Population Health by the Clinical Care System, the Government Public Health System, and Stakeholder Organizations. 2012. Available at: http://www.qualityforum.org/WorkArea/linkit.aspx?LinkIdentifier=id&ItemID=70394.
4. National Quality Forum. Environmental Scan and Analysis to Inform the Action Guide. Washington, DC: NQF, 2013. Available at: http://www.qualityforum.org/WorkArea/linkit.aspx?LinkIdentifier=id&ItemID=74400. Last accessed November 2015.
5. http://www.qualityforum.org/WorkArea/linkit.aspx?LinkIdentifier=id&ItemID=78136.

6. Kania J and Kramer M. Collective Impact. Stanford Social Innovation Review. Winter 2011. Available at: http://ssir.org/articles/entry/collective_impact. Last accessed December 2015.
7. National Quality Forum. Multistakeholder Input on a National Priority: Improving Population Health by Working with Communities—Action Guide 2.0. Available at: http://www.qualityforum.org/WorkArea/linkit.aspx?LinkIdentifier=id&ItemID=80092. Last accessed December 2015.

24

IMPROVING POPULATION HEALTH

Paul Kuehnert and Alonzo Plough

Introduction

The philanthropic sector is a key partner in collaborative efforts to improve population health at the local and national levels. Across the continuum of philanthropy, foundations have different operating characteristics, geographic foci, and priority funding areas, but still serve as critical resources to foster such collaborations. In this chapter, we briefly describe different types of foundations, and provide a few examples of roles that they have played in addressing pressing population health problems. We provide a case study of the Robert Wood Johnson Foundation's role in improving population health, and describe its current strategic focus on building a national Culture of Health. The Culture of Health strategy is intended to be a catalyst for improving population health, well-being, and equity; we will describe how the Foundation is implementing this strategy through the Culture of Health Action Framework, and specific research and programmatic investments.

Overview of Foundations

Foundations have historically advanced the public good. They are "entities that support charitable activities by making grants to unrelated organizations or institutions or to individuals for scientific, educational, cultural, religious, or other charitable purposes."[1] The Internal Revenue Service distinguishes every 501(c)(3) organization, or charitable organization, as being either a public charity or a private foundation.[2]

Public charities typically receive funding from multiple sources, including private foundations. Their design and operations allow them to have fewer legal constraints. Community foundations, a type of public foundations, leverage their funds to systematically address the surrounding community or geographic region; members of the community will likely govern the foundation.[3] Examples of community foundations addressing aspects of health and health care include the Tulsa Community Foundation, the New York Community Trust, and the Oregon Community Foundation.

Private foundations encounter stricter regulations than public charities. They must abide by the Tax Reform Act of 1969, which placed restrictions on political and grantmaking activities, business holdings, and asset distributions, among its many components. These foundations are required to payout 5% of their assets annually. They are often governed by a board of directors or trustees. Most private foundations fall within three categories: independent, family, and corporate. Independent foundations are funded by endowments from a single source; they are not governed by any benefactor. Family foundations are funded by endowments from a family; members of the donor family often govern the foundation. Corporate foundations are funded by a corporation as a separate legal entity; members of the corporation likely govern the foundation. Private operating foundations are the exception to these three overarching categories. They are similar to private foundations in that they must follow similar financial and legal regulation, but tend to operate similar to public foundations.[4] Examples of private foundations include the Kresge Foundation and the Novartis Patient Assistance Foundation.

Conversion foundations have become increasingly popular over the past few decades, and have great implications for the future of public health practice. Conversion foundations are the common result of the conversion of a nonprofit organization to a for-profit one, which leads to a surplus of assets that are then transferred to a new foundation. Some concerns with such a model is the loss of existing social benefits for the community, and an overall lack of regulation on grantmaking and other activities.[5] Examples of conversion foundations include the California HealthCare Foundation, the Kansas Health Foundation, and the Colorado Trust.

Many public and private foundations have played a critical role in addressing population health concerns. For instance, the Commonwealth Fund previously established the Commission on a High Performance Health System that successfully laid the groundwork for health reform. The Commission, first formed in 2005, looked to determine how all individuals, especially the most-vulnerable, could gain affordable access to high-quality care. The Commission's findings and disseminations sparked national dialogue and catalyzed action amongst researchers, policymakers, and practitioners.[6] This led to specific health provisions, aimed at improving population health, being incorporated into the Affordable Care Act. Similarly, the Bill and Melinda Gates Foundation has catalyzed progress in vaccine development and delivery in the global arena. With an end goal of "achieving the vision of the Decade of Vaccines—delivering full access to immunization by 2020 and extending the full benefits of immunization to all people, regardless of where they are born, who they are, or where they live," the Gates Foundation is improving large-scale population health outcomes.[7] They pledged $750 million in 2000 to establish the Global Alliance for Vaccines and Immunization (GAVI), which enables governments and fosters the creation of sustainable solutions.

As the philanthropic landscape continues to evolve, nontraditional leaders are exhibiting interest in charitable efforts greatly aligned with those addressing population health. The Chan Zuckerberg Initiative confirms a new era of corporate philanthropic action. This initiative looks to invest $45 billion to address overarching themes that affect population health, including fostering equality, through a limited liability corporation.[8] This organizational design will reduce the financial and legal restrictions around grantmaking and operational activities, and will inadvertently reduce the transparency commonly associated with the philanthropic sector. However, such a design may enable the Initiative to tackle complex issues by partnering with additional charitable or private funders, in a way that may not be possible for public or private foundations.

Case Study: Robert Wood Johnson Foundation

For more than 40 years, the Foundation has served as the nation's largest philanthropy dedicated solely to the public's health. The foundation transitioned, in 1971, from a local philanthropy dedicated to supporting health care activities in New Jersey, to a national philanthropy. The Foundation's commitment to its home state, however, has continued with many robust programmatic and research efforts to improve population health and reduce inequities.

The Foundation's initial aims, set forth in 1972, were: "(1) improving access to medical care services for underserved Americans; (2) improving the quality of health and medical care; and (3) developing mechanisms for objective analysis of public policies on health."[9] To operationalize these areas, the Foundation devised a strategy to fund demonstration projects that would serve as a proof-of-concept. To address the first area, the Foundation provided its first demonstration grant to develop the Emergency Medical Services program. This program established regional emergency response systems throughout the nation. It resulted in increased numbers of trained emergency medical personnel, improved access to a 911 system, and stronger relationships and knowledge-sharing between hospitals and ambulances. Around the same time, the Foundation also invested in training programs, specifically the Clinical Scholars and Health Policy Fellowship Programs. Both provided leading practitioners an opportunity to engage with and learn from one another, and to develop a stronger understanding of the policy implications of health care.[10] A commitment to growing the field of researchers and practitioners continues today through four Change Leadership Programs.

The desire to tailor research and programming to different sub-groups of the population led the Foundation to identify new objectives in 1980 that addressed:

> (1) access to health care and emphasized programs to expand access for the most underserved groups; (2) costs and stressed programs to make health care arrangements more effective and care more affordable; and (3) chronic illness and focused on programs to help people maintain or regain maximum attainable function.[11]

During this period, the Foundation adapted to the shifting landscape and began to engage community partners through investments fostering the connection of support services for those diagnosed with AIDS, and programs like Health Care for the Homeless, which shed light on the disparities and obstacles faced by those individuals.

By 1986, the Foundation had redesigned its goals to address how to best: "(1) assist the most vulnerable individuals, (2) combat specific diseases of regional or national concern, and (3) address broad national health issues and concerns."[12] The ten priorities set to focus the goals demonstrated that population health outcomes were not solely influenced by practitioners or health care systems and services. Around this time, the Study to Understand Prognoses and Preferences for Outcomes and Risks of Treatment found that even when given supportive care and environments, the dying were often left alone to die a costly death in hospitals. This work sparked the Foundation's interests in further pursuing end-of-life issues, and looking at broad social influences on health outcomes.

With the ongoing interests in focusing equally on health and health care, the Foundation posed the following goals in 1990: "(1) assure that Americans of all ages have access to basic health care; (2) improve the way services are organized and provided to people with chronic health problems; and (3) promote health and prevent disease by reducing harm caused by substance abuse."[13] The third goal was specifically operationalized by the Foundation's large investments to unearth successful tobacco-cessation policy interventions, and to fund demonstration projects, with an emphasis on addressing youth outcomes.[14] A particularly successful investment was SmokeLess States, a national program funding "state coalitions whose aim was to encourage tobacco control policies, such as prohibiting smoking in restaurants and raising the tax on cigarettes."[15] The concerted efforts of the Foundation, at that time, has had lasting impacts on minimizing substance abuse and encouraging health as a factor in policymaking.

The Foundation additionally made an eight-year, $500 million commitment to reversing the childhood obesity epidemic in 2007. Since then, it has made great strides in pushing the healthy choices as the right choices. By engaging with the Alliance for a Healthier Generation, the Foundation has helped grow the Healthy Schools Program into one where thousands can now reap the benefits of healthier options in academic environments.[16]

Recognizing the increasing costs of health care and continued disparities in health status among the population, the Foundation established the RWJF Commission to Build a Healthier America in 2008. The Commission, composed of leaders from diverse sectors, examined the many social, environmental, and economic determinants of health. In *Beyond Health Care: New Directions to a Healthier America*, the Commission's ten recommendations called for "a national culture" where health and wellness would be omnipresent, especially amongst different groups and sectors.[17] The Commission's findings sparked national dialogue and movements to increase cross-sector collaboration. In light of this incremental success, the Foundation reconvened the Commission in 2013 to examine the drivers of disparities within different populations. In their final set of recommendations in *Time to Act: Investing in the Health of Our Children and Communities*, the Commission outlined the roles different individuals, communities, and organizations across sectors have in creating a healthier, more equitable nation. They determined that Foundation resources should be allocated to: "(1) investing in the foundations of lifelong physical and mental well-being in the nation's youngest; (2) creating communities that foster health-promoting behaviors; and (3) broadening health care to promote health outside of the medical system."[18]

The challenges in health and society, at the time, further demonstrated that America was at a pivotal moment of great urgency and unprecedented opportunity. Addressing these challenges required individuals, communities, and sectors to think and work differently. For the Foundation, addressing these challenges provided an opportunity to foster real societal transformation and systemic change. In its 2014 annual message, *Building a Culture of Health*, the Foundation presented ten principles underlying how it could catalyze an evidence-based national movement to build a Culture of Health, one that enabled all in our diverse society to lead healthier lives, now and for generations to come.[19] This report marked the beginning of a new era at the Foundation, where the overarching focus became health and well-being.

Building a national Culture of Health is a long-term initiative. To chart and foster the nation's progress, the Foundation clustered the interrelated principles into a framework. The Culture of Health Action Framework demonstrates the interdependence of the many social, economic, physical, environmental, and spiritual factors of health and well-being. It contains four priority areas and an outcomes area, whereby actions that occurred upstream would affect the long-term desired outcome of improved population health, well-being, and equity.[20]

The four priority areas, or Action Areas, are each connected to and influenced by the others, and are intended to focus efforts and mobilize an integrated course of action by many individuals, communities, and sectors. Each Action Area includes a set of corresponding Drivers and Measures, to help catalyze and track progress. The Drivers provide a set of long-term priorities for national investment. Together, the Action Areas and the Drivers create the key building blocks of the Action Framework that will remain constant over time.

The Measures are uniquely focused on upstream social, economic, and policy indicators that, if improved, should significantly enhance population health and well-being. The 41 Measures were rigorously identified to have the necessary evidence base at a national level, and represent a marriage of different data sources to best engage diverse sectors and reflect the complexity of the decision-making and multipronged approach communities use to address such challenges. They also highlight underlying factors of health, across the lifespan and healthspan, which are not represented in other national reports. The Measures are intended to inspire national movement and illustrate progress, but will evolve to keep pace with changing needs.

In a national Culture of Health, every person has an equal opportunity to live the healthiest, most fulfilling life possible. Thus, equity is the overarching theme of the Action Framework; not to merely highlight health disparities, but to move toward eliminating them.

The Action Framework is designed to establish priorities while also offering a number of entry points that resonate with the nation's many diverse individuals, communities, and organizations across sectors. Action Area 1 is Making Health a Shared Value. This Action Area places the nation's values and expectations about health front and center. It emphasizes the importance of achieving, maintaining, and reclaiming health as a shared priority, defined in different ways by different individuals, communities, and sectors. This will fuel not only a stronger belief that individual actions can make a difference in the well-being of others and a greater sense of community, but also an increased demand for healthy places and practices. The corresponding Drivers are: Mindset and Expectations; Sense of Community; and Civic Engagement.

Action Area 2 focuses on Fostering Cross-Sector Collaboration to Improve Well-Being. This Action Area places a new focus on breaking down silos that separate improving health from the work of sectors beyond health and health care. Successfully tackling urgent and disparate health challenges, from gaps in educational achievement to gaps in access to healthy food, requires creative, cross-sector collaborations. The corresponding Drivers are: Quality of Partnerships, Investment in Collaboration, and Policies that Support Collaboration.

Action Area 3 looks to Creating Healthier, More Equitable Communities. The goal of this Action Area is to encourage communities to fulfill their greatest health potential by improving the environment in which residents live, learn, work, and play. The corresponding Drivers are: Built Environment, Social and Economic Environment, and Policy and Governance.

Lastly, Action Area 4 focuses on Strengthening Integration of Health Services and Systems. This Action Area aims to strengthen a system of coordinated care that integrates and better balances medical treatment, public health, and social services to empower patients and providers. The corresponding Drivers are: Access, Balance and Integration, and Consumer Experience.

As the nation makes progress in the four Action Areas, the Foundation believes the outcome of improved population health, well-being, and equity will be achieved. Individuals, communities, and organizations across sectors will place a higher value on health as the essential building block of a productive, thriving society. Motivated by this shared value, they will collaborate to prioritize and promote well-being so that all people will have access to health and health care services. This will result in an overall reduction in health care spending and the financial and emotional burden placed on caregivers. Policymakers will integrate health and well-being into public policy, giving special focus to increasing equity.

Transforming the health of this nation is a cultural shift that may span a generation or more, and requires the talent, teamwork, and tenacity of many, including those who have not historically seen themselves as impacting health. Recognizing the need to leverage transdisciplinary data in new and novel ways, the Foundation shifted its research and programmatic investments to more strongly align with building an evidence base for a Culture of Health.

In 2015, the Foundation developed three signature research programs: Evidence for Action, Policies for Action, and Systems for Action. These programs emphasize cross-cutting research that highlights emerging themes from the Action Framework. Evidence for Action: Investigator-Initiated Research to Build a Culture of Health (E4A) is a national program that supports innovative, rigorously designed research on the impact of programs, policies, and partnerships on health and well-being, with a particular focus on research that will advance health equity. A smaller portfolio of grants is dedicated to the development and validation of key measures to improve the assessment of population health, well-being, and equity. E4A targets a wide range of fields both within and outside the health sector, especially encouraging collaboration and multi-sector partnerships.

Policies for Action: Policy and Law Research to Build a Culture of Health (P4A) is a national program that seeks to develop research that generates actionable evidence—the data and information that can guide legislators and other policymakers, public agencies, educators, advocates, community groups, and individuals. The research may examine established laws, regulations, and policies as well as potential new policies and approaches. P4A places a special emphasis on innovative research that evaluates and addresses actionable policies that: advance a community's own priorities; highlight collaboration between the public and private sectors, or innovations within the private sector; and foster stability and continuity at the neighborhood, community, state, or federal levels. The program seeks experts from many different fields, including health care, public health, early childhood development, education, transportation, housing, architectural design, the built environment, economics, and beyond.

Systems for Action: Systems and Services Research to Build a Culture of Health (S4A) is a national program that aims to discover and apply new evidence about ways of aligning the delivery and financing systems that support a Culture of Health. It builds on a strong foundation of recent scientific progress in both health services research and public health services and systems research to identify system-level strategies for improving accessibility, quality, and efficiency in the delivery of medical, public health, and social services, and to identify and address inequities in delivery. S4A will expand this evidence base using a wider research lens that includes, alongside public health and health care, the many other spheres of human endeavor relevant to prevention and health improvement, including social services, community services and supports, education, economic and community development, housing, transportation, and criminal justice.

The Foundation has similarly tailored its programmatic investments to foster connections between and across sectors with the ultimate aim of improving population health, well-being, and equity. One such example is their efforts to reshape communities by encouraging collaborative health-promoting relationships among key stakeholders at the community level. For communities to improve population health in an equitable manner, they need to address multiple determinants of health and engage health care, public health, and other community systems.

The first of three key tactics to operationalize this effort is to develop well-connected, person- and community-centric systems and services that protect and promote health and well-being and provide high-quality care. The Foundation accomplishes this by supporting the development of best practices and sharing of those practices with communities and other relevant stakeholders to improve health. For instance, the Foundation supports the Urban Land Institute as they strive to create a typology for urban commercial corridors that will drive change to make them healthier and more equitable places.[21] The second tactic is to support opportunities to improve the availability of capital to create healthier communities and more equitable community development activities. The Foundation is using new and traditional payment mechanisms, federal and private grants, tax incentives, and program-related investments and evolving approaches to develop, test, and refine sustainable financing models that support a shift of resources toward population well-being. The Foundation is exploring how to partner with other philanthropies, community development financial institutions, and nonprofit institutions to influence and enhance capital channels into disinvested communities, and how to create learning coalitions for communities to learn from and implement successful models. The final tactic is to encourage and support active planning and collaboration across multiple sectors to create health-enhancing organizational, social, and built environments. The Foundation is focusing on supporting the development of new measures that can identify both disparity and opportunity at the local level, measuring health outcomes in community development, and building health metrics into other sectors.

Communities can strengthen their ability to improve population health and equity through collaborative efforts that intentionally harness the key tactics to implement common health-promoting agendas, tailored to the unique assets and challenges of the locales or regions in which they are based.

Conclusion

In summary, the active role of foundations in improving population health is critical to the future of this nation. While public and private foundations offer diverse entry points to foster change and catalyze action, there are overarching challenges that will greatly affect their success. The rise of convergence partnerships, lack of longer-term governance structures, and unknown resources to foster sustainability provide key areas of opportunity for individuals, communities, and organizations across sectors to address.

Although the Robert Wood Johnson Foundation made building a comprehensive Culture of Health their central focus, they are well aware that no individual, community, organization, or initiative can change the trajectory of America's health alone, and lasting change will not happen overnight. It will take the collective efforts of traditional and new partners—some of whom may not have previously considered themselves to be influencers of health. It must be championed by diverse sectors like housing, transportation, and finance, but be grounded in the broad social and behavioral determinants of health.

We hope that this overview of the role of foundations, and specifically the case study, spark dialogue about what and who it will take to improve population health as this nation evolves.

Notes

1. "Foundation Basics," Council on Foundations, accessed January 2016, http://www.cof.org/content/foundation-basics.
2. "Life Cycle of a Public Charity/Private Foundation," irs.gov, last modified July 22, 2015, https://www.irs.gov/Charities-&-Non-Profits/Charitable-Organizations/Life-Cycle-of-a-Public-Charity-Private-Foundation.
3. "Foundation Basics," Council on Foundations, accessed January 2016, http://www.cof.org/content/foundation-basics.
4. "Foundation Basics," Council on Foundations, accessed January 2016, http://www.cof.org/content/foundation-basics.
5. Christopher Frost, "Financing Public Health through Nonprofit Conversion Foundations," *Kentucky Law Journal* 90 (2002): 935–972.
6. "Archived: Commission on a High Performance Health System," The Commonwealth Fund, accessed January 2016, http://www.commonwealthfund.org/grants-and-fellowships/programs/archived-programs/commission-on-a-high-performance-health-system.
7. "What We Do: Vaccine Delivery Strategy Overview," Bill and Melinda Gates Foundation, accessed January 2016, http://www.gatesfoundation.org/What-We-Do/Global-Development/Vaccine-Delivery#OurStrategy.

8. "Advancing Human Potential and Promoting Equality," Chan Zuckerberg Initiative, accessed February 2016, http://chanzuckerberg.com/.

9. Joel Gardner, "The Robert Wood Johnson Foundation: 1974–2002," in *To Improve Health and Health Care Volume X*, ed. Stephen Isaacs and James Knickman (San Francisco: Jossey-Bass, 2006), 202.

10. Joel Gardner, "The Robert Wood Johnson Foundation: 1974–2002," in *To Improve Health and Health Care Volume X*, ed. Stephen Isaacs and James Knickman (San Francisco: Jossey-Bass, 2006), 203–204.

11. Joel Gardner, "The Robert Wood Johnson Foundation: 1974–2002," in *To Improve Health and Health Care Volume X*, ed. Stephen Isaacs and James Knickman (San Francisco: Jossey-Bass, 2006), 206.

12. Joel Gardner, "The Robert Wood Johnson Foundation: 1974–2002," in *To Improve Health and Health Care Volume X*, ed. Stephen Isaacs and James Knickman (San Francisco: Jossey-Bass, 2006), 209.

13. Joel Gardner, "The Robert Wood Johnson Foundation: 1974–2002," in *To Improve Health and Health Care Volume X*, ed. Stephen Isaacs and James Knickman (San Francisco: Jossey-Bass, 2006), 211.

14. James Bornemeier, "Taking on Tobacco," in *To Improve Health and Health Care Volume VIII*, ed. Stephen Isaacs and James Knickman (San Francisco: Jossey-Bass, 2005), 3–28.

15. Joel Gardner, "The Robert Wood Johnson Foundation: 1974–2002," in *To Improve Health and Health Care Volume X*, ed. Stephen Isaacs and James Knickman (San Francisco: Jossey-Bass, 2006), 212.

16. "Foundation Dedicates $1 Billion To Healthy Weight for All Children," Robert Wood Johnson Foundation. 2015, accessed January 2016, http://www.rwjf.org/en/library/articles-and-news/2015/02/rwjf_doubles_commitment_to_healthy_weight_for_children.html.

17. "Beyond Health Care: New Directions to a Healthier America," Robert Wood Johnson Foundation. 2009, accessed February 2016, http://www.rwjf.org/content/dam/farm/reports/reports/2009/rwjf40483.

18. "Time to Act: Investing in the Health of Our Children and Communities," Robert Wood Johnson Foundation. 2014, accessed February 2016, http://www.rwjf.org/content/dam/farm/reports/reports/2014/rwjf409002.

19. "Building a Culture of Health: 2014 President's Message," Robert Wood Johnson Foundation. 2014, accessed December 2015, http://www.rwjf.org/content/dam/files/rwjf-web-files/Annual_Message/2014_RWJF_AnnualMessage_final.pdf.

20. "From Vision to Action: A Framework and Measures to Mobilize a Culture of Health," Robert Wood Johnson Foundation. 2015, accessed December 2015, http://www.rwjf.org/content/dam/COH/RWJ000_COH-Update_CoH_Report_1b.pdf.

21. "Building Healthy Places Initiative," Urban Land Institute, accessed February 2016, http://uli.org/research/centers-initiatives/building-healthy-places-initiative/.

25

ENTERING A NEW ERA IN HOSPITAL AND PUBLIC HEALTH COLLABORATION FOR COMMUNITY BENEFIT

F. Douglas Scutchfield, Lawrence W. Prybil, and Rachel Dixon

In 2013, the Institute of Medicine (IOM), now the National Academy of Medicine (NAM), issued one of its most influential reports (Woolf and Aron 2013a). This was followed in 2015 by a Commonwealth Report that had similar findings (Squires and Anderson 2015). In both cases, findings regarding the health status of the United States were abysmal. The reports pointed out that whereas the United States spent more on health care than any other developed country, our health status was among the worst. Our citizens have shorter life expectancies than other developed nations, and we rank near the bottom of the list in morbidity and mortality from several diseases and injuries. Our infant mortality rate is one of the highest of all developed nations, with birth weights that are lower than many of those in comparable peer countries.

Some portion of our poor health can be attributed to ineffective delivery of health services. We do not have universal financial access to health care, and we have a poor primary care system, the keystone of medical care. The quality of care we provide is frequently questioned, with abundant stories of confusion, lack of communication and poor coordination between the various components of the U.S. system (if it could be called a system).

But much of the blame for this condition should not be placed at the feet of the health care delivery system. Major economic, environmental and behavioral issues such as the use of alcohol when we drive, high rates of gun ownership, consumption of calories and high-risk sexual behavior in our young people also contribute greatly to our population's health problems (Woolf and Aron 2013b).

None of this is really new. Whereas the NAM report highlighted the severity of service problems in the U.S. health system, prior IOM reports focused on the issue of health quality received by the American people (Institute of Medicine

1999, 2001). The fact that over 45 million Americans did not have insurance coverage prompted the failed Clinton health reform efforts (Starr 1995), just as previous efforts to assure financial access to medical care had failed since the Committee on the Cost of Medical Care recommended universal access to care in the 1930s (Committee on the Cost of Medical Care 1932).

Multiple factors, in addition to medical care, determine the health of the American people. This is perhaps best illustrated by the relative weight given to each contributor to health status allocated by the Wisconsin County Health Rankings methodology. In their paradigm, health outcomes is measured in regards to length and quality of life. In their method for designating length and quality of life, the Wisconsin County Health Rankings assign 20% of the contribution for health status to health care, 30% to health behaviors, 40% to social and economic factors and 10% to the physical environment (County Health Rankings & Roadmaps, 2015).

Against this backdrop, major changes have begun to occur in the health care system. In fact, the amount and pace of transformation that is occurring within the system is accelerating at an increasing rate. Many would suggest the transformation that is occurring is the result of the Patient Protection and Affordable Care Act (ACA). However, whereas changes may have been catalyzed by this act, they were beginning to occur prior to its passage. Many changes were responses to an evolving economic environment, changes in medical science and the practice of medicine and new trends in health care delivery.

Some of the change is the result of efforts to achieve the "Triple Aim," a paradigm created by Dr. Donald Berwick and the Institute for Healthcare Improvement. Specifically, this aim calls for improving the experience of care and making it more patient-centered, "bending" the cost curve—lowering the per capita cost of care—and, finally, improving the health of populations. Berwick, in discussing the "Triple Aim," describes five components that will allow the aim to be achieved: "partnership with individuals and families, redesign of primary care, population health management, financial management, and macro system integration" (Berwick et al. 2008, p. 759).

The structure of America's health care system is changing dramatically. This is illustrated by several developments, including the consolidation of hospitals, previously independent, into major multi-hospital systems and the affiliation of physicians with these systems, either as employees or through other affiliation mechanisms. We are also experiencing an aging and increasingly diverse population and growth in the number of persons with health insurance as the result of the Affordable Care Act. There is a growing call for patient-centered medical care, with patients demanding a major voice in their care, the movement to value-based purchasing and a call for an increased focus on population health. All of these are substantially altering the hospital and medical care environment.

Consumers of medical care services have become aware of the variation in the cost of medical interventions that exists among various hospitals and physicians for the same service. This, in turn, has increased the demand for transparency in costs and charges for hospitals and medical care services. It has also created a demand for "value-based purchasing" as those responsible for paying the medical care bill, both public and private, are demanding that they receive value, defined as cost and quality, in the services they purchase. Often the principal public payer, the Center for Medicare and Medicaid Services, is providing leadership and has announced that it will progressively increase the amount of services that it will pay for through value-based purchasing arrangements. The Center has also led the way in establishing new methods for this purchasing, such as Accountable Care Organizations or "bundling" of payments for specific episodes of care.

This transformation is occurring rapidly, and the current health system leadership is moving with dispatch to adjust to these changes in health care delivery. It is imperative for those with leadership roles in health care organizations to be aware of these changes and be prepared to adapt their activities to coincide with the rapid transformation that medical care is experiencing. Clearly among the key strategies is the use of collaboration and partnering with others in the system to address larger issues in health care, such as improvement of population health.

Our medical and health care system components traditionally have existed largely in isolation from each other, all in their own silos with little coordination or efforts to work collaboratively toward common health goals (Health Research & Educational Trust 2015). In fact, in a community with more than one hospital or health system, the environment usually is one of competition, not working with others for the better health of all who are served by these organizations. One of the major avenues for improving community health is effective collaboration between two major components of the system, hospitals with their associated resources and the community's other major "anchor" health institution, the local health department (LHD).

Unfortunately, there is a history of estrangement between these two vital health resources in many communities, with exceptions, of course, such as in a natural disaster. Public health was started by those medical professionals who recognized that community disease was a problem requiring whole-community intervention. It was led by physicians who founded the American Public Health Association in the mid-1800s.

However, a split between medicine and public health occurred in the early 1990s, primarily over care of children, as physicians were resentful of public health departments taking on maternal and child health activities that benefitted poor and immigrant children. The federal Shepard Towner Act (1921), creating the Children's Bureau to extend care to children by the government, was vigorously opposed by medicine, as physicians felt that private practitioners should provide children's care. Opposition to the act by organized medicine led to the repeal of the Shepard Towner Act. Title V of the Social Security Act provided governmental support for maternal and child health in the mid-1930s. This rift between medicine and sickness care and public health has worked to the detriment of both sectors and the public at large. This split is well documented and discussed in detail in Paul Starr's classic book, *The Social Transformation of American Medicine* (Starr 1982).

This separation in health is no longer viable, financially or morally. For each component of the health system to stand on its own is no longer feasible or appropriate. In fact, it is likely that if we are to successfully improve population health, we will have to include some strangers under the health umbrella, such as education, economic development and the social services system.

Efforts were made by the American Medical Association and American Public Health Association in the past to address the rift between public health and medicine with an initiative intended to identify and take advantage of potential collaborative efforts between these two segments of the health system (Reiser 1996; Beitsch et al. 2005). This effort, in the late 1990s, is unfortunately quiescent.

In a similar manner, other organizations—including the American Hospital Association, the Robert Wood Johnson Foundation, the Trust for America's Health and the Institute of Medicine—have called for increased collaboration and new partnership models to address the current status of our health described in the NAM report that opened this chapter (Institute of Medicine 2001, 2003, 2012, 2015a; Robert Wood Johnson Foundation 2013; Trust for America's Health 2013; American Hospital Association 2015).

It is apparent that we cannot solve the nation's health problems one patient at a time, or, for that matter, one person at a time. Instead, we must focus our collective energy on working with populations to assess health status, identify and prioritize those contributors to poor health, identify evidence-based solutions to those contributors and implement programs which can impact the health of a population.

Moreover, as we have pointed out, the contributors to poor health status are drawn not just from the medical care sector, but also lifestyle, socio-economic environment and the physical environment. The medical care sector has little experience working in this larger sphere of health determinants, but the organizations that influence and control the non-medical sphere of the nation's health enterprise must be drawn into the collaboration that will be required to address population health problems. Merely relying on improving access to existing medical care resources and assuring their best and most effective application will not, in and of itself, address the larger health issues that our nation is experiencing.

Thus, to achieve the goal of bringing our nation's health to the lead among developed nations and achieve some control of rising health costs will require better collaboration and communication including parties outside of the health sector who have an important contribution to make to the health of the community. This imperative is well illustrated in a key quote from Alan W. Weil, the Editor-in-Chief of *Health Affairs*:

> What does it take to harness community resources to overcome poor health outcomes? In a word: collaboration. Just as health does not arise from a

> single factor, healthy communities emerge from concerted efforts that
> stretch across public and private sectors and break down barriers between
> the long-standing silos of different government agencies and programs.
>
> *(Weil 2014)*

Collaboration is an imperative part of working together to achieve benefits
for all participants. However, cooperation and partnerships between organizations are challenging to build and maintain. The success rate varies by how
often the organizations involved incorporate key characteristics. We did a
thorough literature review of experience in both the business and health
literature, and identified a series of characteristics that affect the success of
community collaboratives (Prybil et al. 2014). A separate study completed by
Mattessich and Rausch showed that of 661 collaboratives focused on improving various aspects of community health, 297 (45%) were successful (Mattessich
and Rausch 2014).

In our examination of this area, we identified two major actors in the community whose collaboration and participation were imperative to successfully
addressing the community's health status: the health department(s) and local
hospital(s). We felt then and continue to feel that these are "health pillars" of
every community and have the resources and commitment, given their missions,
to address community health. We felt that a partnership to improve the health
of their population between these two major players in the public health system
was the first step necessary to begin the process of implementing the collaboration that we have discussed in the preceding section. Moreover, we were struck
by two recent occurrences that have stimulated opportunities for collaboration
between these two partners.

Specifically, in 2012 the Public Health Accreditation Board (PHAB) began
to accept applications from local, state and tribal health departments for their
voluntary accreditation. Among the standards and requirements for this accreditation process was the responsibility of the LHD to complete a community health
assessment and community health improvement plan prior to beginning its
accreditation efforts. In addition, standards written into the requirements for
accreditation specifically looked in detail at this assessment and community
engagement with major health partners, as a part of the LHDs' efforts in assessment, policy development and assurance.

At about the same time, the Patient Protection and Affordable Care Act
(ACA) became law and was implemented. Whereas not-for-profit hospitals have
had a long history of providing community benefits, these benefits were largely
focused on care of indigent patients and loss of revenue in providing for those
with public insurance that did not cover the full cost of their hospital care. ACA
now requires not-for-profit hospitals to undertake a community health needs
assessment (CHNA) and to document how the CHNA was done. Schedule H
of the Internal Revenue Service (IRS) 990 form has evolved to require the

hospital to work with the community to complete the CHNA, to make the CHNA readily available to interested parties and to provide a description of how the hospital intends to address the problems identified in the CHNA.

The IRS regulations associated with this provision of the ACA have been final-ized and have substantial implications for the collaboration between hospitals and health departments. Although a comprehensive look at the new regulations are beyond the scope of this chapter, the final regulations are available for review online (Quesenberry 2011). Many of their requirements encourage collaboration with LHDs in completing their CHNA and in addressing the issues documented within it, for example:

> Treasury and the IRS intend to provide that a CHNA must, at a minimum, take into account input from—(1) Persons with special knowledge of or expertise in public health; (2) Federal, tribal, regional, State, or local health or other departments or agencies, with current data or other information relevant to the health needs of the community served by the hospital facility.
>
> *(Quesenberry 2011, p. 15)*

In addition, the hospital is expected to develop an implementation strategy for addressing issues identified in the CHNA. The requirements state that the

> Treasury and the IRS intend to allow hospital organizations to develop implementation strategies for their hospital facilities in collaboration with other organizations, including related organizations, other hospital organiza-tions, for-profit and government hospitals, and State and local agencies, such as public health departments. If a hospital organization collaborates with other organizations in developing an implementation strategy, the implementation strategy should identify all of the organizations with which the hospital organization collaborated.
>
> *(Quesenberry 2011, p. 20)*

The simultaneous development of these two complementary actions has certainly provided a strong stimulus for health department and hospital partnerships.

In our recent study, we sought to identify and examine successful partnerships between health departments, hospitals and other stakeholders who shared a col-laborative commitment to improve the health of their community (Prybil et al. 2014). We wished to identify key lessons learned from their experiences that could be shared with those pursuing similar collaborative efforts to improve community health. The study had a series of key steps. First, we had to locate those partner-ships, as such a list did not exist. We worked to identify those partnerships who met several key characteristics; i.e., they had been in operation for at least two years (that is, prior to the passage of ACA); had demonstrated successful perfor-mance; and, to enable generalization, were diverse in location, organization and focus. Through a nomination process and exploration by the research team, we identified a total of 157 partnerships that met our basic criteria. Through a stepwise process, we selected 12 partnerships that, based on available information, were both highly successful and diverse. We then did deep-dive, two-day site visits to these partnerships. This involved structured interviews with key individuals and groups and extensive review of organizational documents to gain understanding of their genesis; organization and staffing; mission, goals, and strategies; metrics used to assess performance; and lessons learned from their experiences.

Whereas each of the partnerships was somewhat unique, several overall patterns and key findings emerged. We observed an increased focus in all sectors of the communities on "population health" and improving the health not just of specific individuals but of the entire community. In all communities, we also found a growing interest in prevention, early diagnosis and treatment and the promotion of wellness. We believe this represents a fundamental change in the approach of communities across the nation as they began to realize the importance of focusing on the health of their communities and not just on those with acute ailments. The confusion that frequently exists in understanding and implementing "population health" serves as a corollary to this finding (Sharfstein 2014). In order to succeed, it is important that communities and their leaders, particularly those involved in partnerships, have a clear understanding of population health and the effort that must be dedicated to develop a common base of understanding regarding the principles, concepts and definitions inherent in the notion of population health.

There are multiple circumstances that can result in partnership formation. One of these is a charismatic or visionary individual who can articulate a vision and inspire others to embrace that vision. An interesting corollary of this type of initiation is that the partnerships' leadership models tend to evolve from a charismatic founder to persons who manifest a servant leadership style (Greenleaf and Spears 1998). Actually, in most settings, we observed that the servant leadership style presently seems to prevail. It seems that over time the organizations seek partners who are consensus builders and develop influence through working with people and organizations. This is not surprising, as the work of most of these organizations are undertaken by volunteers and, with few exceptions, the principal partners do not have a large-scale financial investment in the partnership and are relatively "hands off" when it comes to the day-to-day operations of the partnerships.

A crisis situation or traumatic event also can mobilize partnerships to address a community's health. In one partnership studied, realization of the extent of infant mortality in the inner city of one of our nation's major communities promoted collective action. Finally, grant support and its availability also can motivate the creation of these partnerships. As stated above, the new IRS requirements for hospitals or the standards and prerequisites for accreditation of LHDs can serve to stimulate or guide this process, as community stakeholders, through their community assessment, become aware of the problems and issues that affect their communities.

All of the partnerships we studied had a mission statement and 10 of the 12 had some form of strategic plan. The mission statements varied in scope and nature, but there was strong commitment to the partnerships' missions in virtually all locations. The mission statements that were broad in scope clearly challenged the principal partners and staff with their all-encompassing nature, whereas those that were more targeted made the work of the group somewhat easier, as the focus was clearer and allowed for more effort to be expended in a targeted way. The leaders of all of these partnerships agree, however, that the mission, goals, strategies and evaluation of their efforts needed periodic review and reaffirmation in order to remain both current and relevant. With respect to their "strategic plans," there was broad agreement that they needed to be sharpened with clearer goals, metrics and evaluation processes, but in many locations staff attention to this important work had been constrained by more immediate priorities and resource limitations.

Whereas we began by specifically studying hospitals and health departments, believing these are key institutions in any community that must be committed to improving population health, all of the groups that we studied had a much larger constituency of stakeholders than just the two key groups. They involved both public agencies, such as local government and schools systems, and private organizations, such as the chamber of commerce and United Way. In fact, in some situations we studied, the group included competing organizations; hospitals that were competitors for patients and recognition in the community saw the benefit in collaboration to benefit the community's health, irrespective of their competitive nature in other venues.

One of the most concerning findings in our work was the near absence of health plans in the partnership. Health plans, it would seem, stand to benefit from healthy communities in their business models, but, except in a few circumstances, they were absent from the partnerships we examined. In the same vein, whereas individual employees of major companies in the community were actively involved in volunteering as part of the group, a role encouraged by their employers, the employers themselves generally were not full partners in the coalition and did not provide significant financial support. The lack of health plans and local businesses as principal partners in our coalitions was a major concern and disappointment, as they have resources and benefit significantly from these community health improvement efforts.

We were struck by the challenge of developing linkages in logic models between efforts expended by communities and the anticipated impact of interventions. Much of the work of understanding the multiple etiologies of major health problems, particularly the linkage to non-medical goals, is still at an early stage of development, and these knowledge gaps make it difficult for organizations to build effective goals and measures associated with those non-medical health determinants. With goals, measures and metrics not well developed, it is difficult to track progress and produce solid evidence of impact. We are heartened and believe that two new projects may help in this effort. First, the NAM has published a series of metrics which they believe can and should be used more universally in approaching problems of measuring health (Institute of Medicine 2015b).

In a similar vein, the Robert Wood Johnson Foundation, in its Culture of Health efforts, has also published a series of metrics with the potential to improve the concurrence on effective metrics of health (RWJF 2015). It is likely that these publications will assist communities in moving beyond process measures, such as attendance at meetings, and focus more directly on impact and outcomes.

We were also surprised when we examined the organizational models that had been established for the partnerships we studied. In all cases they were organized in various types of coalition models, and not in more formalized non-for-profit organizations, although some were considering moving in that direction. All but one of the partnerships have a policy-and-direction-setting body that is responsible for setting the partnership's overall direction and priorities. Most also have a foundation in the form of one or more "anchor institutions" such as a strong LHD or hospital. These "anchor institutions" are principal partners that have a particularly strong, enduring commitment to the partnership and provide significant economic and/or noneconomic support for it.

As might be imagined from our comments about limited participation by business or health plans as full partners, most of these partnerships are financially challenged. They are constantly striving to achieve financial stability, and many are constantly seeking to diversify sources of funding including grants from foundations and/or governmental agencies. If they are a recipient of grants, they can find themselves driven to a considerable extent by the terms and conditions of the grant, a reality that can divert them from local issues and priorities. Without substantial funding, these partnerships are hampered in their ability to make long-term plans and focus energy on health issues that require a longer time to resolve, but are much more focused on the short range and process activities. This underscores the importance of having reliable "anchor institutions" to stabilize the partnership and ongoing efforts to strengthen and diversify the partnership's funding sources. The commitment by not-for-profit hospitals or an accredited health department to become an "anchor institution" for a multi-sector partnership devoted to community health improvement certainly is consistent with the intent of current IRS and PHAB expectations.

Vitally important in obtaining and maintaining support for all these efforts is demonstrating measurable progress in achieving the specific objectives and metrics the partnerships have established. In all instances, the boards of the principal partners and the coalition's policy-setting body are committed to achieve these outcomes and must be concerned when the partnerships do not demonstrate positive performance and results. In fact, all of these partnerships should strive to produce "impact statements" that specify the evidence-based effects they are having, both to their stakeholders and to the community at large.

From our work, we generated 11 specific recommendations based on our findings and the various observations of the project itself. Rather than discuss those, we have listed them in Table 25.1. Obviously, more information specific to these recommendations may be obtained from the report itself.

TABLE 25.1 Recommendations for Successful Partnerships

1	To have enduring impact, partnerships focused on improving community health should include hospitals and public health departments as core partners but, over time, engage a broad range of other parties from the private and public sectors.
2	Whenever possible, partnerships should be built on a foundation of pre-existing trust-based relationships among some, if not all, of the principal founding partners. Other partners can and should be added as the organization becomes operational, but building and maintaining trust among all members is essential.
3	In the context of their particular community's health needs, the capabilities of existing community organization and resource constraints, the parties who decide to establish a new partnership devoted to improving community health should adopt a statement of mission and goals that focus on clearly defined, high priority needs and will inspire community-wide interest, engagement and support.
4	For long-term success, partnerships need to have one or more "anchor institutions" with dedication to the partnership's mission and strong commitment to provide ongoing financial support for it.
5	Partnerships focused on improving community health should have a designated body with a clearly defined charter that is empowered by the principal partners to set policy and provide strategic leadership for the partnerships.
6	Partnership leaders should strive to build a clear, mutual understanding of "population health" concepts, definitions and principles among the partners, participants and, in so far as possible, the community at large.
7	To enable objective, evidence-based evaluation of a partnership's progress in achieving its mission and goals and fulfill its accountability to key stakeholders, the partnership's leadership must specify the community health measures they want to address, the particular objectives and targets they intend to achieve and the metrics and tools they will use to track and monitor progress.
8	All partnerships focused on improving community health should place priority on developing and disseminating "impact statements" that present an evidence-based picture of the effects the partnership's efforts are having in relation to the direct and indirect costs it is incurring.
9	To enhance sustainability, all partnerships focused on community health improvement should develop a deliberate strategy for broadening and diversifying their sources of funding support.
10	If they have not already done so, the governing boards of nonprofit hospitals and health systems and the boards of local health departments should establish standing committees with oversight responsibility for their organization's engagement in examining community health needs, establishing priorities and developing strategies for addressing them, including multi-sector collaboration focused on community health improvement.
11	If they have not already done so, local, state and federal agencies with responsibilities related to population health improvement and hospital and public health associations should adopt policy positions that promote the development of collaborative partnerships involving hospitals, public health departments and other stakeholders focused on assessing and improving the health of the communities they serve.

The importance of community collaboration to address major health problems is apparent. In fact, we are beginning to understand that community resources and participation beyond the health sector itself are imperative if we are to be successful in achieving the goal of improving community health. Increasingly, we will depend on a number of community organizations, institutions and agencies if we are to improve the community's health. We have tried to outline some of our findings and observations about the ability to focus our community collective energy and achieve improved community health. We hope and anticipate that we have provided some lessons and observations as communities begin their journey to a health community, one with a "culture of health."

References

American Hospital Association. *Leadership Toolkit for Redesigning the H: Engaging Hospitals and Communities.* Chicago: American Hospital Association, 2015: 249.

Beitsch, LM, RG Brooks, JH Glasser and YD Coble Jr. "The Medicine and Public Health Initiative Ten Years Later." *American Journal of Preventative Medicine*, 29, no. 2 (Aug 2005): 149–153.

Berwick, DM, TW Nolan and J Whittington. "The Triple Aim: Care, Health, and Cost." *Health Affairs (Millwood)*, 27, no. 3 (May 2008): 759–769. doi: 10.1377/hlthaff.27.3.759.

Committee on the Cost of Medical Care. *Medical Care for the American People [Report No. 28].* Chicago: Chicago University Press, 1932.

County Health Rankings & Roadmaps, a Robert Wood Johnson Foundation program. "Our Approach." *Health Rankings.* Last modified 2015. http://www.countyhealthrankings.org/our-approach.

Greenleaf, RK and LC Spears. *The Power of Servant-Leadership.* San Francisco: Berrett-Kochler Publishers, 1998.

Health Research & Educational Trust. *Approaches to Population Health in 2015: A National Survey of Hospitals.* Chicago, IL: Health Research & Educational Trust, 2015. www.hpoe.org/pophealthsurvey.

Institute of Medicine. *To Err Is Human: Building a Safer Health System.* Washington, DC: The National Academies Press, 1999.

Institute of Medicine. *Crossing the Quality Chasm: A New Health System for the 21st Century.* Washington, DC: The National Academies Press, 2001.

Institute of Medicine. *Primary Care and Public Health: Exploring the Integration to Improve Population Health.* Washington, DC: The National Academies Press, 2012: 253–254.

Institute of Medicine. *Collaboration between Health Care and Public Health: Workshop Summary.* Washington, DC: The National Academies Press, 2015a: 256.

Institute of Medicine. *Vital Signs: Core Metrics for Health and Health Care Progress.* Washington, DC: The National Academies Press, 2015b.

Institute of Medicine (US) Committee on Assuring the Health of the Public in the 21st Century. *The Future of the Public's Health in the 21st Century.* Washington, DC: The National Academies Press, 2003: 251–252.

Mattessich, PW and EJ Rausch. "Cross-Sector Collaboration to Improve Community Health: A View of the Current Landscape." *Health Affairs (Millwood)*, 33, no. 11 (Nov 2014): 1968–1974.

Prybil, Larry, F. Douglas Scutchfield, Rex Killian, et al. *Improving Community Health through Hospital-Public Health Collaboration.* Lexington, KY: Commonwealth Center for Governance Studies, Inc., 2014. http://www.uky.edu/publichealth/hospital/collaboration.

Quesenberry, Preston. "Part III- Administrative, Procedural, and Miscellaneous: Notice and Request for Comments Regarding the Community Health Needs Assessment Requirements for Tax-exempt Hospitals." *Internal Revenue Service Office of the Division Counsel/Associate Chief Counsel.* 2011. https://www.irs.gov/pub/irs-drop/n-11-52.pdf.

Reiser, SJ. "Medicine and Public Health: Pursuing a Common Destiny." *Journal of the American Medical Association*, 276, no. 17 (6 Nov 1996): 1429–1430.

Robert Wood Johnson Foundation. *Collaboration to Build Healthier Communities: A Report for the Robert Wood Johnson Foundation Commission to Build a Healthier America.* Princeton: Robert Wood Johnson Foundation, 2013: 257–259.

Robert Wood Johnson Foundation. "From Vision to Action: A Framework and Measures to Mobilize a Culture of Health." *RWJF.* Last modified 2015. http://www.rwjf.org/content/dam/files/rwjf-webfiles/Research/2015/RWJF_From_Vision_to_Action_2015-FullReport.pdf.

Sharfstein, J. "The Strange Journey of Population Health." *The Milbank Quarterly*, 94, no. 640 (2014): 640–643.

Squires, David and Chloe Anderson. "U.S. Health Care from a Global Perspective: Spending, Use of Services, Prices, and Health in 13 Countries." *The Commonwealth Fund.* Oct 2015. http://www.commonwealthfund.org/publications/issue-briefs/2015/oct/us-health-care-from-a-global-perspective.

Starr, Paul. *The Social Transformation of American Medicine.* New York: Basic Books, 1982.

Starr, Paul. "What Happened to Health Care Reform?" *The American Prospect*, no. 20 (Winter 1995): 20–31.

Trust for America's Health. *A Healthier America 2013: Strategies to Move from Sick Care to Health Care in the Next Four Years.* Washington, DC: Trust for America's Health, 2013.

Weil, Alan R. "It Takes a Community." *Health Affairs*, 33, no. 11 (2014): 1886. doi: 10.1377/hlthaff.2014.1092.

Woolf, SH and LY Aron, eds. National Research Council and Institute of Medicine. *U.S. Health in International Perspective: Shorter Lives, Poorer Health.* Panel on Understanding Cross-National Health Differences among High-Income Countries. Committee on Population, Division of Behavioral and Social Sciences and Education, and Board on Population Health and Public Health Practice, Institute of Medicine. Washington, DC: National Academies Press, 2013a. http://sites.nationalacedmies.org/DBASSE/CPOP/US_Health_in_International_Perspective/index.htm.

Woolf, SH and LY Aron. "The US Health Disadvantage Relative to Other High-income Countries: Findings from a National Research Council/Institute of Medicine Report." *Journal of the American Medical Association*, 309, no. 8 (Feb 2013b): 771–772. doi: 10.1001/jama.2013.91.

26

THE ROLE OF DATA IN PRECISION POPULATION HEALTH

Brian C. Castrucci, Edward L. Hunter,
J. Lloyd Michener, Theresa Chapple-McGruder,
and Don Bradley

In the past fifty years, DNA sequencing, molecular genetic analysis, human genetic testing, and many other DNA-based techniques have led to the rise of precision medicine—the customization of medical treatment based on an individual patient's genetics or other molecular or cellular analysis—providing even more detailed and specific information to treat patients. We are just on the precipice of this new medical revolution, but it has already made significant inroads to medical practice. The FDA now recommends genetic testing to assist physicians in establishing dosage for Warfarin, a blood thinning drug. In the wake of Angelina Jolie's public double mastectomy, women are increasingly being tested for abnormalities in the so-called "breast cancer" genes (BRCA1 or BRCA2) and making proactive decisions to maintain their health before the disease appears. In his 2015 State of the Union, President Obama announced the creation of the Precision Medicine Initiative. Additional Federal funding is providing the research support to ensure that we capitalize on the potential benefits of molecular medicine.

However, whereas the information related to individual patients continues to grow and become more precise, the information available to the majority of state and local health departments has failed to keep pace. Clinical care only accounts for approximately 20 percent of health outcomes, whereas the other 80 percent (Booske, Athnes, Kindig, Park, & Remington, 2010)—the large majority of what makes us healthy, or unhealthy—is shaped by the social determinants of health—social and economic opportunities, access to quality education, the availability of safe workplaces that provide a living wage, and the cleanliness of our water, food, and air. Despite the clear, outsized impact that social determinants have on whether individuals are healthy or sick, there is a woeful lack of investment in the tools and information needed to improve community health.

Although we mapped the human genome, precise community health data that are geographically specific and timely are often unavailable to health planners and decision makers. Clinicians want as precise and targeted an intervention as possible and seek available diagnostic and treatment data to help inform their proposed treatment plan. But, when governmental public health leaders address community health risks, they are often left to implement non-specific, broad-brush interventions that may not be as effective or efficient as they could be.

If individuals can rightfully expect diagnosis and treatment tailored to their genetics, should there not be the same expectation for communities—data at the neighborhood level that are current and detailed enough for use in customizing interventions? State- or county-wide disease prevalence data may be available, but how can interventions be targeted when that is the only information available?

Just like the mapping of the human genome paved the way for precision medicine, the advent of electronic health records (EHRs) created the same opportunity to access disease data with the appropriate timeliness and geographic granularity needed to target specific neighborhoods that bear a disproportionate burden of disease. By aggregating these data and combining them with other data that provides context about the communities in which individuals reside, public health and community leaders would have the necessary information to achieve improvements in population health and more efficiently use resources. This is **precision population health**, and, without it, true gains in the health of the public will be challenging.

Increases in Chronic Disease Prevalence: Implications for Data

While control of communicable diseases—both longstanding and emerging—continues to be a national health priority (Armstrong, Conn, & Pinner, 1999; Baker et al., 2005; Beitsch, Brooks, Menachemi, & Libbey, 2006; Bell et al., 2004; Centers for Disease Control and Prevention (CDC), 1999; Citron, 1984; McCaig & Hughes, 1995; Mead et al., 1999; Morens, Folkers, & Fauci, 2004), the increased prevalence of chronic disease presents challenges for local health departments (Frieden, 2004; Frieden, Bassett, Thorpe, & Farley, 2008; McCord, 2005; Mokdad et al., 1999; Plescia, Young, & Ritzman, 2005; Stamatakis et al., 2012; Steinbrook, 2006). Chronic disease accounted for four times the proportion of all U.S. deaths in 2000 compared with those in 1900 (Mokdad, Marks, Stroup, & Gerberding, 2004). The top three causes of death in 1900—pneumonia, tuberculosis, and diarrhea/enteritis—were replaced a century later by heart disease, cancer, and stroke (Centers for Disease Control and Prevention (CDC), 1999; Novick, Morrow, & Mays, 2007). As disease prevalence changed, so did the flow of surveillance data.

By 1901, all states required notification of select communicable diseases to local health authorities (Chorba, Berkelman, Safford, Gibbs, & Hull, 1990). The local health authority receives the report, conducts an investigation, and confirms the case before reporting to the state. The state aggregates data across local jurisdictions and reports to the Centers for Disease Control and Prevention (CDC). In some states, the reporting is directly to the state health department, but local detail is still necessary to conduct an investigation into the source and spread of the disease, and to perform public health functions such as partner notification or addressing the source of a food-borne outbreak. This local-level detail is used to monitor disease trends in communities, and individuals with reported diseases receive specific follow-up to ensure appropriate treatment. Health departments provide counseling and partner notification services, as well as diagnostic testing and prophylactic therapy for contacts of individuals with infectious diseases.

As chronic diseases increased in prevalence, laboratory reporting and reportable conditions were less important as the role of personal behaviors in chronic diseases became more widely recognized. Surveillance shifted to large, representative sample surveys to provide data for targeting resources to reduce behavioral risks and their consequent illnesses—such as the Behavioral Risk Factor Surveillance Survey (BRFSS; piloted in 1981, initiated nationally in 1993), the Youth Risk Behavior Survey (initiated in 1991), the Pregnancy Risk Assessment and Monitoring System (initiated in 1988), and the National Health and Nutrition Examination Survey (NHANES; first conducted in 1971, conducted continuously since 1999). Because of their costs, these surveys lack the sample sizes needed to provide estimates below the county level—and in most cases, are limited to the state or even national levels. Health officials do not get data from neighborhoods, census tracts, block groups, or other common sub-city geographic jurisdictions (Centers for Disease Control and Prevention, 2014; Institute of Medicine (US) Committee on Public Health Strategies to Improve Health, 2011; Simon, Wold, Cousineau, & Fielding, 2001). States and even some cities have implemented corresponding efforts to collect estimates of disease prevalence and correlates below the county level (Hughes et al., 2006; Institute of Medicine (US) Committee on Public Health Strategies to Improve Health, 2011), but few mechanisms were developed that had the geographic precision and clinical accuracy necessary to monitor chronic conditions at the local level (Novick et al., 2007; Thacker, 2000; Thacker & Berkelman, 1988).

The impact of these changes in disease patterns and their subsequent impact on data collection and analysis can be understood on a matrix of timeliness and geographic specificity (Figure 26.1).

In a communicable disease context, health departments used current and address-level data (cell 3 in Figure 26.1) to study, understand, and address problems controlling a limited number of communicable diseases. Public health departments were able to address problems effectively because they had the right information available to them (Novick et al., 2007). Timely local data are still the core ingredients to address to public (population) health problems, but as the disease burden changes and the data collection methods change, so do the data. Today, available chronic disease data lack the precision to identify health

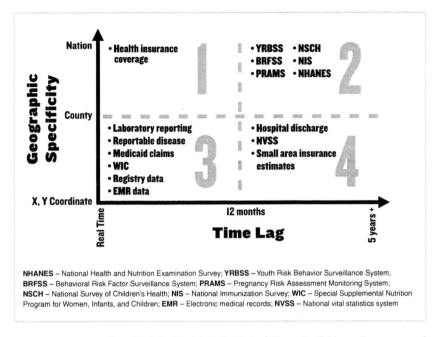

NHANES – National Health and Nutrition Examination Survey; **YRBSS** – Youth Risk Behavior Surveillance System;
BRFSS – Behavioral Risk Factor Surveillance System; **PRAMS** – Pregnancy Risk Assessment Monitoring System;
NSCH – National Survey of Children's Health; **NIS** – National Immunization Survey; **WIC** – Special Supplemental Nutrition
Program for Women, Infants, and Children; **EMR** – Electronic medical records; **NVSS** – National vital statistics system

FIGURE 26.1 Examples of Public Health and Clinical Data Available to Governmental Public Health Agencies by Time and Geography

problems at census tract, neighborhood, or even zip code levels; to provide the necessary evidence base to support programmatic and policy solutions; or to measure the impact of interventions. Chronic disease data are rarely below the county level and often take years to be collated and released, diminishing their potential benefit to strategic planning (cell 2 in Figure 26.1). Even when data are available at an address level, as is the situation with mortality data, the delay in their availability and lack of investment in geocoding drastically limits their impact and places LHDs in the position of implementing solutions today for problems documented more than a year ago (cell 4 in Figure 26.1). Thus, public health leaders have lost much of their ability to accurately monitor the most critical elements in the health status of their communities (Remington, Brownson, & Wegner, 2010; Thacker, 2000).

Whereas disease data are important, without contextualizing data that can measure the socio-economic and environmental factors potentially impacting disease prevalence, the opportunities to implement interventions, improve the environment, and reduce disease burden are limited. However, like disease data, these contextualizing data must also be geographically specific and timely enough to inform planning and decision making. They include public safety/crime data; licensure data; parks and other public facilities locations; businesses such as alcohol sales outlets, farmers' markets, and other business locations that may impact health;

proportion of students receiving free and reduced cost school lunch; and tobacco sales. For example, using census tract data, the Washington State Department of Health was able to assign a lead poisoning risk score to each census tract throughout the United States, information that could be used to target prevention, screening, and community-based lead mitigation interventions (Frostenson & Kliff, 2016).

The Critical Role for Data in Policymaking

Public health interventions for communicable diseases focused on case finding—targeting resources at individuals or groups who are suspected of having or being at risk for a particular disease, and then directing program interventions towards them. The emergence of chronic diseases has shifted attention from treatment to policy solutions, using law, regulation, administrative mechanisms, and legislation to protect communities and establish conditions that can improve health. Scientific evidence and sound data along with social infrastructure and political will are critical to achieving public policy (Richmond & Kotelchuck, 1991, 1993). Data can help identify problems, craft policies that reach their intended targets (and avoid unintended consequences), understand distributional impacts (i.e., winners and losers), and build the case for policy adoption, implementation, and adaptation (Feder & Levitt, 2005).

Issues of timeliness and geographic specificity are as relevant to support effective policy as is the management of programs and the implementation of interventions. Specific data considerations for policy development include:

- **Real time.** Elected officials and other policymakers work on shorter timeframes than many in public health. To make the case that they should invest funding or political capital in a policy intervention, current data are important because they highlight the immediacy of the problem being addressed, and offer the prospect that there will be data to show success within the elected official's tenure in office.
- **Geographically specific.** Elected officials represent specific constituencies, and the frequently used phrase "all politics is local" is relevant to public health. Policymakers desire information that is specific to their jurisdiction, and that compares their jurisdiction to others like theirs. This includes a desire for specificity *within* the jurisdiction, so that resources and interventions can be micro-targeted and subsequently more effective.
- **Illuminating of patterns of impact.** The ability to build coalitions needed to implement policies requires an understanding of those who will benefit, as well as who will bear the cost of an intervention. Data help to assess benefactors and beneficiaries (winners and losers), clarify potential inequitable or unintended impacts, and empower constituents to align interests in policy change.

The Power of Narrative in Policymaking

Whereas policy-relevant data bring a level of credibility to an argument, personal narratives can bring to life the need for and impact of policy changes. Take, for example, this account from a former Massachusetts legislator:

> I was a legislator in the Massachusetts House of Representatives arguing against deregulation and market-based health care as a means of controlling health costs. I carried a nine-inch pile of evidence everywhere—to hearings, press conferences, meetings, and floor debate. Half the pile was made up of empirical, peer-reviewed studies demonstrating the efficacy of state-run hospital rate setting programs. The other half consisted of peer-reviewed studies failing to identify improvements in cost or access from managed care. By contrast, deregulation advocates—corporate benefit managers, insurance and hospital executives, and union welfare fund trustees—had no empirical evidence to support their case. . . . My adversaries spoke from the real world, telling anecdotes describing their actual experiences in controlling costs by becoming active, aggressive purchasers of health care. In the end, their perspective mattered more than the reams of scientific evidence I brought to the debate.
>
> *(McDonough, 2001, p. 8)*

Data alone may not persuade policymakers of the need for governmental intervention, but the addition of personal narrative can illuminate the actions causing a problem and subsequent personal suffering leading to action (Stone, 1989). When policy debates are based in philosophical or values-based differences, the impact of data may also be limited (McDonough, 2001). In these situations, each side may present a compelling statistic or fact that could persuade an opponent, but such information is rarely found persuasive as ideological position trumps empirical evidence (McDonough, 2001). This suggests that policy change is more likely achieved when policy-relevant data are paired with a compelling personal narrative.

Electronic Health Records and Their Public Health Potential

Between 2008 and 2013, Federally-funded incentives have contributed to a five-fold increase in at least basic EHR adoption from 2008 to 2013 (Charles, Gabriel, & Furukawa, 2014). This relatively recent expansion of health information technology has presented new opportunities for the systematic collection and analysis of large-scale healthcare data that inform public health practice (Diamond, Mostashari, & Shirky, 2009). An opportunity exists to leverage the national investment in the EHR infrastructure to enable public health officials to gain access to chronic disease data that are timelier and more geographically granular (cell 3, Figure 26.1) than the data currently available (cell 2, Figure 26.1). The promise of EHRs, however, has yet to be recognized, although progress is being made (Adler & Stead, 2015).

Leveraging Existing Public Data on Economic and Social Factors Affecting Health

Similarly, more administrative data that can measure the social and economic determinants of health are being digitally captured, making these data more readily available. In some cases, these data are collected for the purpose of informing planning and policymaking (e.g., the Bureau of the Census' American Community Survey); in other cases they are compiled as the byproduct of delivery of public services (e.g., law enforcement; administration of food assistance programs). As community health planners increasingly focus on "upstream" social determinants, these data can be important in understanding the patterns of associated health risks, and targeting of interventions, and hold significant promise as an element in "precision public health." Examples include public park location and safety; crime statistics, revealing patterns and geographic hot spots of violence; emergency medical system responses that identify patterns of falls by seniors, or distribution of cases of drug overdose; alcohol sales outlets or other zoning-related patterns to impute alcohol use; housing stock age, lead-lined water pipe locations that relate to risk for lead exposure to children; farmers' market locations and grocery store locations that identify healthy food availability.

The "data liberation" movement has gained attention as a way to make geographically specific data from these public sources more readily available for multiple purposes (Bjarnadottir et al., 2015). Beginning with the U.S. Department of Health and Human Services' Health Data Initiative, Federal efforts have grown to include mandates that all Federal agencies make detailed microdata available in formats readily accessible for development of applications. Some states and local jurisdictions have followed this model (Choucair, Bhatt, & Mansour, 2015), and have begun to use their own internal data sources in a more integrated way. This movement has the potential for making more integrated neighborhood-level data on key health-related variables available to both clinicians and health agencies for the improvement of the health of their targeted populations.

The Importance of Data Flow: A Two-Way Street

Data and data sharing are the foundation for improvements in population health and for public health and healthcare setting goals together. The first step is to use whatever data are available to identify population health concerns. What troubling patterns exist that raise concerns? Has there been an increase in a specific chronic disease over the past few years, or the number of preterm deliveries in a specific geographic area? Does the pattern of flu cases among older adults suggest steps to improve preparedness for the next season?

When establishing partnerships and first examining data, it is important to understand data broadly. Whereas a wide variety of data can be used to establish a partnership, achieving, measuring, evaluating, and monitoring improvements

FIGURE 26.2 Data Flow

in population health will require an improved, mutually beneficial data flow, especially between primary care and public health in order to improve the lives of community members (Figure 26.2). The growing availability of data in electronic formats suggests that population health improvement efforts can be strengthened through expanded cooperation and partnership between public health and healthcare. From the healthcare side, clinical case data generated by medical care encounters need to be aggregated within and between medical practices to yield population-level estimates. From the public health side, useful data can be derived from state and nationally published healthcare encounter data: such as hospital discharge data and all payer claims databases, and numerous public health program-specific surveillance and service delivery datasets covering infectious and chronic diseases and injury, environmental, and maternal and child health services. At the same time, community agencies can play a role in compiling non-health data on the social, environmental, and economic context in which patients live (for example, from public sources described above), and making those data available in ways relevant to healthcare practitioners. Improving community health begins with better utilization and understanding of these data, and that begins with a commitment to sharing information.

Primary Care Data to Public Health

Medical records contain a wealth of health data, but unlocking that information has historically been time and cost intensive. The implementation of EHRs digitized this once previously inaccessible source of information and created an opportunity to monitor trends within a medical practice. Now hospital administrators, payers, and researchers can relatively quickly and easily track a practice's adherence to recommended disease management guidelines and collaborate with public health practitioners by sharing their analyses of patient data to contribute to population-based, geographically specific estimates of disease burden.

From a population health perspective, clinical data can be used to understand the geographic distribution of individuals with various diagnoses and conditions across the community. These data are relatively real-time (when accessible) and provide more geographically specific and timely information on chronic diseases than is available via typical public health surveillance datasets, such as BRFSS or NHANES. Near real-time analysis of clinical data can refine and focus community-level interventions, ultimately leading to targeted public health interventions to reduce the prevalence and severity of disease, cost, and burden on the healthcare system.

Whereas EHRs represent a potential yet largely untapped opportunity for public health practitioners, they have limitations:

- Ensuring patient privacy when sharing these data
- Clinical data excludes those who do not access healthcare
- EHR data are fragmented across different practices
- Medical records from a single practice, hospital, or even health system don't necessarily encompass a complete longitudinal patient record
- Electronic health record systems are not readily interoperable or interconnected
- Data are often collected using different inclusion/exclusion criteria and definitions
- Data may be recorded in multiple locations in the same system, making aggregation of comparable data within systems a challenge, and across systems extremely difficult

Public Health to Healthcare

With increased acceptance that individual health and community health are inextricably linked (Koh & Tavenner, 2012), lacking information about the communities in which patients reside, clinicians are only using a small portion of the information available. Information on housing quality, crime statistics, child welfare, food security, and environmental risks could all be made more readily available to clinicians to provide them with a more complete understanding of the whole patient in the context of her/his family, neighborhood, and community. For example, it would be clinically beneficial to know that a patient with a respiratory condition is living in an apartment whose owner is listed on the city's negligent landlord list. The drive to collect as much medical information before making a diagnosis and plan should be equally applied to the need for adequate social and environmental information. Whereas collecting this type of information remains beyond the scope of clinical practice, it is now central to achieving desired health outcomes.

Public health departments have the data resources and expertise to combine a variety of publicly financed data sources (e.g., census, reports of child abuse and/ or neglect, vital records) with de-identified data from clinical care and place these data into formats (like application program interface (API)) that can be readily accessed through the systems of multiple partners. These resources would allow for simultaneous visualization of social and health information, which could inform clinical interventions, urban planning and land use, community development planning, and policy agendas. Information could also be made available to nonprofit hospitals within the community to include in their Internal Revenue Service-required Community Health Needs Assessment.

An example of this type of activity is found in the Cleveland, Ohio, BUILD Health Challenge site. The BUILD Health Challenge supports "bold, upstream, integrated, local, and data-driven" (BUILD) community health interventions in low-income, urban neighborhoods by stimulating and strengthening partnerships among nonprofit organizations, hospitals, healthcare systems, and local health departments to improve community health and well-being. Cleveland's BUILD site uses data from multiple sectors to contextualize neighborhoods and target homes that may have environmental hazards that negatively impact health. The current data system, Neighborhood Stabilization Tracker (NST), has been in place for over ten years. It is funded by Case Western Reserve health system and contains HUD, building code enforcement (e.g., mold, mildew, and vermin violations), census tract data, and other local regulatory data. The NST data are geocoded and sent to the public health department, and de-identified geocoded data on elevated blood lead levels is added. These data are then sent to the healthcare system Med Health, and they overlay real-time data from ER and ambulatory visits where the primary diagnosis is asthma, COPD-related, or lead toxicity. Data are aggregated and the community partners are given a list of addresses where a member of the household has either elevated blood lead levels, asthma, or COPD, and the house has been flagged by the NST database as having at least one building code violation within the last five years. Community organizers conduct a home visit and identify and then remediate environmental hazards in the home.

Another role for the public health department is to aggregate data. Data collected by any one individual institution is reflective of those who use that system, which may be inadequate to understand the health of a particular community. For example, an analysis of the Chesapeake Regional Health Information System for Our Patients, Maryland's Health Information Exchange, found that for more than half of all frequent visitors to emergency departments (ED) no single hospital had a full picture of a given patient's care (Horrocks, Kinzer, Afzal, Alpern, & Sharfstein, 2016). Hospital-specific analyses alone would have failed to identify 40 percent of frequent ED utilizers (Horrocks et al., 2016). It is in the best interest of the hospital and the community to have more complete, cross-institution data to inform community health planning; however, institutions are reluctant to share "proprietary" information with their competitors. Public health can serve as a third-party, neutral aggregator of data among institutions, allowing each to have more complete information without jeopardizing proprietary information or market position.

The Community: The Center of the Circle

Whereas the information flow between healthcare systems and public health is critical to achieving improved population (and individual) health, sharing those data with key partners and advocates in the community is equally important. The best interpreters of data are those from whom the data has been collected. These stakeholders may recognize patterns and causal factors that are not obvious to those not living in the community. In addition, community constituents can mitigate community concerns regarding the collection, analysis, and/or inappropriate use of data collected. Data showing high rates of obesity in a neighborhood may be due to a variety of possible causes, including a lack of residents participating in recommended levels of activity. A clinical practitioner might be tempted to prescribe increased walking, but a member of the neighborhood may well point out that the neighborhood lacks sidewalks, functioning street lights, and that the neighborhood is not a safe place to walk. Enhanced understanding among community leaders of the information and the patterns and potential inequities it identifies could lead to improved advocacy and activism to change neighborhoods and the systems that contribute to these patterns. Using data to engage the community is a powerful strategy to mobilize a necessary partner in the effort to improve population health. A key challenge is that many community organizations and advocates lack the capacity for sophisticated data management— pointing to the importance of efforts by public health agencies to make data available in easy to visualize and use formats.

Making It Happen: Forging Data Sharing Agreements and the Role of the Data Diplomat

The *use* of data across sectors also presents challenges. Protecting patient privacy is a pre-eminent concern, and discussions about sharing patient information is often hampered by real and perceived statutory and regulatory limits on sharing personal health information for public health purposes. In addition, there may be concerns that aggregated data may reveal clinical practice patterns that could, if known by competitors, lead to negative impact on the practice or financial situation of a healthcare provider. Many public health agencies that partner with clinical providers to address community health issues may also have regulatory authority over those who would provide data, and healthcare practitioners and organizations may fear misinterpretation of fully transparent raw data. Similarly, sharing of detailed data may reveal protected information or practice patterns that trigger political or policy debate.

Most of these concerns can be addressed through a carefully crafted data sharing agreement—the domain of "data diplomats" who can shape partnerships based on mutual interests. Data diplomats can:

- Identify solutions to privacy issues that allow data to be shared at a level of detail that is simultaneously useful, safe, and legal
- Create or cultivate trusted third-party institutions, if needed, to serve as intermediaries or repositories for data—serving, in effect, as safe houses for creating data that can be shared or combined with other sources
- Negotiate the value and use of data with all stakeholders, including the healthcare organization that is being asked to share the data; for example, making clear to a healthcare system how clinical data will be used for constructive public purposes, and how this data combined with other public data resources can help the healthcare system more effectively plan and deliver patient care
- Develop use agreements that provide for significant public health uses of shared data, but don't infringe on the proprietary or policy interests of the source of the data
- Forge agreements on the use of common definitions/standards/vendors where this helps facilitate collaboration

Despite these challenges, the widespread use of EHRs represents great potential as a bridge to improve collaboration between public health and healthcare. In order for robust data exchange, analysis, and use to be possible, however, both sectors need to develop a trusting, collaborative relationship to realize the promise held in these data repositories.

Obesity: The Data Divide Poster Child

Our nation's struggle with obesity provides an excellent example of the data divide that exists in the United States. Obesity surveillance has been primarily conducted through large surveys such as BRFSS, NHANES, the National Survey of Children's Health, and the Youth Risk Behavior Surveillance System. These survey-based obesity data do not have the precision to identify health problems at the census tract, neighborhood, or even zip code levels; provide the necessary evidence base to support programmatic and policy solutions; or measure the impact of local interventions. Some states have attempted to collect obesity data through state-mandated data collection through schools. Whereas school-based data collection overcomes some challenges, data are often limited to only specific grades or populations, the data collected may only be available in aggregate at the school level, and access limited by the Family Educational

Rights and Privacy Act (FERPA) (Longjohn, Sheon, Card-Higginson, Nader, & Mason, 2010).

Whereas population-level obesity data offer a longitudinal view of the obesity epidemic, they have a significant time lag and only reflect large geographic areas. The granular history of the obesity epidemic has been captured and stored in medical records. Data on height and weight, the components used to calculate body mass index, are collected during many medical encounters. If these data could be made accessible, it would provide the specific and timely disease-relevant data needed to develop precise, targeted interventions and to track the impact of community-level as well as clinical interventions. Public health practitioners would benefit from detailed information to evaluate community health and develop targeted health policy. Clinicians would benefit from better information regarding social determinants of health—housing, transportation, available parks, and food security for their patients. Public health-generated, neighborhood-based information provides information to clinicians that they may not otherwise have available to them.

The American Medical Association recognized obesity as a disease in 2013 (Pollack, 2013). In addressing obesity, clinicians confront a condition—obesity—for which social and environmental factors play at least as important a role, and for which there are few effective clinical remedies while working in a system that calls for them to achieve positive outcomes to problems that originate far beyond their reach. This amplifies the need for primary care practitioners to partner with public health practitioners who are skilled in influencing the spectrum of social determinants of health.

The personal and economic costs of the obesity epidemic are staggering. Costs associated with obesity have been estimated to approach $300B, with more than $200B in medical costs and another $66B in indirect costs (Spieker & Pyzocha, 2016). Fortunately, there are signs of progress on ensuring that the appropriate information is available for public health practitioners and clinicians to reverse the curve on obesity. In Denver, Colorado, and San Diego, California, building on the reportable disease model, pilot projects are under way to provide height and weight data to the local public health authority (Kranz, Browner, McDermid, Coleman, & Wooten, 2015; Tabano et al., 2015). In Washington, DC, a pediatrician leader worked with the local public health authority and the National Park Service to incorporate information about available parks and recreation options directly into the EHR, providing patients with detailed information to help them access the parks nearest to them based on distance and public transportation availability (Stead Sellers, 2015). In the past, clinical treatment alone has been unable to prevent or stem the obesity epidemic. Going forward, projects like these and others make good on the promise of gathering, analyzing, and mobilizing the information available to promote healthier behaviors and reduce the burden of obesity and the yet unknown challenges in the future.

All Available Data Are Needed to Address Population Health

Our communities face complex health challenges. Historically, the top causes of morbidity and mortality were the result of communicable diseases—viruses and bacteria. Today, our most pressing health issues are the result of complex, inter-related social and environmental factors that interact in equally complex and sometimes unpredictable, seemingly irrational ways with our genes, medical history, and lifestyle choices. If one's zip code has as much, if not more, impact on health and longevity as genetic code (Weintraub, 2014), then information that supports decision making that equally and simultaneously allows access to disease and geographic data will be needed to improve population health. To improve popula-tion health, public health agencies, clinical care providers, and others who have data on critical social factors in communities need to work together to build data resources that can plan, execute, and evaluate precision interventions.

References

Adler, N. E., & Stead, W. W. (2015). Patients in context—EHR capture of social and behavioral determinants of health. *The New England Journal of Medicine, 372*(8), 698–701. doi:10.1056/NEJMp1413945 [doi]

Armstrong, G. L., Conn, L. A., & Pinner, R. W. (1999). Trends in infectious disease mortal-ity in the United States during the 20th century. *The Journal of the American Medical Association, 281*(1), 61–66. doi:joc80862 [pii]

Baker, E. L., Potter, M. A., Jones, D. L., Mercer, S. L., Cioffi, J. P., Green, L. W., . . . Fleming, D. W. (2005). The public health infrastructure and our nation's health. *Annual Review of Public Health, 26*, 303–318. doi:10.1146/annurev.publhealth.26.021304.144647 [doi]

Beitsch, L. M., Brooks, R. G., Menachemi, N., & Libbey, P.M. (2006). Public health at center stage: New roles, old props. *Health Affairs (Project Hope), 25*(4), 911–922. doi:25/4/911 [pii]

Bell, J. A., Hyland, S., DePellegrin, T., Upshur, R. E., Bernstein, M., & Martin, D. K. (2004). SARS and hospital priority setting: A qualitative case study and evaluation. *BMC Health Services Research, 4*(1), 36. doi:1472–6963–4–36 [pii]

Bjarnadottir, M. V., Agarwal, R., Crowley, K., Jin, Q., Barnes, S., & Prasad, K. (2015). Improving decision-making using health data analytics. In K. Marconi & H. Lehmann (Eds.), *Big data and health analytics* (p. 288). Boca Raton, FL: CRC Press.

Booske, B.C., Athnes, J. K., Kindig, D. A., Park, H., & Remington, P. L. (2010). *Different perspectives for assigning weights to determinants of health*. Madison, WI: Population Health Institute, University of Wisconsin.

The BUILD Health Challenge. (2016). Our mission. Retrieved from http://buildhealthchallenge. org/our-mission/

Centers for Disease Control and Prevention (CDC). (1999). Control of infectious diseases. *Morbidity and Mortality Weekly Report, 48*(29), 621–629.

Centers for Disease Control and Prevention (CDC). (2014). Brfss. Retrieved from http:// www.cdc.gov/brfss/about/about_brfss.htm

Charles, D., Gabriel, M., & Furukawa, M. (2014). *Adoption of electronic health record systems among U.S. non-federal acute care hospitals: 2008–2013*. (No. ONC Data Brief 16).

Washington, DC: Office of the National Coordinator for Health Information Technology.

Chorba, T. L., Berkelman, R. L., Safford, S. K., Gibbs, N. P., & Hull, H. F. (1990). Mandatory reporting of infectious diseases by clinicians. *Recommendations and Reports: Morbidity and Mortality Weekly Report. Recommendations and Reports / Centers for Disease Control, 39*(RR-9), 1–17.

Choucair, B., Bhatt, J., & Mansour, R. (2015). A bright future: Innovation transforming public health in Chicago. *Journal of Public Health Management and Practice: JPHMP, 21*(Suppl 1), S49–55. doi:10.1097/PHH.0000000000000140 [doi]

Citron, K. M. (1984). Trends in tuberculosis. *Postgraduate Medical Journal, 60*(701), 187–193.

Diamond, C. C., Mostashari, F., & Shirky, C. (2009). Collecting and sharing data for population health: A new paradigm. *Health Affairs (Project Hope), 28*(2), 454–466. doi:10.1377/hlthaff.28.2.454 [doi]

Feder, J., & Levitt, L. (2005). Why truth matters: The role of health statistics in health policy. In D. J. Friedman, E. L. Hunter & R. G. Parrish (Eds.), *Health statistics: Shaping policy and practice to improve the population's health* (p. 278). New York, NY: Oxford University Press.

Frieden, T. R. (2004). Asleep at the switch: Local public health and chronic disease. *American Journal of Public Health, 94*(12), 2059–2061. doi:94/12/2059 [pii]

Frieden, T. R., Bassett, M. T., Thorpe, L. E., & Farley, T. A. (2008). Public health in New York City, 2002–2007: Confronting epidemics of the modern era. *International Journal of Epidemiology, 37*(5), 966–977. doi:10.1093/ije/dyn108 [doi]

Frostenson, S., & Kliff, S. (2016). The risk of lead poisoning isn't just in Flint. So we mapped the risk in every neighborhood in America. Retrieved from http://www.vox.com/a/lead-exposure-risk-map

Horrocks, D., Kinzer, D., Afzal, S., Alpern, J., & Sharfstein, J. M. (2016). The adequacy of individual hospital data to identify high utilizers and assess community health. *The Journal of the American Medical Association Internal Medicine, 176*, 856–858. doi:10.1001/jamainternmed.2016.1248 [doi]

Hughes, E., McCracken, M., Roberts, H., Mokdad, A. H., Valluru, B., Goodson, R., . . . Jiles, R. (2006). Surveillance for certain health behaviors among states and selected local areas—behavioral risk factor surveillance system, United States, 2004. *Morbidity and Mortality Weekly Report: Surveillance Summaries (Washington, DC: 2002), 55*(7), 1–124. doi:ss5507a1 [pii]

Institute of Medicine (US) Committee on Public Health Strategies to Improve Health. (2011). doi:NBK209716 [bookaccession]

Koh, H. K., & Tavenner, M. (2012). Connecting care through the clinic and community for a healthier America. *American Journal of Preventive Medicine, 42*(6 Suppl 2), S92–4. doi:10.1016/j.amepre.2012.04.002 [doi]

Kranz, A. M., Browner, D. K., McDermid, L., Coleman, T. R., & Wooten, W. J. (2015). Mapping EHR data to examine neighborhood-level variation in obesity rates in San Diego. Retrieved from https://cste.confex.com/cste/2015/webprogram/Paper4380.html

Longjohn, M., Sheon, A. R., Card-Higginson, P., Nader, P. R., & Mason, M. (2010). Learning from state surveillance of childhood obesity. *Health Affairs (Project Hope), 29*(3), 463–472. doi:10.1377/hlthaff.2009.0733 [doi]

McCaig, L. F., & Hughes, J. M. (1995). Trends in antimicrobial drug prescribing among office-based physicians in the United States. *The Journal of the American Medical Association, 273*(3), 214–219.

McCord, C. (2005). What's needed to fight chronic disease. *American Journal of Public Health, 95*(6), 930–931; author reply 931–932. doi:95/6/930-a [pii]

McDonough, J. E. (2001). Using and misusing anecdote in policy making. *Health Affairs (Project Hope), 20*(1), 207–212.

Mead, P. S., Slutsker, L., Dietz, V., McCaig, L. F., Bresee, J. S., Shapiro, C., . . . Tauxe, R. V. (1999). Food-related illness and death in the United States. *Emerging Infectious Diseases, 5*(5), 607–625. doi:10.3201/eid0505.990502 [doi]

Mokdad, A. H., Marks, J. S., Stroup, D. F., & Gerberding, J. L. (2004). Actual causes of death in the United States, 2000. *The Journal of the American Medical Association, 291*(10), 1238–1245. doi:10.1001/jama.291.10.1238 [doi]

Mokdad, A. H., Serdula, M. K., Dietz, W. H., Bowman, B. A., Marks, J. S., & Koplan, J. P. (1999). The spread of the obesity epidemic in the United States, 1991–1998. *The Journal of the American Medical Association, 282*(16), 1519–1522. doi:joc91119 [pii]

Morens, D. M., Folkers, G. K., & Fauci, A. S. (2004). The challenge of emerging and re-emerging infectious diseases. *Nature, 430*(6996), 242–249. doi:10.1038/nature02759 [doi]

Novick, L. F., Morrow, C. B., & Mays, G. P. (2007). *Public health administration: Principles for population-based management.* Burlington, MA: Jones & Bartlett Publishers.

Plescia, M., Young, S., & Ritzman, R. L. (2005). Statewide community-based health promotion: A North Carolina model to build local capacity for chronic disease prevention. *Preventing Chronic Disease, 2 Spec no*, A10. doi:A10 [pii]

Pollack, A. (2013, June 19). A.M.A. recognizes obesity as a disease. *The New York Times*, pp. B1.

Remington, P., Brownson, R. C., & Wegner, M. V. (2010). *Chronic disease epidemiology and control.* Washington, DC: American Public Health Association.

Richmond, J. B., & Kotelchuck, M. (1991). Co-ordination and development of strategies and policy for public health promotion in the United States. In W. W. Holland, R. Detels & G. Knox (Eds.), *Oxford textbook of public health* (pp. 441–454). Oxford, UK: Oxford Medical Publications.

Richmond, J. B., & Kotelchuck, M. (1993). Political influences: Rethinking national health policy. In C. Mcquire, R. Foley, A. Gorr & R. Richards (Eds.), *Handbook of health professionals education* (pp. 386–404). San Francisco, CA: Jossey-Bass Publishers.

Simon, P. A., Wold, C. M., Cousineau, M. R., & Fielding, J. E. (2001). Meeting the data needs of a local health department: The Los Angeles county health survey. *American Journal of Public Health, 91*(12), 1950–1952.

Spieker, E. A., & Pyzocha, N. (2016). Economic impact of obesity. *Primary Care, 43*(1), 83–95. doi:10.1016/j.pop.2015.08.013 [doi]

Stamatakis, K. A., Leatherdale, S. T., Marx, C. M., Yan, Y., Colditz, G. A., & Brownson, R. C. (2012). Where is obesity prevention on the map?: Distribution and predictors of local health department prevention activities in relation to county-level obesity prevalence in the United States. *Journal of Public Health Management and Practice: JPHMP, 18*(5), 402–411. doi:10.1097/PHH.0b013e318221718c [doi]

Stead Sellers, F. (2015, May 28). D.C. doctor's rx: A stroll in the park instead of a trip to the pharmacy. *The Washington Post.* Retrieved from https://www.washingtonpost.com/national/health-science/why-one-dc-doctor-is-prescribing-walks-in-the-park-instead-of-pills/2015/05/28/03a54004-fb45-11e4-9ef4-1bb7ce3b3fb7_story.html?utm_term=.cb8b4c55e3e2U

Steinbrook, R. (2006). Facing the diabetes epidemic—mandatory reporting of glycosylated hemoglobin values in New York City. *The New England Journal of Medicine, 354*(6), 545–548. doi:354/6/545 [pii]

Stone, D. A. (1989). Causal stories and the formation of policy agendas. *Political Science Quarterly, 104*(2), 281–300.

Tabano, D., Barrow, J., McCormick, E., Bol, K., Anthamatten, P., Thomas, D., & Daley, M. (2015). PS2–20: Obesity mapping in Colorado: A novel system for monitoring and tracking BMI. *Clinical Medicine & Research, 12*(1–2), 83.

Thacker, S. B. (2000). Historical development. In L. M. Lee, S. M. Teutsch, S. B. Thacker & M. E. St. Louis (Eds.), *Principles and practice of public health surveillance* (2nd ed., pp. 1–15). New York, NY: Oxford University Press.

Thacker, S. B., & Berkelman, R. L. (1988). Public health surveillance in the United States. *Epidemiologic Reviews, 10*, 164–190.

Weintraub, K. (2014, May 1). CDC: Lifespan more to do with geography than genetics. *USA Today.* Retrieved from http://www.usatoday.com/story/news/nation/2014/05/01/preventable-deaths-cdc/8570951/

27

SOLVE POPULATION HEALTH ISSUES THROUGH COLLABORATION

The IDEA Model

Sonja Armbruster and John W. Moran

This chapter is designed to provide quality improvement tools to the Community Chief Health Strategist and the Community Health Improvement Team to help them successful identify, decide, execute, and assess community-wide population health improvement. The **I.D.E.A.** model provides the framework and tools to **I**dentify the community health issue, **D**ecide where to focus (prioritize), **E**xecute the project plan to make the improvement, and **A**ssess the process improvement to see if it achieved the outcome desired. Additional Quality Improvement Tools are available in the Public Health Quality Improvement Encyclopedia[1] and the PHF website.[2]

Tools for the Job

> *The first time Sonja hosted a barbecue for her parents and extended family, her mother came early to assist with meal preparations. As they prepared chicken and fresh road-side-stand corn-on-the-cob for the grill, her mom asked for the tongs. She had one pair and shared. Her mom was quietly frustrated that Sonja would use the same instrument for vegetables and chicken, and when it was time for tossing salad, the serving spoon and fork again came up short. Where were the salad tongs? After the meal it was time to clean up, and washing dishes was a family event. When asked for the drying towels, Sonja offered the terry kitchen towels in the drawer. A few months later, Sonja's birthday present included eight different pairs of tongs of varying sizes and materials as well as flour sack tea towels (which are the best for drying dishes). Prominent American psychologist Abraham Maslow, well-remembered for his hierarchy of needs, is also credited with having stated in his book* The Psychology of Science: *"I suppose it is tempting, if the only tool you have is a hammer, to treat everything as if it were a nail." Having the right tools for the job is essential whether you are in the kitchen, the garage, the sporting field, or leading population health improvement.*

FIGURE 27.1 IDEA Model

The IDEA Model, as seen in Figure 27.1, provides a framework for making progress by organizing and categorizing tools in such a way that they can be accessed and used when they are appropriate to the challenges at hand. Models are developed to provide a framework that enables action on appropriate policy, systems, and environmental solutions. Strategic, thoughtful progress that mobilizes partners across sectors to improve population health requires the ability to *identify* population health issues, *decide on solutions*, *execute* a plan for improvement, and *assess* the impact. In short, Community Chief Health Strategists (CHS) are the IDEA people for the community.

The IDEA Model illustrates the steps necessary for solving community population health issues through collaboration. This chapter should be viewed less like a recipe and more like a puzzle or a toolbox. This work is not a linear process. Further, utilizing every tool could be perceived as work avoidance. Instead, the resources provided are designed to help the Community Chief Health Strategist and the Community Health Improvement Team to have options for multiple approaches to the challenges of population health improvement. Each piece (or phase) of the IDEA Model is critical, but different tools can be used to fulfill each phase, which provides adequate flexibility to address myriad health improvement processes. The tools provided include detailed descriptions as well as guidance about when to use each tool.

Identify Population Health Issues

> *"In God we trust; all others must bring data."*
>
> —*W. Edwards Deming*

The first step in solving for population health issues is determining the as-is state. This requires comprehensive information about the community's current health status, needs, and issues. When the phases of the Plan-Do-Check-Act Model for Improvement are broken down into phases[3] as seen in Figure 27.2, the plan phase is the most detailed. So too is the *Identify* phase in this model.

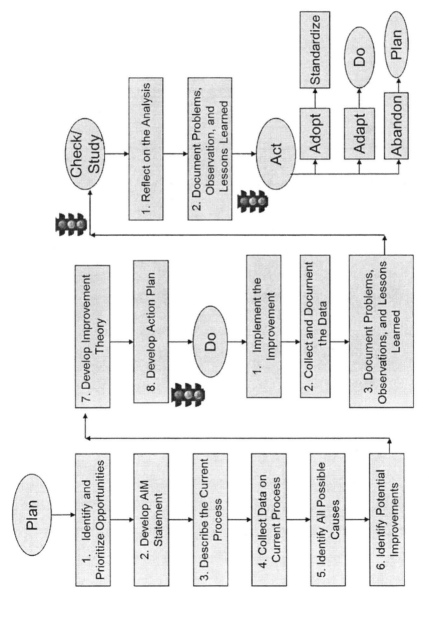

FIGURE 27.2 Phases of the PDCA Cycle

Rushing to action is very seductive as people are quick to praise solutions. However, solving for the wrong problem is common, and in research that is called a Type III Error:[4] the right answer for the wrong question. To assure meaningful and measurable population health improvement, a robust, multifaceted, qualitative, and quantitative data gathering, analysis, and prioritization process must be carefully executed. The tools in this *Identify* phase provide a framework for collecting and analyzing data to be used for mobilizing communities, developing priorities, and planning actions to improve the population's health.

The success of community health improvement initiatives is dependent on clarity of purpose. What are the health issues in the community? What is the prevalence and mortality? What are the perceptions of health? All of these questions get answered through a process that profiles your community. This process clarifies the needs and can be used to catalyze action. Because the health profile is a step in the process toward community mobilization, the community must be engaged in all phases. There are many frameworks and resources for developing Community Health Assessments and Community Health Improvement Plans. The IDEA Model tools are intended to support development, utilization, and action through those plans. This section outlines key frameworks and then introduces tools to support the *Identify* phase.

MAPP—The National Association for County and City Health Officials' Mobilizing for Action through Planning and Partnerships[5] provides a framework for convening the variety of organizations, groups, and individuals that comprise the public health system in order to create and implement a health improvement plan. MAPP was created in 1997 through a collaborative process and has been used among public health practitioners since 2000. This process outlines a six-phase process:

1. Organizing for Success
2. Visioning
3. Assessments—four assessments that include

   a.   Community Themes and Strengths
   b.   Forces of Change
   c.   Local Public Health System Assessment
   d.   Health Status Assessment

4. Identification of Strategic Issues
5. Development of Goals and Strategies
6. Action Cycle

Collectively, the assessment steps result in a Community Health Assessment (CHA), and phases four through six result in a Community Health Improvement Plan (CHIP). The Public Health Accreditation Board developed a resource for Acronyms and Glossary of Terms[6] which provides a widely accepted definition of both the CHA and CHIP and the original sources for those definitions.

Community Health Assessment—*"Community Health Assessment is a systematic examination of the health status indicators for a given population that is used to* *identify key problems and assets in a community. The ultimate goal of a community health assessment is to develop strategies to address the community's health needs and identified issues. A variety of tools and processes may be used to conduct a community health assessment; the essential ingredients are community engagement and collaborative participation."*[7]

Community Health Improvement Plan—*"A community health improvement plan is a long-term, systematic effort to address public health problems on the basis of the results of community health assessment activities and the community health improvement process. A plan is typically updated every three to five years (http://www.cdc.gov/stltpublichealth/cha/plan.html). This plan is used by health and other governmental education and human service agencies, in collaboration with community partners, to set priorities and coordinate and target resources. A community health improvement plan is critical for developing policies and defining actions to target efforts that promote health. It should define the vision for the health of the community through a collaborative process and should address the gamut of strengths, weaknesses, challenges, and opportunities that exist in the community to improve the health status of that community."*[8]

Additional Models for Identifying Population Health Issues—In addition to MAPP, there are many other frameworks recognized to support the *Identify* phase. National models include:

- Assessing and Addressing Community Health Needs (Catholic Hospital Association of the US)[9]
- Association for Community Health Improvement (ACHI) Assessment Toolkit[10]
- Community Toolbox (University of Kansas)[11]
- Community Indicators Consortium[12]
- Healthy People 2020[13]
- NACCHO's Resource Center for Community Health Assessments and Community Health Improvement Plans[14]

No matter which framework is adopted to develop a Community Health Assessment and Community Health Improvement Plan, those efforts are strengthened through the use of tools which can help communities decide where to focus efforts and investigate the change before investing resources. Three tools that support the frameworks mentioned above include:

1. Prioritization Matrix
2. Investigating Change Process
3. AIM Statement

The Prioritization Matrix and Investing Change Process are two tools to help in selecting a focus area, and then identifying challenges that could be encountered. Part of understanding the challenges is to also understand what are the strengths that exist in the community we can draw upon to help facilitate the change and the weaknesses that could derail the desired change.

PH Core Competency	1	2	3	4	Score	Rank	Rating Scale: 0 – No Relationship 1 – Equally Important 5 – Significantly More Important 10 - Exceedingly More Important 1/5 - Significantly Less Important 1/10 - Exceedingly Less Important
1. Analytic/Assessment	■	1/5	10	1/5	5.3	3	
2. Financial & Performance Management	5!	■	10	1/5	15.2	2	
3. Basic Science Skills	1/5	1/10	■	1/10	0.4	4	
4. Leadership & Systems Thinking	10	5	10	■	25	1	

FIGURE 27.3 Sample Prioritization Matrix

Tool Name: Prioritization Matrix

Description: Prioritization matrices are designed to help narrow the focus for an improvement team before detailed implementation planning. The Prioritization Matrix, see Figure 27.3, is used to compare choices relative to decision criteria like cost, service, ease of use, or any other criteria selected by a team. It is a rigorous decision making tool to help make informed, consensus-based decisions. The Prioritization Matrix is a tool for placing a large number of issues, causes, or potential solutions under consideration in rank order based on selected decision criteria using pairwise comparisons.

When to Use: The Prioritization Matrix is useful when the choices are numerous and complex and they have strong interrelationships, or there are very limited resources for improvement activities, forcing concentration on the critical few. The Prioritization Matrix can help teams gain consensus on what is the most important area to focus on. This tool is useful to an improvement team because it can provide a disciplined approach to sort and prioritize items, provide direction to focus limited resources, improve the efficiency or effectiveness of a program, or improve the performance or quality of an organization.

Construction Steps:

- Develop an L-shaped matrix with the items to be prioritized listed on the left side and across the top.
- Select the decision criteria to be used in the prioritization process such as improved quality, less cost, improved productivity, etc. This decision criteria must be used throughout the prioritization process in order to achieve consistency in the scoring.
- Draw a line from the upper left corner of the matrix to the bottom right corner of the matrix. This line will cut through the cells having the same item on the left side and top of the matrix and will make sure we do not compare an item to itself.

- Use a numerical scale to represent each judgment based on the criteria selected such as: 0—no relationship, 1—equally important, 5—significantly more important, 10—exceedingly more important, 1/5—significantly less important, 1/10—exceedingly less important. When facilitating this process it is useful to make a team not default to making everything equal but to push them to make decisions.

- Start with the first and second item and do a pairwise comparison of all the items asking the following questions: Are the related? If No put a "0" in each box and go to the next pair of items. If Yes, are they equal? If Yes put a "1" in each box and go to the next pair of items. If No, ask the following question: Does having _____ contribute more than _____ in achieving the goal? Whichever one contributes more will get a "5" or a "10" and the other one will get the reciprocal score.

- Once the matrix is completed, total the scores for each row, rank order the items based on the highest to lowest score. The team will see which problems or areas are the most important to work on first based on the scoring.

It is best to do the pairwise comparisons quickly because your first inclination is usually correct. Let the experts decide the score and you will see the expertise rotate in the group on different pairwise comparisons. Many find a pre-formatted Excel spreadsheet[15] helpful for developing the Prioritization Matrix.

Tool Name: Investigating Change Process

Introduction: The first step in making change is to understand and articulate to the organization what is the change desired, what are the benefits of making this change, the challenges that will be encountered, and the strategies to overcome expected challenges. Change can often be traumatic for an organization and the individuals involved. Change breaks the status quo that has become a comfortable way of life. Part of understanding challenges includes naming the organizational strengths that can be drawn upon to help facilitate the change as well as the weaknesses that could derail the desired change.

When to Use: Before undertaking a change initiative it is wise to explore what might be the challenges that could be encountered through a paper process.

Construction Steps:

Step 1: Understand the eight change parameters and how they will impact the organization's change initiative:

1. **Benefits**—gains to be made from making the change that should be articulated to the organization. Benefits the organization should promote as an advantage when selling the change.

2. **Strengths**—driving factors we should use to make the change successful and help accelerate it.
3. **Weaknesses**—things we have to improve to make the change. These are restraining factors that are blocking the change from being successful.
4. **Fears**—things that keep us up at night and need to be addressed in the organization. They may not be tangible factors but are feeling of foreboding, apprehension, consternation, dismay, dread, terror, fright, panic, horror, or trepidation of what can go wrong.
5. **External Threats**—outside influences that can cause issues or undermine our change initiatives.
6. **Pot Holes**—minor (distractions) things that could derail our change effort but we can recover from. Clear and regular communications are the ways to fill in pot holes.
7. **Land Mines**—these are crises that could blow up the initiative and end it. These are things we need to avoid at all costs and be prepared for and have contingency plans to minimize their impacts if they occur.
8. **Opportunities**—new things that can only be accomplished after the change. These are future potentials that the organization can exploit when they have mastered the change.

Step 2: Group process:

- Have eight tables.
- Divide the group into eight teams.
- Develop a handout that explains the change initiative to be analyzed.
- Print the eight parameters sheets (for an example see Figure 27.4) on different colored paper.
- Assign one change parameter per table.
- Assign one group to each table.
- Start the process by having the teams at each table discuss the change initiative and then list their ideas on the assigned parameter sheet—20 minutes.
- Now rotate the teams to a new table every 10 minutes, 7 times—each team should add to the existing items that have been recorded or can put a check mark (✓) to indicate agreement and support.
- Next, rotate everyone back to where they started.
- Last round—groups will go back to their initially assigned parameter—20 to 40 minutes—depending on the volume of ideas generated.

  a. Review what has been added.
  b. Prioritize the top three to five issues.
  c. Determine why they exist.
  d. Develop ways to use them or overcome or use them to drive the new change.
  e. Determine the improvement or utilization timeline.
  f. Report out on the eight Change Parameters.

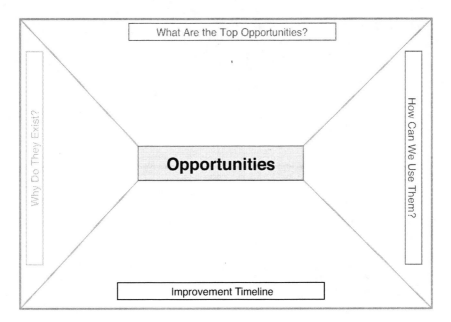

FIGURE 27.4 Investigating Change Process Opportunities Parameter Worksheet

Example: This is a generic sheet and the facilitator would need to develop one for each change parameter. The one shown is for opportunities.

Step 3: Determine next steps, action plans, and future meetings to review progress:

- Once this comprehensive group prioritization process has been completed, it is time to design action plans and next steps. These may be fairly obvious, or they may require additional team work or the use of tools described in the *Execute* phase of the IDEA Model found later in this chapter.

Defining the Community Health Issue Selected

Once the community health change opportunity has been selected, it is important to define it clearly for all those involved in the effort. A clear definition sets the boundaries and defines what will be worked on. An AIM Statement template incorporating a Return on Investment Analysis helps the entire improvement team see why this community health issue selected is so important. This is a living document and can be modified at any time during the project's life as new evidence is uncovered. Modifications to the initial AIM Statement should be documented as revisions and tracked.

Tool Name: AIM Statement Template

This template serves as a guide to assist in formulating the AIM, or goal, of the process improvement. It is a working document designed to evolve over several discussions while the project team works through the problem.

Section 1: Problem Description, Boundary, and Team Composition

• Describe the problem or opportunity to be addressed:

_____

(name process, issue, or area to work on)

This process is important to work on now because of: *(describe the impact this problem or opportunity is having on the agency, program, customers, employees, or the community)*

_____

_____

• Team Sponsor: _____
• Team Leader: _____
• Team Members: Area of Expertise:
  •
  •
  •
  •
  •
  •
• The problem or opportunity starts with

_____

(starting point)

• and ends with _____.

(ending point)

Section 2: Internal and External Benefit and Cost Description

• This opportunity has the following estimated potential benefits internally and to the external community:
  1. **Internal:**   *Tangible Benefits*   *Intangible Benefits*
     •
     •
     •
     •
     •

2. **External:**   *Tangible Benefits*   *Intangible Benefits*
   -
   -
   -
   -
   -

3. Total Tangible Benefits =
4. *Total Intangible Benefits = or Tangible Benefits times multiplier =*
5. The cost of this project is estimated to be: $_____ and is composed
   of the following cost categories:
   -
   -
   -
   -

Economic Impact (EI)

EI = [Tangible Benefits + Intangible Benefits] − Costs/Costs

Estimated EI for This Project =

Section 3: Current State Performance and Desired Future State

- Describe the current state of the problem or opportunity and its current performance (baseline data):
- Describe the ideal future state:
- What are the key driving and restraining forces impacting the current state
  and the ideal future state?

These descriptions can be illustrated by using a Force Field Analysis illustrated
in Figure 27.5.

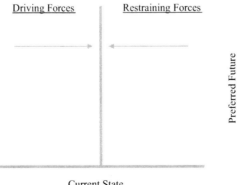

FIGURE 27.5 Force Field Analysis Diagram

Section 4: Improvement Description

• This effort should improve the current state by:

1. Describing the improvement goals to be achieved,
2. Developing the timing of these improvements,
3. Measuring the improvement.

Section 5: Internal and External Customer Identification

• For the following customers/clients *(customers, staff, or those affected by the process under improvement)*

1.
2.
3.

Decide

> *"Management is doing things right; leadership is doing the right things."*
> —*Peter F. Drucker*[16]

Once the issues are fully understood and documented in the AIM Statement Template, it is time to make many decisions. The **Decide** phase has a number of components. Some of these include determining the key community partners, deciding who should be on which teams, identifying the customers for this health improvement initiative, understanding the forces impacting the initiative, and determining the causes of the community health problem. The tools shown in this section will help the Community Chief Health Strategist get the right people involved with the right skills and commitment to ensure a successful improvement initiative.

In the **Identify** phase, the community engaged to help prioritize health issues. Mobilization of the community in the **Decide** phase is even more important to assure successful collaboration and impact. The often-used adage "nothing about us without us" is an important frame for consideration. However, one trap public health practitioners can find themselves in relates to the challenge of serving the whole population, and the impossibility of 100% of the citizenry actively leading the health improvement plan. The tools in this phase offer guidance related to identification of customers and partners. A key principle of quality improvement is maintaining the focus on the customer. In addition to skillfully and strategically bringing the health improvement process to the community, the Chief Health Strategist and the Community Health Improvement Team must also bring their expertise about evidence-based practices.

Communicating effectively with potential community partners to assure the voice of the community in improving a health issue is a key skill for a Community Chief Health Strategist. A Community Chief Health Strategist needs to be an effective communicator of the "Why This Is Important" message. The

Community Chief Health Strategist is a community change leader and must be a consensus builder by pulling together key stakeholders and individuals, and overcoming resistance groups to enlist their support in the community health change initiative. In building this consensus the change leader must clearly communicate a compelling reason for people to change their direction, habits, and current activities. In addition, the change leader must be realistic and describe the challenges and consequences that will come if change is not made.

The most effective change leaders walk the talk, consistently modeling the health behaviors desired that will result in improvement in community health. To do this a change leader must have a relentless passion for the health change they envision and the ability to nurture others to that end state. To do this they must be willing to display the new behaviors on a regular basis, have keen instincts as to when to be adaptable as they move forward, and the willingness and ability to learn new skills. The effective Community Chief Health Strategist is frequently the first participant in wellness programs, regularly reaches out to unusual voices in new sectors, and works to define a compelling case for change.

A process for the Chief Health Strategist to use in order to be an effective community change leader is the PDCA Cycle of a Change Leader as illustrated in Figure 27.6. This Change Leader PDCA Model[17] requires a leader to **Plan** what they are going to say before they speak, **Do** deliver a consistent message at all times to the organization about the change, **Check** to see if what they are saying is inspiring the action required to make the change, and then **Act** to provide nurturing and care to areas in the organization not moving forward as quickly as desired and to ensure that the gains achieved are held as shown in the figure below.

Another tool a Community Chief Health Strategist could use is the Public Health Foundation's "Planning Before You Communicate Spreadsheet."[18] This spreadsheet

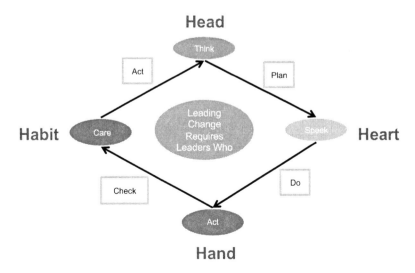

FIGURE 27.6 Change Leader PDCA Model

is designed to help the Community Chief Health Strategist to develop consistent, clear, and crisp communications within the agency and externally with the community. This tool helps design communications focusing on these principles:

- Keep It Simple—If you or someone on your team does not clearly understand, your audience will not either.
- Know Your Objectives—Each strategic communications activity should align directly with a main objective. If it does not, make the decision whether it is still worth doing and why.
- Know Your Audience—What tactics will be most helpful in reaching them with your messages? Where do they spend their time? How do they get their information?
- Be Direct—If you want action from your audience, clearly ask them for it within a given timeframe. Do not wait or hope that they will get around to it later.

Staffing the Community Health Initiative

Getting the message out is one thing a Community Chief Health Strategist has to do, but another important thing is to get the right people on the various improvement teams. The success of any community health improvement project will come down to the quality of the team members working on it. For a community health improvement project team to be effective, it is essential to select the right team members with the right skills. It is not the number of people, but rather how well they function and work together, that makes a team successful. Team members must respect each other, and share common goals, vision, agendas, and timelines to be successful.

Another important thing is that once the improvement teams are formed they must have a clear idea of what they are to do, and this can be modified as they move forward and uncover new evidence. The following three tools have been designed to help with that process.

Tool Name: Stakeholder Analysis

Description: Stakeholder Analysis, illustrated in Figure 27.7, is defined as a process of identifying the individuals or groups that are likely to affect or be affected by a proposed action, and sorting them according to their impact on the action and the impact the action will have on them. This information is used to assess how the interests of those stakeholders should be addressed in a project plan, policy, program, or other action.

When to Use: Stakeholder analysis is used when an improvement team needs to analyze the attitudes of stakeholders towards an implementation plan. It is frequently used during the preparation phase of a project to assess the attitudes of the stakeholders regarding the potential changes. Stakeholder analysis can be

Stakeholder Analysis
Project Name:

Stakeholder (person or group)	Type (primary, secondary, key)	Power Level (high, medium, low)	Support (positive, neutral, negative)	Influence (high, low)	Need (strong, medium, weak)	Drivers (risks, loyalties, losses)	Rank
A							
B							
C							
D							

FIGURE 27.7 Stakeholder Analysis Template

done once or on a regular basis to track changes in stakeholder attitudes over time towards the implementation of change that is taking place.

Construction Steps:

- Draw an L-shaped matrix with seven columns on a flip chart.
- Identify all relevant stakeholders for this improvement or project. List them in the first column.
- Determine if they are **Primary** stakeholders (ultimately affected, either positively or negatively), **Secondary** stakeholders (intermediaries, persons, or organizations who are indirectly affected), or **Key** stakeholders (who can also belong to the first two groups and have significant influence upon or importance involving the improvement or change).
- Determine their **Power Level** as high, medium, or low for this improvement or project.
- Determine their **Support** for the improvement or project as positive, neutral, or negative.
- Decide their level of **Influence** as high or low as it impacts this improvement or project.
- Decide their **Need** for this improvement or project as strong, medium, or weak.
- Consider their **Drivers**. What are the stakeholder's risks, loyalties, or potential losses associated with the status quo or with improvement (change)?

Once the matrix is complete each stakeholder can be ranked and a plan developed to approach them to obtain support or reduce their opposition, or minimize any obstacles they may erect to impede the implementation plan for an improvement or project.

Tool Name: Team Member Selection Matrix[19]

To help a Chief Health Strategist select the right team members there is a matrix on the Public Health Foundation's website that can help guide the process. It is the Team Member Selection Matrix. This matrix can help select the right team members. For an improvement project to be effective, it is essential to select the right team members with the right skills. It is not the number of people, but rather how well they function and work together, that makes a team successful. Improvement team members must respect each other, and share common goals, vision, agendas, and timelines to be successful.

Team dynamics and maturity are central to an improvement team's development, problem-solving ability, and success. The Forming-Storming-Norming-Performing model of group development, by Bruce Tuckman,[20] maintains that these four phases are all necessary and inevitable in order for the team to grow, to face up to challenges, to tackle problems, to find solutions, to plan work, and to deliver results. The best, most effective teams are able to accomplish a lot partly because they've established relationships, they know and understand each other, and they enjoy working together. If you add the wrong person to the team, the whole dynamic can be destroyed. This is why it is important to pick the right people the first time.

Tool Name: Team Charter

Description: The Team Charter is the official document from the executive sponsor that empowers the team to act. It is a written document describing the mission of the team and how this mission is to be accomplished. The Team Charter clearly defines the goals and objectives to be achieved by the process improvement team. The Team Charter is an official work contract. This document delineates the strategic goals, boundaries, measures of success, constraints/limits, and available resources. The Charter provides a framework for ongoing discussions between the team and its executive sponsor with regard to the team's direction and progress.

Overall, the benefits of using the Team Charter are to provide teams with the following:

- Clarity
- Focus
- Alignment
- Permission
- Protection
- Boundaries
- Metrics

When to Use:

- At the beginning of a team project
- As an ongoing reference for the team and related stakeholders on the specific expectations, measures, goals, and objectives of the project
- During project reviews as an audit base for ensuring the project remains on focus
- As a living document for the life of the project to be updated as conditions, requirements, and expectations change

Construction Steps:

- Use the descriptions below as a guide to creating a Team Charter based on the template in the example at the end of this section.
- The Charter can be initially drafted by the project champion, the quality council, or the process improvement (PI) team, although most empowered PI teams create their own charter as part of the forming stage of team development.
- The team leader and team facilitator are instrumental in guiding a new team through the completion of the first draft of the Team Charter.
- The Team Charter is a living document that is reviewed and updated throughout the project to reflect current expectations of the sponsor, process owner, and project customer.

TEAM CHARTER

1. Team Name:	2. Version:	3. Subject:
4. Problem / Opportunity Statement:		
5. Team Sponsor:		6. Team Leader:
7. Team Members:		Area of Expertise:
1.		
2.		
3.		
4.		
5.		
6.		
8. Process Improvement Aim (Mission):		
9. Scope (Boundaries):		
10. Customers (Primary and Other):		Customer Needs Addressed:
11. Objectives:		
✓		
✓		
✓		
✓		
12. Success Metrics (Measures):		
13. Considerations (Assumptions / Constraints / Obstacles / Risks): a. b. c.		
14. Available Resources:		15. Additional Resources Required:
16. Key Milestones:		Date:
17. Communication Plan (Who, How, and When):		
18. Key Stakeholders:		Area of Concern (as It Relates to the Charter):

Identifying the Customers for the Community Health Improvement Project

Before any community health initiative starts it is important for the improvement team to understand who the customers for this improvement are. Customers can be internal to the partner organizations involved, their staff, community organizations, faith groups, community members, etc. The following tools can help the Chief Health Strategist to understand and prioritize the various voices of the customers and make sure the improvement initiative is aimed at the correct community needs.

Tool Name: Kano Model

Description: The Kano Model, illustrated in Figure 27.8, can help an improvement team to uncover, understand, and classify their customer needs for the process they are studying. It also helps the improvement team to understand what causes their customers to be satisfied and dissatisfied with the process.

When to Use: The Kano Model should be used when filling out the Customer section of the SICPOC+CM form to guide the team in understanding the entire customer experience with the process under study. Capturing the Voice of the Customer, both internal and external, is a good first step when designing improvements to an existing process or developing a new process. It allows an improvement team to have an understanding and interpretation of what the customer expects

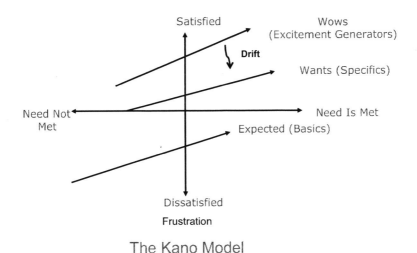

FIGURE 27.8 Kano Model Example

and needs from the improved or new process and build it into the design upfront. This helps keep the team focused on the customer(s) of the process under study.

Construction Steps:

• Draw the Kano Model on a flip chart as shown in the example and determine who the internal and external customers are for the process being studied.
• Indicate on the Kano Model the requirements for each customer grouping in terms of the defined three types of quality:

1. Expected Quality, also called Basic Quality, is the minimum requirements for any process. These basic requirements are not always expressed by the customer because they are expected, but they are obvious to the customer and must be met. If you do not meet the basic requirements the customer is dissatisfied at the outset. These basic requirements are not a source of satisfaction but can cause major dissatisfaction. Because this type of quality goes without saying, it is important to try to uncover these unstated needs in any customer survey the improvement team may conduct.

2. Performance Quality or Wants are specified needs the customer will state when asked what they want in a survey. This category is a strong source of customer satisfaction and should be a priority to meet when an improvement team is developing a solution or improving a process performance.

3. Exciting Quality, or Delighters, is what you design into an improvement process so it can supply delights to the customer. These delighters are unexpected by the customer but something they definitely will like and want in the future. This type of quality is something significantly more than the customer expected to experience. One rule to remember is once you delight a customer they will want it the next time. These delighters that can be an important source of customer satisfaction. If they are not there, the customer is not dissatisfied because they were not expected.

Tool Name: Voice of the Customer Table (VOCT)

Description: The VOCT is a data gathering matrix (see Figure 27.9) to help uncover what customers really want and need. In order to have a customer-centric organization that is delivering what is needed in our community we need to understand who the customers are of our processes that provide products and services. Once we know who the customers are (internal, external, primary, secondary, and etc.) we need to understand what they want and need. The Kano Model is a tool we use in conjunction with the VOCT to discover and understand these needs and wants.

Voice of the Customer Table						
Voice of the Customer	Understanding the Use of Your Process Outputs					
	Who	What	When	Where	Why	How
Customer Type	Who uses it?	What do they use if for?	When do they use it?	Where do they use it?	Why do they use it?	How do they use it?
	Who else uses it?	What else could it be used for?	When else could they use it?	Where else could they use it?	Other reasons to use it?	How else could they use it?

FIGURE 27.9 Voice of the Customer Table Template

When to Use: When we need to have a clear understanding of who our customers are and what they expect of our organization. To develop and complete a VOCT we first need to develop a process to obtain the Voice of the Customer (VOC) on a regular basis. This is not an easy process because we must design and develop a methodology that will track and record the wants and needs of our customer base and alert us to any changes that result and the reasons for that change. Some organizations use surveys, telephone interviews, or person-to-person questionnaires at the touch points in the process.

Construction Steps:

- Develop a methodology to collect the VOC on a regular basis.
- Develop an L-Shaped matrix as shown in the example, Figure 27.10.
- On the left-hand vertical column we enter in the verbatim customer wants and needs obtained from our surveying process.
- Across the top we have columns labeled as who, what, when, where, why, and how which help us analyze the data received from the customer. This also helps us to uncover gaps in our knowledge of the customer, which we can then gather.
- Once we know the customer requirements for our process we need to make sure we have measures in place to track them, and if they are not meeting the customer's requirement, to improve them so they do.
- What excites and delights a customer is a moving target, which requires an organization to be constantly monitoring them and making adjustments in their product and service delivery to meet them.

Knowing which requirements are most critical from a customer perspective is essential if you have to make tradeoffs or sacrifice one requirement to meet another if we have to ration scarce resources.

Voice of the Customer		Understanding the Use of Your Process Outputs				
	Who	What	When	Where	Why	How
Septic System Permit Customer:	General contractor (external customer)	Verification of county approval for installation of septic system for new construction	• For building permits and reviews • At closing for legal documentation	• On the building site • With county inspectors • At closing	• Legal document of services • Formal documentation of regulated activity	• Public document • Freedom of Information • Adjunct to building permits
	EVH septic system unit manager (internal customer)	Completion of permit indicates all information from contractor has been received for processing of documentation	• At application for permit to begin process • Interim documentation for answering questions • Final record of completed permit and closure of file	• In EVH office to drive process • Referral for all permit questions • During internal or external EVH audits	• Record of individual septic system permit • Detailed information as part of public record for deed and land use	• Auditable document • Measurable item for process monitoring • Communication vehicle for sustainability and improvement

FIGURE 27.10 Voice of the Customer Table Example

Design the Kick Off Meeting and Build the Strength of the Coalition

Even with the best data, frameworks, and tools, a community health improvement project can fail if the community engagement efforts are not executed effectively. Chief Health Strategists must carefully plan effective meetings so that the community will stay with them through the challenges of abstract data and the often slow and incremental change processes required for health improvement efforts. Community members are expecting a fair amount of protection, direction, and order from those charged with convening them. Effective coalitions require tools for running effective meetings, including providing participants with a clear tool to clarify the improvement goal and identify root causes.

Tool Name: Tips for Running Effective Meetings

Three Steps to Effective Meetings

a. **Meeting Preparation:**

- Do not meet—avoid a meeting if the same information could be covered in a memo, e-mail, or brief report. Ask yourself the following question: *"Is a meeting the best way to handle this?"* You'll cut down on wasted meeting time and restore your group's belief that the meetings they attend are necessary.
- What is the purpose of the meeting helps determine participants.

    a. Do you want a decision?
    b. Do you want to generate ideas?
    c. Are you getting status reports?
    d. Are you communicating something?
    e. Are you making plans?
    f. *At the close of the meeting, I want the group to decide the following for the next meeting:*
      - Priorities—what absolutely must be covered?
      - Results—what do you need to accomplish at the meeting?
      - Participants—who needs to attend the meeting for it to be successful?
      - Sequence—in what order will you cover the topics?
      - Timing—how much time will you spend on each topic?
      - Date and time—when will the meeting take place?
      - Place—where will the meeting take place?

b. **Meeting Execution:**

- Circulate agenda ahead of time—have participants prepared.
- Ground rules.
- Cover the agenda—contents of the meeting.
- Stick to the time for each topic.

- Keep people focused.
- Limit wandering.
- Summarize what was said, and ask people to confirm.

c.   Meeting Follow-Up

- Debrief, and determine what went well and what could have been done better.
- Evaluate the meeting's effectiveness based on how well you met the objective.

Tool Name: Cause and Effect Diagram

Description: The Cause and Effect Diagram displays multiple potential causes for an effect or problem. The format of the diagram is used to organize the outcome of a brainstorming and affinity session identifying stakeholder ideas concerning the disruptions observed within the process or task under study. Also known as an "Ishikawa Diagram" or a "Fishbone Diagram," the Cause and Effect Diagram allows the user to immediately categorize ideas into themes for analysis or further data gathering.

When to Use:

- When identifying possible causes for an effect, disruption, or problem
- For organizing the result of group thinking around potential symptoms related to a specific effect
- When organizing group knowledge about causes of a problem and displaying the information graphically

Construction Steps:

- Write the issue as a problem statement on the right hand side of the page and draw a box around it with an arrow running to it as illustrated in Figure 27.11.
- This issue is now the effect.
- Generate ideas as to what are the main causes of the effect.
- Label these as the main branch headers.
- Typical Main Headers are:
    - 4 M's—Manpower, Materials, Methods, Machinery
    - People
    - Policies
    - Materials
    - Equipment
    - Lifestyle
    - Environment
    - Etc.
- For each main cause category, brainstorm ideas about the related sub-causes that might affect our issue.

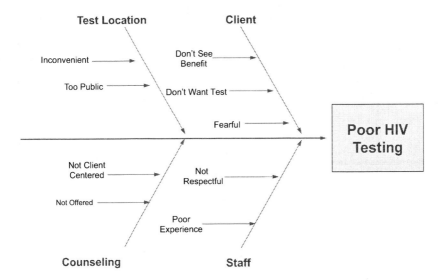

Test Location

Inconvenient ⟶

Too Public ⟶

Client

Don't See Benefit ⟶

Don't Want Test ⟶

Fearful ⟶

Poor HIV Testing

Not Client Centered ⟶

Not Offered ⟶

Not Respectful ⟶

Poor Experience ⟶

Counseling

Staff

FIGURE 27.11 Cause and Effect Example, Analysis HIV Testing

- Use the *5 Why's technique* when a cause is identified.
- Keep repeating the question until no other causes can be identified.
- List the sub-causes using arrows.

Execute a Plan for Improvement

> *"You can't build a reputation on what you're going to do."*
>
> —*Henry Ford*

The **Execute** phase is the one your staff and partners have been waiting for. Utilization of tools in this phase is critical to success. All too often, the first idea from the loudest or most influential partner or staff member is the one selected. Whereas those ideas can yield results, a methodical approach creates time and space for more approaches, nuanced solutions, and innovations that would not have been tested without use of these tools. The **Execute** phase includes three key steps: solution generation, prioritization (see Identify section for a description of the Prioritization Matrix), and project management.

Developing solutions is often a challenging process for any improvement team. The Solution and Effect Diagram gives them a methodology to explore all potential solutions and then narrow those down into a few that will help achieve the AIM of the improvement initiative. The improvement team should sort the various solutions in to categories they control or influence. They should start with the control category because they have the power to make changes in this area. The influence category can be explored later because it will take longer to implement these types of solutions.

Tool Name: Solution and Effect Diagram

Description: The Solution and Effect Diagram uses the same format as the Cause and Effect Diagram. Once the Cause and Effect Diagram is developed, the Solution and Effect Diagram facilitates a closer analysis of potential solutions to priority improvements identified by the Cause and Effect activity.

When to Use: The Solution and Effect Diagram is a logical step in overall Root Cause Analysis. It is used after the Cause and Effect Diagram to explore priority root causes identified by the team during the initial Cause and Effect activity.

It organizes team creativity around changes to existing processes or recommendations for new process design to resolve problems and exploit new opportunities for improved performance.

Construction Steps:

- Place the Solution and Effect Diagram opposite the Cause and Effect Diagram (see Figure 27.12).
- Write the issue as a positive statement on the left-hand side of the page and draw a box around it with an arrow running to it.
- Effect is now made into a positive statement (see an example in Figure 27.13).
- Where the Cause and Effect Diagram statement is: "What are the causes of childhood obesity?"
- The Solution and Effect Diagram effect is now: "Fewer (less) obese children."
- For each main Solution category brainstorm ideas for related sub-solutions that might affect the issue.
- Use the *5 How's technique* when a solution is identified to explore realistic alternatives for root cause resolution.
- Keep repeating the question until no other solutions can be identified.
- List the sub-solutions on the Solution and Effect Diagram using arrows associated with the related major headings.

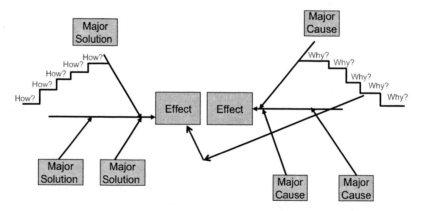

FIGURE 27.12 Solution & Effect Diagram Template

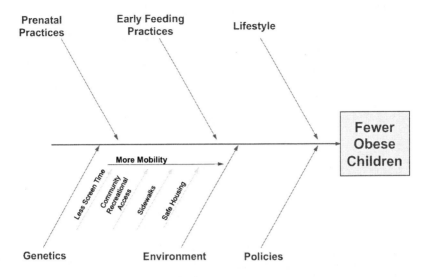

FIGURE 27.13 Solution & Effect Diagram Example

Tool Name: Gantt Chart

Description: A Gantt Chart is a matrix diagram consisting of a collection of horizontal bars plotted against a calendar scale. Each bar represents an activity. The beginning and end of the bar represent the scheduled start and finish dates of the activity, and the collection of all bars portrays a complete schedule for the project, as illustrated in Figure 27.14. These charts are popular because they are easy to construct, and they serve as an effective tool for communicating the project plan to all involved groups.

When to Use:

- To plan projects
- Monitor progress against plan when compared with actual progress of activities
- To show work movement through time
- When communicating the project plan to all involved groups
- As a framework for analyzing interdependencies among processes affected by the project
- To help visualize the connection of project costs to accounting periods
- Assists in identifying and eliminating barriers to project success

Construction Steps:

- Identify the outcome to be achieved by the project.
- Identify the deadline for achieving this outcome.
- Identify the starting point or first activity of the project to be scheduled.

Public Health Department Accreditation Readiness Plan, Phase One Tasks												
Task	Responsible Staff	Week 1	Week 2	Week 3	Week 4	Week 5	Week 6	Week 7	Week 8	Week 9	Week 10
Meet with Consultant	SA, JM, CS, CB	▓			▓			▓			▓
Conduct Self-Assessment Analysis	SA, JM, CS, CB	▓									
Create A-Team Charter	CS, CB	▓									
Convene A-Team	Full Mgmt. Team +	▓		▓		▓		▓		▓	
Design File Organization System	CS, CB + AC			▓	▓					▓	
Domain Team meetings	12 Domain Leads + Teams		▓				▓		▓		▓
Conduct All Staff Orientation	Director + AC + All Staff + SA, JM				▓						

FIGURE 27.14 Gantt Chart Example

- Brainstorm all the tasks or steps to be performed to accomplish the outcome.
- Put the steps in logical order. Identify tasks that must be sequential or can be performed in parallel.
- Assign a length of time to each task.
- Identify the nature of the relationship between steps and adjust timing as required.
- Populate the matrix with appropriate time increments across the top and chart the steps.
- The calendar scale is shown across the top. Units of time may be hours, days, weeks, months, etc.
- The matrix may be created using Excel or other graphic tools using rows and columns.
- Gantt Charts are simple to create manually using graph paper or by drawing the matrix on a white board in the project team work area.

Tool Name: RASIC Chart

Description: The RASIC Chart is an L-shaped matrix which associates tasks to be completed to the roles and responsibilities of those associated with a project. The Y axis of the matrix itemizes the tasks to be accomplished. The X axis of the matrix identifies the functions or individuals responsible for activities within the project. The key responsibilities of a project team are identified in the list below:

R—responsibility—process or outcome owner
A—accountable—approves
S—supports—provides resources to the team (sponsor)
I—informed—notified of results
C—consulted—can help

When to Use:

- At the beginning of a project to identify the essential resources to achieve the strategy or objective
- To identify and agree upon critical roles within the team
- As a summary matrix with detailed matrices to back up each block in the matrix if necessary
- Serves as an easy reference at the beginning of each team meeting and senior management review to reinforce accountability
- Keeps team members focused on task assignments through a visual mapping of responsibilities

Construction Steps:

- Identify all the tasks/processes/activities associated with the problem or project under consideration on the left side of the matrix, as illustrated in Figure 27.15.

	Mayor	National Hurricane Center	Emergency Preparedness Office	Hospital Association	Fire Department	Police Department	Regional Transit Authority	Animal Control	General Public
Coordinate Agency Training	A	S	R	I	S	S	S	S	NA
Communicate Threat	I	R	C	I	I	I	I	I	I
Initiate Evacuation	A	R	A	I	S	S	S	S	I
Conduct Evacuation	A	I	C	I	C	R	C	I	I
Request Additional Law Enforcement	C	NA	R	R	C	NA	C	NA	NA
Coordinate Animal Rescue	NA	NA	I	I	S	S	R	NA	S
Authorize Return to Evacuated Area	A	I	R	I	C	C	C	C	I

Key
R - Responsible
A - Accountability
S - Supporting
I - Informed
C - Consultant
NA - Not Applicable

Individual / Function

FIGURE 27.15 RASIC Chart Example

- List all functions involved in the project on the top of the matrix. Avoid using individual names to minimize adjustments made necessary by personnel movements.
- Assign responsibilities using "RASIC" for each task-involved intersection in the matrix.
- There should only be one "R" designation per task.
- Resolve any overlaps and gaps (no role assigned).
- Expand into sub-matrices to break tasks into smaller implementable activities, communication, or resource requirements.
- Keep the RASIC matrix up to date.

Assess the Impact

> *"Not everything that can be counted counts. Not everything that counts can be counted."*
>
> —*William Bruce Cameron (often misattributed to Albert Einstein)*

The majority of public health work is conducted using local, state, and federal tax dollars and, in some cases, funds from philanthropies (grants from foundations). In either case, the Community Chief Health Strategist must be able to demonstrate accountability. Even if the intervention did not work, the completion of the assessment is important both to the community engaged and the contribution to the larger public health community. The Program Performance and Evaluation Office of the Centers for Disease Control and Prevention[21] offers a number of questions to consider while evaluating programs/interventions:

- What will be evaluated? (i.e., what is "the program" and in what context does it exist?)
- What aspects of the program will be considered when judging program performance?
- What standards (i.e., type or level of performance) must be reached for the program to be considered successful?
- What evidence will be used to indicate how the program has performed?
- What conclusions regarding program performance are justified by comparing the available evidence to the selected standards?
- How will the lessons learned from the inquiry be used to improve public health effectiveness?

This *Assess* phase offers a number of tools for documenting the effectiveness of the chosen solution. These tools are designed to help understand how the trial solutions worked and track the changes observed.

Tool Name: Run Chart

Description: A Run Chart is used to display how a process performs over time. It is a line graph of data points plotted in chronological order in the sequence in which process events occurred. The data points plotted on a Run Chart can represent measurements, counts, or percentages of process output. Run Charts are line graphs of a variable under study over time with a Median Line displayed. The Median Line divides the data into two equal halves. The Median is the middle value in our data sample. Run Charts are used to assess and achieve process stability by highlighting signals of special causes of variation. The Run Chart helps an improvement team to understand what variation there is in a process performance so they can improve it, analyze data for patterns that are not easily seen in tables or spreadsheets, and monitor process performance over time to detect signals of changes. Run Charts do not use control limits and cannot tell you if a process is stable. For determining process stability, a control chart is needed.

When to Use: When there is a need to understand how a process is performing over time to find out if any improvement is required. The Run Chart is easily constructed and simple to understand, as illustrated in Figure 27.16. The plot of a process's data over time will reveal information about a process under study. When observing a Run Chart, it may be possible to see some data patterns such as trends, mixtures, outliers, cycles, instability, or sudden shifts. These data observations can help guide an improvement team to understand how the process is operating and to uncover areas needing improvement.

Construction Steps:

- Define a process to study.
- Determine what is considered a complete cycle of the process to understand how the time ordered data will be plotted. Is cycle per client, hourly, daily, etc.?
- Determine an appropriate sample size to collect in time order.
- Once the data is collected determine the Median value.
- Draw a Run Chart, plot the data in time order, and draw in the Median Line.
- Analyze the chart and determine what you observe from the data plot. Are there trends, fluctuations, or sudden shifts that could indicate process instability?

When analyzing a Run Chart, blend your knowledge of the process with the data displayed and determine if there are any conflicts. Understand the reason for any peaks or troughs that occur and determine the reason for the occurrence.

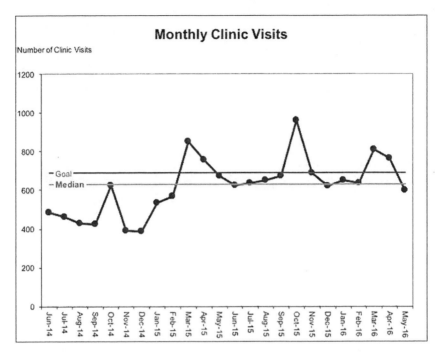

FIGURE 27.16 Run Chart Example, Number of Clinic Visits per Month

Focus on and understand any unusual patterns, shifts, cycles, or bunching of data points and verify if they are real.

Tool Name: Stop-Start-Continue-Improve Matrix

Description: This tool can be used for a quick analysis of a process or problem to see if there are any things currently being done that need to be stopped, any things that should be started, what things that are currently being done that should be continued, and what things that need to be improved and done differently. This tool gathers ideas that need to be individually analyzed to make sure they have merit and will really improve the process or problem under consideration. It is a quick scoping tool to get ideas about what is causing poor performance and how to make improvements.

When to Use: Whenever you need to engage a group around a problem that needs to have a quick scope to see what is really going on. It can also be used when a process is running, and those involved can make notes on what needs to be stopped, continued, or started to make improvements.

Process/Problem: Developing a QI Culture			
Start Doing	Stop Doing	Continue Doing	Improve
Ahas	Learnings	Best Practices	Do Differently
What Should We Put in Place?	What are we doing that is not working?	What is working well & should be continued?	Where can we make improvements in how we do things?
Focus on More QI Projects Based on Performance Management Data	Treating all challenges as formal QI Projects	Sustain senior leadership commitment	Increase training to include advanced QI skills training
	Treating QI as a "check the box requirement" activity	Continue QI training basics to all employees	

FIGURE 27.17 Stop-Start-Continue Matrix, Example

Construction Steps:

- Draw a Stop-Start-Continue-Improve Matrix (L-shaped matrix) on a flip chart and divided it into four columns, as illustrated in Figure 27.17.
- The second column is "What" might work better for us as a team or a process? "What" new ideas or tasks should we try? These are behaviors or tasks that we can **START** doing to improve our performance.
- The first column is "What's" not working in the team or a process? These are behaviors or tasks that we should **STOP** doing immediately to improve our performance.
- The third column is "What" is working well now that we should keep on doing to keep our performance at the current level? These are behaviors to **CONTINUE** doing that are working well for us.
- The fourth column is "What" to **IMPROVE**, and are things that could help the process or problem if they were done differently than they are now. These are things we do not want to stop doing but cannot continue doing in their current state.

Summary

The complex process of community health improvement can require different approaches at different times due to purpose, audience, issue, and context. The Chief Health Strategist and Health Improvement Teams are well served by having a variety of tools to **I**dentify the community health issue, **D**ecide where to focus (prioritize), **E**xecute the improvement plan, and **A**ssess the process improvement to see if it achieved the outcome desired. As illustrated throughout this chapter, sometimes several tools are useful within the various steps. For example, within the ***Execute*** phase, the Solution & Effect model may be paired with Five How's and a Gantt Chart. Further, if a tool is not yielding a result that either illuminates, improves, or assesses the process, having another tool to choose from can keep a process from getting stalled.

The intention of this chapter is to offer a pragmatic set of approaches that empowers and emboldens those who are willing to take on the daunting task of community health improvement. One theoretical concept worthy of consideration is the process of co-construction. In this chapter, descriptions of tools are sterile and teased out from the processes to be improved. When tools are chosen and applied, the result is often a bit messy, and as the tool is deployed, the process changes; both are mutually influenced. A tool that yields results in one context may not prove useful in another. The "When to Use" sections should help guide tool selection, but also hold out the possibility that some efforts at tool selection matching health challenges and audience may fail. Don't let one failed attempt hold back the process. Try another set of tongs. Utilizing tools can move a person from fruitful conversations that admit a problem to action. Having a complete set of back up tools—the right tools for the job—has proven very useful in the kitchen, in the workshop, and in community work. This IDEA Model is a flexible framework for the idea people.

Notes

1. Public Health Quality Improvement Encyclopedia, Public Health Foundation, ©2012.
2. http://www.phf.org/resourcestools/Pages/Tools_to_Supplement_the_Public_Health_Quality_Improvement_Encyclopedia.aspx
3. G. Gorenflo and J. Moran, ABCs of the PDCA Cycle, http://www.phf.org/pmqi/resources.htm
4. Encyclopedia of Research Design, http://srmo.sagepub.com/view/encyc-of-research-design/n483.xml
5. NACCHO, http://www.naccho.org/topics/infrastructure/mapp/framework/mappbasics.cfm
6. http://www.phaboard.org/wp-content/uploads/FINAL_PHAB-Acronyms-and-Glossary-of-Terms-Version-1.5.pdf
7. Public Health Accreditation Board, PHAB Acronyms and Glossary of Terms Version 1.5, Adopted December 2013, http://www.phaboard.org/wp-content/uploads/FINAL_PHAB-Acronyms-and-Glossary-of-Terms-Version-1.5.pdf. Page 10.
8. Adapted from: United States Department of Health and Human Services, *Healthy People 2010.* Washington, DC, 2010.
9. https://www.chausa.org/docs/default-source/general-files/cb_assessingaddressing-pdf.pdf?sfvrsn=4
10. http://www.assesstoolkit.org/
11. http://ctb.ku.edu/en/table-of-contents/assessment/assessing-community-needs-and-resources
12. http://www.communityindicators.net/
13. http://www.healthypeople.gov/2020/tools-and-resources/Tools-for-Professionals

14. http://www.naccho.org/topics/infrastructure/CHAIP/chachip-online-resource-center.cfm
15. http://www.phf.org/resourcestools/Pages/Electronic_Prioritization_Matrix.aspx
16. http://www.phiu.org/documents/LeadershipQuotes.pdf
17. L. Beitsch, MD and J. Moran, Become a Complete Change Leader by Using Your Head, Heart, and Hands: Motivating Employees to Embrace Change and a Culture of Quality Improvement by Varying Your Leadership Style, *Quality Management Forum*, Spring 2014, Vol. 40, Number 1, pp. 1–4.
18. http://www.phf.org/resourcestools/Pages/Planning_Before_You_Communicate_Tool.aspx
19. http://www.phf.org/resourcestools/Pages/Team_Member_Selection_Tool.aspx
20. http://www.businessballs.com/tuckmanformingstormingnormingperforming.htm, accessed 9/22/2013
21. http://www.cdc.gov/eval/framework/

INDEX